NATIONAL INTEGRATION THROUGH SOCIALIST PLANNING

AN ANTHROPOLOGICAL STUDY OF A ROMANIAN NEW TOWN

BY
STEVEN L. SAMPSON
Institute of Ethnology and Anthropology
University of Copenhagen

EAST EUROPEAN MONOGRAPHS, BOULDER
DISTRIBUTED BY COLUMBIA UNIVERSITY PRESS
NEW YORK

1984

EAST EUROPEAN MONOGRAPHS, NO. CXLVIII

To Vibeke

and

To my parents—Dorothy and Horace Sampson

TABLE OF CONTENTS

LIST OF TABLES

LIST OF FIGURES

LIST OF MAPS

PREFACE AND ACKNOWLEDGEMENTS

This book uses the concepts and methods of sociocultural anthropology to examine how socialist planning affects an urbanizing Romanian village. It is a revised version of my doctoral dissertation, which was completed in 1980 at the University of Massachusetts at Amherst. In revising the manuscript for publication, I have had the benefit of anthropological hindsight, which in my case occurred in a completely different intellectual and political atmosphere. I have also benefitted from several subsequent visits to Romania and from the many insightful criticisms offered by Romanian and Western colleagues. Moreover, in attempting to make the present book both interdisciplinary and ethnographically comparative, I have tried to become better acquainted with the Soviet Studies literature and with the burgeoning amount of research done by Western anthropologists in Eastern Europe.[1]

Apart from these new inputs, the revised dissertation also reflects a shift in my own research interests. My initial focus on Romanian planning eventually led me toward a broader range of problems: the anthropology of bureaucracy, the unique character of "actually existing socialism,"[2] the structural problems of local elites in rural communities, and the interaction of formal and informal organization within complex societies generally. In trying to incorporate both these new inputs and research interests, the present book not only includes more recent data, but also clarifies certain conceptual points, elaborates new hypotheses, suggests lines for future research and provides additional references to recent anthropological research on socialist societies.

The sub-discipline called "East European Anthropology" (here meant to include only Western anthropological research on Eastern European societies) has led a precarious existence. This precariousness reflects East European Anthropology's problematic position within the discipline of Anthropology, its marginality to key issues of Soviet/East European Studies, and its vulnerability to political conjunctures (which can limit fieldwork opportunities and influence research conclusions).[3]

The objectives of this book are to help consolidate anthropology's position within each of these three domains. First, as an ethnographic monograph, it seeks to incorporate "the socialist culture area" into the mainstream of contemporary anthropological theory. East Europeanists have themselves acknowledged the limited theoretical impact of their work on anthropology at large. This may be partly attributable to our colleagues' traditional prejudice against those who do fieldwork in Europe, but part of the blame lies with East Europeanists themselves. Through conscious intent, cautious necessity or simple isolation in our field settings, we have tended to avoid examining the most fundamental feature of contemporary East European societies—their political character. It is as if anthropologists fear to tread on ground which has up to now been claimed by political scientists and sociologists. Yet no anthropological study of East European life—be it household economy, ethnic relations or death rituals—can afford to ignore the political culture of socialism. It is by confronting rather than avoiding the explicitly socialist nature of these societies that East European Anthropology can make its most significant contribution to our discipline. Insofar as this task is accomplished, the socialist cultures (including those beyond Eastern Europe) can take their places alongside our traditional ethnographic tribes and peasants from New Guinea, East Africa, Mexico, or the Amazon. Perhaps one day, anthropology textbooks will be discussing the structure of socialist bureaucracies and the symbolism of "the plan" as they now discuss African brideprice, or the potlatch on the Northwest Coast.

The second objective of this book is to bridge the gaps in the field of Soviet/East European Area Studies. Here again, the status of East European Anthropology has been problematic. Our traditional interests in powerless groups, peripheral populations, rural communities, archaic traditions or exotic customs have generated little common ground for discussion with other East European specialists. Our focus on face-to-face relations and our largely qualitative descriptions of East Eurpean rural life are hardly amenable to the macro-oriented, quantitatively inclined social scientists within the Soviet Studies establishment. Moreover, nearly all anthropological studies have focused on countries outside the Soviet Union.[4] Unlike other area specialists, East Europeanist anthropologists find it particularly difficult to transfer local-level results from "Soviet-type" societies to the USSR itself. Because of our disciplinary proclivities and our non-Soviet fieldwork, much of the work of East European Anthropology has been regarded as irrelevant by the Soviet/and East European Studies community. Our foci are seen as misplaced, our methods unscientific, our data noncomparable and our results trivial, or at best, merely "interesting." In discussions with fellow area specialists, the mere fact that an American anthropologist could conduct independent, long-term fieldwork in an East European village generates more discussion than any scientific conclusions we present. Instead of being asked, "What did you find out?", we are asked, "How did you get in?" This interdisciplinary communications gap has also affected anthropologists. Having been brought up with the idea that one understands another culture only by living among its people, we are incredulous to meet scholars who have written whole books about countries they have never set foot in.

Cognizant of these interdisciplinary differences, I have endeavoured in this book to meet my Soviet/East European Area Studies colleagues on some common ground. In this case, it is the subject of "socialist planning." Using what I term a "vertical slice" framework, I examine socialist planning from the perspective of national policy and socialist ideology and try to relate these to day-to-day events in a single urbanizing community. Soviet Studies has already produced detailed analyses of socialist *institutions*—party bureaucracies, central committees, ideological apparatuses, state planning organs and industrial enterprises. Let us not forget, however, that socialist societies also contain "real people." Understanding how these people cope with formal institutions can best be brought out with the eclectic methods, long-term fieldwork, participant-observation, qualitative descriptions and holistic focus which remain the hallmark of sociocultural anthropology.

Within Soviet/East European Area Studies, anthropologists should do more than fill in gaps in the literature, provide "interesting" descriptions of furnish anecdotes about fieldwork. An explicitly anthropological approach must try to bridge interdisciplinary gaps, or better yet, to do away with these gaps altogether.

The third objective of this book is a political one. In examining "actually existing" socialist planning, I am trying to take a step toward a more genuine "socialist anthropology." Socialist anthropology, as I see it, should not be confused with the "Marxist anthropology" which has had over a decade of relative popularity in our discipline. In fact, Marxist thinking has been practically irrelevant for those anthropologists trying to understand how East European societies work.

In both Marxist and non-Marxist scholarship, there has been a tendency to substitute labels and verdicts for more nuanced analyses of Eastern European societies. These labels have come from "official" East European scholars, who persist in calling their societies "socialist" in spite of the manifest contradictions with the visions of Marx and of most Communist Party members. Labelling has also been characteristic of the more critical left-wing scholars, who see East Europe in terms of "state capitalism," "bureaucratic ruling class," "degenerated workers' state" or the nebulous "transitional between capitalism and socialism." In the liberal camp, there is no shortage of paradigms which in themselves carry ideological or political verdicts about Eastern Europe. The "totalitarian" paradigm has been replaced by theories of "convergence," and later by notions of these societies as "bureaucratized," "corporatized," "modernizing" and "neo-traditional." The "convergence" argument has been continually undermined by the enigmatic character of Eastern Europe: its unexpected uprisings, its inexplicable passivity, its "muddling through." Finally, the rhetoric of political commisars does little to help scholars discover how East Europe works. We are dealing with societies which are far from "developed socialism" (Brezhnev) and eminently more complex than "the work of the devil" (Reagan). It is thus gratifying to know that the nuanced data of anthropology, its holistic description of daily life, is particularly ill-suited for making such verdicts.

The societies of actual socialism are new and historically unique social formations, amenable neither to classical Marxist analysis nor to traditional social science theory. Thus the need for a "socialist anthropology," a task which is both scientifically demanding and politically sensitive. The task of a socialist anthropology is to understand how actual socialist societies work, how they "muddle through." Only by understanding socialism as it actually exists—devoid of ideals and shunting aside verdicts—can we forge a better vision of an emancipatory socialism. This book studies one aspect of actual socialism in a single country, using a case study of one urbanizing community. At this modest level, my intention is to show that an anthropology of actual socialism is not only necessary; it is also possible.

In carrying out the research and in writing the original manuscript, my greatest intellectual debt is to my former advisor, Professor John W. Cole. John's continuously expanding research interests, inspiring teaching and provocative criticisms were a constant source of inspiration to me. As chairman of my dissertation committee, as teacher, colleague and friend, John was all that any insecure graduate student could have wished for. Despite the physical distance which now separate us, I am sure that our mutual collaboration will continue in the future.

I also wish to thank other members of my dissertation committee, Ralph Faulkingham, Alan Swedlund and Richard Wilkie, for providing extremely helpful comments on early drafts of the dissertation.

The book was written as part of larger collaborative project, led by Professor Cole, on the Socialist Transformation in Southern Transylvania. Begun in 1973, the project has dealt with socialist planning, ethnic relations, ecological adjustments, household economics and village state relations in both synchronic and diachronic perspectives. My own research thus benefitted from collaboration with fellow members of our Romania Research Group: Sam Beck, David Kideckel, Marilyn McArthur and Steven Randall. During our simultaneous fieldwork and our subsequent collaboration, each of my fellow colleagues has enriched my understanding of Romanian life. Most of all they helped prevent me from making the typical mistake of the anthropologist: assuming that "my village" reflects Romanian society in general.

Most of the field data from this book was collected between 1974 and 1976, largely in the village of Feldioara, Brașov County. My fieldwork received the administrative support and active cooperation of several Romanian institutions. I would particularly like to thank the National Council for Science and Technology, the Academy for Social and Political Sciences, the Center for Sociological Research (Bucharest), the People's Council of Brașov County and the People's Council of Feldioara Commune. The staff at the Brașov Systematization Office was particularly helpful during my weeks spent studying planning documents there.

The citizens of Feldioara, where my wife and I lived for most of our stay in Romania, deserve special thanks for the friendship and support given us from the first day we arrived in the village in January 1974. Having returned to Feldioara yearly since then—for research and for pleasure—we now regard it as our second home, and the Pirvu family as our second family. It is with both anthropological curiosity and personal involvement that I follow the social transformations and minor events which are occurring daily in Feldioara. I have every confidence that the villagers will have the ability to cope with these changes (*a descurca*), in their traditionally civilized fashion.

Alongside government cooperation and village hospitality, I was fortunate to have received generous financial support for fieldwork in Romania and write-up time from the following organizations: University of Massachusetts, European Field Studies Program (1974), International Research and Exchanges Board (1975-76), Fulbright-Hays Doctoral Dissertation Abroad research program (1975-76), and the Ford Foundation (via a grant to the University of Massachusetts Romanian Studies Center, led by John W. Cole, 1977).

For helping to defray part of the costs of preparing and publishing the final manuscript, I am especially indebted to the Danish Social Science Research Council.

Finally, I wish to thank Vibeke Sampson for her companionship and assistance during the fieldwork, for her patient understanding during my prolonged analysis of the data and for her sympathetic prodding during my periods of procrastination. In all these trials of research, Vibeke's constant encouragement proved invaluable. May it remain so in the future.

S. L. S.
Copenhagen, August 1983

NOTES TO PREFACE

1.   The emergence of East European Anthropology is indicated in several ways. Meetings of the American Anthropological Association invariably include formal symposia and informal meetings sponsored by the

East European Anthropology Group or the Socialist Societies Group. In 1982 the semi-annual *Newsletter of the East European Anthropology Group* appeared (ed. by W. Lockwood at the University of Michigan). Recent collections of articles on Eastern Europe have appeared in *East European Quarterly*, *Dialectical Anthropology* and *Anthropological Quarterly*. Finally, Halpern and Kideckel's review article ("Anthropology of Eastern Europe") lists no less than 221 published sources (see *Annual Review of Anthropology 1983*). To this should be added the numerous dissertations, manuscripts and collections now in preparation. While fieldwork possibilities in Eastern Europe are greatly affected by funding limitations and political conjunctures, anthropological writing about Eastern Europe is steadily growing.

2. This expression, originally employed by former East German Party Secretary Walter Ulbricht, was later popularized by Rudolf Bahro in his *The Alternative in Eastern Europe* (London: New Left Books, 1978). The quotation marks denote the conceptual inadequacy of the term "socialism" to these societies. Bahro distinguishes "actual socialism" from a more genuine, "emancipatory socialism."

3. In successive issues of the *Newsletter of the East European Anthropology Group*, John Cole has further discussed the triple dilemma of East European Anthropology: "as Anthropology," "as Area Studies" and as "Politics." See vols. 1 (2), 2 (1, 2) and 3 (1) for discussion, debate and rejoinder.

4. Western anthropological interest in the Soviet Union began with Margaret Mead's and Geoffrey Gorer's wartime studies of Russian modal personality, based solely on literary and emigre sources. Later work was confined to translating Soviet ethnographic works (Benet's *The People of Viriatno*, Dunn and Dunn's *People of Great Russia*). Shorter expeditions were carried out by Benet among the Abkazians and by Balzer among the Siberian Ostiak. Humphrey's recently published *Karl Marx Collective*, which deals with the Siberian Buryat, represents the only instance of long term fieldwork in the USSR conducted by a Western anthropologist. It remains significant, however, that all this recent research perpetuates the anthropological focus on groups which are peripheral rural, powerless and quasi-exotic.

CHAPTER I

INTRODUCTION: THE ANTHROPOLOGY
OF SOCIALIST PLANNING

The Aims of this Study

This book is intended as a contribution to the anthropology of complex society in general and its socialist variant in particular. It describes the articulation of local, regional and national structures within one of Europe's most underdeveloped nations—the Socialist Republic of Romania. In socialist societies like Romania, it is the task of the state planning apparatus to integrate local communities into the national political economy. It follows that the study of national integration under socialism should begin with an analysis of socialist planning.

This study analyzes socialist planning from an anthropological perspective. It focuses on the policy and practice of Romanian settlement planning or "systematization" (Rom. *sistematizare*). The Romanian rural systematization program aims at restructuring the country's entire network of rural settlements: thousands of rural communities will be modernized, hundreds of "irrational" settlements phased out and 300 villages developed into new towns. The first half of this study describes the ideological background and national context behind Romania's systematization program. The second half analyzes how the plan is being implemented in one of the 300 new towns.

1

The explicitly anthropological approach to Romanian planning has several objectives. First, such an approach emphasizes the interconnections between social institutions and individual ideas and behavior. It seeks to explain how people think and act by defining the social matrices in which action occurs. The focus here will be on the planning institution and its effect on planners and on community members in a village undergoing urbanization.

A second characteristic of the anthropological approach is that it seeks to render a qualitative picture of daily life and human relations in concrete societies. This study examines social relations in two disparate settings: the planning office and a community of Romanian villagers.

The third distinguishing feature of the anthropological approach is that it is holistic: it attempts to elucidate the elements of an entire cultural system by showing the interrelations and contradictions among elements of that system. In examining one aspect of Romania's cultural system, the planning institution, both "the culture of the planners" and the culture of the village communities in which they work will have to be analyzed. Only then will we be able to understand the internal contradictions of Romanian society as revealed through the planning process.

To achieve these objectives, anthropologists rely on a variety of field methods, the basic one being long term participant-observation carried out in one or more bounded social settings. Data for this study has been gathered from planning documents and interviews with planners, as well as from fieldwork in planning offices and in the village of Feldioara. Hence, in both basic objectives and research methods, this study of socialist planning in Romania continues the traditions of qualitative, holistic anthropological analysis as set forth above.

As an anthropological study of planning, this study brings up problems which are at once empirical, theoretical, practical and methodological. At the empirical level, this book contributes to the discussion of "socialism as it actually exists" (after Bahro 1978). It describes the ideological and social foundations of Romanian planning, the process by which plans are formulated and executed and the relationship between their intended and unintended consequences. What emerges is a picture of the planning process as the pivotal mechanism for integrating local communities into the larger society. The planning process (and not simply "The Plan") makes for the distinctive characteristics of national integration under "actually existing socialism."

At the theoretical level, this monograph is concerned with the nature of noncorporate social organization in ostensibly bureaucratized societies. Too often we have tended to counterpose bureaucratic administration to noncorporate "corruption." In doing so, we have forgotten that their mutual interaction determines how the system works (and how it fails). An analysis of Romanian systemization in both its formal and noncorporate aspects can lead to more sophisticated ways of looking at socialist bureaucracies and at bureaucratic organization in general. Instead of relegating noncorporate or informal organization to "noise" in the system, we can bring it into its proper place in the social matrix of complex society.

From a practical perspective, this book examines a particular development program in its national and local manifestations. By analyzing planners' culture and the interaction between bureaucratic and informal social structures, we will see that the very nature of development planning generates problems for local communities. An understanding of why these problems arise can help us to explain how planning works in complex societies—East, West and South. With this knowledge, we can be in a better position to design more effective development programs.

Finally, at the methodological level, this book outlines an alternative strategy for studying complex societies. In contrast to approaches which focus on territorial units such as village, region or nation, this book uses a "vertical slice" approach: it focuses on a societal institution in its national, regional and local dimensions. Here the vertical slice method will be applied to a key institution of Romanian society: planning. However, there is no reason why the vertical slice cannot be applied to other institutional domains besides planning and in other settings outside Romania (cf. Nader 1980 for a study of how American business institutions affect children's life chances).

This introductory chapter elaborates some of the issues raised above, beginning with a review of anthropological approaches to national integration. It outlines the logic of the vertical slice approach to planning as a method for explaining national integration processes in Romania and comments on the data base, the fieldwork and the political questions generated from this analysis of "actually existing socialist planning."

Approaches to National Integration

As the mid-1930s, anthropologists had begun extending their inquiry from tribal to state-level societies. In doing so, they were confronted by a seeming contradiction. On the one hand, there existed the relatively self-contained peasant community which had a social dynamic of its very own and a stubborn autonomy that seemed to belie its subordination under powerful states. On the other hand, anthropologists knew that the village was subject to economic, social and political forces which had their origins beyond it. The problem was to reconcile the existence of the social integrity of the community with the pervasive dominance of national-level institutions.

One way to resolve the problem was to conceive of the village as a microcosm of the national society, a perspective first promulgated by Malinowski in his 1938 Preface to Fei's *Peasant Life in China*. "By becoming acquainted with the life of the small village," writes Malinowski, "we study under a microscope as it were the epitome of China at large" (1938: ii, cited in Freedman 1968:146). The major assumption of Malinowski, and of the emerging "community studies" school in general, was the identity between microcosm and macrocosm (Freedman 1968, Leeds 1973). However, the Chinese village is hardly a replica of Chinese civilization. Freedman writes:

> it would seem that from [Malinowski's] patient induction from studies of small social areas would emerge a picture of the social system of China. Of all the biases to which the anthropological approach has been subject, this seems to me to be the most grievous. It is the anthropological fallacy *par excellence* (Freedman 1968:146).

The "microcosm" approach to national integration was prominent in anthropology through the 1960s. In its most controversial forms, Banfield and Banfield (1958) and Foster (1965) used the data of community-based interpersonal conflicts as a framework for explaining the underdevelopment of whole nations.

With the rise of the "modernization" paradigm in anthropology, the microcosm view came to be replaced by a focus on "the changing village community" (summarized in Halpern 1967, see also Dalton 1971). These studies chronicled the consequences of industrialization, urbanization, commercialization and Western innovations as they penetrated "traditional" peasant villages. The key focus was on the post-war changes radiating from the West, rather than on change itself. Stavenhagen notes the ethnocentrism of this approach:

> It is frequently thought that change is a recent phenomenon, perhaps dating from the end of the Second World War, that the so-called traditional communities are only just now, as Hoselitz (1960) puts it, "being drawn into a social framework with much more complex and more highly stratified structures." It is believed, or at least implied, that before the present-day processes of "modernization", rural society was essentially static, and that the term "traditional" is used to refer to some sort of eternal or perhaps slowly drifting type of social organization which is only now awakening under the impact of external innovations (Stavenhagen 1964:316).

Whereas the "microcosm" approach stressed the identity between local and national-level processes, the "changing village community" studies tended to place the village in an exclusively antagonistic relationship with the encroaching state or market. Processes of change were depicted as a struggle between two diametrically opposed entities: the eternal, unchanging villages *versus* the disruptive "outside forces", the folk elements *versus* the urban elements, the Little Tradition *versus* the Great Tradition, backwardness *versus* modernity. The "dualistic" character of the ex-colonial nations was a hindrance to their development. In order to eliminate this dualism, "tradition" would have to give way to innovation. Like the "microcosm" approach, the "changing village community" approach used the individual rural community as the unit of analysis. This stress on the community served to perpetuate the existence of artificial boundaries between village and "outside world", such that "the anthropology of economic development" came to be equated with "The Modernization of Village Communities" (as Dalton subtitled his 1971 book of readings on the subject).

The conceptual flaws of the "microcosm" and "changing village community" approaches have largely been rectified by contemporary anthropology. The village is understood neither as a miniature of the national society nor its dialectical opposite. In fact, the sociological village "community" may be conceived of as little more than a geographic "locality", where supralocal and even supranational forces play themselves out in local space (Leeds 1973). Instead of debating whether or not the village is integrated into the larger society, contemporary anthropology now takes this as an a priori assumption. The task is to describe the varieties of articulation between smaller and larger units and the diverse ways in which local communities are integrated into modern states.

For instance, one form of integration might be via the "unequal exchange" of the market. The role of the market is usually reinforced by integrative social, political or religious institutions, ethnic or regional affiliations, and by noncorporate social relations such as patronage or coalitions. Another form is the cyclical migration of household members who labor periodically on the plantation, in the mines or factories of "the outside world" (Stavenhagen 1964, Amin 1974a).

Early attempts to describe this articulation were made by Redfield, in his "folk-urban continuum" and Great Tradition/Little Tradition dichotomy (Redfield 1941, 1947, 1956). A more successful effort was made by Eric Wolf, who showed how "closed corporate" and "open" communities were integrated into the larger society differently as a result of historical and ecological causes (Wolf 1955, 1956, 1957, 1959, 1966b, Wolf and Hansen 1972, Cole and Wolf 1974). Wolf's view is supported by Stavenhagen, who reminds us that "the Latin American corporate community is in itself a result of Spanish colonial policy" (1964:329). In like manner, Alavi (1973) notes that open and closed corporate communities result from the same general process, i.e. the encapsulation of smaller units by supralocal institutions. Similar conclusions have been reached by diverse groups of social scientists working within the frameworks of "dependency theory" (Frank 1967, 1969, Emmanuel 1972, Amin 1974b), "modes of production" (Foster-Carter 1978, Laclau 1979, Kahn 1981), and "world systems" (Wallerstein, 1974a, 1974b, 1979, Hechter 1975, Schneider and Schneider 1976, Chirot 1976, 1977, Kaplan 1978, Goldfrank 1979, Hopkins and Wallerstein 1980; see also the journal Review edited by Hopkins and Wallerstein). The central message of these "schools" is that the seemingly backward, traditional or "feudal" areas have in fact been integral parts of a complex, capitalist world-economy. The maintenance of folk/traditional isolation is a result of community integration into the world-system. Research within the world-system paradigm centers on explaining how various regions achieved their status as "core", "semi-periphery" or "periphery".

Despite the advances made in depicting how local units are encapsulated by wider systems, we are still left with a problem of studying the system as a whole. Implicit in the world-system approach (as with "microcosm" and "changing village community" studies) is a model for societal integration based on *concentric circles*. Thus, the "individual" and "household" represent the smallest of these circles; they are circumscribed by "village", "region", "nation" and "world-system", respectively. Bringing in units beyond the community generates a dilemma: how do we determine *the* proper units of analysis?

In attempting to address this question, some anthropologists have chosen to simply transfer their field of inquiry from a smaller societal "ring" to a larger one. Thus, the ethnographic study of the bounded community has been overshadowed by the interdisciplinary study of regions or nations (cf. Adams 1967, 1970, Cohn 1971, Fallers 1974, Smith 1976). The tendency to give priority to large-scale units of analysis has led some anthropologists to renounce community studies entirely:

> The community study method is wholly inadequate to the study of state-organized societies, nations, complex societies, countries or whatever one wants to call them (Leeds 1973:19).

Leeds may be correct in his rejection of the theoretical assumptions of community studies (i.e., microcosm equals macrocosm), but he forgets that the community study remains an invaluable *method* for learning how complex societies operate. It would be ill-advised to abandon the study of smaller units solely because these are encapsulated into larger ones. As Lloyd Fallers remarked:

> the microcosmic view contributes something to an understanding of a nation's political life that cannot be gotten from other standpoints and methods of data gathering (Fallers 1974:19).

This is because

> the formal, self-consciously purposive operations [of the nation-state] are mediated through the sociocultural microcosms, interlaced with

internal and external personal ties, that form the setting for day to day life (Fallers 1974:21).

In renouncing the study of one concentric circle (community) we risk becoming trapped by the limitations of another (region, nation, world-system). This would mean that the crucial connections between units— the *essence* of complex society—would be overlooked.

To accept the validity of the world-system perspective should not necessarily render the community study obsolete. On the contrary, the community study method remains essential for revealing how national institutions work in modern society. This is no less true for socialist societies, where national institutions are dominated by the state, the party or the planning apparatus.

The question remains, however, as to the best method of analyzing these links between institutions and "sociocultural microcosms." Within anthropology, the most promising research paradigm is that of "action theory", as reviewed recently by Joan Vincent (1978). Action theory has its roots in the studies of African chiefs under colonialism, village politics in India, political conflict in community arenas, and in the Latin American and Mediterranean "broker" literature (Gluckman 1955, 1963, 1973, Bailey 1960, 1969, Swartz 1973, Wolf 1956, 1966a). Action theory looks at complex society by analysing the behavior of certain key individuals in the local social structure. Examining these individuals' role demands, interpersonal conflicts and social encounters, action theorists attempt to locate mechanisms of national integration and build models of social process.

Who are these key individuals? For Max Gluckman (1963, 1968) they occupy intermediary positions in various local institutions; e.g., industrial foremen, shop stewards, noncommissioned officers, school prefects, local chiefs and district commissioners. For Isaac Schapera, writing over forty years ago, the key individuals were those who lived outside the immediate community but who were in intimate contact with it; thus, "the missionary, administrator, trader and labor recruiter must be regarded as factors in the tribal life in the same way as are the chief and the magician" (Schapera 1938:27, cited in Gluckman 1968:70). The present-day subjects of action theory are those who straddle the interface between peasant community and the national society: patrons, brokers, middlemen, traders, entrepreneurs and local elites.

A major field of interest for action theorists is the study of noncorporate forms of social organization, particularly patron-client relations (cf. Eisenstadt and Roniger 1980 for a comprehensive bibliography). Put in terms of the "concentric circle" model of societal integration, noncorporate social organization serves either to link smaller circles with each other (e.g. household-to-household) or to tie local units into supralocal structures (e.g. political clientelism, peasant coalitions, entrepreneurship).

However, the flexibility of noncorporate organization can generation countervailing processes which hinder full integration between the community and the larger society. This is illustrated in studies of political middlemen, who seek to retain their brokerage functions by restricting local access to national institutions (cf. Swartz 1968, Littlewood 1974, Bax 1975). Similar phenomenon can be found in studies of banditry, mafia, ethnic and regional movements, peasant revolts, political clientelism and "corruption" (e.g. Hobsbawm 1969, 1971, Wolf 1969, Pi-sunyer 1971, Blok 1974, Aya 1975). In trying to account for the contradictory nature of noncorporate social organization, action theorists look for the historical circumstances behind community social structure and the social constraints on interpersonal relations.

Because action theory emphasizes dynamic processes rather than static structures, it represents a clear advance over earlier approaches to complex society. Yet in describing these processes action theory tends to take individuals as the one and only unit of analysis. These individuals unceasingly pursue their various "strategies" by playing according to "the rules of the game" and manipulating their fellow players (Barth 1969, Bailey 1969, Boissevain 1973). As numerous critics have pointed out, this stress on individual "gamesmanship" masks the importance of political-economic constraints on individual decisions (cf. Paine 1969, Asad 1973, Alavi 1973, Sylverman 1974, Vincent 1978). Action theory places too much emphasis on reciprocity and not enough on power; it downplays the class bais of elite hegemony, as it concentrates on the elites' presumed competition for clients. It fails to explain why some people can break the rules of the game whenever they see fit and why entire classes of people are consistently better at "playing the game" than others.

In sum, action theory has two principal weaknesses: first, by focusing exclusively on the individuals who link concentric circles, it neglects the structures which integrate them into larger social systems; second, by its preoccupation with noncorporate social organization excludes the study of formal institutions. Perhaps this second weakness stems from the traditional division of labor between anthropology an the other social scientists. Anthropology studied peripheral or marginal peoples whose small communities were integrated via kinship relations. The study of formal, corporate institutions was left to political scientists, sociologists and economists. This division of labor has tended to inhibit anthropologists from explaining how and why noncorporate social organization functions. This is because noncorporate processes cannot be understood without reference to the formal bureaucratic institutions with which they articulate.

This study employs an alternative approach to the study of national integration. This approach has two principal objectives: (1) to show the structural rather than ideological linkages between community, region and nation; and (2) to maintain equal emphasis on both supralocal institutions and noncorporate social organization in the analysis of national integration processes. This alternative perspective on complex society can be called the "vertical slice" approach.

The Vertical Slice Approach

The concentric circle model of complex society created the problem of deciding on the most relevant level (or unit) of study—e.g., household, village, region, nation, world-system. The vertical slice approach renders this problem superfluous; instead of choosing a specific level, we select a discrete societal institution and examine how it manifests itself through all the levels of society—from the national polity down to the community, household and individual. Where the concentric circle approach highlights individual manipulators and noncorporate relations, a vertical slice perspective locates individuals and groups within the functioning of a formal, corporate institution.

The assumption of the vertical slice method is that rationality and hierarchy are only partial attributes of an institution's structure. Beneath the formal bureaucratic shell exist more subtle structures which determines the institution's real functioning. These noncorporate social relations are embedded even in the most highly bureaucratized organizations. Understanding how noncorporate social relations work can help explain some of the more enigmatic aspects of bureaucratic institutions. The vertical slice perspective helps to reveal the complementary relationship which exists between formally structured corporate institutions and informally structured "supplementary sets" (Wolf 1966a).

The Planning Institution as Vertical Slice

The following chapters describe the national, regional and local manifestations of a single vertical slice: the Romanian planning apparatus and its program to convert 300 of the country's 13,000 villages into urban centers. In both its bureaucratic and noncorporate aspects, the planning institutions will serve as a mirror, reflecting the processes of national integration in Romanian society.

By choosing this particular vertical slice for intensive analysis, we establish a basis for three comparisons. First, we can compare Romania's planning strategy with the settlement planning strategies of other socialist and capitalist countries. Second, we can assess the extent to which the planned urbanization of rural localities contributes to fulfilling Romania's goal of national economic growth. Third, we have the basis for a comparison of socialist and capitalist urbanization.

From a methodological standpoint, the planning slice is well-suited for showing the value of anthropology in the study of complex socieites. On the surface, planning appears to be a technical, rational and bureaucratic activity, quite unlike the traditional communities studied by most anthropologists. On closer examination, we find that the large-scale institutional goals of the planning apparatus and its formally constituted task groups are permeated by personal strategies, cross-cutting interest groups, recessed conflicts and alternative ideologies. These informal aspects are hidden beneath the formal, corporate structure of the planning institution. Analysis of that institution will thus provide a perfect setting for testing the strengths and limitations of the vertical slice approach.

If we were to employ a concentric circle approach to planning, the focus would be on the villagers' reactions to outside inputs as represented by the plan. From the vertical slice perspective, however, planning is seen as a social process which reflects the interaction between the community and the larger society. Hence, planners' activities become as much a part of "local social organization" as do household composition or land tenure arrangements. Analysis of the planning process demands continuous movement up and down the vertical slice: data can come from archives of national planning offices, interviews with regional-level planners, observation of planner-villager interactions and participation in community events connected to plan execution.

Moving up and down the slice does not obviate the necessity to distinguish levels or units of analysis, however. There are clearcut differences between the institution as it appears at the level of the national polity and in its interaction with community social organization. Therefore, it is necessary to distinguish the factors which appear at each level and show how they affect the structure of the institution being studied. Analysis of Romanian systemization requires that we analyze national and regional planning decisions, the way in which these decisions are executed, the relations between planners and the community, and the linkage between local elites and individual households.

It seems reasonable to assume that the key factors influencing planners will be most noticeable where there are heavy demands placed on local communities. This is the case with the 300 villages now being converted into small towns. Hence, one of these villages, called Feldioara, will serve as a case study of planning at the local level. The data from Feldioara indicate that things do not always go "according to plan." The plan may be distorted, corrupted or ignored. In trying to account for these alterations we ask a series of questions: Is it due to some aspect of the plan itself? Does it have something to do with the persons in charge of executing or monitoring the plan? Are the alterations due to idiosynchratic characteristics of the village in which the plan is being executed? By answering these and other questions, we establish the set of constraints and determinants which structure the relationship between the planning institution and the village community. We thus obtain a picture of planning as a bureaucratic institution *and* as a social process which integrates local units into the larger social whole. Moreover, inasmuch as it is the planning mechanism which integrates socialist society, we can better define the natue of "actually existing socialism."

It should be emphasized that this integration can occur even if the plan itself is deemed a failure! This is because it is not "the Plan" which integrates socialist society but the *planning process*. In using the vertical slice approach, we will find that this process involves more than just the formal institutional structure; it involves personalistic ites, noncorporate groups, amorphous social networks, unstated ideologies and conflicting social structures.

This "planning process" can be studied from four different vantage points (these four dimensions are elaborated in Sampson [1983c]). First, we must study the *plan as a physical, social and symbolic model for social-ist society*. Socialist societies are not "planned societies" but "societies with a plan." A study of the planning process in Romania must concern itself with the way the plan affects society as a whole—economically, politically, socially, and even symbolically as a vision for a utopic future.

Second, we must study the *planners as actors in the planning organi-zation*. In anthropological terms, we must examine "the culture of the planners"; how they think, how they act, the rhetoric of planning, or what may be called "planner ideologies."

Third, we must analyze the *planning bureaucracy as an organization*, with its own particular goals, conflicts, interest groups, sections, regions, and social forces, e.g. the technocrats versus the politicians. The planning bureaucracy can be seen as the anthropological "village" as an arena of social action.

Fourth, we must examine the *relation between those in the organiza-tion and those outside it*. Specifically, we must look at the relation be-tween the planners and "the people." From the villagers' standpoint, this is considered as the problem of participation. From the perspective of the planners, it is the problem of mobilizing citizens to achieve national objectives.

In describing the planning process in Romania, it will become evident that there are local-level factors which affect planning as well as institu-tional constraints on community social processes. More importantly, we will be able to demonstrate that alterations in the plan, while they may have been unintended by the planners, are certainly not unpredictable. Alterations in the plan presuppose a purely rational structure which has somehow been "distorted." In fact, such a structure does not exist. Rather, alterations in the plan are logical results of the interaction between institu-tional and noncorporate aspects of the planning process.

Organization of this Study

Using the vertical slice perspective, this study analyzes Romanian plan-ning from the national, regional and community levels. At the national level there are three factors influencing the planning process. These are:

1) *planning-in-general*—i.e. how much of what actually happens in plan
   formulation and execution can be explained by the nature of planning as a technical, social and ideological activity?

2) *the socialist factor*—to what extent is the planning process affected
   by Marxist ideology or the explicitly socialist characteristics of Romanian planning?

3) *national specificity*—what specific social and historical circumstances
   make socialist planning distinctively Romanian, as compared with
   other East European or Third World countries?

The national-level factors are revealed through national policy statements, official documents and the ideologies and actions of national and
county-level planners.

A second set of factors affecting Romanian planning lie at the regional
level. These *regional factors* result from the economic, ecological, ethnic,
demographic and historical circumstances which give each zone its own
special characteristics. In Romania the relevant regional planning units are
the forty counties (*județe*) plus the municipality of Bucharest. This study
focuses on Brașov County as an example of regional-level determinants of
the planning process. Located at the bend of the Carpathian mountains,
in the geographic center of Romania, Brașov County contains a diversity
of settlement types and local economies: uncollectivized pastoral hamlets
in the highlands, lowland collectivized villages, and developed suburban
communities. Like every region, Brașov County has its atypical features:
the level of industrialization and urbanization is higher than most other
counties, and the proportion of ethnic minorities in the County population is above the national average. The exact nature of regional-level
effects on the planning process will vary with the characteristics of each
region; however, Brașov County's high level of development, its ecological
variation and ethnic diversity can provide a more well-defined picture of
how these factors operate.

Planning at the village level is affected by two sets of factors. One is
the *village social organization*, broadly defined as the relation between
local ecology, household economies, social relations and their ideological/
moral functions. Characteristics of village social organization will determine the potential for household mobilization in implementing the plan,
and thus have a direct bearing on planning success.

The second local-level factor involves the village elites. Though an integral part of the social structure, the elites are set apart by their role as executors of state policies and by their "gatekeeper" functions with respect to the planning apparatus, Party organization and the national society at large. The focus here is on the social characteristics, personal goals and concrete mobilization activities of the elites. Understanding elite behavior can help explain how planning works at the local level. Moreover, it will also shed light on the nature of bureaucratic administration in socialist communities.

The vertical slice analysis of socialist planning begins with the higher level institutional factors and descends to the micro-level interactions in one particular locality. Chapter Two discusses theories of regional planning and development, paying special attention to the social constraints generated by any planning scheme.

Chapter Three describes planning in the socialist countries so as to elucidate those factors peculiar to a socialist political economy.

Chapter Four focuses specifically on Romania, its national settlement structure and the development of its rural systematization policy.

Chapter Five describes the regional level factors influencing the planning process by examining the planning organization and regional-local relations in Braşov County.

Chapter Six begins the case study of planned urbanization in the village of Feldioara (Braşov County). This chapter details the historical, social and economic factors which caused Feldioara to be selected as a new town, but which also spawned local processes that transform the plan.

These transformations are shown in Chapter Seven, which deals with the plan for Feldioara's urbanization and its initial implementation in the community.

Chapter Eight focuses on the household-level factors which determine the degree of citizen mobilization in Feldioara.

Chapter Nine examines planning execution from the perspective of local elites, showing why some elites have difficulties in mobilizing the population.

Chapter Ten offers recommendations as to how the planning process could be improved; it concludes with suggestions of how the study of socialist integration and regional planning can help us to understand national development in general and socialist bureaucracy in particular.

Fieldwork in Romania

The need to understand planning from both the national and community perspectives required the collection of extremely different types of data from diverse sources. Long-term fieldwork in the village of Feldioara (1974-76) has been supplemented by extensive consultations with planners and archival research in national and county libraries and offices. More than three of my total sixteen months in Romania were spent in the Brașov County planning office, talking with staff members and analyzing the plans for various communities in the country. In addition, I read through back issues of the county newspaper *Drum Nou* ("New Road"), the national daily *Scînteia* ("Spark") and numerous planning and social science publications to find expressions of national planning ideology.

The fieldwork was not without its frustrations, of course (outlined in detail in Kideckel and Sampson (1983). As I waited nervously outside an office to seek permission to copy a map, or when I attempted to set up an appointment with a county official to ask his views on "socialist cities," I envied my anthropologist colleagues who were using their time to gather extensive data on village social organization and household economy. In retrospect, it is evident that more local-level data could have bolstered my arguments about the influence of supralocal constraints; however, this local data would have been useless had I not spent the time and effort to obtain access to the planning offices, talk formally and informally with planners, browse through Party documents and old newspapers, and to carry out other fieldwork tasks which most anthropologists are neither trained for nor even interested in doing. This is but further evidence that the vertical slice method compels the researcher to use a more eclectic data gathering strategy, to the point where Romanians and even some Western social scientists failed to see anything "anthropological" about my project. This interdisciplinary misunderstanding reflects the generally precarious position of Western anthropologists who study East European societies. Aside from the gamut of fieldwork problems [Kideckel and Sampson 1983], we are faced with the problems of legitimating ourselves to fellow anthropologists, to the East European Area Studies "community" and to policy-makers for whom detailed knowledge of East Europe represents a political liability. These legitimation problems are discussed in a series of articles by John Cole [1982a, 1982b, 1983a].

A final note is in order concerning the time-frame of this study. Since leaving the field in August 1976, I have had the good fortune of returning to Romania for several short visits of 1-3 weeks each. These return visits were extremely productive, in that they served to validate some of my initial predictions while forcing the revision of others. Since the results of these visits are incorporated into this book, it is not possible to present a picture of Romanian planning within a precise "ethnographic present." Besides, Romanian planning policy and its consequences have changed all too rapidly; such fluctuation is a crucial aspect of the planning process. Hence, rather than the usual one-year ethnographic *present*, a five-year ethnographic *period* is used as the baseline for the data. This period stretches largely from 1974 through 1979, but also includes short visits from 1980 to 1983.

On Verdicts and Socialism

Finally, some remarks should be made on the broader implications of this study of "actually existing socialism" in Romania. Regardless of academic interests or political persuasions, all social scientists concern themselves with the question of "how the system really works." This helps to explain "why the system functions the way it does." The reader may wish to begin this book with a more skeptical approach to social systems. This is because there will be revealed a continuing stream of problems, dysfunctions, contradictions and shortcomings in the operation of Romanian planning. Rather than finding out how the system works, the reader may end up asking, "Is there a system at all?"

There is, and this will be demonstrated by showing the system at its points of friction. This is not meant to be an expression of anti-communist or anti-Romanian sentiment; on the contrary, this study is generally sympathetic to the *goals* of Romanian development. Why, then, stress the problems? There are scientific and practical reasons. From a scientific standpoint, elucidating the pressure points in the system can lead to a better understanding of Romanian society, and "actually existing socialism." On a more practical level, explicating the problems of planning and community social organization constitutes a first step toward their solutions. To focus on the dysfunctions of planning is only to admit that all development schemes—socialist or otherwise—create unintended consequences. The problems must therefore by accentuated—so that they can be solved!

This emphasis on the difficulties of socialist development has drawn the ire of Romanian scholars, most of whom would prefer to underline the overall success of Romanian policies, even while they point out its dysfunctions. This is not to imply cross-purposes, but simply a reflection of different social milieus and political contexts. Romanian scholars are justifiably preoccupied with resolving the contradictions that arise from the planning process. The Western social scientist, separated from the immediate responsibilities of policy making, is more interested in discovering why these contradictions appear in the first place. The Romanian approach is both educative and applied, whereas this study is more critical and analytical. There is no reason why these two perspectives cannot serve to complement each other. In order to understand the internal dynamics and external consequences of the planning process, we will find both approaches to be equally valuable and equally necessary.

The critical approach of this study may encourage the reader to formulate a final verdict about socialist planning in Romania, or socialism in general. Rather than leading to verdicts, which would be all too simplistic, the data and interpretations should hopefully lead to the reader to think about solutions to the problems cited. Some of these solutions may be of a more practical nature, in the sense of social engineering. Other solutions may be more theoretical, in that we re-emphasize the importance of informal social organization in the functioning of formal institutions. Finally, there are also political solutions to be considered, solutions which require a restructuring of the kinds of power configurations which spawned the problems in the first place. Some of these political choices are noted in the concluding chapter. While not central to this study, they add yet another dimension to the anthropological analysis of complex societies—socialist or capitalist, East, West or South.

CHAPTER II

PLANNING THEORY, DEVELOPMENT PLANNERS
AND LOCAL COMMUNITIES

Introduction

Romania shares with most other developing countries the opinion that Western European development experience is not an applicable model for the Third World today. There are three reasons for rejecting Western development models. First, whereas West European development was "pristine", Third World countries are trying to develop in the presence of already advanced competitors. Second, whereas West European development was inconceivable without the raw materials, labor and start-up capital extracted from its colonies, the Third World nations must accumulate capital from within their own national boundaries (usually from the peasantry). Third, the development objectives of Third World countries are extremely ambitious; they seek to accomplish in one or two generations what in Western Europe took nearly two centuries.

Because of these (and other) factors, Third World countries have chosen to pursue their goals via deliberately planned, State-directed intervention. For these countries, "planning" has become synonymous with "development planning." This relationship between planning and development will be the focus of this chapter.

It begins with a review of planning theory and practice as it appears in the literature. It then discusses more specific strategies for regional development, especially the complex relationship between optimum settlement hierarchies and economic growth. With this background, the final section of the chapter discusses the problems which planners are likely to encounter in rural communities.

This chapter does not deal with Romanian planning per se. However, some background in the general problems of regional development and planner-community relations will provide a better basis on which to judge Romanian systemization, a policy which contains developmental, socialist and national characteristics.

Planning

There are about as many definitions of planning as there are planners:

> A plan is a program for future action . . . . Planning is then the process of preparing such programs . . . it must 1) involve the future, 2) it must involve action, and 3) some agency must be responsible for causing the future action (Bornstein 1975:2).

> Planning is the process of preparing a set of decisions for action in the future, directed at achieving goals by preferable means (Dror 1963:33).

> Planning is defined here as the application of conscious and deliberate methods to capture the future for the purpose of either altering the present to redirect the future, or changing the future in order to preserve the present (Burke 1979:16).

> Planning is institutionalized and rationalized *ex ante* quantified socioeconomic development, over definite periods of time, carried out by deliberate human activity, on a certain area, and using instruments chosen in advance with the purpose of achieving economic gain by balancing resources with requirements (Bicanic 1967:2).

> Planning is the process [of selecting] a course of action (a set of means) for the attainment of ends. . . . A plan . . . is a decision with regard to a course of action (Banfield 1973:139, 140).

Planning is what planning agencies do. (Faludi 1973:1).

Planning thus encompasses several related activities: the determination of goals, gathering of information and preparation of possible options, choice of a specific alternative and the process by which that course of action is implemented (including the monitoring of its success/failure). Planning should be distinguished from "forecasting," which involves only the prediction of events. Forecasting normally has alternative futures, while planning—because it involves action—selects one of these future outcomes as the most desirable. All planning is done with regard to a course of action, even though in some cases the action may never be implemented. Neither should planning be confused with the selection of alternative options called "decision-making." Finally, planning requires more than simple "administration;" administration is but the implementation phase of planning, whereas planning includes both policy formation and execution. (Davidoff and Reiner 1973:30).

Planning involves certain *ends*, both long-term and short-term, and the choice of alternative *means* for attaining those ends (Bettelheim 1959:3). Debate over which ends or which means to use is not just a technical matter, but political and ideological as well. In fact, goals and the means of achieving them may not be determined by the planner but through administrative fiat or ideological doctrine. Planning is carried out by people with technical expertise *and* individual motivations. "Judgement permeats planning" at all phases of the process (Davidoff and Reiner 1973: 12).

Planning activities take place within a political nexus. According to Bailey, planning is "social control *par excellence*" (1975:19). Options are restricted more by poltiical constraints than by technical or financial limits.

> The exclusions from the debate itself are the most radical proposals and for the planner to imagine that the range of alternatives represents a real range is self-delusion (Bailey 1975:86).

With planning being defined as a complex process of goal determination and action, is it possible to judge a plan as "good" or "bad"? For example, there could be debate over how ends or means are determined;

i.e., how much *participation* was there in formulating policy? A second area of controversy centers on the *validity* of the ends or means selected. Are the "priorities" rational? Is the "public interest" served? Third, one could question the *methods* by which plans are implemented: Does the end justify the means? Finally, one could question the *efficiency* of the plan: Have the means used actually achieved the desired ends? Western critics of socialist planning, for instance, are usually in tacit agreement with the ends of the planners (rapid growth, industrialization, regional equality, etc.). Their criticism usually asserts that planning goals have been formulated undemocratically, that the goals are overambitious in relation to the means available, that the means used are often coercive and that the end results are inefficient (cf. Grossman 1968, Fuchs and Demko 1979).

Critics of capitalism focus on planners' goals: they assert that capitalist planning, in attempting to regulate and stimulate the market forces, benefits only the powerful corporate interests. These critics maintain that lack of centralized State planning under capitalism makes for the endemic chaos of Western economies.

The Yugoslav economist R. Bicanic emphasizes that a plan can only be evaluated in the socioeconomic context in which it is applied. A plan may fail not because it was poorly designed or poorly executed, but because it was executed at the wrong time. As an example he cites Yugoslavia's unsuccessful drive to collectivize agriculture, begun in 1946 and abandoned in 1952. If this plan had been delayed by 10 or 15 years, to allow for the development of industrial base that could support agriculture, it is conceivable that collectivization could have been achieved successfully. Bicanic also makes the astute remark that the overfulfillment of plans is not a sign of success, but a sign of bad planning in the first place (1967: 46).

Centralization versus Decentralization

The advantages of decentralized planning are well known: decentralization reduces delay and inaccuracy in the transmission of information, permits faster and better adaptation to local conditions, leads to resolution of conflicts at lower levels in the administrative hierarchy, frees central planners to concentrate on essential tasks and limits the probability of grand mistakes.

However, decentralized planning may also yield results totally unintended by central decision-makers. It may produce wasteful deconcentration of valuable equipment, and its success is often dependent on centralized allocations of capital, machinery or experts. Moreover, decentralization makes social justice or equity difficult to achieve because there is no way for resources to be redistributed among unequal units. For all its highly touted efficiency, decentralization may lead to a preservation of the status quo instead of redistribution of resources and national development. A prominent example is Yugoslavia, whose decentralized planning mechanism has served to perpetuate serious regional inequalities between rich and poor regions (Hoffman 1967).

It would be wrong to equate central planning with the "authoritarian planning" found in totalitarian societies or war economies (Bicanic 1967: 70, Berliner 1959, Lange 1968). To advocate centralized planning does not mean to advocate a totally planned economy. No country can be totally planned, not even the USSR:

> Of the several million kinds of articles produced in the USSR only several thousand or even several hundred products are planned centrally (Bicanic 1967:75).

At a certain stage of development, central planning becomes a necessity (Bornstein 1975, Mayer, Moroney and Morris 1974, Bicanic 1967). Some plans may fail not because they were overcentralized, but because they were not centralized enough (Friedmann 1968). Friedmann advocates increased government control as a precondition for efficient planning.

The key problem in the centralization/decentralization debate is deciding what gets centralized and what gets decentralized. In order to have successful and efficient plans, certain basic activities (national defense, transport and communications) may be more amenable to centralization, while other sectors (human services, retail trade, intensive agriculture) may run best with the flexibility that decentralization provides. Since changing levels of national development require continuous revision of goals and social needs, it follows that neither centralization nor decentralization alone can be completely adequate over the long term. Consequently, the planning schemes of both Third World and East European states, including Romania, have exhibited a continuous oscillation, whereby decentralizations are followed by re-centralizations and reforms, which lead to new decentralizations, etc. Clearly, there is no one preferred type of planning. What is crucial is that the criteria used in choosing centralization or decentralization include all the relevant political and ideological factors as well as the technical ones.

Planners' Ideologies

Both capitalist and socialist planners are actors in a sociopolitical structure. They are constrained by the wishes of their employer (agency or government), by their own views of the situation both as experts as citizens and by the needs and demands of those who are the objects of the plan. Presumably, the most trouble-free execution would occur where there is complete agreement among the state organization, the planners, the locality and citizens as to short and long-term goals, means to achieve them, and sequence of implementation. Such total agreement is unlikely, however, for each of these parties occupies such different positions in the administrative hierarchy that their fundamental interests will vary immensely and may likely be in conflict.

The anthropology of the planning process involves studying the *structure of planning activity* at each rank in the hierarchy, and the ideology of the plans as they come down from the top. The transmission of a plan invariably involves the transmission of ideologies about that plan. The following is a description of eight of the most common "planning ideologies" as revealed in the literature. Most of these are shared by socialist and Western planners alike. Later chapters will show how these planning ideologies are transformed under the specific conditions of Romanian systematization.

Rational interventionism. This is the belief that the conscious human will can determine the direction of change and influence "the laws of history." Believing in their powers of personal intervention, planners attempt to ameliorate certain negative "trends" (pollution, crime, traffic congestion, etc.) while creating new ones (economic growth, "communism"). The idea that human endeavor can have decisive influence on impersonal social forces is the sine qua non of the planner. This intervention is perceived to be rational and scientific, i.e., based on technical expertise. Though planners readily admit the existence of politics or ideology in society at

large, they rarely admit that these non-scientific factors affect their own
sphere of decision-making. That some planners can operate under the
belief that their activities are only technical surely aids those who know
otherwise.

The public interest. When planners justify their actions in terms of the
common perceived goals and aspirations of an entire society, they are
invoking an ideology of "the public interest" or "common good" (cf.
Apfelbaum 1977, Glass 1973). As Bailey (1975:30) has pointed out, the
public interest ideology assumes a concensus model of society. Yet, the
conception of a single public interest is usually of little practical help to
the planner. This is illustrated by Taubman's (1973) study of Soviet
cities, in which the competition between industrial development and
municipal services becomes a case of "the public interest *versus* the public interest" because both factory and city are formally owned by "the
people." It would be more appropriate to conceive of the planning environment in terms of conflict rather than consensus models. Plans must
be analyzed according to who pays and who benefits. Groups who protest should not be thought of as opposed to the public interest, because
this interest is determined after idological and political precepts and not
rational criteria. Rather, these groups should be thought of as representing
alternative interests, the priority of which must be judged on political
grounds. Recognizing this, Davidoff (1973) has called for the abandon-
ment of the notion of public interest, to be replaced by the planner becoming an advocate of an explicitly chosen interest group, such as the
inner-city poor. Advocacy remains a controversial subject among planners
because it makes explicit the political content of planning. It constitutes
a recognition of the role of non-scientific and external factors in the planning process. For that reason alone it is a threat to those planners who
pride themselves on their "professionalism."

Community. Western planners often formulate programs which reflect
their notion of an idealized community. Planning for cities as if they were
a collection of self-contained neighborhoods and modeling new towns
after rural villages are actions which derive from the planners' "community"
ethos. This ethos persists despite the fact that the idealized rural community never really existed and is especially irrelevant to urbanized, industrialized countries. Although the utopian views of earlier planners (see
Reiner 1963 for summary of these) have been toned down to more realistic

dimensions today, the idea of community permeates planning theory and practice. It assumes that a small population in a limited space will tend to have social relations of a rustic peasant village. Such a notion ignores the numerous other determinants of community behavior, such as the social origins of the residents, their occupational situations, their attitudes toward the settlement, and the community's links to other localities and outside insitutions.

Anti-urbanism. In Britain, Glass (1973), Foley (1973), Bailey (1975) and Petersen (1977) have criticized the anti-urban ideology of most planners. Anti-urbanism is the notion that rural life is natural and city life somehow unnatural or even pathological for human communities. The upshot of this view—which has roots in Rousseau's "noble savage" and U.S. urban sociology (Wirth 1938)—is that the type of settlement most conducive to humanistic social relations will be of low density, low population and evenly distributed space. The ideal settlement is typified by the small family house and garden. The anti-urban ideology was a catalyst for England's "garden city" movement and the subsequent new town program (cf. Howard 1960).

Urban orientation. Counterposed to the anti-urban ideology is the fact that most planning is still urban-oriented. The village exists for the benefit of urban dwellers: it houses the city's surplus labor force and provides a place of recreation for romantic urbanites. Hence, the countryside must meet the demands placed on it by the city. "In the public interest," planners can restructure the countryside with impunity so as to fulfill urban demands. Meanwhile, society's essential functions—industry, services, administration, culture—are to remain within the city. The inferiority of the rural settlement should be reinforced by spatial separation. Thus, the joining of town and country—what we call sprawl—is anathema to all planners, be they socialist or capitalist, in developed or underdeveloped countries.

Architectural determinism. What Bailey (1975:16) has called "architectural determinism" and what Farbman (1960:227) has termed "the physical planning bias" refer to planners' faith in physical design as the most dominant influence on human behavior. As cross-cultural research has shown, however, direct causative links between spatial environment and social behavior are not so easily proven (cf. Hall 1969, Sommer 1969). Social, cultural and economic variables invariably act to neutralize environmental and spatial variables in explaining human behavior in specific social settings. (High density urban living, to take one example, does not *in itself* lead to social pathology, family breakdown or alienation; there is a world of difference between the social patterns of Manhattan, Moscow and Hong Kong despite their relatively similar urban environments. This does not mean that spatial environmental exerts no effect, only that it is rarely the fundamental variable.) Bailey is particularly critical of the way Western planners apply architectural determinism to urban *social* problems. The planners maintain that they can

> manage social relations by physical arranging. Such beliefs bolster professional self-images. . . . Since the only variable which is uniquely within the planners' power to vary is the physical environment, small wonder that they should give it causal priority (Bailey 1975:16).

According to Davidoff (1973:293), the physical planning bias turns city planners into nothing more than land use planners.

Participation. By intervening into an existing social community, the planner becomes enmeshed in a network of interpersonal and interorganizational networks. Since individuals and organizations external to the planner are always involved in the planning process, "it is axiomatic to conclude that planning is participatory" (Burke 1979:65). It is the *form* of this participation that generates debate.

The rise of "citizen participation" in planning has two very disparate origins. One lies in the "community control" movement; this was an attempt to democratize the urban power structure by involving local communities in the formulation and implementation of plans. Thus, "planning with" has replaced "planning for" the people (Faludi 1973). From this perspective, citizen participation is a justifiable end in itself. Yet there is another, more instrumental motivation behind the "participation" rhetoric: planners discovered that citizens could supplement planner expertise. Under the guise of participation, citizens could help planners to achieve *planners'* goals. In this second sense, participation is but a more efficient means for achieving the same set of goals. Conceived in this way, participation carries with it no impetus toward political realignment or democratic power sharing.

Deciding whether planner-citizen contact actually amounts to "meaningful" participation has remained a controversial question for planning theorists. Joe Bailey (1975) cynically maintains that citizen participation is nothing but a sophisticated ploy whereby the citizens are brainwashed into accepting the planners' ideas. In his view, planners are "the soft cops of the system" (Bailey 1975:115). In a widely quoted article, Sherry Arnstein (1969) has formulated a "ladder" of citizen participation. The ladder consists of eight "rungs", the lowest of which are "outright manipulation" and "therapy." Arnstein sees these as forms of nonpaticipation. ("Therapy" is what Bailey would call "brainwashing"; the planner uses his powers of expertise and scientific mystification to make the community members feel that their claims are illegitimate or improper.) The next four of Arnstein's "rungs" are, respectively, "informing", "consultation", "placation" and "partnership"; all these are various forms of tokenism, whereby planners include one or two citizens on their executive committee, but insure that they will be outvoted or outmaneuvered on crucial questions. Arnstein finds genuine participation only at the rungs of "delegated power," where citizens dominate a particular program, and "full citizen control," where the key decisions are in the hands of the community, the planners functioning only as brokers or advisors.

Arnstein's typology is important because she is able to demonstrate that planners might come into conflict with the citizens solely because of a disagreement over the meaning of participation. Arnstein's study showed that planners had envisioned "participation" in terms of the lower rungs of her "ladder," whereas citizens wanted only "delegated power" or "full citizen control." However, the issue of participation should not be reduced to a simple cultural misunderstanding or semantic confusion. In the final instance, participation is an arena of political conflict. The planners' interest is to safeguard their monopoly over expertise and decision-making; hence, any effort by the citizens to increase their participation constitutes a threat to the planners' legitimacy. The awkward relation between citizen participation and planner expertise makes for inevitable conflicts among State, planner and community interests (cf. Conklin 1974 for an example of "participation versus expertise" in Peru).

All of the above-mentioned planning ideologies are to be found in one form or another in any planning scheme. They stem directly from the nature of planning as a process for making and executing decisions, and from the social milieu in which these decisions are made. They are visible in both capitalist and socialist countries, and especially relevant to problems of economic development.

Development

Development entails the systematic increase in the total economic resources of society so as to bring about fundamental improvements in the material and social welfare of its members. Successful development should lead to the alleviation of mass poverty, the reduction of inequalities between regions, social groups, and between city and countryside, and the extension of social benefits and educational opportunities to the vast majority of the population. Development is not to be equated with simple economic growth. Growth is only a precondition for development. An increase in GNP *per capita* does not necessarily produce the basic structural changes associated with development; in fact, high growth rates may even exacerbate already existing inequalities (Seers 1972, Thomas 1974:81-122).

Development is not the same as "modernization," which I define as the increasing integration of a region into the world capitalist economy. Authors such as Frank (1967, 1969), Amin (1974b), Schneider, Schneider and Hansen (1972), Wallerstein (1974a) and Hechter (1975) go to great lengths to show that certain countries (or regions) are "modern" in that they have been intimately connected to the world economy, but are not "developed", because they lack control over their domestic resources and surpluses. Thus, so-called "traditional" or "dual" societies like Indonesia, the West Indies, Sicily, Brazil, or Bolivia are only the other side of the modernization "coin."

Undeniably, the post-war period has seen tremendous change in rural communities throughout the world. It is these post-war changes—urbanization, westernization, industrialization or modernization—that have often been mistaken for the fundamental structural changes of development. Change associated with genuine development is usually not gradual but abrupt; it follows wide-ranging political and social revolutions, class warfare, or national liberation movements.

Development usually entails attitudinal changes, too. The discussion among modernization theorists has in fact centered on techniques of inculcating "modern," (i.e. Western) values so that the proper climate will be created to accept Western technological innovations (Dalton 1971, Goodenough 1963, Barnett 1953, Arensberg and Nihoff 1965, Rogers and Shoemaker 1967). The absence of these values in a given population was seen as sufficient explanation for why development had not occurred (in anthropology the most well-known examples being Banfield and Banfield 1958 and Foster 1965). Modernity was equated with Westernization; social phenomena which did not appear Western were relegated to the catch-all category of "tradition" (Tipps 1973). Such a notion is contradicted by the emergence in the last fifty years of developed nations with highly diverse value systems (e.g. the U.S., USSR, Japan). Furthermore, their development was successful partly because it incorporated such traditional values as Protestant ethic (the U.S.), peasant cooperation (USSR) and patriarchal discipline (Japanese corporations, cf. Rohlen 1974).

Most of the countries of the Third World and a large part of Eastern Europe were at one time colonies or neocolonies of the West, producing cash crops for Western markets, and consequently subjected to the vagaries of the world economy. Recognizing this common historical attribute may be of more importance than any attempt to establish a dichotomy of "traditional" versus "modern" values. These historical conditions mean that the economic development of those nations in the "periphery" cannot occur without a major restructuring of their dependency relation with the "core" societies of the West. Within the Eastern bloc itself, similar types of dependency relations exist between the raw-materials-exporting Balkan states (Romania included) and the more industrialized countries in northern Eastern Europe. As long as this dependency is perpetuated, full-scale development in the periphery cannot occur. Planning in the Third World (as well as Romanian planning) has functioned partly to perpetuate this dependency and partly to help them break free of it (cf. Conklin 1974, Thomas 1974, Boesen and Raikes 1976).

Development Planning

Given their limited capital resources and ambitious goals, most underdeveloped countries (socialist and nonsocialist) have relied on centralized State-level planning strategies to pursue their goals. These goals generally include a rapid degree of economic growth, diversified agro-industrial economy, modernized infrastructure, extensive service sector, modern health and educational institutions, and financial security against fluctuations on world commodity markets.

Let us re-emphasize the difference between Western capitalist planning and the development planning of the Third World. In the West, planning functions to *restore* proper entrepreneurial activity, to *correct* the aberrations of the market during periodic downturns (Bicanic 1967:57). Even the so-called "indicative" planning popular in countries like France (Cohen 1968, Hansen 1968) is little more than a sophisticated forecasting mechanism which only supplements the micro-planning efforts of individual enterprises or industries. Thus, planning in the advanced countries is designed chiefly to keep the economy running smoothly.

Planning in the developing countries is more radical. It takes off from the existing system. They want to do more than simply "correct" the market; they want to stimulate it, or in the case of socialist states, to dominate it. Western development planning *readjusts* resources; planning in the development countries attempts to mobilize completely *new* resources (Hermansen 1972).

Such differences should be recalled when trying to assess Third World development efforts using Western indices. Because development planning is a means for effecting structural change, it will be more ambitious than Western capitalist planning; however, it will also be more difficult and more prone to mistakes and inefficiency.

Development planning is normally implemented either by sector or by spatial unit. Sectoral planning involves allocation of resources for portions of the economy, e.g. agriculture, heavy industry, services, transport, etc. However, inasmuch as sectoral plans must be implemented on a regional/spatial plane, we will concentrate on the regional/spatial aspect of planning. *Regional planning* will be defined as the allocation of given resources for future development over a bounded space. *Spatial planning* will refer to programs dealing with changing the size or hierarchy of settlements. Spatial planning is a key element of any regional development strategy.

Regional and Spatial Development Strategies

The fundamental assumption of regional/spatial development strategies is that a given level of economic development necessitates a specific type of settlement hierarchy. From this assumption, it follows that (1) lack of development can be attributable to an "inadequate" or "irrational" spatial organization; and (2) economic development can be achieved only if this "irrational" spatial organization is restructured. E. A. Johnson (1970) is a well-known proponent of the latter view, going so far as to assert that

> The village of four or five hundred people is an archaic extravagance that a developing country cannot afford (Johnson 1970:375).

To facilitate urban growth, Johnson states that the

> raising of average incomes in underdeveloped countries will require town building programs. . . . Until this task of spatial restructuring is understood, resources will continue to be wasted (ibid.: 177).

As will be shown in subsequent chapters, Johnson's assumptions about a "proper" spatial pattern have largely been accepted by Romanian planners; however, these assumptions have generated debate among regional science theorists. Darwent (1969) believes that it would be impossible to obtain such a precise correlation. Other planners have been content to emphasize the need for a national settlement policy as an adjunct to development. They avoid the issue of whether spatial reorganization (e.g. growth centers) generates development or whether development automatically produces the required spatial transformations (Friedmann 1968: 371, Rodwin 1970, Logan 1972, Brutzkus 1975).

Regional development discussions bring up numerous contradictions: city versus country, core versus periphery, concentration versus dispersal, developed versus backward region, immediate benefits versus ultimate goals. Lloyd Rodwin (1970), in his comparison of urban/regional development strategies in six countries, stresses the necessity of having a national policy to organize the allocation of resources. Urban growth strategies are intimately linked to the achievement of national development goals. Rodwin cites four preconditions necessary for establishing an urban growth strategy. These are (1) a stable government; (2) an intelligence mechanism for analyzing problems and suggesting solutions; (3) the central power of the principle incentive and control mechanisms; and (4) a reliably efficient civil service. Whereas the advanced countries already meet these four preconditions, the underdeveloped countries usually do not. The problem, then is to establish the preconditions for good planning,

a task which unfortunately is beyond the realm of Rodwin's book. Yet his
analysis remains valuable because it links urban policy with national economic development and because he illustrates the inapplicabilty of map-
ing Western development models onto underdeveloped countries.

Urbanization and Development

One of the key issues in the debate over regional development is that
of "generative or parasitic cities" (Hoselitz 1955, 1960). This is attached
to another problem; namely, whether increasing urbanization is inherently beneficial for development. Planners who favor urbanization see urban
growth regions as "innovative and economic seedbeds for much larger
concentrations" (Rodwin 1970:26). John Friedmann (1968) advocates
a "strategy of deliberate urbanization" which can relieve hyper-urbani-
zation and social pathologies of Latin America's giant metropolises. Konrad and Szelenyi (1976), analyzing the Hungarian experience, attribute
the social problems of large cities like Budapest to a deliberate *under*-
urbanization, where planners have consistenly given priority to the industrial sector over urban infrastructure and housing; in their view, economic development (of Hungary) can only occur if these priorities are
reversed and urbanization increased. Hoselitz is typical of those planners
who see urban growth as the key to development:

> One must look, therefore, to the cities as the crucial places in un-
> derdeveloped societies in which the adaptation of new ways, new
> technologies, new consumption and production patterns and new
> social institutions are achieved (1960:163).

The "generative city" approach has its roots in the historical experience of Western Europe, where urban-rural interdependence was an essential factor in the development of West European capitalism (Pirenne
1925, 1936, Merrington 1976). However, the town/country relationship
in today's Third World and in parts of Eastern Europe is vastly different
from that of early modern Europe. Western European towns

> grew up as a function of growing efficiency in agriculture, transport
> and storage. . . . In the case of developing countries [however],

towns grew up and developed for other reasons, and often represent
alien political and cultural systems (Lundqvist 1975:23).

The spatial networks of excolonial countries developed largely to serve
the needs of their former colonial masters; infrastructural development
was often centered on a coastal port or international trade center. As out-
posts of colonial domination, the ports of trade were genuinely parasitic
on the surrounding countryside. When infrastructural linkages were established between the cities and the inland areas, it was only to facilitate the
export of raw materials from planations or mines. The central places
that were developed fostered further capitalist penetration into the countryside and thus served to perpetuate the dependency relation between
developed and underdeveloped zones ("core" and "periphery") of the
world-system (Doherty 1975).

Many of the colonial cities have now become national capitals, but
their skewed locations, oversized populations and weak productive sectors
work against their having a generative affect on their immediate hinterlands, or on the nation at large. The legacy of colonialism and ongoing
dependency between ex-colonies and the core states has made these towns
not only dysfunctional in their environments, but genuine hindrances to
overall national development (Hay 1977). Colonial policies left their mark
on rural settlements as well, restricting outmigration from areas where
plantation labor was needed and maintaining scattered hamlets in areas of
cash crop or animal production (Hay 1977, Wolf 1959).

The noncomparability of Western and Third World urbanization is illustrated in Murphey's (1975) study of Western European and Chinese
spatial networks. Murphey finds that Chinese cities tend to be parasitic
on the countryside while West European cities have been generative and
well-integrated into their rural networks. Quadeer (1974), examining the
Indian experience, sees little evidence that cities serve to modernize the
developing countries; he finds that scarce resources are squandered on a
small portion of the urban middle class while the problems of the rural
poor are ignored. Quadeer notes that these rural problems are well known.
However, because rural areas are less visible to government officials and
foreign observers, urban centers receive higher priority. Logan (1972) attempts to resolve the "generative *versus* parasitic" debate by postulating
an evolutionary continuum: growing cities tend to be at first parasitic on

the countryside, but as they develop they generate "trickle-down" benefits on their hinterlands. Logan's scheme suffers from the same implicit assumptions as others in the debate; namely, that one can place a normative value on a spatial unit. Rather than drawing verdicts about the generative or parasitic character of a given city, it is more useful to analyze the city in the context of its spatial hierarchy, spatial development processes and political-economic processes as a whole.

Sovani (1964) and Kamerschen (1969) both question the assumed correlation between high degree of urbanization and high level of economic development. They find underdeveloped countries with high urban populations and highly industrialized countries with low urban populations. The implication is that we should disgard the notion of an ideal pattern of urban growth which can be universally applied to all developing countries.

Growth Poles and Centers

Reservations about the role of primate cities have led planners to emphasize intermediate or small-sized urban centers, rural towns, central villages and frontier settlements (Hansen 1971, Logan 1972, Masser and Stroud 1973, Weitz 1973, Dahlberg 1974, Shah 1974, Brutzkus 1975, Johnson 1975, Lundqvist 1975, Lăzărescu 1976, Corwin 1977). These schemes, of which Romanian systemization is just one example, aim to reduce the perceived social costs of "exaggerated uncontrolled urbanization" (Ioanid 1974:5) by dispersing development throughout the countryside in the form of smaller settlements. The idea of concentrating economic activities in a particular settlement so as to eventually stimulate development in its hinterland has come to be known as "growth pole" or "growth center theory."

The notion of growth poles and growth centers was first elaborated by Perroux in 1955 (for reviews and critiques of growth pole theory see Hansen 1967, 1969, 1971, 1972; Darwent 1969; Hermanson 1972; Kuklinski 1972; Moseley 1974; and Rodell 1975). Perroux defined *growth pole* (*pole de croissance*) an an economic activity, normally an industrial enterprise or group of enterprises, which generates growth in one sector of the economy. Growth poles have no geographic locus. The *growth center*, on the other hand, is a recognizable spatial unit, typically a new town, growing town or key industrial city. Economic growth (which is equated with "development" by most regional theorists) is supposed to diffuse outward from the center of the hinterland. The key problem for growth center theory is to find those factors, sectors, or enterprises which can set this growth process in motion.

This has led to a search for the "optimum size" of a growth center. Optimum size is that population whereby the generative effects on the hinterland are maximal while the parasitic effects and social costs of urbanization are minimal. Since criteria for "generative," "parasitic" and "optimum" are either vague or subjective, it is not surprising that suggested optimum sizes have ranged from 10,000 (Howard 1960, Weitz 1971) to three million (Le Corbussier 1971). The most frequently cited figures lie between 50,000 and 300,000 persons (Robinson 1969:xvi, Hansen 1971:84, Moseley 1974:160). These intermediate-sized cities are presumed to have all the advantages of larger cities without the accompanying social pathology. There is a crude demographic determinism evident in the "optimum size" discussion. This is one reason why researchers have taken to re-examining growth pole and growth center theories themselves, the mechanisms of "polarization" and the preconditions for "propulsive growth" (Darwent 1969, Nichols 1969, Hansen 1967, 1971, 1972, Kuklinski 1972, Rodell 1975).

Not all planners are enamoured of growth-center strategies, however. Hirschman (1958), Nichols (1969) and Hansen (1971) are skeptical as to whether growth centers actually stimulate development, or only appear to do so. A growth center may in fact end up *depressing* the level of economic development by attracting immigrants and capital resources from their hinterlands. Instead of generating a "spread effect" to its hinterland, the growth center may become attached to urban centers in other regions. To use Hirschman's terms, the growth center's "polarization" effects become stronger than its "trickling-down" effects. Consequently, Hirschman, Nichols and Hansen all argue for unbalanced growth strategies. This view is unequivocally reaffirmed by Robinson, who, after reviewing the state of regional development programs in both Eastern and Western Europe, concludes that, "the peppering of backward areas with large numbers of small projects has come to be regarded as a recipe for failure" (1969:xv).

The controversies over concentration/dispersal of growth centers and balanced *versus* unbalanced growth both reflect the unstated assumptions behind growth center/growth pole theory. Economic growth is equated with genuine development; spatial units are confused with economic processes; and large cities are seen to spawn social pathology. The most pervasive assumption is that of equalizing "backward" and "advanced" regions. The choice is often put in terms of

1) investing in already developed zones to obtain certain and immediate benefits OR

2) investing in lagging regions with great initial expenditures which can be recouped only in the distant future.

Both these alternatives contain assumptions which cannot be controlled by the planners' decisions. Choice 1) implies that development in the advanced zone will somehow diffuse to the backward zone, i.e., economic growth will produce regional development. This ignores the fact that advanced regions may have reached their high level as a result of their having "exploited" underdeveloped regions as part of a core-periphery relationship (Massey 1979). Choice 2) implies that advanced and lagging regions are politically and economically independent of each other, with the advanced region being but a step ahead in the development foot-race. However, regions are tied not only to each other but to larger national and international systems. To stimulate growth in one zone usually means appropriating material and human resources from another. Thus, the ostensibly technical problem of whether to maximize short-term or long-term gains hides important political and ideological questions. Perhaps this is why decisions about which regions or growth points should have priority are rarely left to the planners alone.

To summarize: the discussions about growth centers are preoccupied with modeling and technical factors, neglecting the larger political and ideological implications of spatial restructuring. The generation of economic development is reduced to a search for technique rather than the formation of a coherent policy.

Rural Development Planning

In response to the uncertain benefits of growth centers, some development experts advocate less glamorous policies which focus directly on the rural hinterland. Logan (1972) calls for strengthening the agricultural sector by providing irrigation, rural credit associations and technical extension. Quadeer (1974) and Shah (1974) emphasize the improvement of rural transport, communication, health and education services. Brutzkus (1975) recommends a "decentralized urbanization" using "central villages" and their small hinterlands, rather than the large urban centers advocated by growth center theorists (it can easily be argued that this amounts to a miniaturized growth-center argument). Johnson's (1970) strategy is to locate "promising growth points" from among the hundreds of villages in the spatial hierarchy. Even John Friedmann (1968), known for his faith in urban-rural diffusion models, sees the only hope for sustained development to come from "concentrated decentralization," in which certain backward hinterlands are turned into growth regions by establishing an "integrated" urban/rural hierarchy. Hansen (1972) proposes that growth centers be replaced by a policy of "decentralized concentration." Mangione (1977), examining the Chinese experience, lauds their overt anti-urban bias which encourages rural communes to reduce their dependency on the towns.

The strategy of revising the key foci downward from large cities to small villages has several advantages: it constitutes a more direct attack on the root *causes* of underdevelopment and urban migration; these processes are only *manifested* in the cities. It also leads to a necessary interaction and, hopefully, collaboration between the planning administration and the rural populace, who in most underdeveloped countries compose the bulk of the population.

An emphasis on rural planning strategies also entails new kinds of problems, however. The most difficult task is to transmit development policy across a wide range of settlements, i.e. from the capital to the regional center to the thousands of villages in the provinces. Lundqvist (1975), in analyzing Tanzanian experiences, notes that planners' ostensibly well-intentioned development policies have often been interpreted differently by the rural population. This may be due either to traditional suspicion of urban experts or because the plan compels the peasants to take risks which they deem unacceptable. In light of the numerous studies of development projects that failed due to a lack of understanding of local conditions, the Tanzanian experience is hardly exceptional (cf. Epstein 1965, Fraser 1968, Mamdani 1972, Holmberg 1965, 1971, Dalton 1971).

Several obstacles confront Third World rural development programs: there is invariably a shortage of capital; machinery and technology must be imported; trained experts are lacking; and the administrative organization is a far cry from Rodwin's (1970) requirement of a "reliably efficient civil service." Thus, plans will succeed only if there is substantial local/national cooperation and the active participation of the local population. Under these circumstances, conflicts can emerge at any point in the planning process. For instance, the planners and the local population may agree as to long-term goals, but the schedule of implementation may conflict with the day-to-day needs of local households. Even with total agreement on goals and their sequence of implementation, the means used could arouse opposition from the population, as illustrated by the USSR's collectivization campaign during the 1930s and Tanzania's coercive villageization program known as *Ujaama* (cf. Raikes 1975). Other possible difficulties may include inefficient use of local social organization in implementing planning decisions, inadequate monitoring of their consequences, bureaucratic incompetence and covert or overt corruption.

Problems with "the locals" have been a common concern of the planning profession. The move toward "citizen participation" was partly an attempt to ameliorate some of these problems. Lundqvist typifies the optimistic view that participation of rural dwellers in development planning efforts will make the planners responsive to local needs (1975:28). Though an admiral ideal, it only begs the question of whether there can *ever* be total concordance between national goals and local development needs. Two structural features seem to determine the existence of contradictions between local and national systems in planning efforts. First, development plans—including most community development plans—are invariably formulated at the national level, even if they are executed locally. Consequently, there will be a variance between the program's usefulness to the nation and its utility to the community at hand. Second, contradictions may arise because of competition between diverse regions in the national system, most obviously between rich and poor regions. The issue, then, becomes one of determining how and why these contradictions have arisen in the particular forms that they take.

Making this kind of assessment is all the more difficult because it clashes with the role behavior of planners in the local setting. Cohen's (1977) analysis of small town planning in the U.S. is especially pertinent to the discussion of planner-citizen relations in rural development, where expertise must come from outside the community. Cohen speaks of two kinds of "distance" between planners and clients. When planners are sent

out by large agencies and make contact only with the leading officials
of the small town, they may become the victims of "administrative distance." These individuals may not be the actual beneficiaries of the plan
or may be wholly unrepresentative of the community. Administrative
distance also occurs because planners often assume that because a community is demographically small, that it must also be socially and ideologically homogenous. Planners who enter the rural milieu are subject to
"social distance" as well. Social distance is a result of the physical and
cultural separation between the city-dwelling, urban-oriented planner
and the small town clientele. Small town planners often do not reside
in the area for which they are planning. Their values, beliefs, and lifestyles are often markedly different from small-town or rural folk. The
planners' preoccupation with grand development schemes may conflict
with local desires to maintain small-scale (traditional) features of community life.

Cohen maintains that small town planning may result in even less local
participation than big-city planning as long as planner-citizen contacts
are restricted to a few local elites and the "small-population-equals-social-
homogeneity" idea holds sway. In the urban situation, disagreement
among competing interest groups is expected. Small town planning may
not leave room for this kind of competition.

Cohen's remarks about small town planning in America have equal
relevance to development efforts in Third World rural communities. The
social distance between planner and villager may be even wider than in
the American situation; the planner may have been born and raised in the
capital and educated abroad; he or she may even be a foreign expert and
suffer from an additional "cultural distance." Training in the advanced
West may have been irrelevant to the needs of the home country. The
planner may look with distaste on treating local villagers as equals; and
national demands for speedy implementation and spectacular results may
end up sabotaging well-intentioned programs, engendering citizens' resentment and disillusioning the planners.

Thus, despite the most well-designed and well-intentioned programs,
development planning in rural areas will present special problems for planners. Like other developing countries, socialist Romania does not escape
these problems, for they reflect the contradictory nature of local social
organization in rural communities and the way they articulate with supralocal political forces.

Development Planning "versus" Local Social Organization

As they extend their activities from urban centers to village communities, development planners encounter forms of rural social organization which, because they are unfamiliar, also appear to be unstructured, inefficient, irrational or even corrupt. Seen as especially problematic are the hidden powers of noncorporate social relations, as manifested through kinship, ritual kinship, social networks, patron-client relations, brokers, factions, coalitions, or "nongroups" (Boissevain 1968). The social links established through kinship, friendship, and residence are strong enough to retain their hold on villagers who have migrated to urban areas (Graves and Graves 1974, Simic 1973, Little 1963, 1973); this latter process amounts to a "peasantization of the town" (Halpern 1967).

In certain sectors of life in the advanced capitalist and socialist countries, and overwhelmingly in most underdeveloped countries, these informal social networks are so pervasive that the formal bureaucratic institutions could not function without them (Wolf 1966a). This is especially so in rural areas, where formal institutions are not only fragile and overburdened, but viewed with suspicion by many villagers. Placed within rural communities are the local leaders, who are simultaneously actors in the local social network and executors of national directives. Straddling their dual roles and allegiances, the elites seek to resolve (or at times exploit) the potential contradictions between the local and national arenas (cf. Fallers 1956, Richards 1960, Gluckman 1963, Sylverman 1965, Littlewood 1973, Bailey 1971, Swartz 1973, Bax 1975, Romanian Studies Collective 1977).

What exactly are these potential contradictions? Planners seem to view local social organization with a degree of ambivalence. They readily acknowledge its crucial importance in fostering the acceptance of a plan, but they nevertheless see it as an impediment to rational planning activities. Local social organization is necessary, but it is a necessary *evil*; its "inertia" must be transformed into innovation; its "hold" over the population must be somehow released and its powers of mobilization put to "rational" ends; the stubborn attitudes which it engenders must be swayed or neutralized. From the planners' perspective, local social organization is seen as an obstacle to be overcome.

Social scientists—particularly anthropologists—take a much more benevolent view of community social structure. They point out how informal social arrangements are adaptive responses to the political-economic forces impinging from the region, nation or world-system. For example, Schneider, Schneider and Hansen (1972), in their comparison of regional elites and noncorporate groups in Sicily and Catalonia, assert that noncorporate social organization is eminently suited to societies that are "modernized" (i.e. integrated into the world capitalist system as complex peasant societies) but not genuinely "developed." Shifting coalitions and amorphous social networks are the mechanisms by which society's have-nots (in cities and villages) gain access to constantly shifting political and economic resources. Rather than being the cause of friction in these societies, noncorporate organization functions more as a "lubricant," controlling and restructuring the flow of resources among members through short-term dyadic or polyadic coalitions. Other scholars on the Mediterranean seem to echo Schneider, Schneider and Hansen's view that these particular social forms are characteristic of underdeveloped societies (cf. especially Boissevain 1968, 1973, Blok 1974, Sylverman 1965 and Schneider and Schneider 1976; for a dissenting view see Pi-Sunyer 1974, 1975 and the reply by Hansen, Schneider and Schneider 1975). Presumably, real development renders noncorporate social forms obsolete, transforming them into corporate groups, e.g. voluntary associations, political parties, trade union bureaucracies. Sylverman (1965) sees this process occurring in central Italian villages; local "mediators" are gradually being replaced by formally constituted "intermediaries." The same process is presumed to occur in Eastern Europe, where the gradual corporatization of society into a single grand Party-State apparatus encapsulates or subordinates noncorporate forms of social organization (Jowitt 1978, Chirot 1980, Wiarda 1981).

Let us apply this hypothesis—that noncorporate groups are adaptive for the "periphery" while corporate groups/institutions predominate in the "core"—to the situation of development planners encountering local social organization. Both planners and social scientists agree that plans can succeed only by virtue of (or at least by not threatening) the noncorporate social forms. However, if plans are successful and "development" results these forms suddenly become dysfunctional, irrational, even threatening! Here lies the potential point of contradiction between national planning schemes and local social organization. The combination of

1) planners' suspicions that local social organization is something to be overcome rather than integrated,

2) empirical observations about the ability of local social organization to thwart planners' goals, and

3) the social science assumption that noncorporate forms are maladaptive in developed societies

all produce an atmosphere of confrontation between planners and the local community. This atmosphere could easily result in conscious attempts by the state to destroy the fabric of local social organization under the aegis of eliminating irrationality, inefficiency or corruption. Needless to say, the more intense the atmosphere of confrontation, the more probable it is that we will see coercive methods, local resentment, failed plans and frustrated planners.

Even if we reject the hypothesis about the evolutionary function of noncorporate groups, there remains the task of explicating the relationship between development planning and local social organization. To see this relationship solely in terms of "struggle," "obstacles," and "hindrance" only perpetuates the confrontation mentality. Considering development planning's affect on local social organization, it is safe to assume that planning actions will cause informal groups to alter their forms or functions, without necessarily leading to their absolute demise.

As for the effect of local social organization on development planning, it is evident that the *local* orientation and *noncorporate* nature of rural community organization stands in structural opposition to the *superlocal* goals and *formal* structure of most development efforts. Because of this structural opposition, it is hardly surprising that plans are sometimes altered, transformed or bitterly resisted by their target populations. The task of the planner (with the aid of the social scientist) is to determine why community members are compelled to use their "locality power" (Leeds 1973) to restructure national inputs to their own needs. This involves recognizing that local needs may not be congruent with the national goals. Rather than try to understand the continued validity of noncorporate forms, planners have tended to account for the alteration or stonewalling of their plans by blaming the rural communities themselves. Among both Third World development experts (as will be shown later) and Romanian planners, one hears of "backward mentalities," "provincialism," "corruption," "inefficiency," or simply "traditionalism" as explanations of why plans fail. Yet such explanations say more about how planners (mis)perceive village communities than about why plans fail. Such explanations do little to bring about more effective planning efforts.

At the juncture of community social organization and planning institutions stand the local elites. They are supposed to mediate the local/superlocal relationship, transmit planning goals, monitor their execution, and mobilize the community to accept and/or implement the plan as their own. It would seem reasonable to assume that the elites must be well integrated into the local social organization if planning goals are to be achieved. Yet here another potential contradition arises: the more the local elites are integrated into local social networks and obligations, the less disposed they may be to supporting the superlocal interests of the planners. Moreover, elites may use their "gatekeeper" functions to perpetuate mutual suspicion or conflict between the community and the planners. Planners might seek to replace such elites with more pliable administrators, but this would not prevent the problem from arising again. This is because the new elites can achieve their political goals only through community alliances. Even if planners found local leaders who were their genuine allies, community pressure might compel village elites to resist the plan for fear of losing local legitimacy. Without adequate linkages to local elites, planners will be more likely to experience the social and administrative distance described by Cohen (1977). Most planners know this, but the constraints of planning in rural areas often prevent these linkages from being formed.

The potential contradictions between local social organization and development planning should not be put into a framework of "weakening," "reinforcing" or "corrupting" a plan.

We should instead try to understand the kinds of social processes within the community, the range of short and long-term household strategies and the factors which impinge on the local leadership from below. It will then be possible to analyze how these factors interact with the planning apparatus, which is itself equally complex, and similarly composed of opposing forces and competing ideologies. Rather than a confrontation, the relationship between local social organization and development planning should be conceived as an interaction of structures, processes, social groups and ideologies over time.

Summary: The Planning Factor

The preceding review of planning, development planning and local social organization began by defining planning as a combination of technical, social and ideological activities involving the determination of goals and the choice of possible means for achieving these goals. Evaluating planning in terms of its ends/means or its degree of centralization/decentralization was found to be problematic. Regardless of where it is carried out, planning has a distinct ideological content. This chapter described seven common planning ideologies: rational interventionism, the public interest, community, anti-urbanism, urban orientation, architectural determinism and participation. As ideological constructs they could be manipulated by both planners and target populations to suit their own purposes.

The development planning of the Third World (as well as that of socialist countries) attempts to bring about fundamental structural change in the whole of society. Hence, it is more ambitious, more radical and more difficult than the planning of the advanced capitalist countries. The history of Western economic development and particularly the role of West European cities in stimulating rural development were found to have limited applicability in the Third World, whose economies and spatial structures were shaped by their dependency relations with the West.

Strategies for regional and spatial development proceeded from the premise that a given level of economic development demands a particular kind of settlement hierarchy. Establishing optimum sizes for cities so that they would be "generative" instead of "parasitic" and creating growth centers in backward regions were two methods by which spatial restructuring was supposed to generate economic development. However, these were only partial solutions because the roots of underdevelopment lay in the rural sector. Thus, from large cities and grand regional strategies, development planners have altered their focus to rural settlements. In carrying out activities in the countryside, the inherent contradictions of development planning (city vs. country, backward vs. advanced regions, short-term vs. long-term needs) took on forms which conflicted with the planners' ideology of rational interventionism.

Specifically, planners encountered unfamiliar social structures of a localized and noncorporate nature. These social structures could interact in both conflicting and complementary ways with the national priorities and administrative rationality of the planners. Where the contradictions between local social organization and planners' ideologies were acute, the result would be social and administrative distance, citizen nonparticipation, local elite resistence and corruption, community resentment, and unintended alterations or transformations of the plan.

Much of the preceding analysis of planning-in-general can be applied to the practice of rural systematization in Romania. Like other *planning* schemes, the plan to abolish irrational villages and build 300 *small* urban centers is interventionist, anti-big city, urban-oriented, and requires the mass participation of the rural citizenry in its implementation. Like *development planning*, it is an ambitious strategy for restructuring the relationship between city and countryside, eliminating the disparity between backward and advanced regions, and raising the level of services directed at the rural population. As a *spatial development strategy*, systematization lays great stress on an optimum size—about 250,000 for larger cities, down to 5,000 for future urban centers and 2,000-3,000 for the ideal rural village. The plans to build 300 new towns are an ambitious example of a "growth center" strategy, with its accompanying problems, especially one being the tenuous connection between establishing particular *settlements* and stimulating regional *economies*. Like other development strategies, Romania's systematization carried with it its own logic—the logic of "rational" and "irrational" settlements. In common with radical development planning elsewhere, Romanian systematization puts new kinds of demands on regional planners, local elites and community members. The success of the plan will in large part depend on the way the implicated parties cope with these new demands.

In view of the ambitious goals of development planning, how should we go about evaluating the success of such development efforts? Commenting on the Romanian case, both Montias (1967) and Gilberg (1977) sound a note of caution: Romania's developmental achievements and shortcomings should be evaluated not in the context of what *we* think is proper for a developing socialist state, but in terms of the country's proclaimed objectives and the degree to which these are achieved. This chapter has tried to place Romanian systematization in the context of general planning and development. From the above analysis, it can be seen that many of the problems of Romanian planning are not generated by socialism per se, nor by particularly "Romanian" failings. Rather, these difficulties reflect the generalized features of planning when applied to rural communities and the inherent contradictions which arise in trying to realize structural change.

Although knowledge of general planning and development problems is necessary for understanding the Romanian situation, it is obviously not sufficient. Systematization must also be analyzed as a distinctly socialist planning strategy. In examining Romanian systematization as *socialist* planning, a crucial difference emerges. It is the difference between building new towns, which many countries have tried, and building 300 new towns, something which can be attempted only under special political and economic conditions. The next chapter discusses these conditions in more detail.

CHAPTER III

PLANNING IN THE SOCIALIST COUNTRIES

A "Socialist" Planning?

This chapter presents a general model of socialist planning using data drawn principally from the USSR and Eastern Europe, and where relevant, China and Tanzania. (For lack of data, North Korea, Mongolia, Cuba, Vietnam, Kampuchea and Laos are not included.)

In view of their wide diversities in history, social composition and economic level, is it valid to group these countries into a single category? Planners and officials from the individual countries repeatedly emphasize how they each must cope with unique national conditions. These conditions mean that Marxist principles can serve only as a general guide. American scholars, on the other hand, have been more than willing to lump socialist countries together, using phrases like "command economies," "Soviet-type economies," or "centrally planned societies" (cf. Feiwal 1968).

It has also been argued that the similarities of planning in the USSR, East Europe, China, Cuba or Tanzania have little to do with Marxism-Leninism per se, and hence do not merit a common designation as "socialist." For instance, Grossman (1969), Lange (1968) and Erlich (1967) classify East European planning as the "war-economy type." Maoist dogma asserts that so many deviations from Marxism-Leninism have taken place in the Soviet bloc that these nations are irrevocably capitalist. These

48

semantic problems are growing more and more acute as Third World governments proclaim their particular national styles to be simply "our kind of socialism" (cf. Aaby 1977 for a distinction between "socialism in Africa" and "African socialism").

This chapter will try to demonstrate that these "deviations" do not constitute a fundamental break with the tenets of socialism as elaborated by Marx, Engels, Lenin and to a degree Mao and Stalin. Rather, they are based on pragmatic adaptations of Marxism to specific conditions of each country. This means that instead of looking for a truly "ideal type" of socialist planning we delimit a range of strategies which use socialist principles and praxis as their point of departure. As such, this chapter approaches socialist planning from three vantage points. First, what has Marxist theory to say about the nature of planning in a socialist or communist society? Second, what are the characteristics of socialist planning ideology? And third, how does this ideology interact with the concrete realities of planning cities, new towns and rural settlements?

Marxist Planning Principles

In their 1848 *Manifesto of the Communist Party*, Marx and Engels assert that a revolution in the mode of production will occur only through the

> combination of agricultural with manufacturing industries; gradual abolition of the distinction between town and country, and a more equable distribution of the population over the countryside (Marx and Engels 1955:32; cited in Lonsdale 1977:591).

Some years later, Engels noted the destructive effect of the separation of town and country. In *Anti-Duhring*, he calls for "the most equal distribution possible of modern industry over the whole country," the result of which would be to avoid creating the large towns necessitated by capitalist concentration (Engels 1962:406-408). These views are reiterated by a Soviet spokesman for Marxist planning theory, who maintains that the USSR follows "Marxist principles of expansion and technological development, balanced and national development and centralized planning" (Kudinov 1975:12).

Since Marxism places highest priority on the role of material production, and since the mode of production is supposed to determine the

corresponding social and spatial arrangements with which to exploit material resources, it can be expected that socialist *economic* planning should
take precedence over *social* or *spatial* planning. Moreover, Marx's con-
tempt for "the idiocy of rural life" (Duggett 1975) and his conviction that
industrial production was the key to economic growth both lend an under-
standable bias toward industrial rather than agricultural development. The
presumed inevitability of large-scale enterprises combined with a faith in
a vanguard modernizing elite lead Marxists to place a high value on coordination and centralization. Centralization was seen as a natural result of
capitalist development and a more efficient organizational form.

Finally, Marx's and Engels' personal disgust at living conditions in large
cities disposed Marxist planning theory toward intermediate or smaller
sized towns, where "lumpen elements" could be brought under better
control. Due to inevitable changes in the mode of production, however,
the priority of urban over rural life would be maintained. Since rationalization of agricultural production stimulates an increasing concentration
of settlements, there is no place at all for the village in Marx's scheme.
Socialism would produce

> changes of a qualitative nature resulting. . . in the final disappear-
> ance of the village as a distinctive unit of settlement. . . . This is
> the process by which social, cultural and economic differences be-
> tween town and countryside are eliminated, the inevitability of
> which was argued by Marx and Engels (Pallot 1979:215).

Marxist planning theory also brings with it a utopian element. Many of the
Soviet and East European new town experiments, in seeking to create an
entirely new life for their residents, echo the utopian planning schemes of
the 19th century Owenites.

As inspiration for achieving a classless society, Marxism sanctions certain methods while ruling out others. For instance, the maintenance of a
class of casual laborers (the "reserve army") might conceivably reduce
labor costs and foster job mobility; however, such a strategy implies the
existence of a permanent underclass and is ruled out at the level of principle. On the other hand, the transitional period from capitalism to socialism
necessitates a "redistributive" planning mechanism whereby surpluses are
transferred from a class of owners to society as a whole. The redistributive

ethic, because it calls for total social equality, underlies regional development strategies in all the socialist countries (Koropeckyj 1972, Lonsdale 1977, Fuchs and Demko 1979).

Marxist-Leninist "theory of the transition" (Sweezy and Bettelheim 1972) acknowledges that there will be a period when the fledgling socialist state is in a position of weakness *vis-a-vis* its developed capitalist neighbors. To limit these ties of dependence, a socialist development strategy sanctions a temporary withdrawal from the world market (Amin 1974b, Thomas 1974). Even though none of the socialist countries can truly isolate themselves from the world capitalist system, Marxist-Leninist principles stipulate that foreign investment be restricted only to those sectors where it is deemed absolutely essential for development. As a consequence, the amount of foreign investment and volume of foreign trade in socialist countries is well below that of comparable capitalist states. Restrictions on foreign trade and national control of investment and purchasing decisions help to insulate the population from drastic fluctuations in the world market. However, this means that domestic resources (human and material) must substitute for the foreign capital or expertise that would have freely entered the country under a nonmarxist development strategy. The increased reliance on domestic resources makes citizen mobilization and participation *imperative* for the successful execution of socialist planning.

Marxist planning theory still leaves room for deciding how strictly the above conditions can be applied to actual planning practice. For example, there is no precise way to determine just when foreign investment has become foreign control; there are no guidelines as to how much of the market should be left in individuals' hands, or whether to rely on material or moral incentives to achieve long-term socialist goals. These determinations must be made during the actual *practice* of socialist development.

Features of Socialist Planning

Orthodox Marxism was predicated on the idea that socialist revolution would first occur in the advanced capitalist nations of the West. The establishment of the USSR as the first socialist state meant that Marxist theory had to be adapted to the USSR's immediate needs. This task was made difficult not only by the ravages of the civil war but by years of diplomatic and economic isolation. The most pressing need was to rebuild and develop the economy.

Under Lenin and Stalin, the USSR was forced to carry out the historical task assigned by Marx to capitalism. Instead of waiting for "the laws of capitalist development" there was a determined intervention to sustain the economy via War Communism and the New Economic Policy (NEP) and later to industrialize through Stalin's Five-Year Plans. The USSR was "building socialism," a notion which Marx, waiting for revolution in Germany or England, never envisioned (Aspaturian 1974:13).

Decades later we have seen the East European states, China, North Korea Cuba, Tanzania and other African and Asian countries formulate planning strategies for "building socialism." For these countries, *socialist* planning has become their *development* strategy. Thus, many of the problems they have experienced derive from the general nature of development planning rather than from socialist planning in particular. The flaws are magnified because the goals of socialist development planning are usually overambitious in relation to the available resources.

Hence, planning in the socialist countries has taken on different characteristics than those envisioned by Marx. The following lists describes some general characteristics of socialist planning as it is practiced today.

Active planning. Because socialism came to largely underdeveloped or warravaged countries, new resources had to be rapidly mobilized and new socioeconomic infrastructures created. This had to be done without resort to outside capital. The active element has persisted through the transition from extensive to intensive economic growth. Socialist planning uses highly diverse forms of conscious intervention (including crude coercion at times) to achieve its goals. It strives to go beyond the mere forecasting of trends and instead dominate them (Fisher 1962, Zeitlin 1972).

Long-term planning. Socialist planning is oriented to long-term as well as short-term goals. Resources are allocated based on the anticipated development of a sector/region and not solely on the basis of existing needs. Long-term planning implies that stimulating economic growth is only a means to an end, the end being the creation of a classless communist society as defined by Marx, Engels, Lenin, Mao or the national leadership. Socialist plans can extend for 10, 25, or even 50 years. In some cases such plans are only predictions or propaganda statements. In others, however, they constitute policy decisions and courses of action having the force of law and the backing of the national bureaucratic and political institutions.

Wide scope planning. Socialist planning is both comprehensive in scope and integrative in execution. All sectors of the society—production, housing, commerce, services, health, education and culture—are brought into the planning apparatus. In spatial planning, for instance, plans focus on particular localities as a part of the total planning framework. To say that all sectors or localities are integrated into the plan does not imply that they are brought in on an equal footing, however. Generally, (though not universally) material production has priority over services, heavy industry over agriculture and light industry and towns over villages (Fisher 1962, 1967, Osborn 1962, Taubman 1973, Fuchs and Demko 1979). Disputes over these priorities (as occurred in the USSR in the 1920s, China in the 1950s and Cuba in the 1960s and 1970s) have generated innumerable factional quarrels and even schisms in the international communist movement (Erlich 1967, Frolic 1976).

National scale. Despite socialism's internationalist ethic, socialist planning is still nation-oriented (Dragomirescu 1977). Resource allocation is determined on the basis of the long-term national interest, putting in second priority the needs of individual localities or regions. The "national interest" is merged with "the public interest." Conflicts among regions, between regional and national planners, or between the State and (what remains of) the private sector are considered extraneous to the planning framework. The immutable hierarchy of national over local interests means that there is *no such thing as a local plan*. There is only a national plan executed in various localities. If national goals or planner strategies are challenged by local level units, planners can respond by invoking the ideology of "national interest," and by using their technical expertise and monopoly over information to dismiss local objections as uninformed or narrowminded.

Now it is undeniable that conflicts between planners and citizens also exist in nonsocialist countries. However, it is only in the socialist states that these conflicts are never *institutionalized* because of the Party's political monopoly and the dogmatic insistence that conflicts are impossible once private property is in the hands of the state. Furthermore, the national scale of planning means that any decentralization will affect the plan only at the level of implementation. Decentralization must not lead to genuine local self-determination, for this would be viewed as antithetical to the national interest. Communities may thus *protest* plans, but they can never formally *reject* them.

Economic primacy. Virtually all plans are subordinated to the goal of increasing material production (Osborn and Reiner 1962), as this is the means by which the ultimate goal of communist society is to be achieved. Social and spatial policies are designed to support primary objectives of economic (usually industrial) growth and productive efficiency. To this end, there is an absolute primacy of sectoral interests over territorial (regional) interests. Regions, cities and villages are seen as epiphenomena of the productive forces. Cities are planned to serve the needs of industry (Osborn and Reiner 1962, Taubman 1973). Villages are organized so as to maximize agricultural production and provide cost-effective services (Ioanid 1966). The "primacy of the economic" helps support planners' ideas that humans are somehow capable of arranging themselves in irrational patterns of settlement. Economic primacy provides socialist planners with the pretext to revamp, rebuild or even abolish localities according to the presumed needs of the national economy. For example, the Soviet planner Voskresensky states that "the scattered rural population is the biggest barrier to industrialized agriculture" (1976:535). And in fact, the USSR has reduced the number of rural settlements from 700,000 to 115,000 (Jarvesoo 1974, Khodorev 1972, Zaslavskaya 1978, Pallot 1979). The Soviet idea of the "expendability" of spatial units is replicated in the village resettlement schemes of the other East European countries, in Tanzania's *Ujaama* (villageization) program, and even in the infamous emptying out of Cambodia's cities by the Khmer Rouge (see the section on "Rural settlements" later in this chapter for more details).

Not only can settlements be abolished, but economic policy can determine that residents be required to remain in their localities via internal passport systems or migration restrictions. Decisions as to the future of settlements are taken away from individuals and localities and placed under the control of the planning administration.

Ideological/moral foundation. Like all plans, socialist plans combine technical with ideological legitimation; in this case it is with the help of Marxist-Leninist theory and national development ideology. Plans can always be rationalized as being in the national interest. Short-term (one or two generations!) sacrifices by the population are justified by invoking the long-term benefits. The ideological component of planning means that some options are openly discussed, others dismissed and still others ignored as irrelevant. For example, socialist planners make a strict separation of town and country, with the intermediate size city being the preferred settlement unit over either the large metropolis or the peasant village (Osborn and Reiner 1962, Enache 1973, Matei and Matei 1973). The Chinese, with a longer tradition of "parasitic cities," are more ardently anti-urban, to the point where middle school graduates (not intellectuals) are "sent down" to the countryside for both ideological and economic reasons (Ma 1976). Frolic (1976:150) summarizes the difference when he distinguishes between the "new Soviet man, who is a worker, and the new Chinese man, who is a peasant." The anti-metropolitan ideology of socialist planners is well documented.

> It appears that most of the arguments for limiting urban growth are ideologically based, derived in part to counter the "bigness" and thus inhumane conditions supposedly characteristic of major Western cities, as well as the belief that, by means of size limitations, one can somehow equalize the differences between the city and the countryside. [In any case] detailed socioeconomic analysis is not one of the determining elements. (Fisher 1967:1080.)

In contrast to the prejudice against large spatial units, a "bigger-is-better" mentality seems to dominate many industrial plans, especially in the Soviet Union and the Balkans. A final example of the ideological/moral foundation of planning, lies in the millenarian orientation and elitist feelings of omnipotency on the part of some socialist planners. These tendencies seem to foster the ideology of ends justifying means, no matter how great the immediate human costs (cf. Stalin 1940b).

Reduction of spontaneous market forces. Socialist planning is intended to become progressively dominant over the market forces of society. The market comes under the control of the planning apparatus via policies of taxation, expropriation, discriminatory pricing, rationing or administrative allocations. One way of controlling the market is to centralize decision-

making. However, the periodic reforms in the socialist countries (especially
in Hungary, Poland and Yugoslavia) indicate that centralization itself is
neither necessary for, nor specific to socialist planning (Feiwal 1968,
Bicanic 1967).

Regional balance. As a manifestation of class equality and as a means for
furthering overall economic development, socialist planning aims for a
"balanced and judicious distribution of the productive forces over the
entire national territory" (Dragomirescu 1977:5). This drive toward spatial
homogenization, derided by Western observers as dullness, is well illustrated by the standardized apartment complexes, the policies of eliminating
town/country differenes, and the programs to industrialize backward
regions (Fisher 1967, Koropeckyj 1972, Sawers 1977). Because investments in backward regions may be costly and unprofitable for long periods,
the ideology of regional equality can come into conflict with the need
for rapid accumulation (Fuchs and Demko 1979). High cost enterprises
placed in backward areas may become "enterprises parasitic to the economy" while smaller-sized villages may be branded as "irrational settlements without perspectives for development" (Blaga 1974:197). The
regional balance ideology brings with it conflicts between regional interests. However, these conflicts are perceived as totally contrary to the
national interest and not accorded any kind of institutionalized channel
for expression. Instead they are dealt with on an ad hoc basis.

Necessity for citizen participation. Since socialist planners conceive of
their activities as benefitting society as a whole, they fell more than justified in calling for the active participation of the entire citizenry. Moreover,
the low level of economic development, limited State resources, and the
scale of the plans make citizen participation not only a moral duty, however, but an economic necessity. The socialist planner's dependence on
citizen help is much greater than under capitalist planning, where State or
private contractors obviate the need for direct client participation in plan
execution. The difference can be expressed with the following example:
An advanced capitalist state may decide to build a road which is unwanted
by the local residents; this would be done by hiring a contractor. A socialist state may also decide to build the road, but it will ask that the villagers
participate in its construction, *even if they do not want it* (for reasons
which the planners do not find valid).

Types of participation can range from "consultation with the masses," which is an educative technique for helping them to understand the rationale behind planning *policies*, to citizen labor contributions in planning *execution*. In general, national policy makers determine the major goals while regional and local units help in their implementation. While one can criticize the actual workings of the participation process in socialist countries, it is undeniable that

> there is planned integration of the citizens' participation beyond periodic election of political candidates . . . . This is a systematically integrated constitutional principle (van Putten 1971:11).

Citizen participation seems to be more essential when the level of national development is very low and State resources scarce. Cuba's sugar harvesting brigades are one example. China's constant mobilization of urban neighborhood residents is another (Salaf 1971, Frolic 1976). In Tanzania the "participatory ideology" is especially developed, being a reflection of long-standing African consensus traditions, part of the national ethic, a fundamental feature of democracy, an essential characteristic of Tanzanian socialism, and an effective means for helping to execute plans and achieve development. Participation is seen as a *prerequisite* for development and as the decisive factor affecting planning success or failure (see Samoff 1979 for further comments on the relationship between participation and development in Tanzania).

The Essential Difference

Many of the preceding characteristics of socialist planning are also present in the planning of the advanced or underdeveloped capitalist countries. The national scale, ideological foundation, emphasis on industrialization and efforts to transform lagging regions have all been part of capitalist planning strategies.

What distinguishes socialist planning is not any particular quality among the nine features elaborated above. Rather, it is the sum total and wide scope in which they are applied, combined with Marxism's ideological legitimation and the practical necessities of "building socialism." Socialist planning is more ambitious and more pervasive than capitalist or nonsocialist development planning. It penetrates through all regions and all sectors of the society, intervening at any level. In theory there is no aspect of life that is beyond its scope.

Not only are planning goals more comprehensive, but with State control over land, raw materials, capital and labor allocations, socialist planners have more means at their disposal. This can lead to spectacular successes as well as massive blunders. For the planners, conflict of interest is kept to a minimum because there is no other possible client but the state and no "private sector" to impose its organized will on the "public sector." Socialist planning is not total planning, but it is the *dominant* mode of social, political and economic action, to which individuals, households, localities and enterprises must adapt. Moreover, socialist societies should not be considered planned societies but instead "societies with a plan." The dominance (without omnipotence) can be illustrated by examining socialist city and regional planning in Eastern Europe.

Socialist City Planning

Following the socialist restructuring of their governments, East European city planners were confronted with several key problems, the most pressing being the massive war devastation, low levels of industrial output and acute shortage of urban housing. Unlike today's Third World, where industrialization generally lags behind urbanization, the situation in Eastern Europe was the reverse; countries were industrializing without urbanizing fast enough (Benet 1974, Konrad and Szelenyi 1976, Szelenyi 1977).

Those urban infrastructural inputs which failed to generate economic growth were downgraded in favor of direct industrial investments. City plans were regarded as mere appendages to industrial production plans (Osborn 1965, Taubman 1973, Fuchs and Demko 1979). While villagers were clamoring to fill city factory jobs, the urban housing shortage made it necessary to restrict immigration. This gave rise to a class of commuting villagers who combined factory wage labor in the city with household agricultural production and/or collective farm labor: the so-called "peasant-worker" or "worker-peasant" (Fischer 1962, Frolic 1963, 1976, Mihailovic 1972:82-100, Taubman 1973, Sarfalvi 1975, Cole 1981). The state employed a variety of administrative measures to restrict the growth of urban populations, but "administrative barriers were broken through and very few countries succeeded in regulating the inflow of the labor force" (Mihailovic (1972:100). Summarizing the Soviet experience, the American planner Jack Fisher is particularly unimpressed: "Despite fifty years of socialist planning in the USSR, population restriction has been unsuccess-full" (1962:262). Fisher's remarks apply equally well to Romania, where between 1966 and 1977 the population of Bucharest grew by 33% and the industrial town of Brașov by 60%, rates that were wholly unexpected by State planners (Sampson 1979).

Along with the administrative measures, socialist city planners led a multi-pronged attack on the urban housing problem. Detached single-family homes were deemed economically and even ideologically unsound. Standardized (and thus cheaper) apartments of four, six and ten stories were built instead. Planners constructed self-contained urban neighborhoods (*microrayon* in the USSR, *cartieri* in Romania, etc.) of 5,000 to 15,000 persons, each having its own complex of services, schools, and clinics. The city's former residential and business center now began to take on increased political, administrative and symbolic functions (cf. Fischer 1962, 1967; Frolic 1963, Pioro 1965, MacMurray 1971, Binns 1979, 1980). Though cities were expanded, socialist planners retained their antipathy toward large urban agglomerations, extolling the virtues of intermediate sized cities with their lower infrastructural costs and higher productivity (Fisher 1967, Abrams and Fracavighia 1975). This applies to Chinese planners as well (Frolic 1976).

The rapid construction and massive inputs into housing have not solved all the problems of developing socialist cities. Stvan (1973) attributes some of the deficiencies of socialist urban planning to an arbitrary pricing policy which blinds the planner to the "true" land values. The extension of public transport and disappearance of slum areas is now over shadowed by complaints of "barren neighborhoods, travel fatigue and lack of parking" for citizens who live on the giant housing projects at the edge of socialist cities (*New York Times*, June 10, 1977). Fisher criticizes the spatial uniformity in urban construction, arguing that cost cutting in nonproductive investments led to waste, inefficiency and a "dull unimaginative grayness in the urban landscape" (1965:40). For the Polish planner Z. Pioro (1965:32), however. "Fisher's 'uniformity' is nothing but an expression of Socialist equality" (see also French and Hamilton 1979 for further viewpoints on socialist cities).

Socialist urban development has also been hampered by the Party's single-minded emphasis on industrial growth (Fuchs and Demko 1979).

Referring to the factory vs. services conflict in Soviet new towns, Taubman concludes that "one public interest has been sacrificed for another" (1973: 46).

In addition, Western criticism of socialist planning should be seen in light of Western views of socialist societies as dull, bureaucratic and unresponsive to individual needs. In this respect, their criticism of the Party's "politicization" of planning is a fatuous criticism. After all, artificially low rents, subsidized food prices, free medical care and cheap public transport are equally "political." The issue is not politics but policies. Behind Party preferences for economic growth lie both Marxist principles and practical necessities: "building socialism" requires a developed economy, without which the cities would become parasitic.

Socialist Spatial Planning

Spatial planning appeared in Eastern Europe only in the early 1960s. At that time the main objective was to reduce the flow of migrants into the larger, established cities by means of rural industrialization and new town construction. Despite frequent pronouncements about the need for developing backward regions, East European planners have been forced to concentrate key investment in specially selected growth centers having the most promising development potential.

In China, regional policy has focused on consolidating the rural commune (population 50,000-100,000) as the basic administrative, economic and social unit of society. Not only are the communes to be made as self-sufficient as possible (Lee 1977), but this is supplemented by the systematic expulsion of urban dwellers for permanent resettlement in the countryside (Frolic 1976, Ma 1976, Mangione 1977).

New Towns. Ash (1977) has pointed out the major difference between the Western (especially English) model of new towns and the new town policies of the socialist countries. English new towns are suburban settlements meant to siphon off urbanites who would like to leave the city. Socialist new towns are built to attract rural outmigrants who would otherwise enter the older, established cities. Where the English new town is in an adversary/competitive relationship with the older, established city, socialist urban centers relate in a more complementary fashion, being subsumed under a broad national economic plan and integrated into a unified spatial hierarchy and planning administration.

The country with the most experience in new town construction is the Soviet Union. Since 1917 between 800 and 1,000 new towns have been built (Rugg 1971:98; Taubman 1973:54). By comparison, England has built 32 new towns, housing a total of two million inhabitants (Diamond 1977). Bulgaria has imitated the Soviet experience, building 66 new towns, half since 1964 (cf. Carter 1975). Soviet new towns vary in size from 30,000 to 400,000. Most are linked to extractive industries or mines, while others are part of a general program to populate the sparsely inhabited area east of the Urals; the famous Akademgorodok research complex in Siberia is a prominent example

The Soviet achievement was not without difficulties, of course. A common problem was that new town growth often exceeded the original plan; new towns began experiencing the same urban dysfunctions which they were supposed to alleviate (Taubman 1973). Other problems occurred because of the enormous costs of locating new industrial plant and transport facilities in relatively isolated areas (Lonsdale 1977). New town construction was hampered by squabbling between the industrial and housing/service interests. The socialist "laws of spatial location" (Hamilton 1970) which stressed high immediate return clashed with the costly and often inefficient long-term investments represented by new towns. Planners suffered from lack of information about far-off conditions, "administrative distance" from the new town's citizens, "social distance" as to their real needs (after Cohen 1977) and an arrogance about the possibility of unintended social consequences.

Similar problems are noted in the Polish debate over city planning. Especially prominent are the problems of the new migrants. In many instances, after a short stay in the new town, the new urbanities sought to migrate to larger, better-provisioned metropolitan centers; this directly counteracted the new town's purpose (on the Polish experience see Fisher 1962, 1965, 1967, Pioro 1965, MacMurray 1971, Regulski 1972, Murray 1974).

Rural settlements. Though debate over "socialist settlement hierarchies" dates back to the first decade of Soviet power, concrete actions did not take place until the late 1950s, when Khrushchev announced his "agro-town" proposals (see Pallot 1979, on which much of the following debate is based). The agrotown policy sought to redress the inequality between town and countryside by converting selected villages into miniature towns.

Developing new urban centers in rural areas would presumably encourage young and ablebodied residents to remain in the countryside, where they were needed for agricultural modernization.

To this end, planners established a minimal viable population of 1,000, below which the provision of services was judged prohibitively expensive (this minimum was raised to 2,000 in 1972). To implement the proposals, villages were designated as either "viable" or "nonviable." The viable settlements were earmarked for growth while nonviable localities would either die out naturally or have their populations resettled. In keeping with the urban orientation of Soviet planners, construction in the viable settlements included blocs of five story apartments and communal buildings built to the same specifications as those found in Moscow and Leningrad's urban "microdistricts."

As for the nonviable villages, over 200,000 of them disappeared between 1959 and 1970; the vast majority contained fewer than 100 persons. In north-central Russia, for example, half of the 142,000 communities held fewer than 50 persons, so that kolkhoz labor had to be drawn from an average of 20 different settlements (Voskresensky 1976). To bring urban-type services to the 16 million collective farmers in this zone, the 142,000 villages would be regrouped into 29,000 agrotowns. Village consolidation and the need to relocate is "wholeheartedly welcomed" by the residents, according to Voskresensky (1976:535). To take a second example, in the Iaroslavsk region of Great Russia, where 43% of the settlements have fewer than 800 people, the 7,770 villages will be consolidated into 522 population centers according to the size and needs of their associated collective farms (Ioanid 1968:6-9). The Iaroslavsk plan reflects the ambiguities in Soviet spatial policy, in that it calls for the construction of localities which will be torn down a few decades later! In Soviet Estonia, also characterized by dispersed hamlets, the existing 7,000 villages are to be regrouped into 700-800 agrotowns with sizes of 2,000 or more (Jarvesoo 1974). The peasants will retain small gardens next to their apartments, with larger private plots at the village outskirts.

Attempts to recreate the city within the village has spawned considerable discussion among Soviet planners (Pallot 1979). Geographers pointed out that concentrating agricultural settlements produced increased labor time for the peasants in getting to and from their fields. Moreover, the costs of establishing the new villages have been much higher than expected. In some new villages, those residents whose household plots were expropriated for apartment construction migrated to outlying villages in order to obtain new plots. The simplistic dichotomization of villages into "viable" and "nonviable" proved too restrictive.

In 1968, the number of viable villages was doubled, and today there are gradualist classifications using "degrees of viability" as a planning index. Rather than planning for settlements on an individual basis, programs are formulated and executed for entire groups of localities. This so-called "Group" or "Unified" system incorporates a diversity of settlement types into an integrated spatial hierarchy. Soviet architects and planners have finally recognized that urban solutions will not always work on what are essentially rural problems:

> The principle source of conflict [remains] the seeming incompatibility of the policy of concentration with the need to safeguard the interest of both socialized and private agricultural production. If the result in terms of the plans formulated has been imperfect, it is perhaps as much a reflection of the intractable nature of the problem as of poor planning *per se* (Pallot 1979:226).

Soviet village resettlement programs and problems are replicated –albeit on a reduced scale—in other East European countries. In Hungary, where geographical characteristics make for generally larger villages, the grain belt between the Danube and Tisza rivers will be restructured so that only 300 of the existing 657 localities will remain. Optimum sizes for these villages range from 3,000 to 6,000, depending on topographical and agricultural characteristics (Ioanid 1968:11; see also Dienes 1973 and the comprehensive review by Fuchs and Demko 1979).

In Bulgaria, the projected rural settlement network will consist of large villages with 5,000-6,000 population, surrounded by smaller ones of 2,000-3,000, and still smaller villages containing 800-1,000 people located close to the fields. These needs are dictated by the labor intensive conditions of Bulgarian agriculture, which specializes in fruits, vines and roses, and by the topographic variations between mountain and plains zones. In addition, the Bulgarians plan an intermediate "town-village" settlement to occupy the niche between villages and new towns (Hoffman 1964, Carter 1975).

In Czechoslovakia, reducing the number of villages is a priority item for rural development. Between 1949 and 1964, the number of villages dropped from 14,803 to 10,608. This was due both to the expulsion of Germans from Bohemia and to normal rural outmigration (*Radio Free Europe Situation Report* March 3, 1976, pp. 5-8). In the 1970s, the role of the "central village" has been emphasized; this is a hazily defined unit of about 2,000 persons which would serve as a point of attraction for those migrating from less viable localities (ibid.).

Not all the East European countries are willing to abolish "unwanted" settlements, however. In Poland, for example, there are plans to develop 10,000 of the country's 69,000 rural settlements, but there is no program to actually phase out the remaining 59,000 (Ioanid 1968:5). In East Germany, a highly industrialized country with an ostensibly "irrational" settlement pattern characterized by tiny villages (average population 350), there are no major plans to revamp the settlement structure. Rather, the East Germans seek to strengthen the existing network of settlements (Krambach and Muller 1978). Finally, Yugoslavia has not developed a comprehensive rural settlement strategy. Location of industrial enterprises and regional imbalances are still approached as economic problems requiring infrastructural investment and not as problems of settlement reorganization (Macesich 1964, Mihailovic 1972, Hoffman 1967). It is testimony to the variety of socialist development strategies that massive settlement reorganization is considered counterproductive both in one of the richest and most homogenous of the socialist countries (East Germany) and in one with considerable regional inequality and in which the backward regions are among the poorest in Europe (Yugoslavia). This is further evidence for the view that the correlation between economic development and a proper settlement strategy is difficult to make from a purely technical standpoint.

In applying Marxist principles to their specific national conditions, socialist settlement strategies have also generated their own difficulties. The speed, urgency, scope and centralization of the plans, the inexperience and overambitiousness of the planners, their urban orientation and administrative and social distance from the rural populace all led to various miscalculations and unintended consequences. Another set of problems developed because the success of certain plans failed to generate corresponding changes in the planning apparatus. In Hungary, for instance, the success of industrialization and agricultural collectivization brought on the "underurbanization" crisis (Konrad and Szelenyi 1976). In Yugoslavia, Denitch (1970, 1974) has noted that the causes of rural-to-urban migration have changed from rural "push" to urban "pull"; thus, plans aimed at neutralizing "push" factors—which might have worked in decades past— are not effective today. In Romania the gradual industrialization of labor-exporting regions has produced a labor shortage for those regions which formerly recruited workers from these zones.

As a result of problems in applying socialist planning strategies there remain considerable disparities in living standard between town and countryside and between backward and advanced regions. This is especially true where the inherited regional disparities were greatest, i.e., the USSR and the Balkans (Lonsdale 1977, Fuchs and Demko 1979). In Yugoslavia, the Republic of Dalmatia has a GNP five times higher than that of backward Kossovo (Hoffman 1967). And in Romania, the proportion of total production contributed by the backward areas rose only 4% during the period 1950-1964 (Turnock 1977). Whereas some authors (Fuchs and Demko, especially) conclude that this is evidence of the failure of socialist planning, it is undeniable that a wide gap exists between the ideology of spatial equality and the harsh realities of regional disparity. Few planners from socialist countries would deny this fact.

Summary: The Socialist Factor

This chapter began with two assertions: first, that the similarities between the planning strategies of the Soviet Union, East Europe, China and Tanzania were based on a common ideological foundation of Marxism-Leninism; and second, that their divergent planning practices constituted the pragmatic adaptation of Marxist theory to the exigencies of "building socialism."

Marxist theory brought with it an emphasis on the productive over the social and spatial aspects of society, on the town over the countryside, and on large-scale, redistributive over small-scale, incremental planning. Like all ideological systems, certain means were ruled out at the level of principle, while other means could be justified by the ultimate ends—to construct a classless, communist society.

Put into practice, the Marxist principles were applied to the task of building socialism in war-torn, underdeveloped countries. Socialist planning

became a special form of development planning. The combination of Marxist principles and the necessities of building socialism generated several
similar characteristics in the planning of socialist countries: the active
element, the long-term element, the wide scope, national scale, economic
primacy and settlement "irrationality," ideological/moral foundation,
reduction of spontaneous market forces, regional balance, and necessity
for citizen participation. These features were designated "socialist" because they were founded in Marxist ideology and the desire to construct
a socialist society.

The practice of socialist planning in rebuilding cities, constructing new
towns and revamping settlement hierarchies showed the dominance of an
urban orientation and the priority of intermediate cities and new towns.
In the rural areas this was paralleled by a stress on upgrading "viable"
settlements and abolishing "nonviable" ones. Notwithstanding the ambitious goals of these programs, they confronted problems that could be
solved only by a continuous restructuring and flexibility in the planning
apparatus. The problems include the serious inequalities between town and
country and between advanced and lagging regions, inequalities that will
take a long time to alleviate.

This chapter has tried to show that there indeed exists a "socialist"
planing sui generis. It includes both common ideological principles and
shared practices. However, each of the socialist countries has had to apply
these principles according to their specific historical, economic and political circumstances. Hence they have emerged with a variety of programs,
some eminently successful, others only partially, still others unsuccessful.
The idea of irrational settlements, for example, was taken to its extreme
in the Soviet Union but ignored in East Germany. Romania, as we shall
see shortly, appears to follow Soviet policies in some domains while applying East German and Yugoslav solutions to others.

Those who would deny that there is a socialist planning point to similarities with development planning in general. The common elements include preoccupation with growth centers, anti-metropolitan ideology,
and urban prejudice toward rural settlements. However, these characteristics must be considered in their totality. In this perspective, the ostensible similarities fade in contrast to the divergence in long term goals. Development planning in the West is simply "planning for development,"
while development planning in the socialist countries is a means by which
they *build socialism*. Both types of planning employ similar means to

achieve their ends; only one goes further to try and create an entirely new social order.

Socialist planning is not carried out in a vacuum. It must confront and incorporate specific national circumstances in order to achieve long term goals. The next chapter deals with these national specificities by examining Romania's policy of rural systematization. In analyzing Romanian planning at the national level, the linkage between planning-in-general, socialism and national specificity will become clear. Only then can the analysis proceed downward, to the regional and local levels of the "vertical slice."

CHAPTER IV

SYSTEMATIZATION:
ROMANIA'S NATIONAL SETTLEMENT STRATEGY

Introduction: Historical Preconditions

This chapter begins by outlining the historical circumstances which shaped the evolution of Romania's settlement structure. It then goes on to describe the evolution and current status of Romanian settlement planning (*sistematizare*). The final section of the chapter summarizes the key contradictions in Romania's planning ideology, showing how these relate to "planning-in-general" and to "the socialist factor" discussed in previous chapters. The chronology of systematization policy decisions may be tedious for some readers (they are advised to skip to the concluding sections of the chapter). However, this debate over policy formation in fact foreshadowed many subsequent contradictions when systematization was put into practice.

Historically, Romania may be seen as a "war-ravaged buffer state between the major powers of southeastern Europe" (Turnock 1970:541). Geographically, the landscape is dominated by the Carpathian mountains, which, because they traverse the middle of the country rather than its perimeter, have served as a refuge for Romanian peasants fleeing the lowlands. in times of military invasion, feudal persecution or political turmoil. The presence of hundreds of tiny hamlets in the highland areas attests to the fact that such ocasions were quite frequent. Until the mid-20th century,

Romania's peasantry was its main social class and the peasant village the principal settlement unit. Romanian history, like that of the Balkans generally, is dominated by the presence of foreign powers and outside interests. The southern and eastern provinces of Wallachia and Moldavia were under Ottoman domination until 1878. Czarist Russia ruled the northeastern province of Bessarabia until Romania managed to reclaim it in 1919. The ethnically mixed province of Transylvania had been a part of Austria-Hungary until Romania acquired it after World War I. Romania's subjugation to foreign powers continued in the 1930s, when it was brought into the orbit of Nazi Germany. After the War, having lost Bessarabia to the USSR, Romania became an obedient Soviet satellite. In the mid-1960s, it gradually emerged as a "maverick" in the Eastern bloc, both in terms of political independence from Moscow and in economic links with the West, especially West Germany. Romania's continued orientation toward outside patron states is indicative of its status as a "periphery" in the European division of labor (Chirot 1976, Wallerstein 1974). The desire to rise above this dependency on foreign powers (east or west) has become an integral part of Romania's foreign policy, economic programs, and the national consciousness in general.

Both topographic variability and the legacy of underdevelopment influenced the structure of settlements in Romania. The country is about evenly divided among mountains, hill/plateau areas and plains, with corresponding variations in the size and structure of rural settlements. Highland communities tend to be smaller and dispersed, while lowland settlements vary from highly nucleated agrotowns in the plains and border zones to sprawling "tentacle villages" hugging roads and valleys (a classic Habsburg settlement scheme).

Indicative of Romania's underdevelopment before 1945 were the low level of urbanization, the inequality between town and countryside, and the wide disparities between a few advanced and many underdeveloped regions. Though its position in world commerce was as supplier of grain and agricultural raw materials, the country also possessed rich resources of ferrous and nonferrous metals, coal, natural gas, oil and forests (Turnock 1970). The lack of an industrial base and an underdeveloped infrastructure prevented these resources from being fully exploited, however. Through the interwar period, industrial development in Romania was confined to the east-west axis of southern Transylvania (from Timișoara to Brașov) and a north-south axis from Sighișoara to Ploiești and Bucharest. Except for isolated pockets of wealth, the rest of Romania was largely agricultural and desperately poor. The regional contrast between the older industrial areas of Transylvania and the agrarian zones of Oltenia and Moldavia persists today, although new towns and factories are being constructed in the backward areas.

The low level of development and the regional inequalities both aggravated the rural/urban imbalances in the settlement structure. Up to 1948, nearly three-fourths of Romania's population lived in villages. Urban centers were few with Bucharest being the dominant "primate city." Most of the towns contained below 20,000 inhabitants and could not provide extensive services to their own populations, much less to their rural hinterlands. Urban/rural links were grossly underdeveloped due to a lack of transport arteries. Even where adequate transport and communication lines existed, their purpose had been to serve the commercial needs of the Ottoman or Habsburg empires (or foreign firms) rather than the needs of the emerging Romanian state. The rural/urban imbalance was most acute in Romania's less developed regions (Moldavia, Oltenia). Not only were towns lacking, but villages in these zones were generally smaller, more dispersed and less accessible, education and health services were minimal and infant mortality as high as any of the poorest countries in the Third World. In more developed regions (Braşov, Sibiu, Prahova), villages were more nucleated, their average populations greater, and communications with neighboring towns more frequent and reliable.

This brief review indicates five principle features which have influenced the formation of Romania's existing rural settlement structure. These are 1) the low overall level of economic development, 2) the legacy of economic and political domination by more foreign powers, 3) the existence of regional disparities between industrially developed and backward agrarian zones, 4) imbalances between rural and urban settlements, lack of urban infrastructure, and 5) extensive topographic variation due to political and ecological factors. These five features should be recalled as the present day rural settlement structure is described.

Romanian Settlement Structure

The post-war period has seen a steady increase in the general level of economic development, as shown by the rapid rise in industrial production (admittedly from a very low base), the urbanization of the population and the transfer of the labor force from agriculture to industry (see Table 1).

TABLE 1

ROMANIA'S OCCUPATIONAL AND SETTLEMENT PATTERNS

Category	Year						Projected	
	1930	1948	1956	1966	1973	1978	1985	2000
Populations (in millions)	14.3	15.9	17.5	19.0	20.8	21.8	25	30
Index of Total Industrial Production (1948 = 100)	85	100	388	1200	2800	4900		
Agricultural[1] work force (%)	80	75	70	57	42	34	25	15
Proportion dwelling in urban areas (%)	21	23	31	38	42	49	65	75

1   Agricultural work force in the post-1948 period includes salaried workers in state and cooperative farms (470,000 in 1978), cooperative farm members (2.4 million in 1978), and individual farmers in the highland areas (600,000 households in 1976).

Source: *Anuarul Statistic al R. S. România 1978.*

With industrialization and urbanization, the network of urban settlements has also been transformed (see Table 2). Below the still-dominant capital of Bucharest (population 1.9 million) there is now a group of 18 urban-industrial centers with populations ranging from 100,000 to 320,000 inhabitants. These large cities have received the greatest influx of urban migrants from the countryside. Of the remaining 217 towns, sixty percent (150) have populations below 20,000. These 150 towns hold only 18% of the total urban population. The number of towns has risen steadily, and by the end of 1985 an additional 120 villages will be declared "urban centers." Because of the high density of localities in the landscape, the construction of completely new towns has been rare in Romania. The three

TABLE 2

ROMANIA'S URBAN SETTLEMENT STRUCTURE—1930-1978

Category		Year			No. of towns
	1930	1948	1966	1978	1978
Proportion of total urban dwellers who live in towns with:					
Under 20,000 inhabitants	32.9%	26.7%	20.9%	15.1%	144
20,000-100,000 inhabitants	36.1	39.1	29.5	30.2	75
100,000-320,000 inhabitants	10.0	6.2	28.1	35.7	18
Bucharest	21.0	28.0	21.5	19.9	1
	100.0	100.0	100.0	100.0	236
Total number of towns	142	152	183	236	
Mean urban population	21,487	24,429	39,922	44,915	
Urban as percentage of total population	21%	23%	38%	49%	

Sources: Dragomirescu 1977:5; *Anuarul Statistic al R. S. Romania 1978.*

major examples are Dr. Petru Groza (population 8,225 in 1978), Victoria (8,596) and Gheorghe Gheorghiu-Dej (43,282).

Romania's rural settlement network consists of 13,124 villages grouped into 2,706 communes. The number of villages has declined from 14,203 in 1966 due to consolidation of scattered hamlets (*catune*) into single village (*sat*) units. The principal characteristic of the rural settlement structure is the large number of small, scattered population clusters dispersed along hillsides, valleys and roads. According to a 1966 study, over 70% of Romania's villages have under 1,000 persons (see Table 3).

The Romanian literature on rural settlements is almost singlemindedly preoccupied with pointing up their inadequacies (Bold, Matei and Sābādeanu 1974, Matei 1974, Enache 1973, Turnock 1976). Villages are seen as too dispersed over the landscape with houses being separated from one another by large plots of unproductive green space. Average village population sizes are considered too small to justify state investments in services

TABLE 3

VILLAGE SETTLEMENT STRUCTURE—1966

Category	No. of villages	As percentage of all villages	As percentage of total rural population
1-199 inhabitants	2263	14.9%	2.1%
200-499 inhabitants	3934	27.7	11.5
500-999 inhabitants	4134	29.1	25.0
1,000-1,999 inhabitants	2695	19.0	31.4
2,000-4,999 inhabitants	1081	7.5	25.3
over 5,000 inhabitants	96	0.8	4.7
TOTALS	14,203	100.0%	100.0%

Source: Ioanid 1968:12.

and infrastructure for all of them, and the total number of villages in the settlement network is considered too great. This overabundance of settlement is highly variable from region to region. Some counties (e g Braşov, Tulcea and Vaslui) have from 120-150 villages on their territory while others (Vîlcea, Argeş, Alba) have from 500 to 600. Counties with large numbers of localities have greater difficulty and added expense in trying to supply rural residents with services, transportation and communication. It appears that such "irrational" settlement patterns are most pronounced in the mountains or highland regions; these zones have greater numbers of villages with smaller average populations, great dispersion of individual homesteads, a low urbanization percentage, and a lower proportion of their workers in nonagricultural occupations. This correlation between settlement structure and economic level (echoing that of Johnson and other Western regional theorists) is greatly emphasized in the Romanian planning literature (Bold, Matei and Săbădeanu 1974, Lăzărescu 1976, Turnock 1976).

To summarize, it appears that the Romanian settlement structure reflects four kinds of inequalities:

1) between economically developed and economically backward regions
2) between larger, better endowed urban-industrial centers and smaller provincial towns;
3) between the towns as preferred settlement units benefiting from state investments in industry, infrastructure and housing and the villages which often lack modern services and workplaces;
4) between villages which are large, nucleated and with higher potential for viability in the future spatial network and the mass of small, dispersed, isolated hamlets in the highland areas.

It would be tempting to cite the historical legacy of underdevelopment as the sole explanation for the perpetuation of these inequalities in the socialist period. Such an explanation is necessary, but it is hardly sufficient; for these inequalities have also been reproduced under the specific conditions of socialist development in Romania. At the close of World War II, Romania began the task of "building socialism." Primary emphasis was placed on restoring and expanding the productive base of society. This led to an intentional channeling of investment into industry, especially heavy industry. Seeking the quickest and most certain return on investment, state planners looked first to those cities and zones which already possessed plant and infrastructure. Consequently, through the 1960s, a disproportionately high amount of investment went into the traditionally advanced areas, most particularly the industrial towns in Transylvania, to Ploieşti, and to Bucharest. The share of industrial production contributed by these advanced areas fell only four percent over the period 1950-1965 (from 62% to 58% of the total national output; Turnock 1970:555).

The industrialization of the older towns led to the concentration of housing inputs and services to these preferred localities. The expanding industries were compelled to import labor from underdeveloped regions or from their immediate rural hinterlands. The consequences of this rapid socialist industrialization were increased labor time for peasant commuters, social alienation for the new migrants and the persistance of inequalities between town and village and between the advanced and backward (i.e., labor exporting) regions.

As Romania's economy expanded, there was an increased need to exploit new resources (especially mineral wealth and energy sources) in areas far from established industrial centers. Rural industrialization thus became a key element in Romania's strategy for economic self-reliance. The necessity to reorganize the settlement structure became more obvious in 1963, after the completion of agricultural collectivization. From the amalgamation of agricultural holdings it was a short step to the consolidation and systematization of rural settlements.

To achieve rapid and sustained industrialization and to upgrade the quality of life of the villages, it was necessary to restore the imbalance between urban and rural settlements, bring backward regions up to the level of advanced regions, relieve the stress on overburdened large cities, and provide industrial jobs and social services to all the rural areas.

Thus, as a result of both the historical legacy of underdevelopment and the contradictions generated by socialist industrialization, there emerged a new set of priorities, encapsulated in the policy of *sistematizare* as articulated in the late 1960s and early 1970s.

Evolution of Systematization Policy in Romania

Definition. The term "systematization" (*sistematizare*) will be used to refer to planning activities which apply to particular localities or regions, especially their physical transformation. In the Romanian context, *sistematizare* is more than just a method for the physical transformation of villages and towns. It is, firstly, an *ideal* of how spatial planning should be integrated with economic planning (*planificare*) and socialist development. Second, systematization is a *program* for developing (or in some cases phasing out) each settlement in the country, from hamlet to metropolis. Third, systematization involves an *organizational structure* in which national objectives, regional imbalances and local potentialities are to be harmonized into a centrally administered State policy, codified by law. Systematization activities may be carried out by economists, draftsmen (*proiectanți*), architects, engineers or by the (more rarely heard) *sistematizator* ("one who systematizes"). In this book, the words "planning" and "systematization" will be used interchangeably, though the reference will always be to the physical/spatial planning connoted by *sistematizare*.

A preparatory phase. Activities of rural settlement planning in Romania date from the late 19th century, when land reforms generated calls to revamp the structure of localities (Bold, Matei and Săbădeanu 1974:29-30). Planning legislation was also enacted in 1904 and 1920, and was again linked to agricultural land consolidation. During the 1920s and 1930s

Romania's Liberal and Peasant Party governments each formulated policies for upgrading the villages. Some policies sought to concentrate peasant homesteads while others preferred to disperse them so that they would be closer to their parcels. The work of C. Sfințescu (1933, 1942) emphasized the need for an optimal settlement design to facilitate economic growth. Nevertheless, the policy discussions led to few concrete actions. Romania's economic resources did not permit the expense of village consolidation on any significant scale, while government instability, the world recession and Romania's subjugation to Nazi Germany all relegated planning to a low priority item on the national agenda.

After the emergence of a socialist government in Romania, major efforts were directed at restoring the war-shattered economy, building new factories, reclaiming lands along the Black Sea and in settling virgin lands on the steppes of the Baragan and Dobrogea. Several new mining towns were built up and in Bucharest giant self-contained neighborhoods of up to 200,000 persons were constructed.

It was not until 1960 that Romanian settlement planning was given its first institutional foundation, with the formation of the State Committee for Construction, Architecture and Systematization (CSCAS) and the establishment of Systematization Departments in each of the Regional and Municipal People's Councils. Plans were soon elaborated for the restructuring of twenty-five villages, and the first theoretical work began to appear on the subject of rural settlement planning (Matei 1960). This was followed by a major project around the town of Slatina and the development projects in other backward regions such as Vaslui and Călărași (Bold, Matei and Săbădeanu 1974:36-38).

The emergence of Romania's more autonomous political stance within the Warsaw Pact, the consequent need for economic self-reliance (1964-65), the drive for rural industrialization, and the completion of collectivization all contributed to upgrading the priority of village settlement planning. In November 1965, the Central Committee of the Romanian Communist Party created the Central Commission for Village Systematization. For the first time, plans were mandated not just for individual localities, but for entire networks of settlements (Bold 1965a, 1965b, Ioanid 1967). Collectivization of agriculture had brought forth new social and economic conditions of production. Successful rural development required a rural infrastructure which would (1) make optimum use of all agricultural lands, (2) provide rational placement of industries close to their sources of raw materials and labor force, and (3) assure an optimal level of services and living conditions for village populations. The final impetus for the emergence of systematization policy was the territorial administrative reorganization carried out in October 1967. Romania's sixteen macroregions (*regiune*) were reformed into 39 counties (*judeţe*) (increased to 40 in 1981), the lower-ranking district units (*raione*) were dissolved, as was the Autonomous Magyar Region. In addition, the number of rural communes was reduced from 4,259 to 2,706, with most communes containing from three to seven villages. The commune (*comună*) became the unit of rural administration, with one village in each commune (usually the largest) designated the commune center (*reşedinţa de comună*).

With Romania divided into a larger number of administrative units the economic inequalities between counties became even more noticeable. Some counties were highly urbanized and industrialized, while others had virtually no major towns within their boundaries. The 1967 reforms led to the creation by decree of 49 new towns, some little more than minor market centers (Turnock 1974:40). New enterprises were located in the more backward countries, but enormous start-up costs and lack of transport links hindered their productivity.

Policy Formation 1969-1974

The Tenth Party Congress. The Tenth Congress of the Romanian Communist Party, held in November 1969, saw the formation of a "General Program for the Organization of Regional and Locality Planning" (Cardaş 1970). The Program served as the basis of activities for the next three years. The previous State Committee was now upgraded to a State Institute for Construction, Architecture and Systematization (ISCAS). The Institute began to centralize data and issue technical guidelines for County-level planners (see their *Buletin* 1969). Based on the General Program, zonification studies were begun in which each settlement was evaluated with respect to its available raw materials, work force, population distribution, development prospects and tourist potential. "Proper" settlement hierarchies were established, and villages were placed in classifications ranging from "excellent potential for growth into a small town" to "total lack of development potential" (Cardaş 1970). Each county was asked to select from three to ten villages for transformation into towns.

In the meantime, counties were called upon to calculate optimum sizes for all towns and villages and develop plans for the most effective use of their material and human resources.

In March 1971, in a speech before the Union of Architects, Party First Secretary Ceauşescu stated that the creation of new towns was an essential condition for Romania's development (*Scînteia* March 3, 1971, p. 1, also Bold, Matei and Sābādeanu 1974:43). The ISCAS office was expanded to include a Center for Documentation which culled foreign planning literature (both East and West) and published summaries of key articles for Romania's planners and architects. (This publication was closed in 1974, ostensibly because of the "paper shortage" of that year.)

The National Party Conference. The outlines of systematization policy took shape during the Communist Party Conference of July 1972. Mr. Ceauşescu called for a sustained drive for economic development so that by 1990 Romania would be an urbanized, industrial country with per capita incomes being raised from an existing $1,100 to $2,5000-3,000 (the exact proportions used were 80-85% in nonagricultural employment and 85% urban dwelling (see Ceauşescu 1972:37-38). To accomplish this, growth rates were to be maintained at 10-12% yearly, 32% of Romania's GNP being channeled back into investment (ibid.). Along with new industries and the modernization of agriculture would come an integrated national policy for regional, town and village planning. By placing industrial plants in the countryside and supplying modern utilities and services, villages would become "true agrotowns" (ibid., p. 45).

The existing network of 236 towns would more than double by 1990, with the expansion of 300-350 villages into urban centers. Each of these new towns would become a central place for three to four surrounding communes, which could mean anywhere from five to 30 villages. Ceauşescu emphasized, however, that this policy could be accomplished only by "mass consultation and intense participation of the working people in the entire planning activity"—under the guidance of the Romanian Communist Party (Ceauşescu 1972:45).

At the Party Conference, a special Section on Regional and Locality Planning was held in which 265 were present and 39 participants actually spoke (*Editura Politică* 1972:279-91). The speeches, which constituted the first public debate over systematization, foreshadowed many of the problems which would confront planners when they tried to implement policy in rural communities. Particular importance was placed on turning low density, dispersed villages into high density, urbanized localities, creating vertical (2-4 story) construction and reclaiming village residential or waste land for agricultural use. Some speakers cited as their biggest problem the need to attract state industrial development into their communities so that they could remain viable. Other participants commented on the grossly inadequate social, cultural and retail facilities in their villages. While generally supportive of the goals of systematization, many speakers indicated skepticism about the planners' ability to actually achieve them. Speakers cited state expropriations of privately held land or houses as a particularly sensitive problem. A collective farm president feared that poor organization would mean that "some people construct, while others come afterwards with bulldozers to tear down" (ibid., p. 284). Foreshadowing some of the consequences of urban transformation in rural areas, he warned further that:

> we should not transform the peasant from a producer to a consumer; the peasant must continue to produce for himself in his garden all the vegetables he needs, while the surplus is sold on the market (ibid.).

Additional topics mentioned by the speakers included more follow-up on implementing the plans, restricting the number of demolitions and expropriations, establishing strict zone boundaries to prevent sprawl, regulating the construction of new private housing on publically owned lands, more local autonomy in determining local needs, and environmental protection. By far the key issue was rationalizing land use; "putting accent on vertical construction (ibid., p 290) was seen as a key to bridging the city/country distinction.

In addition to the speeches in the Section on Problems of Regional and Locality Planning, the National Conference also heard a short address by Natalia Stefanescu, a commune mayor from Botoșani County, one of Romania's poorest areas. The comments of Mayor Stefanescu were indicative of some of the future problems which local elites would face when planning decisions were executed at the village level.

She complained of lack of assistance from county engineers, architects and other specialists in implementing the plan for her community. "Such

people rarely come into our commune," she said (ibid., p. 405). These
people persisted in making up urban-oriented desings which she felt were
inapplicable to rural conditions. Finally, she asked that the ideas of systematization be introduced into the national educational system, so that
citizens could understand the scope and importance of planning activities,
act responsibly and work with "increased discipline" for the fulfillment
of plans (ibid., p. 406).

Emerging from the Party Conference were the "Directives of the National Conference of the Romanian Communist Party Concerning the
Planning of Regions, Cities and Villages and Their Social and Economic
Development" (ibid., pp. 476-99). The "Directives" are perhaps the most
significant and detailed official statement of rural problems and rural
planning strategies. They begin by emphasizing Romania's regional disparities, acknowledging that the goal of even distribution of the productive forces across the country has yet to be achieved. They note "serious
shortcomings" in the network of localities; they had developed "in an
anarchic way", with all too many scattered villages, urban sprawl and
consequent inefficient land use in the agricultural sector (ibid., p. 477).
Commune administrators were castigated for "lack of responsibility concerning the use of land, our national heritage, strictly tied to material
production and the welfare of the entire nation (ibid., p. 480). The dispersed small towns and villages led to exaggerated State expenses in installing telephone, heating, electricity, sewage and gas lines, as much as
fifty percent above what were considered "rational" cost. Village densities were appallingly low (8-10 persons per hectare), and the number
of villages much too high. Moreover, 40% of the 13,149 villages had populations below 500 persons. According to the Directives, "raising the level
of organization and civilization of villages [could] be obtained only by
a concentration of localities and buildings" (ibid., p. 479).

As a first step toward this goal, the Directives called for a rational distribution of resources according to a unified national plan. A country-
wide network of settlement, transport and communication links was to
be established. Strict land use was to be an absolute necessity, with fixed
perimeters around each locality, beyond which no construction would
be permitted. In this way, valuable land would be reclaimed for agricultural use. The environment was to be protected from air, water and
traffic pollution. Within each locality population density would rise by
mandating vertical construction. Three hundred to three hundred-fifty

would be selected to become "economic and social centers with urban character." In selecting these future towns, the key criteria would be "material and human resources, geographical position in the territory, relation with surrounding localities, access to means of communication and previously existing local facilities" (ibid., p. 485). Each urban center would have a population of at least 5,000 persons and serve 4-5 nearby communes within a radius of 15-20 kilometers.

As for citizen participation in the plans, the Directives state that

> citizens are to be kept permanently informed about the main problems and actions of systematization and these activities should be sustained on a permanent basis. 'Systematization Commissions' in each locality will contain citizens elected by assemblies of their factory, neighborhood and workplace (ibid., pp. 486-87).

Village planning guidelines reflect the preoccupation with high density living characteristic of urban planning. Like the cities, every village is to have a designated "civic center" (*centru civic*) where key administrative offices, services and stores would be located. The proposed new urban centers would be endowed with factories, food processing units, commercial centers, cinemas, pharmacies, schools, clinics and utilities so that they "constitute a model of organization for the surrounding communes" (ibid., p. 493). New enterprises would be located only in those localities with maximum development potential. Concurrently with the upgrading of 300 villages into towns would come

> a reduction in the number of villages within a commune, as well as regrouping of population of small and dispersed villages—lacking in the preconditions for development—into those localities which have these possibilities. This action will be long term, and, besides the economic and social advantages, will make for a better network of rural localities (ibid.).

The Directives stipulated that by the end of 1973, zonal studies were to be completed and all localities classified as to whether they would be developed into towns, maintained at current levels or phased out completely. Government planning commissions were to be formed and local People's

Councils were to be given the responsibility of seeing that plans be fulfilled. Each national ministry was to coordinate its activities with the
planning apparatus: agricultural experts were to consult with rural planning officials, road and rail networks were to be built in concert with the
future network of localities, and educational institutions were to assure
that enough specialists would be trained to carry out the tasks of systematization efficiently. The Directives also called for the elaboration by the
end of 1972 of a "National Program for Systematization" (by 1977 the
Program was still in draft form, however). Finally, and also by the end
of 1972, a "Systematization Law" was to be elaborated and enacted.

The Systematization Law. It was not until late 1974 that Romania's Grand
National Assembly passed Law Number 58, "Concerning the Territorial
Planning and Systematization of Urban and Rural Localities (see *Buletin
Oficial*, Nr. 135, November 1, 1974; reprinted in Miu 1977:31-50). Whereas the 1972 Conference "Directives" were more goal-oriented, the systematization law set out legal and administrative mechanisms for executing
the plan. To facilitate the optimization of land use and reclamation of
valuable agricultural land, the law specifies that each locality establish a
strict "building perimeter" (*perimetru construibil*) beyond which no construction is permitted. Towns and especially villages are encouraged to
make this building perimeter as small as possible, to the extent that houses
lying outside it must be torn down.

Guidelines for city planning stipulate that buildings be five stories high,
and never less than two stories. Energy-saving housing designs which make
optimum use of space and building materials will be furnished by architects attached to the local People's Councils. Roads and public transport
will be built to better link the central and peripheral zones of large cities,
and apartment neighborhoods will be placed as close as possible to the
factories so as to ease commuting time.

For rural planning the law stipulates that a "civic center (*centru civic*)
be established in each of the 2,706 villages serving as commune centers.
The civic centers will contain political, administrative, cultural, educational,
medical, retail and service establishments, as well as offices for industrial
or agricultural enterprises. Paralleling the centralization in urban areas,
these offices should be grouped into a single building or group of buildings. Industrial, manufacturing or other economic units all will be preferentially placed in the commune centers rather than in outlying villages,

with priority being given to the 300-400 commune centers which are to become towns. Similarly, all infrastructural investment—water, sewage systems, electric power, phone, gas lines and roads—will be concentrated in the commune centers and new towns. To insure optimum land use, all village housing *must* be at least two stories, with 2-5 stories in the *centru civic*. House lots may not exceed 250 square meters; any land in excess of this can be expropriated without compensation. Garden lands within the household compound are calculated in the "private plot" allotments to collective farmers. Expropriations or demolitions are permitted "in the public interest" but only after "just compensation" (Article 33). The law also requires that local enterprises (including collective farms) provide monetary and labor assistance to help implement the plans. At the local level there is to be coordination between the activities of the enterprises and the Commune Peoples' Councils.

Organizationally, the law establishes a centralized planning administration led by the "Committee for the Problems of People's Councils" which is itself supervised by a Central Commission of Party and State for Regional, Town and Village Planning. Each of the 40 County People's Councils and the Municipality of Bucharest will have their own Planning Institutes which will elaborate the plans in detail. At local levels, citizens participate through the Systematization Commission. Each community plan should include a background profile of each settlement (*Studiu de Sistematizare*) to determine its possibilities for future development, a locality plan (*Schiţe de Sistematizare*) which outlines the spatial and socioeconomic development in several alternatives and a detailed plan (*Detalile de Sistematizare, Studiu de Amplasament*)—showing the actual placement of each and every building, street, store and other facility plus detailed economic and demographic projections. As stipulated by the law, the President of the Socialist Republic of Romania must personally approve all county-level plans, those of county seats, Bucharest and other municipalities, plus any large-scale housing, commercial, cultural or tourist facilities. The plans for the 300 villages which are being converted into towns are ratified by the Council of Ministers, though the "Detail" studies and the plans for other villages are approved at the County level only. After the plans have been discussed by the local Systematization Commissions and ratified by higher authorities, responsibility for plan execution is left in the hands of the local (town or commune) People's Council.

Popularization of Systematization Policy 1974-1977. Almost coinciding with the publication of the systematization law, the Eleventh Congress of the Romanian Communist Party was held in late November 1974. As part of its drive toward "multilateral development," President Ceaușescu stated that at least 100 new towns would be declared during the forthcoming 1976-1980 Five Year Plan (Ceaușescu 1974:51). This was later revised upward to 120 (*Scînteia* February 5, 1976, p. 4). Statements on systematization were also published in the first "Program of the Romanian Communist Party for the Building of a Multilateral Society and Romania's Advance Toward Socialism" (*Editura Politică* 1974:614-789; published in English by Agerpress and Merdiane Publishing Houses, Bucharest). In a short section on territorial, urban and village planning the program emphasizes the need for the "harmonious" development of towns and villages so as to eliminate both the urban/rural distinction and regional inequalities. There would be "harmonization" of industry, agriculture, transport and communication and "optimum densities" for villages and towns. Villages would be equipped with modern utilities, health, cultural and commercial facilities.

During 1975 and 1976 other laws and decrees were enacted to support the systematization policies. These concerned agricultural land use (Law no. 59/1974), industrial location and investment (Law no. 29/1975), road construction (Law no. 37/1975, 73/1975), water resources, housebuilding, apartment ownership and migration permission.

As the systematization policy was put into practice, the creation of new towns and the efforts to redistribute productive forces throughout the entire country became common themes in the mass media (see *Scînteia* October 10, 1975; November 14, 1975; November 18, 1975; December 23, 1975; January 17, 1976; February 3, 1976; February 5, 1976; February 24, 1976; March 7, 1976; September 1, 1976). A national television program on October 23, 1975 described five of the prospective new towns and interviewed local residents about the forthcoming transformations. Similar education/publicity campaigns were carried out by County newspapers, party journals and scholarly publications (Lazarescu 1976).

In February 1976, the entire complex of commune, town and county plans was approved by the newly formed National Congress of Deputies of People's Councils and Commune and Town Mayors. In his keynote speech (*Scînteia* February 1, 1976, p. 4), President Ceaușescu again linked the judicious use of land with the development of the national economy. While holding up the plan as yet another example of the Party's concern for multilateral development, ultimate responsibility for its success rested with the local officials rather than with the national planning apparatus.

Romania's earthquake of March 4, 1977, while it may have slowed down systematization efforts in some areas, also served to re-emphasize the national importance of settlement planning. The destruction of the small Danube port town of Zimnicea immediately brough forth a national campaign to rebuild it as a conscious symbol of socialist commitment. Resources and expertise that would have been employed in villages and urban neighborhoods throughout Romania were now channeled into those areas hit hardest by the earthquake, specifically Bucharest, Craiova and Zimnicea. To recoup the losses, President Ceaușescu asked for an increase in the plan for construction of apartments—from 815,000 to one million units by 1980. As another symbol of national commitment, Romania honored the nine villages which had sparked the 1907 Great Peasant Uprising by adding them to the list of future towns. During the summer of 1977, Mr. Ceaușescu examined many of the county systematization plans and actually rejected several of them; this caused a considerable degree of consternation among county planners. Nevertheless, on October 19, 1977, all the county plans were ratified and systematization policies began in earnest (*Scînteia*, October 19, 1977).

Current Systematization in Romania

Regional and urban planning. The official policy of systematization is to raise the level of the backward regions. These priority regions include the southwest, the northwest (Bihor, Arad Counties), the Dobrogea area near the Black Sea, and Moldova in the northeast (Dragomirescu 1977). The city is still the preferred development locality in Romania, with rural policies subordinated to the needs of cities much like city plans are subordinated to economic plans. All urban localities come under the national planning apparatus rather than the County. For example, cities receive state fiscal aid for facilities which villages must furnish with indigenous or voluntary resources. While urban planning in Romania presupposes a gradual increase in the overall urban population, large cities are still restricted as to who may move in (Decree No. 68/1976 published in *Buletin*

Oficial, reviewed in *Scînteia* April 13, 1976, p. 2). Urban population levels are determined by the labor force needs of the city's factories and service establishments. If the local work force is insufficient—as it is in some older industrial towns—a limited amount of in-migration will be permitted. However, efforts will be made to seek out commuting workers from sub-urban villages. For the fourteen largest cities in Romania, urban residence permits are given only to those persons who live more than 30 kilometers from the city. Planners do not believe that such "closed" cities will be a permanent feature of Romanian life. They look forward to a time when people will want to move to other locations beside the largest cities, or when living conditions in villages improve to the extent that both the necessity and the desire to migrate disappears.

In the meantime, commuting serves the state as a more efficient and less costly form of labor recruitment than migration. The commuting worker's labor is used by the city, while food, housing needs and social services are supplied back in the village. Negoescu (1974:121) calculates that rural-based commuters save Romania more than eight billion lei ($730,000,000) yearly on food alone, since they normally obtain most of their food resources from garden or collective farm plots (this calculation is based on a theoretical immigration of 60,000 families from rural to urban locations, with each family relinquishing their food production of 20 lei ($2.20 per day). Also, the state saves an additional six billion lei ($540,000,000) per year in apartment construction costs. By comparison, the costs of subsidizing the rural-urban commuting lines are miniscule. It should be emphasized, however, that while commuting may be economically efficient for urban enterprises and inexpensive for the state, it burdens the individual worker with increased travel time (often more than two hours daily, six days a week), the cost of the monthly train ticket (1-2 days salary), and the need to work a "second shift" in agriculture (cf. Konrad and Szelenyi 1976, Cole 1981).

Within the cities, systematization seeks to maximize land use by means of vertical construction. By extending more services into residential neighborhoods, the burden on urban transport can be reduced. New apartment housing will be dispersed among existing buildings rather than placed on peripheral lands as in the past. There are no plans for one-family detached housing for the cities, but diverse types of apartments will be built to blend in with the urban landscale. Lazarescu (1976) states unequivocally that monotonous rows of 10-story blocks are not the goal of urban systematization.

Rural settlements. For the group of villages which will neither be made into towns nor phased out, systematization policies will concentrate on upgrading the 2,706 commune centers. This includes modernizing water, sewage and heating facilities, asphalting principal streets, building irrigation dikes and rationalizing land use by adhering to the building perimeters. Each county will build two or three "model villages" (*sate model*), which will have new construction and exemplary services. By the year 2000, 85% of the communes are to have piped-in drinking water and 82% modernized sewage systems; the magnitude of this endeavor is indicated by the present situation, where only 846 of Romania's 13,124 villages have piped-in drinking water and only 206 are connected into the natural gas network (*Anuarul Statistic* 1979:600, 605). Official policy also emphasizes the retention of local architectural styles and their utilization in the plans. Optimum village populations are determined to be 3,000 inhabitants; this will furnish enough children to maintain a middle school and provide efficient utilization of retail and health services which would be "unprofitable" in a smaller locality. By concentrating population and restricting settlement boundaries, rural population density would increase from the present 14 to 50-70 persons/hectare.

Dissolving of "irrational" villages. A settlement is a prime candidate to be phased out (*dezafectat*) and have its population "regrouped" if it is low in population, widely dispersed over the landscape, isolated from roads or other villages, and without prospects for economic development or demographic growth. Estimates as to the number of such settlements range from 3,000 (Lăzărescu 1976:86) to nearly 6,300 (Lăzărescu 1977: 36), or between 25% and 50% of the total number of villages now existent. (Because of the large number of tiny villages, the number of rural inhabitants affected would be between 1.0 and 1.5 million persons.) While the perspective new towns will be evenly distributed across Romania, the "nonviable" villages are concentrated in those regions with extensive highland and forest areas. The five counties of Bacau, Botoşani, Maramureş, Olt and Vrancea, for example, will see 926 (53%) of their 1,801 villages phased out by 1990 (Bold, Matei and Săbădeanu 1974:166). Ilfov, Teleorman and Ialomiţa counties will lose a total of 200 villages (Vernescu 1972:

62), while Argeș County alone will lose 107 villages (*Scînteia,* November 14, 1975, p. 2). At the lower end of the scale, Salaj County will phase out only 50 of its 281 villages and Brașov County only 10 of its 150 villages (*Scînteia,* December 23, 1975, p. 2; Institut Proiect-Brașov 1972, vol. 2:108).

The vast majority of the nonviable villages are located in the mountain zones, especially in the Western Mountains (*Munții Apuseni*) of Translyvania. Others are scattered Gypsy hamlets usually located on the edges of Romanian villages; still others are former pastoral settlements now being depopulated. Most of the villages have populations well below 500 persons. They are deemed "irrational" because they are too difficult or too expensive for the state to reach with services or transportation.

While there exist many guidelines for the planning or building of new towns, there are as yet no instructions for planners on how to dissolve a village. While there have been rumors of bulldozers coming on a few days' notice (as happened when Bucharest's Gypsy quarter was razed in 1956), planners insist that the process will be slow and completely voluntary. Families will be induced to move to those localities which can provide them with better working conditions, new housing and advanced schooling for their children, etc. One planner conceived of the regrouping process as one of "self-destruction" (*autodezfiinţare*), in that villagers would voluntarily succumb to the "pull" of other, better endowed communities.

Planners recognize, however, that older families will not want to leave their natal homes; hence, the intention is not to completely abandon these villages but to maintain a minimal level of services while prohibiting new housing. While acknowledging that the regouping process is a very delicate task with complex social ramifications (as shown in a recent study by Gheorghe and Gheorge 1978), Romania's planners emphasize that this process occurs simultaneously with the upgrading of other settlements. The creation of new towns will thus absorb the surplus rural population.

The three hundred new towns. The conversion of three hundred villages into new towns is the most dynamic, most expensive and most codified part of the systematization policy. The most likely localities to be selected for urbanization are the five percent of Romania's villages which contain over 3,000 persons or any locality which is the site of a new factory. A 1976 statement on new town development (*Scînteia*, September 1, 1976, p. 1+) indicated five general criteria guiding the selection of the future urban centers.

1) Degree of present economic development *and* possibilities for future development.
2) A healthy demographic profile and the possibility for eventual population growth.
3) Central location, or the capacity to provide adequate communination and transport links to serve 4-5 surrounding communes.
4) Preexisting social and cultural facilities, retail establishments, school, clinic, etc., so that initial state investments are reduced.
5) "Traditional and positive influences" as central places for other villages; former market centers or district administrative centers (*plase*).

These selection criteria can be applied with varying degrees of strictness. In Iaşi County each village was evaluated according to a point system: two points for a population over 3,000 inhabitants, two points for a middle school, one point for each retail establishment, five points if near a rail line, and so on. The ten villages with the most points were then designated as future towns (Miftode 1978). In certain cases, villages may be relatively equally endowed, so that choice of which village to urbanize becomes more subjective. Objective criteria may be waived entirely if urbanization assumes a more symbolic character. For example, it is hardly accidental that President Ceauşescu's home village of Scorniceşti is on the list of future towns; and the recent commemoration-through-urbanization of the nine villages which sparked the Great Peasant Revolt of 1907 is a second example. Other selections were simply anomalous (Turnock 1982).

In keeping with the ideology of regional equalization, the 300 new towns are to be evenly distributed throughout all of Romania's counties. Each county was asked to develop 2-5 new towns in the 1976-1980 Five Year Plan and 2-5 more by 1990. One hundred-twenty localities were to be declared in 1980, but due to Romania's economic retrenchment (limitations on new investment, etc.) these have now been delayed until 1985. Some composite information on these 120 localities was provided in a long article in *Scînteia* (September 1, 1976, p. 1+). The article noted that

37 of these villages already have over 5,000 inhabitants. Taken together they possess 400 industrial units, of which 170 were large enough to be classified *"republican"* level (the remainder, classified *"industrie locala"*, comprise small-scale milling and food processing operations, handicrafts, light manufacturing and service cooperatives). On the average, the 120 localities have 52% of their total work force in nonagricultural occupations; this compares with the Romanian rural average of only 30%. The villages also possess a high degree of preexisting social and cultural facilities: 80 of them have high schools and 50 have hospitals or clinics; most have an above average number of retail and service establishments because of their large size and prior central place functions (Turnock 1982).

The projected changes mandated for these new towns are as follows:

1) *productive investments*—The 120 new towns will receive 200 new industrial units over the 1976-1980 Five Year Plan, so that each locality will have at least one *republican* level enterprise. These industries will include mining, manufacturing, animal husbandry, food processing and, for women, light industry ("women's industry" is a commonly used designation which planners apply to food processing and textiles, both of which have overwhelmingly female labor forces; when men migrate to heavy industrial work in new communities, their wives constitute a newly available "reserve army"; hence, the necessity for "women's industry"). Eventually, 71 of the 120 villages will become either "industrial" or "agro-industrial" towns, each with at least 50% of their labor force in nonagricultural occupations; another 40 will become "agro-towns" with highly mechanized farming, dairying, beef or pork processing plants. The remaining nine localities will be developed as tourist centers or health spas.

2) *population growth*—all new towns will increase to at least 5,000 persons, with growth coming from both normal population increase and in-migration from surrounding settlements. An especially important social segment will be new professional cadres (doctors, teachers, engineers, technicians) who will begin to reside in the urbanizing localities as more industry and services are placed there.

3) *new services*—In 1976, the average rural commune had 10 commercial units; by 1980, this was to have risen to 15. In contrast, the new towns will have a projected 40 commercial establishments (*Scînteia,*

January 27, 1976, p. 2), and the proportion of work force in the service sector will reach 15%, more than double the present rural average. Each new town will be endowed with a bakery, shoemaker, barbershop, restaurant, post office, bank, veterinary services, public bath, pharmacy, culture house, cinema, bookstore, dispensary/ polyclinic, new schools, kindergartens, nurseries and tourist facilities. The urban centers are to attain the appearance of genuine towns, with offices and buildings concentrated in a central plaza, homes placed in a residential zone and green space on the periphery.

4) *new housing*—Of one million housing units to be built in Romania by the end of 1980, over 300,000 were to be in rural areas; most of these were to be concentrated in the new towns. State investment in housing consists exclusively of apartments, usually 4-6 stories, with central heating, kitchens, bathrooms, hot/cold running water, etc. Most of the apartments will house in-migrant industrial workers, specialists or intellectual cadres. In all villages, privately constructed housing must be of the two-story variety in order to conserve land; housing plans and technical advice are furnished free of charge by the Systematization Section of the County People's Council.

5) *utilities*—as concrete evidence of modernization, the new towns will be provided with piped-in water, sewage lines, phone lines, road resurfacing and central heating in public buildings and apartments (virtually all of Romania's villages are already electrified).

In theory, the industry, service, housing and utility investments are to be carried out concurrently. In practice the tendency has been for "productive "investments (factories) to take precedence over the building of "unproductive" housing or services. Even when housing is provided, it often remains unfinished, and the accompanying stores and services are often delayed. These priorities are determined by what planners consider to be their primary immediate objective: rapid accumulation through industrialization. Only when this objective is accomplished can the more long term goal, "raising the material and spiritual living standard of the population" (as repeated in the Party Program), be achieved.

Implementation and Administration of Systematization

FIGURE 1

ORGANIZATION OF PLANNING ADMINISTRATION IN ROMANIA
("Planning" is to be understood as "Systematization" here)

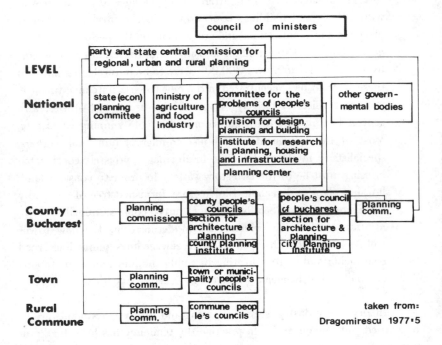

taken from:
Dragomirescu 1977:5

Figure 1 above is the official view of how systematization is executed administratively. Under the guidance of the Council of Ministers and Party/State Commission for planning, the Committee for the Problems of People's Councils (CPCP) approves and supervises the plans for each locality. Because of its relatively small staff, however, the CPCP does little more than act as a clearing house for the thousands of local planning dossiers submitted to it for approval. The CPCP offers practical help through its Institute of Planning Research. Working in conjunction with the 40 county planning institutes, it provides technical guidance, surveys, maps, building specifications and the like. For example, county planners receive standardized models for certain types of public buildings so as to make efficient use of prefabricated construction techniques. Thus, most Romanian nurseries have a standard capacity of 240 beds, kindergartens of 100 pupils, and apartments are usually four, six or ten stories. While this may appear to restrict the creativity of the plans, the planners are instructed to use the models so that they blend in with local architectural styles, and to carry out their plans as an ensemble rather than as a set of individual alterations in buildings or roads (Ioanid 1969, *Scînteia*, September 1, 1976, p. 1+, Lăzărescu, 1976, Gheorghe 1977).

Planning at the county level is managed by the Sections for Architecture and Systematization attached to each of the 40 County People's Councils and to the People's Council of Bucharest Municipality. The Section collects important baseline data of demographic, economic and geographic nature. This data is provided to the associated County Planning Institute ("Institut de Proiectare") whose staff actually makes up the planning dossier and then resubmits it to the Section for approval.

A completed dossier for a locality normally consists of several types of documents. The background study (*Studiu de Sistematizare*) gives the geographic, economic, and demographic profile of the community. Special emphasis is placed on the structure of the work force and the locality's projected labor needs. Plans for large cities have statistics on commuting; those for rural localities usually have a separate "Agricultural Profile" (*Studiu Agricole*). Common problems cited in these background studies are the lack of a local agricultural work force or its aging or feminization, lack of nonagricultural employment for surplus rural population, irriga tion problems, dispersed settlement structure, inadequate sewage, poor roads for transport facilities, poor housing quality, declining population, and lack of social services.

On the basis of the background study the actual plan (*Schiţe de Sistematizare*) is prepared. The *schiţe* will contain detailed land use maps of the locality and a written statement outlining 2-3 alternative proposals for its future development. Each alternative proposal is divided into an immediate five-year projection and a 10-15 year projection. The long-term projections are often meticulously worked out even though the actual plan may change radically over the years. Alternative proposals do not usually differ from each other very much. They may vary in their forecasts of population growth, projected speed of construction, or in the placement of new buildings. Included with the planning maps, charts, graphs and text will be cost estimates, technical specifications for large buildings and utilities, memoranda with ministerial officials over land use or industrial locations, and signed approvals by the chief planner, local officials and eventually by the President of the County People's Council.

The systematization law mandates citizen participation during all phases of the planning process. This takes place during periodic village assemblies, intermittent progress reports by planners to community leaders, and consultations with individual citizens affected by certain planning decisions, e.g. those whose houses are to be expropriated. On the basis of local inputs, the County Planning Institute formulates a plan. This is approved by the Systematization Section of the County People's Council, and then sent down to the locality to be approved by its own People's Council. At this stage it is still possible to suggest revisions. These may come from either the locals or from county officials. When approved, the County submits the plans to the Committee for the Problems of Peoples' Councils in Bucharest, which forwards them to the proper authorities for final approval.

The Role of the Citizen

While villagers may not have final say in their plan's formulation, they are expected to aid in its implementation. This can be done by participating in meetings, by contributing money or labor time equal to 4-6 days per year (*"contribuție în bani și în muncă din partea populației"*) through additional village taxes and extraordinary voluntary work campaigns (*"muncă voluntară"*). These obligations, required for all adult villagers up to age 55, may also be carried out through one's enterprise. In addition, children can stand-in for their parents in certain cases. Typical village contributions to the plan would be the following: constructing a nursery school, kindergarten, or village "culture house" (for weddings and assemblies), road resurfacing, irrigation construction, beautifying parks, planting trees and helping to improve the local agricultural output by contracting to deliver pigs, calves, or milk or eggs to the consumers' cooperative. Voluntary contributions by community members form a crucial part of all rural planning activities, such that planning dossiers normally specify exactly which new endowments in the villages will come out of state resources and which will come from local contributions of labor or cash.

National planners accept the importance of their tasks in the rural planning sector but they have mixed feelings about their ability to fulfill these duties. Many planners viewed village planning as a deadly chore, ill-suited to their grand architectural training and uninteresting when compared to building magnificent hotels, plazas or tourist complexes. An architect planning a new town complained that local interest in the plan ceased as soon as villagers found out that *their* houses would not be expropriated. Many plans need continuous restructuring so that meetings with local officials often prove impractical and time-consuming. Planners visit the village by train or bus, tramp through the mud, and wait around for a mayor or local official, all with a resulting loss of time and energy on the planners' part. This is not to say that the plan does not receive some citizen input. Ioanovici and Popescu (1977:19) tell of the exhibition in Bucharest where dozens of local plans were shown to the public; these exhibitions attracted 120,000 visitors, with 20,000 "cards of appreciation and suggestions" on topics such as environmental protection, buildings and transport, social and cultural facilities and use of green space.

Citizen participation is continually requested in mass media campaigns. Newspaper articles, usually written by either the County planners or the local mayors, detail the components of a community's plan, describe meetings which took place to criticize and approve it, and give examples of conscientious citizen activity. One commune mayor described measures taken to assure that local youth will want to remain in the village; by upgrading the "cultural level" of the community, he hopes to attract more intelligentsia to live there (*Scînteia*, October 10, 1975, p. 3). Another mayor lauded citizen suggestions for improving the plan and detailed his efforts to assume that the revisions are carried out "with firm discipline" (*Scînteia*, November 18, 1975, p. 1). Local People's Councils are frequently reminded to respect the provisions of the systematization law and to sanction those who build their houses outside the designated building perimeters (*Scînteia*, February 3, 1976, p. 1; August 2, 1976, p. 2; August 6, 1976, p. 4). Numerous articles attempt to explain to rural citizens the advantages of building modern two-story houses, despite the cost (*Scînteia*, March 27, 1976, p. 1). Through frequent restatements of systemization policy in press reports, high-level speeches and Party journals, Romania's citizens are encouraged to take an active part in building up their communities to help the country achieve its objective of "multi-

lateral development." National campaigns are replicated in county newspapers, with citizens being instructed to attend meetings, make proposals
and engage in voluntary labor contributions. Citizen participation in the
execution of systematization is more than an economic necessity for the
state: it is the civic duty of each and every citizen,

Some Contradictions of Systematization

Romania's rural settlement planning policy exemplifies many of the
characteristics of socialist planning depicted in the previous chapter. The
plan is clearly an *active* policy which seeks to restructure the urban/rural
hierarchy, achieve economic development, prevent hyperurbanization in
a few large cities, and spread urban amenities into the rural areas. The
plans to double the number of towns, remove or regroup thousands of
tiny hamlets, and rectify the serious regional inequalities are indicative
of systematization's *national scale, wide scope, long range* and desire for
regional balance. The policy is grounded in Marxist ideological precepts
about reducing town/country distinctions and regional inequities, and
by specifically Romanian demands for rapid economic growth in all sectors
of the economy. To this end, the existence of individual localities is predicated not on their ability to adapt to local ecological or sociopolitial
conditions, but on their usefulness to the *national interest*. Systematization is both highly *centralized* and high bureaucratized, with national
directives filtering down to the local level and local intermediaries feed-
ing information back up the chain of administrative command. Finally,
to achieve these ends, citizen *participation* in planning execution is not
only encouraged but required. Without doubt, Romanian systematization
is a synthesis of general planning strategies, socialist planning, and national specificities.

At the national level, we find four major contradictions permeating
Romania's systematization policy. These are: 1) economic efficiency
versus regional equity, 2) rational versus irrational settlements, 3) the
individual versus the general interest, and 4) the problem of popular participation in a highly structured planning bureaucracy. These will be dis-
cused in turn.

Regional equality versus economic efficiency. The "socialist" aspect of
systematization consistently highlights the objective of achieving social

and economic equality between rich and poor regions. However, national priorities for rapid accumulation take precedence over alleviating inequalities. Spokesmen for systematization (e.g. Ion Blaga 1974), are explicit in stating that the "harmonious and judicious" development of the productive forces will not necessarily lead to full regional equality. This is because "different possibilities determine not only different solutions, but in the last analysis different levels of industrialization in different zones and localities" (Blaga 1974:162). The emphasis on economic development over regional equity manifests itself in Romania's systematization practice: "the county or locality offering the highest efficiency will be preferred even if it is already developed" (Blaga 1974:192). New industries will be placed in underdeveloped areas "only if the efficiency they offer is greater or at least equal to the more developed zones" (ibid.). The "inevitable outcome" (ibid.) of this policy, says Blaga, is the development of extractive industry, forestry and tourism in the underdeveloped zones/localities, and their use as labor reserves for the advanced zones/localities. Thus, to the extent that state investments go only to zones with immediate economic returns, systematization may not only perpetuate regional inequalities but actually aggravate them.

Even more troublesome is that systematization policy denies any recognition of genuine regional interest. Regional development problems are subsumed under national priorities. The pursuit of regional equality can never be permitted to cause a slow-down in the rate of national growth. There is "a priority of the interest of all members of society rather than the interest of certain groups—counties, geographic zones" (Blaga 1974:39). Any manifestation of regional dissatisfaction with a plan can be considered to be an attack on the "interest of all members of society" and therefore a political threat. A region or locality which expresses open discontent with its place in the planning hierarchy can be vulnerable to accusations of "chauvinism." Even more volatile is the fact that some industrialized zones (e.g. Transylvania) are populated by non-Romanian ethnic groups (e.g. Magyars). Were these zones to be downgraded for purely economic motives, this could be interpreted by them as ethnic discrimination as well. Since the plan does not recognize the existence of regional (or ethnic) competition, these interests lie just below the surface. They can emerge during the implementation of the plan, and cause it to be transformed, distorted or otherwise "corrupted."

Rationality and irrationality. Planners quote several "objective criteria" which determine whether individual localities will be maintained, expanded or abolished. Behind these ostensibly technical calculations, however, lie typical "planners' ideologies": explicit or implicit assumptions about the value of centralization, concentration, urban orientation, "optimum size," anti-rural bias, etc. At the core of systematization lies the assumption that humans are capable of arranging themselves in irrational forms of settlement, which the planner is obligated to make rational again. The rationality of spatial centralization leads the planner to replicate the political centralization of the State, the leading role of the Party, and the administrative dominance of Bucharest. Each locality must fit into the spatial and social hierarchy of Romanian society. The emphasis is on separating and demarcating each locality. Villages sprawled along hillsides—an adaptive pattern which allows households to be close to key resources—are now deemed irrational according to the Romanian planning ideology.

Planners' rationality criteria are dominated by a pronounced *urban orientation.* With their civic centers, residential zoning, mini-office buildings and four-story apartment houses, villages are to become miniature versions of large cities. At the same time, rural localities are subsidiary to the towns. Villages not fortunate enough to be "rewarded" by urbanization are maintained at a reduced level of services or are abolished altogether. State investment plans are executed to meet the needs of urban areas. Suburban villages are turned into urban dormitories in order to supply the cities with cheap labor.

This *anti-rural bias* is in striking contrast to the anti-metropolitan bias of many Western planning schemes. Where Western planners seek to recreate village communities in giant urban agglomerations, Romanian planners are trying to insert the city into the village. The contrast is partly a reflection of Romania's historical conditions, where "urbanism" has been synonymous with "civilization" and "modernization." As in the Mediterranean, an urbanized village (*un sat urbanizat*) is also *un sat civilizat.*

The underlying tendency toward centralization, concentration and urbanization has direct implications for planning actions in rural communities. The typical peasant dwelling in rural Romania is a multifunctional one: it is a residence for a large (often three-generation) family;

it houses cattle in barns and lets fowl and other animals thrive by letting them browse in courtyards and "waste areas"; and it is a workplace for peasants to carry out productive tasks, repairs, gardening, etc. With their urban oreintation, planners tend to view the village house solely in terms of its residence function. Large courtyards and seemingly unproductive waste areas are seen as incompatible with the urbanization of the countryside, an irrational use of space. Instead, planners give preference to vertical construction, especially apartment housing. They resolutely supply the apartments—*only* apartments—with the amenities of "civilization" while denying these to rural homes because of their irrationally large physical layout. When installed with hot running water, central heating, baths, sewage and asphalted areas, the apartment indeed *becomes* the ideal residential unit for the simple reason that this is where the State chooses to concentrate its investments. As symbols of *un viaţa civilizat* ("a civilized life"), the rows of blocks so proudly displayed in Romanian newspaper and television are indeed "beautiful"; but their aesthetic is as much social as it is physical. The apartments are where the State chooses to place the physical symbols of modernization, symbols which have been accepted by the villager and planner alike.

In view of the limitations on State investment and the competition for scarce resources, the imposition of planners' "rationality" almost guarantees the existence of conflict between "viable" and "nonviable" localities, between those living in preferred and those living in "irrational" residential units, between the home-owning peasant and the apartment dwelling worker or specialist, and between villagers' ideas of rational land use and those of the planners. The competition between localities or between rational and irrational households is neither a retrograde "survival" from the past nor an example of local traditionalism. Rather, it is a logical outcome of the Romanian planners' assumptions about efficient planning. These assumptions are grounded in ideological premises which are not wholly accepted by those localities the planners are attempting to "civilize."

General versus individual interest. The prevailing assumption behind all Romanian planning is that the needs of communities and individual peasant and worker households will inevitably "harmonize" with the needs of Romanian society as defined by the planners, Party or President Ceauşescu.

Sometimes this indeed happens, as when the state encourages peasants to produce more agricultural goods by offering them higher prices, and the households increase their production accordingly. However, should the *interes particular* (alternately translated "individual", "narrow" or "particular" interest) come into conflict with the *interes general*, the latter must predominate. As in the West, the *interes general* (or what we know as "the public interest") can be manipulated by planners to achieve their own ends. This can be more critical in a country like Romania, where the plan is centralized at the national level and where planners possess a monopoly on most key information. Thus, planners can invoke the "general interest" to condemn as "chauvinistic" the protests of villages who see themselves judged "nonviable." They can dismiss objections to expropriation or to the State's preferential treatment of apartment dwellers by citing the dissenting individuals' "retrograde mentality" or by inferring that they do not (and cannot) understand "the big picture."

The "general interest" is, in fact, an all-embracing rationale for the *planners'* interest. Insofar as planners' allegiances lie with the State bureaucracy and the villagers' allegiances to their kin and community, conflicts between planners' and local interests are unavoidable. These structurally based conflicts are concealed by the rhetoric of "general interest" versus local "chauvinism." Neither can they be resolved by the planners' arrogant protection of their information on the basis of technical expertise or "working secrets." In both cases, these are devices by which the planners preserve their authority to define the general interest and by which they bolster their legitimacy and authority.

The "general interest" is, in fact, an all-embracing rationale for the is a rhetorical device and not a scientific concept. It is politically and not rationally defined.

Especially problematic is that some planners see the conflicts as mere dysfunctions of planning rather than as being intrinsic to the systematization process itself. From this perspective, manifestations of local or individual interests will always be considered unacceptable. A few planners deny the possibility of conflict altogether. One emphatically told me that the very notion of regional competition for state resources is "impossible, period."

The "general interest" meets "individual interests" most sharply in situations where a locality is to be phased out. Regrouping small localities may result in economies of scale for the State, but this is hardly consoling for those citizens unlucky enough to be dwelling in a locality classified as "irrational." The problem with "general interest" is that it is always used for particular ends. When this occurs, contradictions will arise: these can take the form of conflicts among individuals, competition between localities, or conflicts between localities and the planners, Party and State. Refusing to recognize these contradictions only makes them more intractable.

Power and participation. Citizen participation—either as suggestions for formulating the plan or as labor contributions in executing it—is both encouraged as a civic duty and required as a supplement to State inputs. Citizens are to be "consulted" by the planners and "informed" of ongoing developments. Yet there are problems with the *form* of participation. Recalling Arnstein's (1969) "ladder of citizen participation" discussed in Chapter II, it is clear that informing, consultation and citizen suggestions still leave decision-making in the hands of the planners. Behind the debate over participation lies the problem of *power*. Planners can "consult" with the citizens or hear their suggestions, but there is not a single guarantee that the planners will be obliged to accept them. While citizens may be called upon to actively participate in the *execution* of the plan, the fundamental decisions about goals are made by higher organs to which citizens have little formal or informal access.

What makes the exercise of local power particularly volatile is that Romania really has no such thing as a "local" plan. Rather, there is a single national plan executed in different localities. Some localities (e.g. the new towns) will benefit disproportionately, while others (the "irrational" highland villages) will suffer.

Just as there are no local plans, neither are there autonomous local planners who could be employed by the community apart from the State apparatus. For a locality to contest (or reject) its plan is not just a matter for local debate, but a threat to the national plan itself. The national aspect of every local plan provides the basis for county planners to have the last word in village decisions; it enables national planners to intervene in any county decision. If there are no local plans—or local planners—there is no legitimate basis for (institutionalized) local power. As long as the planners envision local participation to be *only* "informing" or "consulting", as long as citizen participation consists of helping to execute the *planners'* objectives rather than formulating their own, as long as this local power is not institutionalized, then the danger of alienation between local residents and state policymakers is very real indeed. This does not mean that local power will not be exercised at all. It means only that this power will be exercized informally, in ways which the planners may be unable to comprehend. It is this informal community power which enables villagers to ignore, transform or corrupt the original plan to suit their particular interests.

Summary: Romania's Planning Ideology

The Romanian systematization of rural settlements is an ambitious endeavor to combine spatial change with economic development. Systematization determines the location of future settlements, what they will look like, how investments will be made, whether populations will be required to move, and the speed at which changes take place. Behind the ostensibly technical, rational judgements of planners are the historical preconditions of Romania's settlement structure, the national requirements for political independence and economic self-reliance via rapid industrialization, and underlying planning ideologies which generate major contradictions. Some of these contradictions may be seemingly resolved, but the structural features of Romanian planning will cause them to reappear in other forms. It is in this sense that the analytical separation between the four contradictions is truly an artificial one. Debates about regional inequality inevitably touch on the idea of rational and irrational settlements, which testifies to the lack of citizen control over key planning decisions, all of which is articulated in terms of subordinating the "particular interest" to the "general interest."

What is important here is the realization that these contradictions, though unanticipated or dismissed by the planners, are quite predictable when seen as part of a larger planning process. At the national level of the "vertical slice," this process has been shown to include aspects of planning-in-general, socialist ideology and practice and the unique characteristics of Romania's own systematization policy and planning ideology.

The exact form these contradictions take, however, will depend on factors below the national level. The next chapter examines how systematization is applied to the problems of a specific region: Brașov County.

This examination will then set the stage for a more detailed analysis of how one village in this county—Feldioara—undergoes conversion into a new town.

CHAPTER V

REGIONAL FACTORS IN THE PLANNING PROCESS:
THE CASE OF BRAȘOV COUNTY

Introduction: Brașov County as a Region

This chapter focuses on the planning process within Brașov County (pronounced "bra-SHUV"). This process is affected by (1) the county's specific characteristics as a region and (2) the county planners' relations with both the national administration above them and the local communities below. The chapter begins with a brief regional profile of the county highlighting the problems confronting the planners. It then discusses the evolution of systematization policy in the county and the organization of planning practice. The final section describes the relations between county planners and local communities, focusing particularly on the factors affecting local participation.

Brașov County's complex political history, developed economic structure and unique ethnic make-up all serve to lend it an unequivocal regional identity. While the county is an administrative unit within Romania, this unit is not arbitrary in the case of Brașov County. The county seat of Brașov City (*Orașul Brașov*), has dominated the region economically, politically and culturally for centuries (Dunare 1972, 1974). The integrative role of Brașov City has been maintained despite fluctuations in county borders over the last century (Helin 1967). The present borders of Brașov

County date from 1968, when Romania's sixteen Soviet-style *regiune* were reconstituted into thirty-nine *judeţe* (counties) (increased to 40 in 1981).

Braşov County is located in the geographic center of Romania, between the bend of the Carpathian Mountains and the winding Olt River (see Map 1, next page). The county's area of 5,351 km² and its population of 600,000 inhabitants are about average for Romania's 40 counties. Aside from the county seat of Braşov City (population 300,000), there are eight smaller towns all with populations below 50,000.

The county contains 150 villages, grouped administratively into 43 communes (*comune*). Like all regions, Braşov County has its atypical features, the most important of which are its high degree of economic development, large proportion of urban-dwellers, and its diversity of ethnic groups and ecological zones.

Economic Development and Ethnic Diversity

With the exception of the mountain zones to the south, most of Braşov County's settlements lie on the Transylvanian plateau, at altitudes of 300-600 meters. More than 65% of the land is covered by mountains or forests; only 25% is cultivated at all. Capricious weather conditions and highly variable soils give fluctuating yields of grain. Potatoes and root crops generally give average or above-average yields (compared to the national average), but these vary with soil composition, rainfall and fertilizer inputs.

Braşov County's importance derives not from its agricultural productivity, however, but from its industrial development. It is Romania's leading industrial county, producing three times its proportion of industrial output per capita (compared with the other 40 counties, Bucharest excepted, *Anuarul Statistic* 1979:94). It is also Romania's second most urbanized county, with 71% of its population living in towns (ibid.:48). Braşov's urban and industrial level is roughly ten years ahead of what Romania's planners have forecasted for the entire country. The national plan for 1990 projects 10-15% of the population in agricultural occupations and 70% living in towns and cities. This level has already been attained in Braşov County.

The county's industrial preeminence is not solely the result of socialist development. Until 1919, Braşov City and its immediate hinterland functioned as a prosperous border zone for the Austro-Hungarian empire. Since

MAP 1

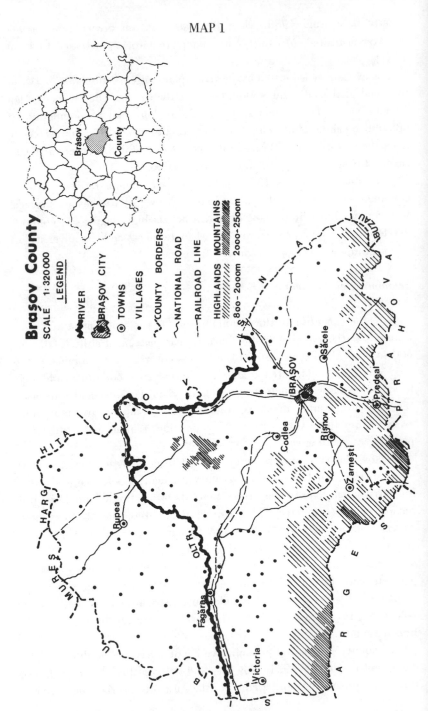

the Middle Ages, the area had been the intersection of trade routes connecting Central Europe with the Ottoman Empire and the Near East. Romanian historians depict the Braşov zone as a social and economic arena which integrated Romania's three historic provinces of Transylvania, Wallachia and Moldova (Dunare 1972:85-106).

Braşov County is the home of four major ethnic groups: Romanians (75% in 1966), Hungarian-speaking Magyars (15%), German speakers known as Saxons (9%) and an unknown proportion of Gypsies. Since 1966, the proportion of ethnic Romanians has risen due to proportionally lower birth rates among Magyars, emigration of Saxons to West Germany, and in-migration of Romanians from other regions. Within the city of Braşov, for instance, the absolute number of ethnic Germans has shrunk from 30,000 in 1930 to 9,000 in 1977, from 35% to 3.6% of the city's population.

The ethnic diversity of the county is well attested in the historical record and in the structure of rural settlements. The Magyars first entered the Braşov zone in the tenth century A.D. They occupied the area around Săcele and three villages north of Braşov City (Apaţa, Satu Nou, Crisbav). In the 13th century, the Hungarian King Andres II invited German-speakers from the Rhineland to settle his southeastern frontier and establish trade and agricultural settlements. These German speakers came to be called (and call themselves) "Saxons." While urban life and trade were dominated by Saxons and Magyars, the indigenous Romanian population was confined to transporting goods across the Carpathians or carrying out pastoral activities in the mountains. Romanians also settled less fertile lands in the northwest, and many worked as agricultural laborers for the Saxons.

Up until the socialist period, there was a general ethnic stratification between better off Saxons and the poorer Romanians. The Magyars existed at all levels, from serfs to nobles. Gypsies occupied the lowest ranks of the social ladder (for further details on ethnicity in Transylvania see Beck 1979, Romanian Research Group 1979, Beck and McArthur 1981, McArthur 1981, Cole 1981a and Verdery 1983). The ethnic stratification was mirrored in the structure of settlements. Saxons occupied the towns and established large, nucleated, multifunctional villages in the fertile plains around Braşov. Magyars lived in Braşov City and in the nearby forest and pastoral areas to the east. The Romanians were left those zones unwanted by the Saxons, mostly in the west or in the highlands. Finally, the Gypsies, true to their pariah status, occupied the margins of villages or had outlying hamlets of their own.

After the emergence of a socialist Romania, there were preferential investment policies aimed at the developed counties like Braşov (Turnock 1974:131). As a result, the county is today a major industrial producer of trucks, chemicals, metals, electrical instruments, textiles and paper/pulp. More than 70% of industrial production is concentrated within Braşov City itself and in the nearby towns of Săcele, Zărneşti and Rîşnov. The western part of the county contains important chemical works at Făgăraş and Victoria. Textiles are produced in Braşov and in some suburban villages.

Ninety-five percent of the arable land in Braşov County is owned by State or collective farms. The first State farm was formed in 1948 in the village of Prejmer, and the first collective farm in nearby Hărman in 1949 both of which had been Saxon villages. Because Saxon farmers had had their lands expropriated on grounds of being kulaks or Nazi collaborators, collectivization proceeded more rapidly in the Saxon settlements. By contrast, the ethnically Romanian Făgăraş zone, which was home to various fascist groups and even an armed resistance, was collectivized only in 1963-1965.

Braşov County today contains several types of agricultural units: there are mechanized State agricultural enterprises which specialize in dairying or beef/pork/fowl production; three State farms (with 50 sections scattered in various communes), specializing in livestock or fodder crops; 72 multi-village collective farms which raise grain, potatoes, sugar beets, industrial crops and livestock; individual holdings of collective farm members (roughly 0.15 hectares/member), which are used for members' own needs or for growing fodder; finally, in the uncollectivized highland areas, there are "individual" agricultural households producing fodder, potatoes and livestock under State contracts. Despite the relatively poor production of some agricultural units (particularly the collective farms in the western part of the county), the agricultural sector is extremely important because it must supply the 426,000 persons living in urban areas. Braşov County remains a net food importer, however.

By any index, Braşov County's economic level is superior to the other 40 counties in Romania (Bucharest excluded). It has the highest total industrial production, the largest proportion of its population in the industrial work force, and contributes the biggest share of total industrial output of any county (*Anuarul Statistic* 1979). The 12.9% of its work force is agriculture is the lowest in Romania. County industrial output in 1978 was 54.2 billion lei, 16 billion more than its nearest competitor (Galați County). Brașov's industrial output can also be contrasted with that of the 16 least developed counties in Romania, all of which had less than 10 billion lei annual industrial production in 1978 (*Anuarul Statistic* 1979:145).

Brașov County's high level of development is also reflected in indices of living standards. Compared to other counties, it has the third lowest rate of infant mortality, highest number of specialized high schools, most professional schools, complete electrification of its 150 villages, second highest number of settlements supplied with drinking water and the greatest number of telephones, radios, televisions and autombiles per capita (*Anuarul Statistic* 1979).

While Romania's national economy is relatively underdeveloped, Brașov County is highly industrialized and a pacesetter (if not a predictor) for the rest of the nation as a whole. Although considerably developed in the pre-socialist period, it has clearly benefitted from thirty years of socialist industrialization. Of the 40 counties, Brașov ranked 4th in amount of investment funds received from the state during the 1971-1975 period (*Anuarul Statistic* 1977:339). The industrial development of Brașov is also reflected in the structure of its urban and rural localities.

Brașov County's Settlement Structure

Urban settlements. Nearly three-fourths of the county's urban population (300,000 out of 426,000) live in Brașov City, whose population has nearly doubled since 1966. Of the county's eight other towns, five are located within 15 kilometers of Brașov City. These smaller towns house industrial workers unable to find housing in Brașov City itself. The Brașov urban agglomeration has increased its population largely due to in-migration: the proportion of in-migrants to natives within Brașov City was 71% in 1966. In the suburban towns the in-migrant percentage ranged from 44% in Rîșnov to 79% in Predeal (*Anuarul Demographic* 9174:470, 480).

Rural settlements. Brașov County stands out as having a very low density of settlements (2.8/100 km^2 *vs.* a national average of 5.5/100 km^2). While distances between villages may be great, average populations per village are high (over 1,200 persons *vs.* an average 980 for rural Romania as a whole). Brașov County's central geographic position has given it a dense network of road and rail lines. The county ranks sixth in density of rails ber 1000 km² and seventh in length of roads modernized (*Anuarul Statistic* 1979:441, 443). These arteries help deliver goods and services to the most peripheral villages and bring rural commuters to the cities for industrial jobs.

The structure of rural settlements in Brașov County is less problematic than Romania's rural settlement structure generally. Table 4 indicates that the number of inhabitants in villages with under 500 persons is negligible, while a significant proportion (12.7% in 1970) resided in villages containing more than 4,000 inhabitants. This is very much higher than the Romanian average of 4.7% as shown below.

TABLE 4

RURAL SETTLEMENT STRUCTURE IN BRAŞOV COUNTY (1970)

Village Size	No.	Percent of all Villages	Total Population	Percent of Total Population	Romania Average (1966)
Under 500 inhabitants	30	20.0%	9,351	5.2%	13.6%
501-1,000 inhabitants	58	38.6	43,087	23.8	25.2
1,001-2,000 inhabitants	41	27.3	57,173	32.0	31.4
2,001-3,000 inhabitants	9	6.0	22,063	12.3	25.0
3,001-4,000 inhabitants	7	4.7	25,149	14.0	25.0
4,001 + inhabitants	5	3.4	23,200	12.7	4.7
TOTALS	150	100.0%	200,023	100.0%	100.0%

Sources: Institut Proiect-Brasov, 1972, vol. I, p. 5 (for Brasov); Ioanid 1968:18 (for Romania 1966).

Subregional variation. Based on ecology, economy and ethnicity, Brașov County can be divided into four major subregions. These are the Bîrsei plain around Brașov, the Fagaraș zone in the west, the Rupea zone in the northwest, and the mountain zones around Bran in the south and Vama in the southeast (see Map 2, next page).

The Birsei plain (*Țara Bîrsei* or *das Burzenland*) is the most populous and most developed of the four regions. It contains virtually all the original Saxon frontier villages and five of the county's towns (plus Brașov City). Villages are large (many with over 3,000 inhabitants), and highly nucleated. They are also multifunctional, possessing both viable collective farms and numerous industries, e.g. brick factory, sugar beet refinery, food processing, minerals extraction, forestry and textiles. The proximity of these villages to Brașov City and their location along rail lines enables them to function as dormitory communities for urban workers. Two villages in this region (Feldioara and Prejmer) are scheduled to be upgraded into towns by the end of 1985.

The Făgăraș zone (*Țara Făgărașului* or *Țara Oltului*) centers around the city of Făgăraș (population 50,000 in 1980). Făgăraș and Victoria (population 8000) are the only towns. Village sizes in this zone range from 800 to 1,200, and the populations are almost exclusively Romanian, with some Gypsies. Agriculture is collectivized, but low fertility of the land gives relatively mediocre returns. Many of the villages lie along the Brașov-Făgăraș-Sibiu rail line, so commuting to these cities is common for the villagers.

The Rupea zone is the most underdeveloped area of Brașov County. The only urban center is the small town of Rupea (population 7,000); the area lacks rural employment with which to retain its population. The Rupea zone is actually a hinterland between Brașov to the south and Sighișoara to the north. It lies too far from either to take full advantage of these cities. The villages are small, dispersed, and the land is not productive. The road network and services are poor to inadequate. Except for Rupea and a few Saxon villages, the population is almost all ethnically Romanian. Outmigrants from Rupea migrate to Brașov (or villages near Brașov if unable to obtain permission to live within the city), to Sighișoara in the north or to Baraolt in the east. County planners acknowledge serious problems in providing services to the Rupea zone; they are trying to establish central places to strengthen the settlement network. The only major investment project at the moment, however, is the recently completed cement factory in the village of Hoghiz, located just to the south of Rupea.

MAP 2

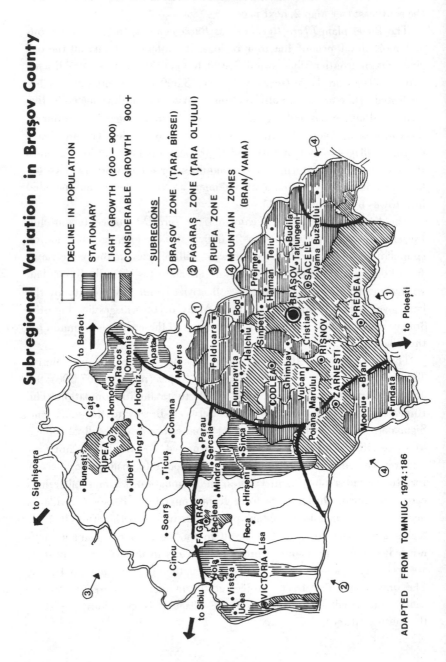

Subregional Variation in Braşov County

DECLINE IN POPULATION

STATIONARY

LIGHT GROWTH (200 – 900)

CONSIDERABLE GROWTH 900 +

SUBREGIONS

① BRAŞOV ZONE (ŢARA BÎRSEI)

② FAGARAŞ ZONE (ŢARA OLTULUI)

③ RUPEA ZONE

④ MOUNTAIN ZONES
   (BRAN/VAMA)

ADAPTED FROM TOMNIUC 1974:186

The fourth subregion consists of the thirteen villages in the area of Bran-Zărneşti, and five villages in the eastern border of the county, near Vama. These are scattered hamlets, often far from main roads. Populations are totally Romanian. The land is uncollectivized, and the individual farmers raise sheep, cattle, fodder, and potatoes for household consumption, contract to the State, or for sale on the private market. Household production is supplemented by wage labor in nearby mills, mines or quarries. Some residents have shifted completely to industrial employment, moving their houses into the village center, but transportation to work and the seasonal demands of the pastoral economy are still problematic (Beck 1979). Braşov's mountain villages also derive income as weekend recreation and tourist centers for urban populations. One tourist village, Bran, is scheduled to be upgraded into a town by 1985.

Summarizing the regional profile of Braşov County, two points remain to be brought out. First, the four subregions have had symbiotic relationships with each other for several centuries. The Făgăraş and Rupea zones once supplied labor to the Saxon farms near Braşov; today these workers are employed in the State farms and factories. Lowland peasants used the mountains as a refuge from feudal obligations and political upheavals, while mountain peasants came down into the lowlands as traders, village shepherds, seasonal laborers, and, after 1945, as colonists taking over expropriated Saxon farms. The open markets in the towns have served as an arena of interaction for Saxons from the Braşov area, peasants from the Fagaraş or Rupea zones and the mountain folk from Bran or Vama.

The second point worth noting is that the advantages of one subregion over another tend to be cumulative rather than complementary. The Braşov zone, for instance, not only has several towns and considerable opportunities for factory employment, but the best agricultural land and the most developed villages. A the other end of the scale, the Rupea zone lacks fertile agricultural land, has very little industry and is without adequate transport or commercial infrastructure. Consequently, as Map 2 indicates, outmigration has been particularly heavy from the Rupea zone; the Fagaraş and mountain zones are relatively stable, and the Braşov zone is a net importer of population.

Planning Conditions in Braşov County

Braşov County's ecological variability, high level of economic and urban development, and subregional inequalities have generated specific regional-level problems for county planners. The problems center around (1) urban-rural relations, (2) the special interests of mountain populations, (3) the ethnic factor, (4) investment efficiency versus spatial equity, (5) the social heterogenity of the county's population and (6) the status of Braşov County in the national planning scheme.

Romania's effort to control large urban populations has meant that thousands of urban workers live in surrounding villages. Communities as far as 45 kilometers from Braşov City send over half their populations to Braşov as commuting workers. Migrants unable to find housing in the city itself reside in these commuter villages or in the small towns lying along the railroad lines. Because of the large amount of in-migration, housing and services in these villages are often overcrowded or inadequate. The planners responsible for these suburban communities must recognize that their importance derives almost exclusively from their linkage to Braşov. If Braşov "opened up" so that all who work there could also live there, many of these villages would be rapidly depopulated.

Over the 1966-1967 period, the population of Braşov County increased by 32% (vs. 12% for Romania as a whole; *Scînteia*, June 1, 1977). This increase, due largely to in-migration from underdeveloped regions, has led to a hetereogenous population and consequent social frictions between inborn residents, migrants and commuters (Sampson 1979). Residents of cities or suburban villages around Braşov City recite numerous anecdotes about the countrymen recently arrived from far-away Moldova. Commuter villages are heavily populated by in-migrants who, as transients, have no long-term interest in remaining in these communities. This makes citizen participation especially problematic.

Regional inequality presents another serious problem for the planners. How much investment should be made in the desolate Rupea zones or the marginal mountain areas? One strategy would be to emphasize economic efficiency and develop the Braşov zone even further; another would be to build up the regional economy/infrastructure around Rupea or Bran, but years would pass before concrete benefits could be seen. By investing in backward zones, further outmigration might be prevented.

This would help relieve overcrowding in suburban villages and large cities, bit it would also force urban industries to become more efficient or to seek out labor from other areas.

Planning for the mountain zones presents special problems because of the presence of relatively more autonomous land-owning households, the ostensible irrationality of mountain settlement patterns, and the historically tense relationship between mountain peoples and the State. Despite good intentions, the planners' actions could be construed by mountain groups as an attack on their household economy; this occurs with the periodic rumors that the state is going to collectivize mountain village "X" or when planners discuss the amalgamation of scattered settlements. In cases like this, suspicions about the State bureaucracy can produce apathy or resistance to the planners.

The role of ethnicity in the development process is especially sensitive. Since the large, nucleated Saxon villages have the greatest potential for development. Saxons as an ethnic group will benefit more from urbanization than the majority Romanians. Folk stereotypes do not go unnoticed in this process: on more than one occasion I have heard it explained that the preference for modernizing Saxon villages is based partly on the Saxons' traditional propensity for hard work, sobriety, thrift and community effort, all of which are necessary if Romania's development goals are to be achieved.

To take a contrasting example, the county's Gypsy population is adversely affected by plans to amalgamate settlements. Gypsies have often located themselves in (or been relegated to) undesirable locations on the peripheries of villages or towns. In 1976, Braşov County planners recognized the particular hardships of Gypsies. Planners proposed that the Gypsies rebuild their houses using inexpensive one-story designs euphemistically called *"casa simplu"* (simple house). Even though the one-story *casa simplu* violated the systematization law, it represented a clear improvement over the current decrepit condition of Gypsy dwellings in some settlements. By 1977, however, it appeared that the Gypsies had ignored the planners' help; they preferred to invest their time and energy in other endeavors than home improvement. Moreover, the revised regulations to upgrade the plans stipulated that Gypsy zones would be moved back inside the central "building perimeters" of their respective villages. Hence, the *casa simplu* plans, despite their good intentions, went unused.

These two examples indicate how the ostensibly objective criteria for evaluating a given locality may also involve subjective ethnic criteria as well. Any plan which makes it *appear* that a given ethnic group is being differentially affected—positively in the case of Saxons, negatively in the case of the Gypsies—can generate tensions among affected segments of the population. The tendency to interpret judgements about settlements in ethnic terms lies latent in the planning process. In the same fashion, the competition between settlements engendered by Romanian systematization may also generate competition between ethnic groups.

The final condition affecting planning decisions in Braşov is the relationship between planners' regional allegiances and their duties as executors of national policies. The planners would naturally prefer that Braşov County retain its leading position in the Romanian economy: however, this may clash with national priorities for regional equity. The potential for conflict may increase if planners feel that the county deserves special treatment because of its migration/commuting problems, social heterogeneity, subregional inequalities and ecological and ethnic diversity.

Systematization Activities in Braşov County

Up until the late 1960s, regional planning in Braşov County had concerned itself largely with the expansion of Braşov City itself. After the War, industry was greatly expanded and retooled. Entire neighborhoods of apartment blocks were built to accommodate streams of in-migrants. While Braşov City expanded, the new town of Victoria (population 8,000) was built on the site of a Nazi chemical factory, a group of seven Magyar villages was consolidated to form the town of Sacele, and the resort area of Poiana Braşov was enlarged for domestic and foreign tourists.

Rural planning activity began in earnest following the national territorial reorganization enacted in 1967. Directives were issued calling for each locality to determine its development potential; counties were told to select from three to ten villages to be converted into towns. Since the main problem was (and still is) controlling the growth of Braşov City, the new towns were conceived as a way of relieving pressure on Braşov. By dispersing urbanization throughout the county, the strict migration controls in Braşov City might eventually prove unnecessary.

The selection of new towns was carried out by analyzing the existing economic, demographic and geographic characteristics of each locality.

This was combined with projections which would result from investments in industry, mining, forestry, agriculture, infrastructure or services. The stated objectives were to equalize the regional imbalances within the country, regulate urban growth by reducing outmigration from the backward zones and assure Braşov City's work force by maintaining large numbers of commuters in the surrounding villages (Institut Proiect-Braşov 1972).

After collecting relevant data, each locality in the county was classified according to economic profile and development potential. This classification scheme is shown in Table 5 (following page).

Concerning the ten villages to be phased out (i.e. Bogata Olteana, Cutuş, Dalghiu, Ioneşti, Ludişor, Luţa, Lupsa, Maliniş, Savasteni, Vilcea), the decisive factors were their extreme dispersion, isolation from rail, road and service networks or unsafe proximity to new plants or mining operations. Four of the ten are located in the Rupea zone, four in the Făgăraş zone, one in the southeastern highland area near Vama, and one in the Bîrsei plain north of Braşov. Four of the settlements have large Gypsy populations; most are uncollectivized. While some villages would be joined administratively to nearby larger villages—thus disappearing in name only—most will be physically eliminated over time. Their residents will be provided housing in other villages or in the towns (Institut Proiect-Braşov 1972, II:108).

In those villages which will not be phased out, "building perimeters" have been established within which all future construction must take place. The most important investments in the rural sector will consist of infrastructural improvements: piped-in water and sewage lines, flood control, extended electrification, modernizing roads, etc. New stores, schools, clinics and public buildings will be constructed. The village of Măeruş has been designated as Braşov County's "model village" (*sat model*) and will receive exemplary utilities and services. Located along a well-traveled highway, Măeruş will function as a visible symbol of rural development. To date, the principal work in Măeruş has been a flood control program for the nearby Olt River.

From the list of villages with development potential, seven localities were chosen to be transformed into towns. Once urbanized, these would help form a future network of fourteen "areas of polarization," such that no rural community would be more than 10 kilometers from an urban (see

TABLE 5

VILLAGE DEVELOPMENT IN BRAŞOV COUNTY 1975-1990

Category	No.	Subtotal	Average Population
I. VILLAGES TO BE PHASED OUT	10	10	260 inhabitants
II. VILLAGES THAT WILL BE RETAINED BUT ARE WITHOUT DEVELOPMENT PROSPECTS		80	
A. Villages with small declines in population	49		580 inhabitants
B. Villages which will experience mild growth	31		1,000 inhabitants
III. VILLAGES THAT WILL GROW		53	
A. Due to internal development of agricultural or dormitory functions	40		1,500 inhabitants
B. Agrarian or dormitory villages which could be made into towns except for one criterion which is lacking	13		2,000 inhabitants
C. Prospective new towns		7	
1. Tourist functions only	1		2,000 inhabitants
2. Agricultural and dormitory functions	3		900-2,200 inhabitants
3. Multifunctional, i.e. industry, agriculture and dormitory	3		1,400-5,600 inhabitants
TOTAL VILLAGES	150	150	

Source: Institut Project-Braşov, *Schţte de Sistematizare a Judeţului Braşov*, Vol. II, January 1972, p. 104.

MAP 3

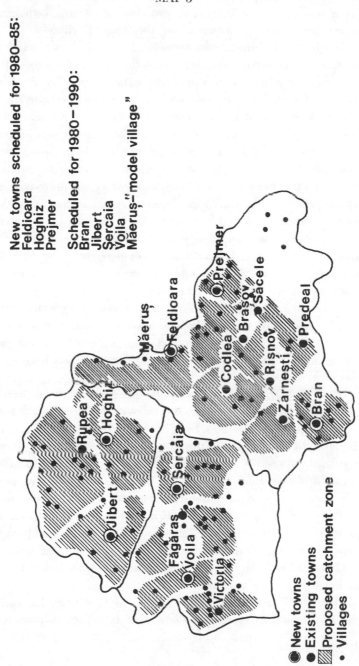

New Towns in Braşov County 1975–1990

New towns scheduled for 1980–85:
Feldioara
Hoghiz
Prejmer

Scheduled for 1980–1990:
Bran
Jibert
Şercaia
Voila
Măeruş–"model village"

● New towns
● Existing towns
▨ Proposed catchment zone
• Villages

Map 3 on preceding page). During the 1976-1980 plan, about one-third of all rural investment was to focus on just three new towns, with remaining resources presumably spread out among the other 147 villages.

According to the original plan, formulated in 1972, the seven new towns would be scattered relatively evenly over the County's territory. Table 6 gives pertinent information as to their characteristics. By the time the plans were finalized in late 1975, however, two important alterations had occurred. First, one of the future towns—Lovnic—was eliminated and replaced by neighboring Jibert. According to the conversations with county planners, residents of Jibert were angry at having been passed over, and vehemently contested the decision to urbanize Lovnic. No formal complaint was filed, but country officials received verbal protests whenever they happened to visit the village. Planners maintain that Lovnic had no significant advantage over Jibert other than a slightly more central geographic placement in the relatively desolate Rupea zone. Jibert, however, was a commune center (*reşedinţa de comună*), and its residents felt (justifiably) that the village would stagnate if neighboring Lovnic were made into a town instead. Jibert's interests were apparently spurred on by former natives of the village who worked in the Braşov planning offices. By 1975, Jibert had replaced Lovnic on planners' maps. It is not unreasonable to expect that similar conflicts have occurred in other parts of Romania when relatively equally endowed villages compete for scarce State investment.

The second significant change in the plan was in the sequencing of urbanization. Initially, the villages of Feldioara, Prejmer, Şercaia and Bran were to achieve urban status by 1980, with Hoghiz, Voila and Lovnic being delayed until 1980 (Institut Proiect—Braşov 1972, vol. II, p. 85). By 1975, however, the sequence had shifted: the construction of a giant cement factory in Hoghiz pushed this locality up to a priority position. Şercaia and Bran were relegated (together with Voila and now Jibert) to the 1980-1990 period. It appears that in the contest between spatial equity and economic efficiency, State and County planners opted for efficiency. The lesser-developed localities, those needing the most investment, were *all* put into the post-1980 phase. This only served to consolidate Braşov County's inequalities.

In late 1975, at the close of the 1970-1975 Five Year Plan, each commune and town in Braşov County was asked to debate the plans for their

TABLE 6

NEW TOWNS IN BRASOV COUNTY

Village	Major Functions	1970 Population	Projected Population 1985	No. of Villages in Catchment Area	Total Population Served
Feldioara	factory agriculture commuter	2,921	5,000	9	18,000
Bran	tourism	1,950	3,000	13	15,640
Voila	agriculture service	900	4,125	12	16,085
Hoghiz	factory	1,441	4,000	14	15,450
Prejmer	factory agriculture commuter	5,535	8,000	5	18,990
Sercaia	service	2,175	4,325	16	16,975
Lovnic	service	939	2,050	11	9,820

Source: Institut Proiect-Brasov 1972, vol. II:114-122.

locality and approve them. While the County newspaper *Drum Nou* carried daily accounts of these meetings, there are indications that some citizens were either overwhelmed by the plans or at least misinformed about them. Thus, *Drum Nou* (November 22, 1975) cited the towns of Victoria and Rupea, where meetings were postponed because "local administrative organs were unprepared for discussion." In Hoghiz, residents requested that their plan be revised, so that additional stores and child care facilities would be built immediately, rather than being delayed until the post-1980 phase (Institut Proiect-Braşov 1976a). In Prejmer, local officials and planners discussed what to do about Gypsy hamlets lying outside the village perimeter (Institut Proiect-Braşov 1975a). As the deadline for approving the plans approached, most localities held meeings, and all approved their plans.

Following several postponements, a conference of the Braşov County People's Council finally ratified the community plans and sent them on to Bucharest (*Drum Nou*, February 2, 1976). During 1976, however, the plans were revised several times. In fact, there were so many revisions that local voting or discussion of each would have been too time-consuming.

In Spring 1977, President Ceauşescu re-examined plans from all counties of Romania, focusing especially on those for the large cities and for prospective new towns. The ostensible purpose for this re-analysis was to evaluate the effect of the March 1977 earthquake on the systematization program. However, on a visit to Braşov City, Mr. Ceauşescu's criticisms went far beyond mere technical modifications. According to planners who heard his remarks, Ceauşescu complained that the plans were not "ambitious" enough; they were limited to the placement of buildings or apartment houses when they should really be plans for new, socialist cities. Many of the plans, he said, were "sterile," "repetitive" and "monotonous;" they failed to reflect diversification in settlement structure and neglected to utilize local architectural traditions. He suggested that the planners' ideas should be more "grandiose," and that the scale of the plans be greatly enlarged. More emphasis was to be placed on consolidating, organizing and intensifying land use via vertical construction in the villages; especially important was that everyone should build two-story houses.

Ceauşescu's comments were variously interpreted by those in the Braşov County Planning Institute. Some planners thought that a minor upgrading would be sufficient, while others felt that they had to begin all over again. There was considerable debate over the need to demolish existing village housing in order to create the new "civic centers" in the villages. Originally, housing demolitions were supposed to have been kept to an absolute minimum.

As a result of President Ceauşescu's criticisms, several revisions were made in the plans, many of which were never officially presented to local communities. In the planners' views, these alterations constituted not substantive changes but technical modifications of a previously approved plan. Informing the mayor and local officials of the revisions was all that was necessary. Ceauşescu's new directives were especially relevant for the three new towns being constructed during 1975-1980: Feldioara, Hoghiz, and Prejmer.

Analysis of the New Town Plans

Feldioara, which will be discussed in later chapters, has been a service center for surrounding communes. Presently containing newly 4000 persons, it lies on main road and rail lines, and houses commuters who work in Brașov. It also has a brick factory nearby and a minerals processing facility under construction.

Hoghiz (population 1500) is the site of a large cement plant, and its urbanization is meant chiefly to service the factory's workforce.

Prejmer, with over 5500 persons, is like Feldioara a multifunctional village; it has a textile factory, a mechanized state farm, and houses hundreds of commuters to Brașov.

The plans for each village are roughly similar. Each will grow to a population of 5,000-10,000 persons; high density civic centers with administrative, economic and service functions will be constructed; several hundred apartments will create an urban ambiance; dormitories will be built for unmarried workers coming from other locations. Light industry and food processing units will be started to provide work for the "surplus female labor force," i.e., wives of men working in heavy industry. With strict adherence to the "building perimeters," valuable agricultural land will be reclaimed. Large gardens once in the centers of the villages will be moved to the margins. Utilities, especially running water and sewage, will be extended.

Central heating will be provided for apartment dwellers, and in administrative and commercial establishments, but state priorities preclude investing in the construction of heating lines to heat individual homes, much to the dismay of most villagers. Natural gas, commonly used to heat urban homes, will be used only in industrial enterprises.

The three new towns will obtain or expand upon a number of services: clinics, schools, nurseries, kindergartens, retail units, outdoor marketing areas, restaurants, workers' clubs, culture houses, recreation areas, asphalting of roads and landscaping of parks all appear on the new town plans. However, the amount of new services and facilities does not accord with the projected demographic or economic growth of these localities. While population growth will occur in the early stages of the plan, the service investments are not scheduled until the later phases (post-1985, or even post-1990).

The selection of Feldioara, Prejmer and Hoghiz as the first new towns is clearly linked to their industrial functions. In fact, it might be said that their priority ranking resulted not so much from a county decision but from ministerial level decisions to build factories in these three locations. In contrast, the remaining four villages (to be urbanized after 1985) have no industry and none planned: Şercaia, Jibert and Voila will contain service functions while Bran will be developed as a tourist center for mountain vacationers.

The construction of a new town uses three kinds of financial resources. First, there are State investment funds alloted directly from Bucharest; these pay for building most factories, major roads, irrigation works and other installations deemed to be in the national interest. Second, there are county investment funds controlled from Braşov and subject to discretionary use by county officials. Such funds are used for county roads, maintenance of infrastructure, apartment construction, and schools and clinics. Third, there are local contributions which may consist of a) funds taken from the commune budgets; b) local taxes which villagers pay in either cash (100-150 lei) or labor (4-6 days per adult), what is officially called "contributions in money and labor from the population" (*contribuţie in bani şi în muncă din partea populaţiei*); and c) extraordinary contributions of money or labor for specific projects, called "voluntary work" (*muncă voluntară*). Citizen contributions are particularly important in contructing new public facilities, landscaping the village center, maintenance of irrigation works (dikes, etc.) and contracting animals to deliver to the consumers' cooperative. Because the implementation of planning in Braşov County's villages entails the active participation of the citizenry, the linkage between the planner and the community takes on crucial importance.

Planning Organization in Braşov County

Plans for all villages, towns and future towns are drawn up by a team from the Braşov County Planning Institute (Institut "Proiect"–Braşov); the dossier consists of a 25-75 page monograph describing the village's existing geographic, economic and social structure, and its future development. Also included are an agricultural profile, statistical summaries, planning maps showing two or three alternative proposals, detailed maps of the "civic center," and notations of meetings between planners and citizens, including any suggestions put forward. Most of the suggestions request more utilities or services to be added in the initial phase of the plan instead of being delayed until the post-1980 or post-1985 phases. In addition to the dossier, a three dimensional model is also constructed. The model is stored at the Planning Institute and used mainly for ceremonial (exhibition) purposes. Like most such models, it is extremely ambitious, to the extent that buildings are inserted which are not to be constructed until well after the year 2000.

The County Planning Institute maintains contact with the County People's Council through the Council's Section for Architecture and Systematization, which examines and certifies the plans. There is a periodic exchange of staff between the two agencies, part of Romania's ubiquitous system of "rotation of cadres" (*rotaţie cadrelor*). The intention behind rotation of cadres is to broaden the individual's work experiences, but rotation is not all that systematic. Within both the Planning Institute and the Systematization Office there are almost periodic rumors of reorganizations, lay-offs or transfers of personnel which invariably do not materialize. In fact, no major reorganization of Braşov's planning organs has occurred since the county itself was reconstituted in 1968.

As the plan for a new town is designed, revised and implemented, county planners are affected by several factors: their links to the national bureaucracy; the actions of colleagues in other domains of political activity, personal, social and cultural traits which influence the way planners articulate national planning policy; and the planner's relationship to local communities.

The Planner and the State

In executing directives from the national planning administration and in passing local information back up the administrative ladder, county planners must make special efforts to keep abreast of state investment programs which may directly affect their work. For example, if a ministry decides to build a new factory or expand an old one, the resulting increase in labor force will require new county plans for housing, food supplies and social services. Similarly, state agricultural officials may have approved an irrigation scheme whcih will unknowingly disrupt planned housing construction in the county. However, planners' access to this needed information is impeded by Romania's constantly shifting administrative arrangements, by the centralization of so much data in Bucharest, and by the fact that much valuable economic information is considered of strategic importance and is thus kept secret.

Planners are also concerned about how Romania's national development priorities affect county status. One planner, proud of Braşov's high level of economic development, was disappointed that the Hoghiz cement factory would be the only major new investment in Braşov County during the coming five-year plan. Others felt that even this one plant was unnecessary, and that the resulting cement dust would pollute a potential recreation area. Apprehensive about the negative consequences of industrialization and urbanization, these planners seemed more concerned with what they called "the quality of life" (calităţii vieţii) than continued economic growth. These concerns are hardly unfounded; several Romanian sociological studies—some dealing with Braşov itself—cite unwanted results of rapid urbanization: high labor turnover, housing shortages, inadequate services, lack of recreational facilities, alcoholism and delinquency among youth (Dragan et al. 1968, Bogdan et al. 1970, Herşeni 1970, Tunaru and Rujan 1975, Banciu and Banciu 1977). Hence, Braşov's planners try to steer a course between the two extremes: they compete for state resources so as to retain the county's leading position, while lobbying with the state so that over-industrialization does not lead to adverse consequences.

County planners must also be vigilant about obtaining extra state financing and support services when they feel it necessary. For example, the construction of workers' housing may be paid for out of factory funds, county funds or via loans and credits to private citizens. Thus, there is considerable manuevring among citizens, localities, counties and the state to share the burden of such activities. In early 1977 the planners sought to convince authorities in Bucharest that Braşov City needed more stores and service establishments. They did this by showing that the number of unofficial, uncounted or illegal in-migrants in Braşov was so large, and the number of rural commuters buying their goods in Braşov so great, that the existing facilities were inadequate. The publication of detailed census results later in the year confirmed the ugency of the planners' request, which was ultimately granted.

In line with their varied opinions about state investment priorities, county planners also had differing perceptions of the Systematization

Law (Law No. 58/1974) and how it should be used. One highly placed official objected to the Systematization Law's strict guidelines for vertical construction and spatial centralization; he called it "an iron law" (*legie de fer*) which constricted planner creativity rather than stimulating it. A close colleague, however, saw the Law in completely opposite terms: it was so flexible that it allowed maximum operational movement; regulation by Bucharest served to guard against making mistakes. Whether or not the Systematization Law is "iron" can only be judged by its application in specific cases. Nevertheless, such differing perceptions on the part of two high-echelon planners (who presumably cooperate in making up the plans) might lead to plans which are either contradictory or inadequate. In fact, the desire for creativity and flexibility conflicts with higher level imperatives for economizing and discipline. At best, this leads to compromise plans. At worst, this conflict generates improvization and confusion.

Planners' actions are also affected by their perceptions of socialist ideology. One planner, when asked about the role of the detached single-family home, saw this type of dwelling as antithetical to the idea of a socialist city. He thus excluded it from his planning inventory. His colleague, while agreeing that the one-family home is a luxury (given Romania's existing needs for mass housing), nevertheless saw it as the healthiest living environment for families with young children, and an absolute necessity in the future. Unmarried youth could live in dormitories, he said, and smaller apartments would be sufficient for childless families or pensioners, but the socialist city of the future should provide a variety of household forms. The use of either of these contrasting ideals for a genuine socialist *urban* structure could have drastic effects when applied to *villages*, where the single-family residence constitutes the main type of housing. At the moment, State funds in the countryside are used exclusively for constructing apartments. Single families must spend exorbitant amounts to build two-story homes, sometimes sharing the costs and labor with another family.

Another problem for county planners is the general uncertainty and open-endedness of planning. Planners lack information about those options being discussed at the highest level. The data which they feed to Bucharest is not equally reciprocated. Bucharest is where national policies are formulated. The Braşov planner is expected to put these policies into action. Policy changes occur, of course, but while these "reforms" may relieve bottlenecks at the national level, they yield anxiety and frustration for planners at the county level. Weeks or months of work may be wasted, causing frustration in the planners offices and cynicism or apathy in the affected communities.

For example, President Ceaușescu's surprise rejection of several plans for Brașov County's urban and rural localities (in 1977) resulted in having to redesign the future town plans, the plans for existing towns in the county, and for Brașov City itself. Construction activities were halted. Village land saved for recreational purposes was suddenly slated for new construction. Trees that had been cut down in the name of urbanization were suddenly to be replanted, while sturdy houses and barns were now scheduled for demolition. For those localities already skeptical about the county's bureaucratic procedures, these revisions led only to further disillusionment.

Constant revision of the plans—flexibility as it were—is a valuable asset for adapting to new conditions. Plans will be improved, *provided* that there are open channels of communication and congruent perceptions of goals and means at local, regional and national levels. However, when information is inaccurate or incomplete, where the gap between levels is wide, the goals contradictory, the pace of the plans rapid and the turnabouts abrupt, the advantage of flexibility gives way to uncertainty and confusion. Planners are themselves of diverse opinions; they approach their communities with plans which they expect will be altered, or with plans which do not consider local conditions. Such planners will have difficulty mobilizing citizens.

The Planners and Their Collaborators

Planners contact local communities to gather preliminary data, confer with the local elites and monitor the progress of their plan. However, they are not the only outside officials who visit the village. Almost daily, technicians, experts, auditors or trouble-shooters sent out by the County, the Party or a ministry may be seen walking through the streets or fields, talking with the local mayor. Of particular importance are two individuals whose chief task is to ensure that the village develops according to the plan; thus, they function as collaborators of the planner. These are the Party activist and the journalist from the County newspaper.

The Party activist. The Party activist (*"activistul de partid,"* formally called *"instructor de partid"*) is a salaried, full-time functionary of the County Party Committe. The activist may be assigned to a locality or to an enterprise. An activist in the rural sector will normally work out of the offices of the County Party Committee in Brașov City. Each activist is responsible for 7-10 villages (3-4 rural communes). He or she will visit the village on an average of once a week, though localities having special problems or important activities—prospective new towns, for example—may be visited more often. Though their official duties are to articulate Party policy to the community and see that it is carried out, the activist does more than just oversee local Party affairs. Duties may include monitoring the results of the collective farm's harvest (and reporting these to the authorities), looking for bottlenecks in the administration of the local consumers' cooperative, corrdinating the linkage between the factory management and commune administration, attending meetings of the local school committee, and helping local elites mobilize the population to achieve the plan.

During meetings of the village's enterprises, Party organization, labor union, Women's Council or Party Youth Organization, the activist sits as a representative of the County, often giving a final summation speech or pep-talk to the assembled audience. Activists are well-versed in both the Party line and State priorities. Many of them possess the zealousness of the "true believer," and a few have the kind of elitist arrogance which alienates local citizens or community leaders (and at times, visiting anthropologists).

When entering the village, the Party activist is considered to be the social equal (if not the superior) of the local Party secretary (who is also the mayor). Most activists roam freely through the mayor's office, sit in the mayor's chair and use the telephone. In visiting the village, activists gather information, identify any local problems and root out corruption or malfeasance on the part of local elites.

County Party activists also function as network organizers and brokers, helping the village to obtain scarce resources from the county. Living in Brașov City, activists can easily contact the key persons or offices necessary for procurement of desired goods and services. Village leaders take the brokerage and patronage powers of the activist quite seriously. The activist may be asked to procure scarce building materials for the commune, obtain schoolchildren from Brașov to help with the harvest on the collective farm, intervene with State planners to build a new road, or to help the community secure a delay in repayment of a debt to the County or State. The activist may also be approached by ordinary villagers to help resolve their personal problems, e.g., certifying disability benefits, arranging travel permissions, obtaining admission for their children into Brașov's high school, and the like.

The activists' success depends greatly on their style of work and their relation with the community. In this connection, they suffer from some of the same problems as county planners. Activists are outsiders, with their own career objectives. They are oriented toward the Brașov social and political setting rather than to the local one. Even though they may visit the village often, they never actually live there; hence, their contacts are limited to those villagers whom they meet during the course of their daily rounds. This does not preclude a drink at the local bar and a friendly chat with local residents. Nevertheless, the activist usually establishes the most meaningful ties with local elites and village Party cadres. Other villagers may hardly know their local activist's name.

The inability to forge long term links with the village is further inhibited by the activists' social and spatial mobility. Their job often serves as preparation for a more permanent post in an urban enterprise, in Party administration or as a commune mayor. Activists are rotated to new posts or new communities every twelve months, giving little opportunity to establish deep-going relations with a representative segment of community members. In extreme cases, the activist comes to be perceived as just one in a long line of outsiders who are prying into local affairs, constantly imploring villagers to work harder, do more, sacrifice for the future, but who themselves return each night to their modern, urban apartments in Brașov City (often in their own cars). There *are* understanding and sympathetic Party activists, with imaginative ideas for improving community life; individuals who on some days remain late in the village long after they should have returned to Brașov. In rare cases, activists even become partisans for their zones. However, the nature of their position and the demands made on them from above keep them locked into roles as agents of the County Party apparatus, rather than as advocates for the communities they oversee. For this reason most activists are destined to remain "outsiders," with corresponding limitations on their mobilization effectiveness.

The journalist. The County newspaper *Drum Nou* ("New Road") is received by nearly every second household in Braşov County; this proportion
increases still further if the newspapers of the Magyar and German nation-
alities are added (i.e., *Brassoi Lapok* and *Neuer Weg)*. Planners and officials
turn to *Drum Nou* each morning (after reading the national Party daily
Scînteia).

The typical method for reporting on rural life in *Drum Nou* is the "raid-
inquiry" *(raid-ancheta)*, in which the journalist makes a surprise visit to an
enterprise or locality. In reality, the journalist usually contacts the factory
chief or mayor on his arrival, and only then proceeds to investigate such
matters as whether all the workers are actually working, the plan is being
met, the crops are being harvested on time, the restaurant is actually serving what is on its menu, the youth organization is having regular meetings,
or whether volunteer work is showing good results. Like the Party activist,
the journalist helps to mobilize the population and seeks to identify
breaches of socialist ethics and legality. Agricultural mobilization is the
prime task of the rural journalist. The collective farm's plan must be
achieved and peasant deliveries of milk, eggs and livestock to the con
sumers' cooperative must be assured. The journalist's mobilization tasks
also include pointing out poor moral examples in the village: the housewife who does not cultivate every square meter of her courtyard to attain
self-sufficiency, the peasant who constructs a barn in violation of the systematization provisions, local intelligentsia who neglect to take active
roles in village cultural life and so forth.

In addition to mobilization, the journalist also has a control function.
Corruption or crime can be pursued after receiving anonymous tips, signed
citizen complaints or directives from the County Party Committee. If a
local official has recently been censured by the Party or removed from
office, the journalist may write an exposé of the culprit's "abuses." How
ever, "criticizing local Party leaders is a Party matter" as one journalist
told me. Since blame for local shortcomings cannot be attributed to Party
policy, and only rarely to the local Party secretary, difficulties are invariably attributed to lower echelon foremen, brigade leaders or other
specific individuals. When things are going well, however, these "little
people" are also hailed and their contributions justly recognized. The most
commonly expressed causes for dysfunctions or shortcomings are "indiscipline," "poor organization," or "weak leadership." The general

solution to these problems is to increase ideological vigilance and to take "organizational measures" so that they will not recur.

The role of the newspaper in furnishing the planners with information should not be underestimated. Sometimes it is only after a scathing critique of an intolerable situation that planners will rush to the village and try to rectify the situation.

The Planner in the Village

Several factors structure the way planners relate to village communities. One of these is the standardization of many local plans and building guidelines. The effect of this standardization is to limit the planners' creativity and reduce the options which they can offer local communities. With the amount of creative work reduced, county level planning degenerates into administration and monitoring, something which many planners—educated as architects and engineers—find to be uninspiring.

The intensity of planner-village relations is also affected by the degree to which planners seek to overcome the physical, social and administrative distance between themselves and the rural communities. Some planners truly relish leaving their offices for the trip to an outlying rural community. Others find the long rides on overcrowded buses to be a deadly chore. The physical distance means that there is little likelihood that planners will visit the rural localities except during the course of their duties. Physical distance also contributes toward a social distance between the planner and the community. Whereas villagers would much rather see sewage, heating and utility lines installed, the planners' urban orientation emphasizes monumental architecture in the villages. Long-term ties between planners and villagers are also inhibitied by the planners' social and spatial mobility. Some planners, realizing that they will be changing jobs or leaving the area, are uninterested in forming close relations with the villages under their jurisdiction. About half of Braşov Coounty's planners were born outside the county; of those born locally, most were raised in Braşov City and have somewhat less familiarity with the current concerns of rural residents. Finally, planners may suffer from administrative distance: field visits are often haphazardly planned; village officials may be unaware when the planner is coming and delays may result in obtaining key local information. More important is that planners may be unaware of the wide social diversities in even relatively small communities; this is particularly true of the suburban villages around Braşov City, which contain collective farmers, private peasants, commuting industrial workers, educated professionals, long-time residents and young migrants of four different ethnic groups (Romanian, Saxon-German, Magyar, Gypsy). Administrative distance is most severe when planners choose to rely solely on the local political leader for their information about community needs. The local leaders may themselves be subject to the same social/spatial mobility patterns as planners.

The consequences of the physical, social and administrative distance produce incomplete or incorrect knowledge of local conditions. In many cases, planners leave the communities either misinformed about local conditions or ignorant of citizen concerns; even worse, they might be apathetic to these concerns.

Despite frequent consultations with local elites, intermittent meetings with village representatives in Braşov, and rare public debates, the villagers are generally ignorant of all but the general outlines of the plan. Only one copy of the planning dossier is kept in the village and it is never made available to the public. Moveover, it is rarely kept up to date with current revisions. Most villagers get their information from occasional posters, news articles or uninformed gossip. (There is reason to believe that citizen misinformation about local plans is widespread in rural Romania. A sociological study of a village in Maramureş County (Dumitru 1977:142n) revealed that very few residents were acquainted with the different alternative proposals for their local plan. Even more serious was the fact that 62% of the villagers were wholly unaware of any plan for their village whatsoever!) The lack of information has direct bearing on the degree of citizen participation which the planner can expect from the community.

The Planner and Citizen Participation

Braşov's planners realize that their duty is not to form State policy in the county but to implement it. One planner summed up their position in the administrative hierarchy: "As planners, we can offer options. The solutions are not ours. They are political," meaning that they are decided outside Braşov County. Thus, no matter how much "consultation" takes place between village and county levels, no matter how many proposals the planner receives from the villagers, the *ultimate* decisions still rest with Bucharest. For virtually all planning activities, it is the national interest which is paramount. This is why there can never be "a plan *for* Village 'X,'" but only a "national plan which is executed *in* Village 'X'." Centralization of key decisions perpetuates the conflict between the "particular" and the "general interest." This conflict is acted out on several levels: between Brașov County and the central authorities, between villagers and county planners, between villagers and their local elites, and even among villagers themselves.

Within the community setting, these conflicts become visible in the activities of citizen participation and mobilization. To the planners, citizen participation means taking part in the execution of centrally determined policy. Yet the centralization of the planning apparatus and the planners' physical, social and administrative distance prevents them from formulating plans that could foster local participation. In reaction to their own inabilities, Brașov County's planners echo the complaints of the development expert: "the villagers are apathetic, lazy or unduly hostile to progress;" "they are narrow-minded and provincial;" "they don't understand the benefits they will ultimately receive;" "they will not let us help them to a better life."

Grudging acceptance rather than enthusiastic voluntarism is the usual type of citizen relation with the planner, this according to the planners' experience. Citizens participate, but only until their individual interests are served. "They will go to a meeting, but stay only until they find out that their house is not to be subject to demolition," as one planner stated. Brașov's planners complained that the peasants will not adopt any of the 42 different house designs that they provide free of charge to any villager planning to build a new dwelling. But since all the designs use the required two-story format, which actually increases some of the costs, the "irrational" peasants build using designs which contradict the systematization provisions.

Under pressure to achieve their targets, without substantial links to the community, county planners enter the village not in routine monitoring visits, but in an emergency, patchwork atmosphere, using information provided by the Party activist or spurred on by a superior who has heard the frustrations of an irate villager or read a scathing commentary by the journalist. Such conditions are not conducive to systematic decision making. They hardly give villagers the feeling that the plan is being channeled to community needs.

Most planners have a genuine desire to see that optimum plans are formulated and carried out effectively. Many have real sympathy for communities' needs and wants. But because of their structural position in the planning bureaucracy, the ideological constraints of socialist planning, their social characteristics and urban-oriented world-view and numerous local factors of which they are destined to be unaware, community mobilization can fall short of the goals and the plan will go unfulfilled. While it is true that some villagers may exhibit apathy, indiscipline, laziness, skepticism or conservatism, these are not the causes of plan failure. Rather, they reflect the structural contradictions in the planning process.

Summary: Regional Factors in the Planning Process

The planning process at the regional level is affected by (1) specific economic, social and geographic characteristics of the region and (2) the structure of regional-level planning administration. For Braşov County, the key regional characteristics were its high degree of economic development, large proportion of urban dwellers, diversity of ecological zones and ethnic groups, and sub-regional inequalities. The chief problems facing planners thus centered around the intensity of urban-rural links (commuting, migration), the special interests of mountain populations, the disproportionate effect of planning policies on Saxon and Gypsy ethnic groups, the conflict between efficient investment in advanced zones and the goal of regional equity, the social heterogeniety of the county's population and the status of Braşov County in the national planning scheme. The process of selecting future new towns generated competition between invidual localities; it also illustrated the priority which factory investment has over service investment; this was especially true of the county's backward regions, which will receive new towns only in the post-1985 period.

The second factor which affected regional level planning was the structure of the county planning apparatus and the corresponding role demands it placed on the planners. Planners were required to keep abreast of central ministerial decisions for industrial investment and to compete with other

regions for scarce State funds. Their perceptions of the systematization
law, their education as urban-oriented architects and engineers, and their
political training as *socialist* planners all structured the way plans for villages were formulated. Obtaining information from Bucharest and having
a meaningful influence on policy formation were particularly difficult for
Brașov County planners. Continual revision of the plan was often spurred
on by central authorities or by the President himself. This tended to generate skepticism or uncertainty on the part of those affected.

In the villages, the planners received assistance from local elites, the
Party activist and the visiting journalist. Village plans were constricted
by the centralization and standardization of construction, by the urban
orientation of the planners and by requirements to build vertically. Planner-village contact was hindered by the sheer physical distance between
outlying localities and the planners' offices, spatial and social mobility of
planners, and by a lack of coordination with local administrative organs.
The consequence of this "distance" was that planners were ignorant or
misinformed about local concerns. This generated adverse effects on the
level of citizen participation in the plan's execution. While they may have
had good intentions, the regionally generated constraints and planners'
structural position in the planning bureaucracy often caused them to over-
look the crucial elements needed for effective planning implementation.

The dysfunctions of planning at the regional level are not caused by
individual shortcomings or retrograde peasant mentalities. Rather, regional
planning in Romania reflects the structural aspects of the Romanian planning process. The "planning," "socialist" and "national" features are
given specific form by regional characteristics and the way national plans
are administered by county planners. What seem to be dysfunctions are
really logical outcomes of the planning process.

Planners combine the roles of visionary, expert, broker and bureaucrat.
After they reconcile their relations with Bucharest and with their own
planning ideologies, they must deal with the individual localities themselves. In the following four chapters, the implications of Romania's socialist planning strategies are brought down to their local setting, with a
case study of Feldioara, one of the three villages in Brașov County now
being transformed into a town.

CHAPTER VI

THE LOCAL CONTEXT OF PLANNING:
FELDIOARA VILLAGE AND ITS "ORGANIZED FLOW"

Introduction

As part of the select group of 300 future towns, Feldioara (pronounced Fel-dee-WAll-ra) can hardly be called a "typical" Romanian village. However, it can be assumed that (1) Feldiora will be typical for the group of 300 future towns; and (2) that the local level factors affecting the planning process will be most prominent in places where the state chooses to concentrate its inputs. Feldioara is such a place. Analysis of planned urbanization in the community can serve to illustrate how local social structures interact with supralocal political forces. This chapter sets the stage for such an analysis by outlining the ethnographic background and social conditions of Feldioara during the mid-1970s. Subsequent chapters deal, respectively, with plan formulation in the village, the relationship between household economy and local participation, and the village elites' role in plan implementation.

The historical and ethnographic description of Feldioara will employ the "organized flow" framework developed by Watson (1970) and Vincent (1977). "Organized flow" is a model for describing communities not as self-contained units but as intersections of demographic movements and social activity fields. As individuals enter, filter through and leave the community, they are subject to economic and social constraints. The "organized flow" framework helps to reveal how these constraints affect the village. This forms the basis for a subsequent discussion of household strategies and elite-citizen relations.

Early History

The village of Feldioara (population 3600 in 1980) is located along the main highway 22 km north of Brașov City, on the west bank of the Olt River, which forms the eastern border of the county. Together with Colonia Reconstrucția (pop. 1100) and nearby Rotbav (pop. 1000) the three villages comprise Feldioara Commune, of which Feldioara village is the commune center ("reședința de comună") Colonia Reconstrucția sprang up in 1936, when a brick factory was built on the road 2 km north of Feldioara. Feldioara and Rotbav are both former Saxon frontier settlements dating from the mid-thirteenth century.

The historical interaction of Feldioara's ethnic groups, its high level of economic development, and extensive demographic fluctuations have given the village a high degree of ethnic complexity. This is apparent in Feldioara's toponymic history. Originally named "Marienburg" by its German founders, it acquired the Hungarian name "Foldvar" as it came under (Austro-) Hungarian suzerainty; from this came the Romanian "Feldioara." Today all three names are used interchangeably, depending on the language of the speaker.

While archaeological and linguistic evidence indicate ethnic Romanians (Geto-Dacians) to have dwelled in the vicinity of Feldioara (Dunare 1972: 57), the village itself was founded in the year 1211 A.D., by Teutonic Knights returning from the Crusades. In return for protecting his southern border against marauding nomads, the Hungarian King Andreas II granted the Knights the territory north of Brașov, what is now called Țara Bîrsei (Bîrsei Country or Burzenland). The Knights immediately began construction of a castle ("Castrum Sankt Marie" or "Marienburg"), and Andreas invited German-speaking Rhinelanders to colonize the area. Though not from Saxony, these German speakers came to be known as Saxons.

Fourteen years after founding Marienburg, Andreas expelled the Knights for conspiring against him. However, he continued to invite the Saxon colonists, offering them "free peasant" status and tax privileges. Between

1211 and 1270, several thousand Saxons migrated to the Burzenland, establishing fifteen free villages (Teutsch 1965, Dunare 1972). The Saxons who came to Marienburg built earthen fortifications around their settlement, from which originated the Hungarian name "Foldvar" ("castle of earth") and eventually the Romanian "Feldioara." The village's fortress-like character is still evident today. It sits atop a hill overlooking the Bîrsei plain; houses adjoin each other on each side of a long tree-lined street; stretching back of each house are garden "strips." At one end of Feldioara there stood a fortified gate, now destroyed. Still standing at the other end, however, are the remains of the Knights' unfinished castle. Next to it is the Saxons' (Lutheran) Church.

Earliest documentation for Feldioara after the expulsion of the Knights appears in a 1240 A.D. proclamation by King Bela IV bestowing tax privileges on the Cisterian Order of monks (Zimmerman 1892, Dc. 76). In 1379, King Ludwig I designated Feldioara a weekly market town (Zimmerman 1897:509), a function which it maintained intermittently up until 1950. In 1380, it was declared a haven for runaway serfs (ibid.: 529).

Located on a trade route and on the border to the (Hungarian) Szekler lands to the east, Feldioara came to assume toll-collection fundtions. Dozens of proclamations by Hungarian kings and voivods reflect the importance of the frontier villages near Braşov. Some of the proclamations sought to stabilize economic functions, especially taxes, tolls and mills. Others were intended to keep the unstable peace between the Saxon colonists and the Hungarian Szeklers; in 1442 Feldioara was ordered to pay a 300 Guilder fine for killing six (marauding?) Szeklers (Gundisch 1937:109). There were also military threats: in 1529, Romania's Prince Petru Rareş fought a bloody battle against Cuman armies on the plain below the village. In 1612, 14 of Marienburg's Saxon youth were killed defending Braşov against the army of the Hungarian Gabriel Bathory. A moument to these martyrs stands at the far end of the village.

Ethnic and Class Stratification

Feldioara's 800-year history is marked by the interaction of several ethnic groups and their varied adaptations to changing macroeconomic and macropolitical conditions (see Romanian Research Group 1979, Beck and McArthur 1981, McArthur 1981 and Verdery 1983 for a more comprehensive treatment of ethnicity in Transylvania). Though it was one of 13 "Saxon" villages, Feldioara in fact contained equal numbers of Romanians and Saxons by the year 1800. In addition, there were a few Magyar families and some dozen Gypsy households. Like the Saxons, Feldioara's ethnic Romanians were free peasants. Yet the Saxons dominated the local economy as middle-peasants, craftsmen and traders linked with markets in nearby Braşov and through it to Budapest and Vienna. Saxon dominance in Feldioara is reflected in the village settlement pattern: they occupied the central core of the village while Romanians dwelled in hovels at the edges or out in the fields. After 1880, Romanians gradually moved into the village proper, but even then they were confined to smaller house lots, down the hill from the Saxons, literally out of their sight. This topographic and social boundary persists today.

By the 19th century, a rough class stratification of Feldioara along ethnic lines had been established. Saxons were middle peasants cultivating from 5-15 hectares of land, with a few landowners holding over 50 hectares. Romanians, on the other hand, rarely held over 5 hectares; a high percentage were either landless or held tiny scattered plots (see Tables 7 and 8, following page).

A major event in Feldioara's economic history was the building of a sugar beet refinery in nearby Bod village in 1889. Sugar beets grew well around Feldioara, and a transition from three-to-four field agriculture was quickly made. The peasants could deliver their sugar beets directly to the factory, thus avoiding the financial burden of the middleman. For those lacking sufficient land, the factory provided seasonal employment after the harvest. Nearly all Romanians in Feldioara have had family members who have worked in the sugar beet refinery: this seasonal work continues today for dozens of villagers.

Coinciding with the factory came land reclamation along the Olt River. In 1889, Feldioara was chosen as a test site for Transylvania's major land consolidation. This reform awarded ownership of common lands to private Saxon owners, and enabled local Romanians to put pasture land under the plow. Sugar beets could be cultivated on smaller plots; they yielded both cash benefits and gave surplus fodder for household livestock. Feldioara's Saxon farmers modernized their agriculture by importing Swiss dairy cattle, Yorkshire and Landrace pigs and sugar beet strains from Denmark and Germany.

Ethnic stratification was reflected not only in landholdings but in demographic rates: church records for the 25-year period 1867-1895 show the

TABLE 7

LANDHOLDINGS FOR ETHNIC GROUPS IN FELDIOARA–1896

	Romanians	Saxons	Total
Total population	1,182 (54.2%)	997 (45.8%)	2,179 persons[1] (100%)
Hectares owned	1,978 ha.[2]	3,956 ha.[2]	5,934 ha.
Percent of land held by	33.3%	66.7%	100%
Hectares per person	1,7 ha.[2]	4.0 ha.[2]	2.7 ha.[2]

1. excludes 247 Magyars and 55 Gypsies, landholdings minimal.
2. these figures are about double what would be expected, probably due to the inclusion of church, forest and pasture lands; it is the proportions owned which should be emphasized.

Source: Podea, *Monografia Județului Brașov*, 1938, p. 149.

_____

TABLE 8

LANDHOLDINGS FOR ETHNIC GROUPS IN BRASOV COUNTY–1910
(15 Saxon Villages Only)

	"Non-German"[1]	"German"	Total
Total No. of landholders	6,972 (52%)	6,646 (48%)	13,618 (100%)
Of which:			
No. holding *over* 3.0 ha.[2]	557 (8%)	3,209 (48%)	3,766 (28%)

1. includes Romanians, Magyars, Jews, Gypsies.
2. the original measures was 5 *"joch"* (Rom. *jugare*), where 1 joch = .577 hectar.

Source: F. Teutsch, *Kleine Geschichte der Siebenburger Sachsen*, 1965 (orig. 1915), p. 341.

infant death rate for Romanians to be 39% higher than that of the Saxons (12.9/1000 vs. 7.9/1000).

With Saxons controlling most of the land in Feldioara, the Romanians could enter Saxon households as laborers, migrate to Brașov or Bucharest, or emigrate abroad. Between 50 and 100 Feldioarans went to America or Canada during the early 20th century, the majority never to return. Roughly three-fouths of the adult male Romanians worked as farm hands in Saxon households until they had saved enough to establish their own holdings. Strong affective ties could develop between individual Romanian laborers and their Saxon masters. Saxons occasionally served as godparents at the weddings of their Romanian servants. Despite their different religions (Saxons were Lutheran, Romanians were Othodox), Saxons baptized about 10% of the Romanian children born during the 1867-1895 period. Some Romanians have even inherited the nicknames of their Saxon masters: "Wagner," or "Kaller" (cellar).

Saxons cutomarily prevented Romanians from purchasing Saxon-owned lands. Nor were Romanians allowed to attend the regional agricultural school located in Feldioara. Nevertheless, local Romanians can readily recount that they "learned from the Saxons" how to improve their farming techniques. Despite the objective facts of ethnic stratification, it is significant that Feldioara's history lacks any incidents of overt ethnic conflict. Romanians were still the butt of Saxons' humor and denigration; for a period they were not even permitted to walk freely in Feldioara's central (Saxon) quarter.

By the early 20th century, Feldioara had become (by Romanian standards) a prosperous village of middle peasants, with a population of about 2500. According to census lists, the number of agricultural laborers fell from 153 in 1857 to only six in 1910. The peasants benefitted from the natural high fertility of the land, good quality seed and livestock strains, the proximity of the sugar refinery, and income from suppling Brașov with vegetable and dairy products. With close economic and cultural ties to central Europe (via the Saxon ethnic consciousness) and a railroad line begun in 1873, Feldioara had lost all semblance of isolation.

Cultivation of sugar beets required additional labor for weeding and harvesting. With local Romanians owning their own land or migrating, Saxon farmers began to recruit seasonal laborers from Magyar villages to the north and east, supplementing them with transient Gypsies.

While Saxon farms prospered, Braşov's industrialization provided opportunities for local Romanians to enter the city's work force. In addition, Feldioara itself became the site of several small enterprises. The local barley crop was absorbed by two local breweries (one founded by a Bohemian Jew, the second by a wealthy Romanian from Braşov). There was also a small paint and lacquer works, a vinegar refinery and a local mill. In 1930 a gas bottling plant opened. Transit traffic through Braşov enabled Feldioarans to open inns and cafes, while local Saxons specialized in carting goods and people to villages across the Olt River. There was also the weekly market, attracting as many as 200 buyers of livestock and fodder. Feldioara is the only former market place in Braşov County which has not yet become a town.

The occupational profile of Feldioara from 1910 illustrates the degree of economic diversity (Table 9, next page). Even at this early date 30% of the local work force were employed in nonagricultural occupations.

Political and Economic Change in the Interwar Period

In 1919, the Austro-Hungarian province of Transylvania ("Land of Magyars, Szeklers and Saxons") was incorporated into Greater Romania. The Saxon ethnic group united with the Bucharest administration and were welcomed as hardworking farmers who could aid the agrarian economy of the new Romania. At this time, Feldioara elected its first ethnic Romanian mayor. This coincided with the rise of a small local Romanian elite, consisting of about half a dozen landowners having 12-15 hectares, plus one individual (nicknamed "The Baron") who supposedly held as much as 40 hectares. Regardless of whether the Romanian mayor was of the Liberal Party or National-Peasant Party, he was still elected by the grace of the Saxon voters. Under the "assistance" of the Saxon notary, the Romanian mayors remained under effective Saxon influence, if not total control.

Romania's 1921 land reform had little effect on Feldioara, as there were no giant estates to be divided. A consolidation of parcels was carried out, and this helped both Saxon and Romanian farmers to rationalize production. Feldioara's prior market function as well as its geographic placement enabled it to be named as one of Braşov County's four district administrative centers (*plase*) during the 1920s and 1930s. (Feldioara is the

TABLE 9

OCCUPATIONAL PROFILE OF FELDIOARA IN 1910

Category	Number of producers	Percentage of producers
Agriculture, horticulture	724	70.9%
Industry	153	15.0
Commerce, credit	20	2.0
Transporting, carting	22	2.2
Public services and free professions	41	4.0
Dayworkers (Rom. *zilieri*)	6[1]	0.6
Servants	30	2.9
Others, including five gendarmes	25	2.4
TOTAL	1021[2]	100.0%

1. Compare with the figure of 152 *zilieri* listed in the 1857 occupational census.
2. An additional 1470 "dependents" are recorded. Total village population at the time was 2491.

Source: Podea, *Monografia Judeţului Braşov*, 1938, p. 149.

only former *plasa* which has not become a town.) Another notable "first" for the village was the installation of an electrical generator in 1924. By virtually 1960 all houses had been electrified.

In 1936, the Bohn family from Timişoara built a brick factory at what is now the Colonia Reconstrucţia. Like the sugar refinery, the brick factory gave supplemental employment to local residents, though most of its work force was recruited from other parts of Romania.

The Ethnic Factor

It is no exaggeration to say that ethnicity crosscut the social and economic life of each individual—circumscribing occupational mobility, social networks, marriage possibilities, even where one could take a walk. Using landholdings as a measure of economic power, the Saxons held the dominant position over the Romanians, Magyars and Gypsies (the latter two groups comprising but 10% of the village population). Only a half-dozen Romanians and no Magyar or Gypsies owned more than ten hectares of

TABLE 10

LANDHOLDINGS IN FELDIOARA IN THE INTERWAR PERIOD

Sizes of holding	No. (percent) of Saxon households	No. (percent) of Romanian households
0-5.0 hectares[1]	70 (39.8%)[1]	205 (91.0%)
5.1-10.0 hectares	51 (28.9%)	15 (6.7%)
10.1-1-15.0 hectares	24 (16.5%)	3 (1.3%)
15.1-20.0 hectares	18 (10.2%)	1 (1.5%)
20.1-25.0 hectares	4 (2.3%)	1 (0.5%)
25.0-33.7 hectares	4 (2.3%)	1 (0.5%)
TOTALS[2]	176 (100%)	225 (100%)

1. Subdivided into 32 households (18.2%) with 0-3.0 ha.
   38 households (21.6%) with 3.1-5.0 ha.
2. An additional 295 ha. in small plots was held by 99 outsiders.
   The Saxon Church held 45.2 ha. and the agricultural school 19.7 ha.

Source: Village archives of Saxon landholdings before expropriation, May 4, 1945.
Data for the Romanian group is based on interviews and is only approximate.

land. In contrast, 50 Saxon households were in this category, as Table 10 indicates. The disparity would be even more striking if qualitative criteria were included, for Saxon lands tended to be of higher fertility and closer to the village than corresponding Romanian holdings. Saxon farmers could also count on social and financial assistance from their ethnic brethren, especially from those holding more land than they could farm alone. While Saxons employed day laborers or seasonal workers from all four ethnic groups, no Saxon ever worked for a Romanian, Magyar or Gypsy farmer.

It would be tempting to postulate a pure class-ethnic equivalence among Feldioara's ethnic groups, with Saxons on top, Magyars and Romanians in the middle and Gypsies on the bottom. However, such an equivalence would hide the overlapping in the stratification system as well as the class differences *within* each ethnic group. As Table 10 indicates, some Saxons were relatively poor, and there were Romanians who were relatively well-to-do. The internal class stratification was represented in village spatial organization: rich Saxons generally lived on the front main street (*"în centru," "Zentrum"*), while poor Saxons dwelled in the back street (*"die*

Gasse"). Prosperous Romanian families would move "up the hill" (*"in deal"*) and thus distance themselves both socially and spatially from the poorer Romanians living at the bottom (*"sub deal"*). For each ethnic group, social mobility and economic status were affirmed by the movement between the two areas. Internal stratification was less marked for Feldioara's small Magyar population. As for the Gypsies, they occupied the bottom rung of the social ladder, and dwelled in a special quarter of the village.

Interethnic relations in Feldioara were governed by several types of social markers which lent each group its own ethnic personality. These markers were not only locational, as has been mentioned, but physical, behavioral, linguistic, religious and economic. When these were combined with folk stereotypes and local naming customs, membership in one of Feldioara's four ethnic groups could be determined precisely.

For example, although the principal *occupation* for all Feldioarans was agriculture, the Saxons dominated in the domains of crafts, shopkeeping and petty trade. Even today the village consumers' cooperative and local public services contain disproportionately high numbers of Saxons on their sales or clerical staffs. Occupational specialization also characterized the Gypsies, who took on tasks rejected by other groups, such as making brooms or straw baskets, tinkering, fortune-telling, day labor, music making or peddling.

Language was a pivotal ethnic marker for the Saxons, who prided themselves on their ability to converse not just in Saxon dialect and High German, but also in Romanian, Hungarian and the Gypsy dialect. Feldioara's Romanians, on the other hand, were generally monolingual; for the Saxons this was further evidence of Romanian racial inferiority.

Since all Saxons were Lutheran and all Romanians (and Gypsies) Orthodox, the *religious* life of the two groups coincided with demonstrations of ethnic solidarity. This was particularly true for the Saxons, whose conversion to Lutheranism in the 16th century marked their consolidation as a Transylvanian German ethnic group (McArthur 1981). Saxons' obligations to their church have always been more strict than those of Romanians. The financial and social burdens have increased today because Feldioara's Saxon base has been steadily dwindling.

Together with the more discrete markers of occupation, language and religion, there were beliefs about *"race" and "blood"* which permeated ethnic relations in Transylvania. There were many fair-haired Saxons and *brunet* Romanians, but skin pigmentation in itself was insufficient as an ethnic marker. There were also swarthy Saxons and blond Gypsies to be found in Feldioara. Marriage between Saxons and Romanians was virtually forbidden in order to (so say the Saxons) "keep their blood pure." In Feldioara, there are today 18 villagers of mixed Hungarian-Saxon parentage, and eight Romanian-Saxons. All were born after 1945.

Finally, there were widespread *folk stereotypes* attached to the behavior of each ethnic group. Saxons were known as hardworking, passive, reserved, clannish and money-conscious. Romanians described themselves as passionate, emotional and aesthetic, though to Saxons they seemed undisciplined and sentimental. Magyars prided themselves on their Austro-Hungarian roots; like the Saxons, they tended to look down on the Romanians. The lowly Gypsies took on the most unflattering characteristics: they were considered insolent, shifty and prone to violent criminal behavior; they debased themselves by using their women and children as beggars. While envied for their musical abilities and carefree ways, Gypsies were considered thieves and, therefore, not to be trusted. These folk stereotypes were a vivid part of ethnic relations in Feldioara. They have largely been retained today, though in more attenuated form.

One could also cite Romanian/Saxon differences in folk costume, house-type and culinary traditions (Romanians cook sour, Saxons cook sweet), but these are relatively insignificant when compared to differences in social organization between the two groups.

Aspects of Pre-World War II Social Organization

As in virtually all agrarian societies, the fundamental unit of production, consumption and socialization was the co-resident domestic group. This entailed a "developmental cycle" (Fortes 1958) whose highest stage was the three-generation lineally extended family. While the vagaries of the life-cylce often precluded many families from reaching this stage, or holding it for very long, it was still the working deal.

For both Romanians and Saxons, marriage was largely endogamous within the village. There were no lineage restrictions, but as in all agrarian communities, there were "better" and "worse" families, with the more well-to-do Saxons and Romanians living in the center. Hence, marriage patterns were territorially skewed: Saxons in the center shunned those in the back street (*Gasse*), and Romanians living "up the hill" were cautious in allying with families "down the hill." Within both groups, however, bride and groom each received a parcel of land from parents to establish a holding. Post-marital residence was ideally patrilocal, at least during the early years.

Intergenerational transmission of resources was ideally carried out via partible inheritance, in which both sexes were given roughly equal shares of family property. The parents' house and courtyard were usually transmitted to the youngest son, who would then care for the parents in their old age. Children living permanently outside the village would eventually sell their share to a sibling who remained. Aside from inheriting land, Saxon children might also be set up in a nonagricultural occupation such as storekeeper or craftsman. The size of Saxon land holdings made their inheritance system more flexible. Romanian families, because of their more limited resources, usually could afford to set up only two of their children in agriculture. A third child might inherit the parents' own house and fields, while remaining children would be forced to take up a trade in Braşov or go abroad.

Over and above the domestic group, however, the Saxons and Romanians had quite different forms of social organization. Saxon values of *zusammenhalten* ("holding together") and *harmonie* (McArthur 1976) were reinforced through ties with their Lutheran Church, their schools and their many voluntary associations. These associations included neighborhood groups (*Nachbarschaften*), ladies' *Krenschen* and corresponding men's clubs, and age groups for confirmands and post-confirmands. Much of a Saxon's free time, and even some of their work-time, was spent in the company of one of these groups.

If the church could be seen as that institution which maintained Saxon ethnic identity, the Saxon school was that institution which forged it. Saxon teachers gave their pupils the linguistic training and the historical consciousness with which to deal properly—even cordially—with the lower social orders (i.e., Romanians). The better pupils attended German language high-school in Braşov. On finishing their schooling, Saxon boys might take a *Vanderreise* to Austria or Germany to rediscover their Teutonic roots. In virtually every domain of social life—from separate neighborhoods, churches and schools to commerce, marriage, political parties and separate cafes—Saxons of all economic levels were bound together vis-a-vis the Romanians.

The Saxons' voluntary associations had no counterpart among the Romanians. Instead, Romanians functioned in what can best be described as a system of amorphous networks, including the bilateral kindred (*familie*, *rude*), ritual kin (*naş/fin*) and neighborhood ties (*vecini*). The Romanians' use of well-to-do Saxons as godparents helped supplement those resources unobtainable through normal kin and friendship networks. (Work- and age-groups (*clacă*, *ceată*) which were highly elaborated throughout Romania, were insignificant among Feldioara's Romanian population. A possible explanation for their absence is the corresponding absence of feudal corvee obligations among the free peasants of Feldioara; it was these obligations that originally gave rise to *clacă* and *ceată*.)

From this cursory description of pre-World War II social organization, it can be seen that the ethnic differences between Saxons and Romanians were not mere epiphenomena of class stratification. They encompassed a whole gamut of distinct social forms, socialization mechanisms and folk beliefs. The profound differences between Saxons and Romanians were dramatized and reinforced during the years of World War II and its prolonged aftermath.

"The War Years"—1939-1954

In 1939, Romania fell under the economic and political domination of Nazi Germany. Saxons in Feldioara joined either the Hitlerist organization or the more moderate Bund, both led by wealthy landowners. The Hitlerist group eventually won out, but only after tempers had reached such a pitch that brawls occurred between members of the two groups. (In view of Feldioara's potential for acute class/ethnic contradictions, it is ironic that the only recorded instance of local political violence occurred *within* the Saxon group, which was normally so concerned with maintaining its unity and *harmonie*.)

The link between the Germans of Romania and the Third Reich gave Saxons expanded political and economic powers during the war years. Saxons were appointed to posts in the Civil Guard, and became conduits for Nazi ideology. Transferring their loyalty from Bucharest to the *Reich*, Saxon families sent their sons to fight in special *Volksdeutsch* divisions on the Russian front. A few were even sent for SS training in Germany. Feldioara's Romanian youth were attracted to the Romanian fascist organization

(The Iron Guard) but only to the extent that they wore the uniform and sang various patriotic hymns as they paraded around the village.

After Romania's antifascist uprising of August 23, 1944, and its alliance with oncoming Soviet armies against the German army, there was little doubt that the Saxons' "mandate" would soon be terminated. As Soviet occupation forces advanced, some local Saxons retreated with the German army to the "motherland" that they had left 800 years earlier. It would be an understatement to say that Feldioara experienced political turmoil after the war. More accurately, the social structure was turned upside down. Reflecting the volatile history of Transylvania, the revolutionary transformation of the local social structure was carried out on two fronts: one could be called "ethnic," the other "class."

Following Soviet demands for reparations, and with the acquiescence of the Romanian government, male Saxons between the ages of 18 and 40 and females between 18 and 30 were deported to Soviet labor camps, where they remained for three to five years. In addition to those subject to forced deportation, several older Saxon men volunarily accompanied their younger wives to these camps. Even in their darkest hour, Saxons demonstrated an extraordinary degree of community solidarity.

Romania's official justification for sending the Saxons to the USSR was to punish them as Nazi collaborators. However, the sole evidence used was their collective membership in an organization called "The German Ethnic Group" (*Grupul Etnici German*). The German Ethnic Group had been a relatively innocuous interest group organization which predated the fascists' rise to power. Though only a few of Feldioara's Saxons were genuine Nazis, all were nominal members of The German Ethnic Group and thus subject to deportation as collaborators. About twenty exemptions were given to Saxons in poor health or for those who had participated in anti-Nazi activities.

As soon as the Saxons departed Feldioara, their homes, tools, wagons, livestock and farmlands were taken over by local Romanians and "colonists" brought in from the highland villages around Bran. In many instances, remaining Saxon residents were shunted to the back rooms or barns of their own homes in order to make room for the new occupants. About 180 of the 235 Saxon homes were "integrated" in this way.

The years 1945-1952 thus saw Feldioara without a substantial portion of its adult Saxon population. Many died in the Russian labor camps;

others became "displaced persons" and remained in eastern or western Germany after their release. In 1954 the Romanian government issued the Saxons a formal apology. The Party and State admitted their mistake in deporting the Saxons *as an ethnic group* rather than because they were guilty of collaboration with the Nazis. It was further implied that Soviet occupation forces had given Romania no choice in the matter. With the apology, Saxons again received title to their houses and lands (except for large holdings which had been permanently expropriated). Conveniently for Feldioara's Saxons, all but about 30 of the shepherd "colonists" had returned to their natal homes, having been unable or unwilling to remain in Feldioara. Official Romanian policy now relegated the Saxon trauma to "history." Saxons were now a "co-inhabiting nationality," working alongside Romanians and Magyars for the construction of socialism.

While this declaration may have "solved for all time" (to use Party rhetoric) Transylvania's *ethnic* predicament, the *class* struggle in the countryside continued unabated. Because of the economic inequality between ethnic groups, many of the "class enemies" in Feldioara happened to be Saxons; hence, the class struggle also took on ethnic overtones.

Saxon economic and political dominance had already been undermined by expropriations and deportations. Former Saxon elites had gone to Germany, died in the camps, been jailed or otherwise deprived of influence. Some Romanian political leaders had also been harassed and jailed for short periods. During the "transitional period," the dominant political groupings in Feldioara were the poorest Romanians, outcast Gypsies, and the recently arrived shepherd colonists from Bran; all were under the direction of Party cadres sent from Braşov City. Feldioara's class struggle was carried out most directly in the agricultural sector.

Collectivization of Agriculture

Even before the War officially ended, all farmers and landlords holding over 50 hectares had been expropriated. Along Soviet lines, the Romanian peasantry was divided into the familiar triad of "kulak," middle and poor peasants (*chiaburi, ţaran mijlocaşi, ţaran mici*). In Feldioara, about ten Romanians and 15 Saxons holding above 10 hectares were declared *chiaburi*.

The *chiaburi* were burdened with forced delivery quotas and high land taxes. Threats and jailings were received by those who had been politically active in noncommunist parties before the War. In addition, *chiabur* classification itself was used to threaten some middle peasants regarded as "stubborn." As a result, virtually all of Feldioara's *chiaburi* joined the local collective farm (the two exceptions continued carrying on small private agriculture and raising horses).

According to the "theory" of collectivization, the cadre of poor peasants should begin the collective farm enterprise, whereupon the more conservative middle peasants follow suit. Yet observers with both Marxist and non-Marxist political persuasions have agreed that the practice of collectivization is hardly that harmonious (cf. Stalin 1940a, 1940b, Mitrany 1951, Cliff 1965, Shanin 1972).

Feldioara's collective farm began in 1949 with 19 families and 143 hectares. With the existing base of fertile land, draft animals, tools and eight tractors (!) involuntarily donated by the now-deported Saxons, Feldioara was an ideal location for one of Romania's first collective farms.

For several reasons, collectivization proceeded slowly in Feldioara (see Table 11, next page). The village had been relatively prosperous before the war so that poor peasants were not the dominant social class. The Communist Party was viewed with suspicion by most of the peasants. The shepherds, Gypsies and Party functionaries in Feldioara had neither social prestige nor political legitimacy. The pre-War elites, who might have bridged the gap between citizens and the new leadership, had been deported to the USSR or condemned as class enemies. Consequently, most Feldioarans joined the collective farm only when they saw no other option. The precipitating cause could be a family labor imbalance (no children at home) which, given restrictions on hiring farm labor, made household agriculture impractical or impossible. Other peasants joined the collective after being discouraged by the poor quality lands they had received, lack of aid from the machine tractor station and burdensome taxes and quotas which the State had imposed on private farmers. A few Feldioarans entered the organization in lieu of punishment for petty crimes. Finally, many residents joined in order to insure university admission or job promotion for their children; that is, to insure that the children came from "healthy social origins."

The State was hardly oblivious to the middle peasants' resistance to collectivization. As a consession, the villagers were encouraged to form "agricultural associations" known as *întovărăşire*. (In Feldioara, the *întovărăşire* was commonly referred to by its Russian acronym *"TOZ,"* which

TABLE 11

EVOLUTION OF COLLECTIVIZATION IN FELDIOARA, 1950-1977

Year	No. of families	No. of active members	Total arable land	Comments
1950	39	70	161 hectares	
1955	167	375	531	
1958	224	307	620	
1960	563	598	1367	collectivization com-
1961	477	605	1375	pleted in Fall 1959;
1962	746	735	2033	Union with Rotbav
1967	854	933	1912	collective farm 1962.
1969	845	577	1919	
1972		433	1919	
1974		392	1919	
1975		355	1929	
1976	501	365	1929	
1977		227	1929	purging of inactive members from "active" list.

Source: *Dare de Seama al lui Cooperativa Agricole de Producţia Feldioara* (Collective Farm Yearly Summaries).

stands for *Tavarishchestvo po obshchestvennoi obrabotki zemli*. It might also be added that Feldioara's collective farm or *cooperativa* is often referred to as the *kolhoz!*). Both the *întovărăşire* and collective farm organizations had amalgamated agricultural holdings. Unlike the collective farmers, however, *TOZ* members retained their livestock and tools as personal property and were paid according to the amount of land they had donated. The *TOZ* peasants thus received the benefits of cooperation while maintaining control over means of production and the labor process. Additional advantages of joining an *intovarişira* were a reduction in land taxes, possibilities to obtain technical aid from the State and access to the Machine Tractor Station.

Feldioara's first *intovarişira* was begun in 1952 with 20 families, each possessing from three to eight hectares of land. Stringent, locally administered entrance requirements barred all but land-owning middle peasants from entering the organization. The first *întovărăşire* proved so successful that two more were formed the next year. Like the original, these were relatively small (40 and 80 households, respectively) and locally managed. One consisted of a group of neighbors and kinsmen from a specific neighborhood in the village; the other was composed of Saxons. Former *TOZ* members in Feldioara uniformly speak of high incomes during this period (40,000-50,000 lei per year, or twice that of collective farmers).

Through the 1950s there existed four different types of agricultural production units in Feldioara: the State farm and collective farm had the best lands and highest degree of mechanization, though not necessarily the highest productivity; the three *întovărăşie* had consolidated lands but retained household ownership of tools and livestock; the individually-owned farms occupied low quality land, far from the village and were without the benefit of mechanization.

In 1959, collectivization was "completed" in Feldioara by disbanding the *întovărăşire* and compelling virtually all the remaining peasant families to enter the collective farm. In 1962 the collective farms of Feldioara and neighboring Rotbav were merged into a single unit containing over 800 families and 2,000 hectares of arable land.

Despite the "administrative measures" used to recruit members, most villagers speak well of Feldioara's collective farm up to about 1970. Members were paid on the "labor-day" system, with payments averaging 4-5 kg. of grain per labor-day, plus vegetables, fodder, sugar and the option of harvesting the collective's hay fields to secure fodder for one's own animals. Since the labor-day was a unit of payment and not a physical day, it was possible for some families to receive payment for 800-900 "days" per year. This was particularly true for those working in the zootechnic sector, where there was year-round work.

After 1970, however, Feldioara's collective farm experienced a series of difficulties which brought about a stagnation in real income and an exodus of members. These difficulties originated not only within the local setting but in societal changes over which the village had no control. The most important external factor was the availability of industrial employment in nearby Braşov City. Despite the time-consuming demands of commuting, working in Braşov's factories guaranteed villagers a year-round, cash income and pension benefits much superior to those offered by the collective farm. The result was that many of the collective's most productive members left the organization to become industrial workers. The local labor force was further depleted by the aging of the original members. As they began to go on pension, their children, preferring to pursue nonagricultural occupations, failed to replace them. Feldioara's labor shortages occurred just as the collective farm had been given the task of supplying Brașov City with more vegetables and industrial crops, which were labor-intensive (especially menthol and lavender plants, used for producing medicines). These new obligations forced the collective to hire as many as 200 migrant laborers, paying them not only high cash wages, but food and lodging as well. The expenses for these seasonal migrants came out of the pockets of remaining collective farm workers. This engendered local resentment toward both the migrant workers (who were seen as lazy) and the collective farm's managers (who were seen as incompetent). As a result, members began to look for jobs elsewhere.

Collective farmers' payments were further reduced by a series of floods, droughts and hail storms which occurred between 1970 and 1977. As work-day payments fell from five kilograms to two kilograms of grain per day, as vegetable payments were eliminated, more collective farmers left the organization and more laborers had to be hired to replace them. This led only to new burdens for those members who remained, and increasing discontent with the leadership.

The difficulties of Feldioara's collective do not derive purely from local causes. Studies of collectivization elsewhere in Romania (cf. Kideckel 1979, 1982) have shown that problems of collective farms mirror changes in the relationship between the organization and Romanian society as a whole; one such change is the spread of industrial opportunities to rural areas. The problems plaguing Feldioara's collective farm may thus be replicated in other communities subject to industrial influence.

That there are structural causes for the collective farm's problems should not imply that competent leadership is unimportant. In 1976, for example, Feldioara's collective passed into the hands of a well-known, hardworking, locally born brigade leader. His first act was to pass out grain to the pensioners as an indication of his good faith (see Chap. 9).

Feldioara's collective farm began to revive, but like its previous decline, there were several explanations. Crop investments in menthol and lavender finally began to pay off. State buying prices increased and the weather was benevolent. The State placed a moratorium on the collective's debt and wrote off some of the loans. The collective's new president began to instill confidence in remaining members by guaranteeing minimum payments and increasing pensions, a move that was impossible without State backing. Finally, the collective introduced a new type of share-cropping system called *acord global* ("global accords" or "large-scale piece-work"). Under the *acord global* arrangements, collective farmers are made personally responsible for cultivating and harvesting a given plot of land. In essence, this allows the families of collective farmers to help cultivate land, saving labor costs for the organization. With increased mechanization and better utilization of the local labor force through *acord global*, the number of migrant workers has dropped significantly.

Yet the problems of Feldioara's collective farm come into focus during each harvest period: schools and shops close so that all villagers—students, teachers, clerks, housewives and pensioners—can be put into the fields to bring in the crops. Collective farm members are painfully aware that agrarian incomes cannot compete with those offered by Brașov's factories; what keeps most members within the organization are the (noncash) benefits provided by the private plot and access to collective pastures, fodder and production materials. However, the conflict between household requirements and the State's need to centralize grain yields has led to a reduction in grain payments to collective farmers in favor of cash benefits. Since members remain in the organization largely for the noncash benefits, this policy has tended to demoralize some members. It has also made it more difficult for the collective's leaders to mobilize the membership. In 1981, the president resigned for reasons of health. His post has now been overtaken by the village vice-mayor, an electrician by profession. Despite the leadership changes, and especially due to reduced grain payments, the problems of the collective farm continue. Members tend to produce not so much to help the organization fulfill its plan, but to supply their own households with food. Were Romania to markedly increase its ability to supply food products to rural communities through its network of rural shops, the motivations to remain in the organization would be further reduced. At present, with Feldioara's new minerals plant offering a local alternative to agricultural work (as well as preferential rations of meat for its workers), there is serious questions as to who at all will be left to work the collective farm ten years from now, when most existing members will have reached retirement age.

Political Changes in the Socialist Period

In the late 1940s, Feldioara's political vacuum was filled by newcomers from the mountain areas, low status Gypsies and Party cadres from Braşov City. In the 1950s there was a succession of mayors and Party secretaries, none of whom lasted very long. There was also a considerable rotation of leading posts among local cadres. For example, one of the "colonists" from the mountain village of Bran became Party secretary in 1952 and mayor in 1954. By 1958 he had become president of the collective farm, even though he had little acquaintance with lowland agriculture. To take a second example, a recently deposed mayor of Feldioara was made president of the local consumers' cooperative, even though he lacked any sort of commercial training. Finally, the current president of the collective farm is a former vice-mayor. An electrician by trade, he is considered totally unacquainted with running an agricultural enterprise. Hence, it appears leadership posts in Feldioara were (and are still) allocated on political qualifications rather than on the basis of technical expertise.

A Party official might reply to this assertion by saying that Party cadres do indeed have expertise: they are experts at mobilizing the population and taking "organizational measures." Such abilities are necessary for running any local enterprise in Romania, but they are not sufficient. As these enterprises grow more complex and more specialized, dynamic mobilization abilities will be ineffectual if they are not combined with technical expertise.

In analyzing Feldioara's political situation, two questions must be posed. First, why the fluctuations in leading positions? Second, why did so many leaders come from outside the community? The two questions are in fact related to each other; because so many leaders came from outside the community, there was a higher propensity for fluctuations in leading positions. By comparing Feldioara's local elites with those in other Romanian villages (Romanian Research Group 1977, Sampson 1982, 1984), one can isolate four key factors which seem to have facilitated a non-local elite.

First, the Saxon emigration and deportation had deprived Feldioara of a large pool of potential local leaders who might have eased the transition from middle peasants to collective farmers. (This continuity is clearly evident in Kideckel's study of collectivization in Hirseni [1979, 1982]).

Second, those villagers who were originally attracted to the Party organization (which allocated leading positions) were of a social status which discouraged other villagers from joining the Party. This initial core of Communist Party members included poor peasants, Gypsies, opportunists, colonists from the mountains and refugees from other parts of Romania. Feldioara was large enough and economically developed enough to attract such immigrants.

Third, Feldioara happened to be close enough to Braşov City so that urban political cadres could serve in the village without actually having to live there. Consequently, Feldioara received many administrators who regarded their positions as temporary and had little long-term commitment to the village (this situation has changed little today; with increasing private car ownership, commuting from Braşov is even more attractive). Hence, geographical proximity led to outside leadership being perpetuated.

Fourth, the effect of collectivization on Feldioara's political situation cannot be underestimated. In particular, it should be noted that Feldioara was one of the first villages to be collectivized (in 1950) and one of the earliest to be collectivized completely (in 1959). The consequent abuses and mistakes by Party organs in the village, "the penalty of being first," probably caused a higher degree of alienation between the citizens and the local political institutions than in communities where collectivization was delayed.

In comparing Feldioara with other Romanian villages, the influence of these four factors is clearly evident. Thus, the ethnically homogenous villages did not experience the loss of entire groups of potential leading cadres as occurred in Saxon villages. Similarly, communities in the mountains, those which were underdeveloped, or those far from large cities were more egalitarian and less subject to influxes of stigmatized social groups which would have been attracted to the Party in the early stages. Finally, villages which never experienced collectivization (the mountains) or those villages which underwent collectivization in later phases had simply more time to adjust to new conditions, and the State more time to attract and recruit competent locally born cadres (Romanian Research Group 1977).

Feldioara Today: Demographic, Economic and Social Transformation

We can isolate four principal factors which have structured the relations between Feldioara and the planners. These include:

1) the demographic consequences of the prolonged "War years" experienced by the Saxons;
2) the political restructuring brought about by class struggle and collectivization;
3) the village's regional importance in the Brașov zone and the consequent in-migration of worker families pursuing industrial jobs;
4) the exodus from agricultural work to industrial employment among the local population.

To designate these as "local" factors would be somewhat deceptive. More accurately, these conditions are a local reflection of Romania's general political and economic transformations. While the local arena is the setting where they are manifested, their ultimate cause lies outside the community itself. Factors 1) and 2) have been covered in the historical account. Hence, the rest of this chapter will focus on factors 3) and 4), examining them in the context of Feldioara's current demographic, economic and social situation.

Demographic growth and replacement. Though hardly a boom town, Feldioara is one of the few villages in Romania that can boast a growth rate of 50% since 1945 (see Table 12, next page). The net increase of 1,200 persons is all the more striking in light of the national statistics, which show an absolute decline in the rural population (*Anuarul Statistic* 1977:45).

When we examine Feldioara's population *composition*, however, the change becomes even more radical. Table 12 shows that the number of ethnic Germans in Feldioara has declined from a prewar high of 1,100 to well under 400 today. The emigrating Saxons are being replaced by Romanian, Magyar, and Gypsy in-migrants. The demographic situation in Feldioara reveals a combination of population *growth* and population *replacement*. The actual number of in-migrants is much greater than would appear if only aggregate statistics were used. Moreover, the emigration from Feldioara has left behind an increasingly aging Saxon population (see Table 13). All indications point to a continuing Saxon decline.

The combination of Saxon emigration and the sustained in-migration has made locally born Feldioarans a minority in their own village. As Table 14 (see page 162) indicates, the first wave of migrants came immediately after the war. These included: (1) refugees from Moldova and Bessarabia who found work in Brașov's factories and (2) pastoralists

TABLE 12

POPULATION GROWTH IN FELDIOARA, 1832-1977

Year	Total	Of Which: Saxons	Source
1832	1560		
1838	1953	895	Census records for Kronstadt
1849	1816	800	District (National Archives
1850	2048		Brasov).
1857[a]	1926	900	
1857[b]	1883	836	Religious census (National
			Archives, Brasov).
1869	1898	836	Wachner 1934: 231-32
1880	2021	933	Podea 1938:179
1890	2212	983	Wachner 1934:231-32
1900[a]	2527	1032	Jekelius, 1929:361
1900[b]	2479		*Podea* 1938:179
1910	2486	993	Wachner 1934:231-32
1919	2491	997	Podea 1938:179
1930[a]	2505	1052	Jekelius 1929:361
1930[b]	2505	1014	Wachner 1934:231-32
1945	2242		Village archives, Feldioara
1956	2826	850	Institut Proiect-Brasov 1974
1966[a]	2798	600 (?)	Osaci et al. 1968:33
1966[b]	3143		Institut Proiect-Brasov 1970
1970	2821		Institut Proiect-Brasov 1974
1972	2950		Institut Proiect-Brasov 1974
1974	3040	543	Registru Agricol (street list), Feldioara
1975	3305	520	Institut Proiect-Brasov 1975b
1977	3455	500	Official census records, Feldioara (unofficial: 4000)
1980 proj.	5140	450(?)	Institut Proiect-Brasov 1975b
1990 proj.	6200-7000	?	Institut Proiect-Brasov 1975b

TABLE 13

AGE STRUCTURES OF ETHNIC GROUPS IN FELDIOARA (1975)

	Age Group		
	0-16	17-59	60+
Feldioara (N = 3103)	23.6%	60.7%	15.7%
Of Which: Non-Saxons[1] (N = 2258)	24.1%	62.1%	13.8%
Saxons only (N = 543)	21.1%	54.3%	24.6%

1. Includes ethnic Romanians and a small minority (15%) of Magyars and Gypsies.
Source: Local census data.

from the Bran highlands who had been brought in to take over Saxons' farms (while Saxons were in Soviet labor camps). The continued industrialization of the area around Brașov City has brough a second wave of in-migrants to Feldioara. The brick factory at Colonia Reconstrucția provides 600 workplaces. Migrants have also come to work in Feldioara's State farm (125 workplaces), the Machine Tractor Station (30), the intercooperative pig raising complex (35), the railroad siding (25) and the new construction site (200, varying seasonally). At present, the principal magnet for migrants is the newly opened minerals extraction plant, whose projected labor force will exceed 1,000. While an increasing number of local youth are renouncing their jobs in Brașov to work at the minerals plant, most workers have been recruited from other areas of Romania (Moldova, Oradea). These workers, technicians and engineers have begun to settle in Feldioara as *permanent in-migrants*.

In addition to those working in local enterprises, Feldioara's proximity to Brașov has transformed it into a staging-area for hundreds of *temporary in-migrants* hoping to find housing in the city. For these families, living in Feldioara is part of a long-term migrant strategy. Expecting to leave within a few months or years, many show little concern for the community or its future.

TABLE 14

IN-MIGRATION INTO FELDIOARA BY YEAR AND LOCALITY OF ORIGIN
(Adults only, 1976)

Community of Origin	Category	Total	Year of in-migration into Feldioara										Year unknown
			1975-76	70-74	65-69	60-64	55-59	50-54	45-49	40-44	35-39	before 35	
25 km radius[1]	Males	73	10	14	7	7	13	6	8	1	1	4	2
	Females	101	14	10	11	11	17	6	9	3	8	4	8
	Totals	174	24	24	18	18	30	12	17	4	9	8	10
26-50 km radius[2]	Males	44	–	3	7	4	2	2	25	–	–	–	1
	Females	59	–	5	6	6	6	4	29	–	–	–	3
	Totals	103	–	8	13	10	8	6	54	–	–	–	4
beyond 50 km radius	Males	136	28	21	14	20	10	6	10	14	4	2	7
	Females	123	21	18	15	22	11	6	8	10	2	3	7
	Totals	259	49	39	29	42	21	12	18	24	6	5	14
origin unknown, but probably over 50 km	Males	159	91	28	6	2	1	–	–	–	–	–	31
	Females	144	77	21	4	2	2	–	–	1	1	–	36
	Totals	303	168	49	10	4	3	–	–	1	1	–	67

ALL MIGRANTS (adults only)												
Males	412	129	66	34	33	26	14	43	15	5	6	41
Females	427	112	54	36	41	36	16	46	14	11	7	54
Totals	839	241	120	70	74	62	30	89	29	16	13	95
Households where *both* spouses are in-migrants												
TOTAL	223	70	42	21	19	10	6	16	6	2	1	30

Note: Due to the higher number of transients, the actual number of in-migrants are probably higher than those listed here. Data come from the author's interviews with key informants.

1 Includes all those communities in the northern part of Brasov County plus those lying east of Feldioara along the Olt River, in Covasna County (27 villages, 1 town, and Brasov City).

2 Includes all remaining communities in Brasov County plus areas in Covasna and Buzau to the east.

The same is true of the *transient in-migrants,* who are seasonal agricultural or construction workers. Despite their considerable numbers (300-400 during summer), the transients play no active role in the community and are neither expected nor asked to do so.

Feldioara's population growth, demographic replacement and various categories of in-migrants all make it difficult to achieve an adequate amount of community integration. As will be shown later, this has direct implications for citizen participation.

From agricultural to worker village. From a peasant community with small industry and crafts, Feldioara has evolved into a worker village. It has acquired its own industrial workplaces and become a dormitory settlement for nearly 1,000 residents who commute daily to Brașov City. Feldioara's agricultural work force has dropped from 70% in 1910 to 42% in 1968 to some 20-25% today (depending on seasonal demands). Within the agricultural sector itself, there are fewer collective farmers and more and more wage laborers and specialists. The latter two groups are employed on the collective farm, the State farm unit (which raises livestock), the pig-raising complex (presently housing over 30,000 pigs) and the Machine Tractor Sector (see Table 15, p. 166).

The existence of so many worker households in Feldioara is partly a reflection of the attraction of wage-labor, which gives villagers more stable incomes, pension and sick leave payments than agriculture. However, the high number of commuting workers in Feldioara is also attributable to state legal restrictions on outmigration from suburban villages into large cities. Since Feldioara lies less than 30 km. from Brașov City, villagers may move there only if they marry a Brașov resident or inherit a house there. For hundreds of Feldioarans, then, the village is their place of residence but not their place of work.

Feldioara not only sends commuters but receives them as well. Teachers, engineers, clerical staff and technicians come daily from Brașov City. Their conspicuous absence after working hours leaves a serious gap in community cultural life, a subject of frequent comment by journalists. Besides intellectual and skilled workers, about 250 employees from Feldioara's minerals plant commute directly from Brașov to the factory. Except for a pause in the local cafe, they are basically strangers to the village itself.

Feldioara's pre-existing level of development and new industrial opportunities have given the village one of the highest living standards in rural Romania. With 40 enterprises or services, it contains twice the average for a village of similar size. These include a general store, vegetable shop, butcher shop, bakery, pastry shop, two cafes, a hardware store, a clothing/textile shop, book store, furniture outlet and services offered by the local consumers' cooperative—tailor, seamstress, shoemakers, barbers, beauticians, photographers, bricklayers, electricians, radio-TV repair, watchmaker and the like.

Public services include a local savings bank, the main offices of the regional credit union, post and telegraph office, pharmacy, lottery office and fuel deposit. There are three physicians and two dentists serving the commune population of 6,000. Child care facilities include a day care center for women working on the collective farm and two kindergartens (in Romanian and German, respectively). There is an elementary school now running in two shifts (also with dual language classes), and a high school which has recently been re-profiled for training in chemistry and natural sciences. About thirty pupils from surrounding villages board in Feldioara in order to attend the high school, which is the only village-located high school in Braşov County.

The large number and variety of shops, the high school, the credit union, the machine tractor station and frequent rail and bus links all give Feldioara central place functions for villages to the north, east and west. Up until 1977, Feldioara also held the central office for the regional consumers' cooperative, but this has since been reorganized in smaller, commune-wide units.

The increase in living standards is reflected in the new houses being constructed and the purchases of consumer goods (see Table 16). Most now houses have gas ranges (using bottled gas), garages, bathrooms and, in a few cases, central heating units. However, the large Saxon houses in the village center have remained unmodernized and fallen into disrepair. Their owners—many of whom are elderly or waiting for emigration permits—care little about improving their properties, especially in view of possible demolition in the future.

Summary and Recapitulation: "Organized Flow" in Feldioara

Adapting a concept used by Watson (1970), Joan Vincent (1977) has suggested that agrarian society be analyzed within a framework of "organized

TABLE 15

WORK PLACES IN FELDIOARA (1975)

SECTOR Work Place	ORIGIN OF EMPLOYEE				
	From Feldioara	incoming commuters	temporary migrants ("flotanti")	total "permanent" employees	additional seasonal employees
AGRICULTURE					
1. Collective Farm	168	3	80	251	280
2. State Farm	118	43	20	181	50
3. Machine Tractor Station	26	10	—	36	—
4. Intercooperative Pig Raising Complex	20	20	58	98	—
Total Agricultural Work Places	332	76	158	566	330
INDUSTRY-CONSTRUCTION					
5. Minerals Factory	22	75	646	704	—
6. Support Maintenance Unit	26	35	55	116	—
7. Food Processing (regional bakery)	8	1	—	9	—
TRANSPORT-TELECOMMUNICATIONS					
8. Factory Trucking Unit	32	36	—	68	—
9. Road Maintenance Station	12	5	—	17	—
10. Railroad Station	20	3	—	23	—
11. Feldioara Post Office (incl. telephone)	20	3	—	23	—
12. Electricity	12	7	—	19	—
COMMERCE					
13. Consumers Cooperative (retail stores, services, fuel)	75	42	—	117	—
HEALTH					
14. Polyclinic	22	2	—	24	—
EDUCATION					
15. Nursery, Kindergarten, 2 Schools	55	23	—	78	—
ADMINISTRATION, MISC.					
16. Town Hall, Fire, Police, etc.	30	—	—	30	—
Total Non-agr. Work Places	342	229	701	1,226	—
TOTAL WORK PLACES IN FELDIOARA	674	305	859	1,792	330

Source: Institut Proiect-Brasov, *Schiţa de Sistematizare Com. Feldioara,* August 26, 1975, p. 70.

TABLE 16

SOME INDICES OF RISE IN LIVING STANDARDS IN FELDIOARA
1967-1977

	1967	1970	1977
1. No. of houses built since 1945	370		
Of which: owned by memers of			
collective farm	198		
2. No. of indoor baths	86		
3. No. of TVs	250	450	950
4. No. of Telephones	4	57	185
5. No. of Automobiles	7	25	75
6. Total households	800	950	1185

Sources: Osaci et al., *Monografia Comunei Feldioara*, 1968. Village statistics for 1970, 1977.

flow." Vincent asserts that anthropologists should use the community study method to discover the "activity fields" of the residents. She criticizes the one-sidedness of "peasant studies" which focus on man-land relations, thus excluding groups such as women, youth, artisans, traders and middlemen, for whom the boundaries of the village may be relatively unimportant. Following Watson's conclusions from New Guinea, Vincent suggests that migration flows are essential for maintaining the seemingly stable structure of rural communities.

Vincent's framework can be profitably applied to Feldioara, where social, demographic, economic and political changes have created numerous social categories. These categories have both overlapping and contradictory interests with each other, related to the degree to which they move into and out of the village. In the following scheme, Feldioara is broken down into the elements of its "flow" using criteria of class, ethnicity and natal origin. The social categories reflect the complexity of the village:

I. Class/Occupation Categories
  A. Locally
    1. Collective farm peasants
    2. Salaried farm and industrial employees
    3. Clerical and service workers
    4. Administrative-Party leaders, professionals
    5. Temporary unskilled workers, migrant workers
    6. Non-salaried household workers, i.e., housewives, pensioners, private peasants
  B. Commuting to Brașov
    1. Industrial workers
    2. Clerical and service workers
  C. Commuting from Brașov to Feldioara
    1. Professionals (teachers, engineers, specialists)
    2. Skilled and clerical workers
    3. Industrial workers brought directly to the factory

II. Ethnic Groups
  A. Romanians (demographic majority, increasing)
  B. Saxons (declining, emigrating, intermarrying with Romanians)
  C. Maygars (increasing via in-migration)
  D. Gypsies (slightly increasing)

III. In-migrant Flows
  A. "Colonists" brought in after the war
  B. Permanent in-migrants employed locally (at the new factory)
  C. Temporary in-migrant families who commute to Brașov waiting to move there or elsewhere
  D. Transients, i.e., seasonal in-migrants in construction or farm labor
  E. Local youth returning or re-assigned to the village after schooling, training, army service
  F. In-marrying spouses

IV. Out-migrant Flows
  A. Local youth out-migrating permanently or temporarily for school, work, army service
  B. Saxons emigrating permanently to West Germany
  C. Out-marrying spouses

V. Commuting Flows
  A. Local workers who commute to Brașov

      B. Temporary in-migrants who commute to Braşov (IIIc)

      C. Professionals, skilled, clerical workers commuting from Braşov

VI. Household Status

      A. Purely agricultural (both spouses members of collective farm)

      B. Mixed (one spouse in collective farm, one in industry, children in school, industry)

      C. Purely proletariat (both spouses salaried workers)

      D. Professional, administrative, "prestige" households

      E. Self-employed craftsmen

Members of some of these social categories (those in which natal origin, resident and workplace overlap) have intense interactions within the community arena (the circle represented in Figure 2, next page). Other groups are tied to the village in a more tenuous fashion: their kin, workplaces, natal homes or future homes lie outside Feldioara. Figure 2 is a schematic representation of the dynamics of organized flow in Feldioara.

Within the "flow" of village life, there are two relatively homogeneous groups. The largest of these are the industrial commuters to Braşov. The vast majority are males, and they are of all ethnic groups. Most will be required to live in Feldioara because they cannot obtain a residence permit for Braşov City. Some will be able to move to Braşov by marrying someone from that city, moving in with a relative, or obtaining a permit for "special motives" or illegally. Other commuters will be content to remain in Feldioara after having weighed the inconveniences of commuting with the benefits of having parents, kinsmen and friends next door, the possibility to own one's own house, and (in view of Romania's chronic food shortages) to have one's own garden plot and animals.

The second relatively homogeneous group are the emigrating Saxons. Judging from the disproportionately high number of elderly persons in the Saxon population (24.6% over 60 years of age, vs. 13.8% for non-Saxons, see Table 13, p. 161), it is the younger, able-bodied Saxons who are emigrating. Saxon emigration does not go unnoticed among the members of Feldioara's other ethnic groups: upon receiving emigration permission Saxon houses and possessions go up for sale. Even after emigrating to West Germany, many Saxons return to Feldioara for summer visits. Saxon emigration has two serious consequences: first, maintenance of Saxon ethnic identity is made more difficult as their number declines; second, it

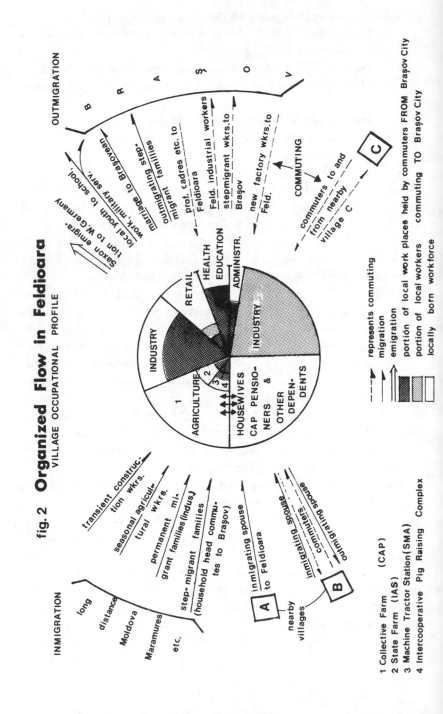

fig. 2 **Organized Flow in Feldioara**
VILLAGE OCCUPATIONAL PROFILE

OUTMIGRATION

B R A Ş O V

Saxon emigration to W. Germany

local youth to school, work, military serv.

marriage to Braşoven

outmigrating families

migrant families

prof. cadres etc. to Feldioara

Feld. industrial workers

stepmigrant wkrs. to Braşov

new factory wkrs. to Feld.

COMMUTING

commuters to and from nearby village C

C

RETAIL
HEALTH
EDUCATION
ADMINISTR.

INDUSTRY
INDUSTRY
AGRICULTURE

HOUSEWIVES
CAP PENSIO-
NERS &
OTHER DEPEN-
DENTS

2
3
4
1

INMIGRATION

long distance
Moldova
Maramureş
etc.

transient construc-
tion wkrs.

seasonal agricul-
tural wkrs.

permanent mi-
grant families (indus.)

step-migrant families
(household head commu-
tes to Braşov)

inmigrating spouse
to Feldioara

A

nearby
villages

inmigrating spouse

commuters

outmigrating spouse

B

represents commuting
migration
emigration

portion of local work places held by commuters FROM Braşov City
portion of local workers commuting TO Braşov City
locally born workforce

1 Collective Farm (CAP)
2 State Farm (IAS)
3 Machine Tractor Station (SMA)
4 Intercooperative Pig Raising Complex

becomes more difficult for Feldioarans as a group to maintain some kind of community solidarity vis-a-vis the new immigrants.

Within the social arena of Feldioara, the sharpest distinction is made not betweeen classes or ethnic groups, but between those who are local (*bastinaşi, localnici*) and those who are "outsiders" (*straini*) or "newcomers" (*venetici*). This distinction permeates the entire spectrum of social relations and daily interactions in Feldioara (Sampson 1976). Thus, locally-born Feldioarans insist that "our collective farmers work harder than the migrant farm workers," that "a locally born leader treats people better than an outsider," that Feldioarans are "civilized" while the newcomers are "uncivilized."

Local Feldioarans tend to classify (or denigrate) the newcomer group as a whole; however, as the organized flow diagram indicates, the inmigrant group itself is extremely heterogenous. Seasonal migrants, for example, are stigmatized both because of the nature of their work and their origins from the province of Moldova. In contrast to the transient or temporary migrants many of the permanent migrants are trained specialists who have been assigned to Feldioara as technicians, engineers, teachers or political-administrative leaders. Despite their educational level, they rank lower on the social prestige scale than locally born villagers. Those migrants who have come to Feldioara with their spouses and children have a better chance to establish multiplex social relations than those who have come alone. For the unmarried construction workers (already stigmatized as irresponsible) there is little to do but spend evening hours among themselves, either at the local bar or in their dormitory rooms. A similar type of social isolation exists for migrant couples, especially where both spouses commute to Braşov City. The best situation is found among those inmigrants who arrive as individuals and marry into local families. However, this has occurred on only few occasions.

The various "flows" into and out of Feldioara structure the ways in which each group copes with social changes in the community, be they spontaneous or consciously planned. For example, one can expect that soon-to-emigrate Saxons, temporary and transient migrants will be relatively apathetic about community efforts in connection with Feldioara's urbanization. One could also expect a disharmony of interest among local villagers who seek to maintain household agricultural production and migrant industrial workers whose interests are tied to increasing consumer goods. The fluctuation in leading posts and predominance of nonlocal elites mean that local leaders may become mis-informed, ill-prepared or mistrusted in their tasks, at least during their initial adjustment period in the village. For the temporary migrants, their interests in the community's improvement will last only until they have achieved transfer or promotion to Brașov City or another large town. Hence, the social structure of the village has direct ramifications for how the community will react to the plan, and the degree to which various social groups will help to implement it.

Organized flow into and out of Feldioara is more than just local demographic movement. It is a concrete expression of the way wider social and economic forces act on the community, household and individual levels. Changes in birth, death or migration rates can be considered only in their social-historical context. In the case of Feldioara, this context includes the political changes of the post-War period, ethnic re-organization, collectivization of agriculture, and the industrial opportunities available locally and in Brașov's factories. As a result, the community of Feldioara has lost much of its corporate character. It is now a social arena where the divergent interests of numerous social categories—classes, ethnic groups, locals and outsiders—now play themselves out.

The emergence of Feldioara as a developed worker village gave it distinct advantages over other settlements in the competition for urban status. However, it has also resulted in tension between diverse types of households, social groups and between local citizens and a foreign leadership cadre.

It would be inaccurate to assert that local factors simply "confront" the national or regional-level factors in the planning process. Instead, local factors in Feldioara "work themselves out" partly though over social conflict, factionalism and tension, but also via integration, assimilation and pure entropy. If some of the changes in the community have little in common with the stated desires of the planners, this is but further evidence of local social forces with which planners must ultimately come to terms. Putting the existing social conditions in Feldioara into the "organized flow" framework has helped to reveal the potential contradictions between supralocal constraints and the local social organization. The next chapter examines the implications of these local social factors on planning activities in Feldioara.

CHAPTER VII

THE PLANNING PROCESS IN FELDIOARA

Chronology of Planning Decisions 1970-1979

This chapter begins by tracing the history of planning decisions concerning Feldioara's urbanization. This is followed by a discussion of planner-village interactions and an analysis of the plan itself. Data for this historical reconstruction derive from four sources: 1) plans and documents made available to me by Feldioara's People's Council, the Brașov County People's Council and the County Planning Institute; 2) newspaper accounts published in *Drum Nou* (organ of the Brașov County People's Council and County Party Committee); 3) supplementary interviews with villagers, local officials and planners; and 4) participant-observation at local meetings and in County Planning Offices. Although each of these four data sources is subject to misinterpretation or misuse, the varied data base can serve to fill some of the gaps left by unavailable sources, incomplete files or blurred memories.

The earliest available document concerning Feldioara's future urbanization was prepared in 1970 (Institut Proiect-Brașov 1970). This *Studiu de Sistematizare* noted Feldioara's industrial, agrarian, dormitory and administrative/central place functions and proposed a population increase from an existing 2,700 to 3,400 by 1980 and 4,000 by 1985. (These projections were already exceeded by 1977, when the census revealed an offical village population of 3,455, and an additional 400-500 uncounted residents.)

173

The study also proposed that 365 apartments be built, half of which were to be completed by 1975.

On the basis of the 1970 *Studiu*, Feldioara was officially proposed to become one of Brașov County's seven new towns. This decision was soon followed by the first and only public meeting between planners and citizens, in 1971. I was told by citizens and local officials that over 300 persons attended, virtually filling the seats in the village assembly hall. At this meeting, for which there is not a single archive and of which memories are understandably blurred, the Brașov planners presented the villagers with a myriad of charts, graphs and statistics. The assembled audience contributed numerous questions and comments. Some of these reflected personal worries about future demolitions; others were concerned with obtaining more retail and service establishments for the village. Though several problems were undoubtedly raised, the meeting resulted in no major changes. The plan for Feldioara was approved.

At this time, hundreds of migrant workers were being brought into Feldioara to construct the minerals factory and its adjoining railroad siding. Most were housed in "temporary" barracks or in newly constructed apartments at the edge of the village. It is apparent that the ministerial decision to build the factory overrode any local reservations about accepting it. Although Feldioara's plan was being debated by the villagers, the factory was being built anyway. One could conclude that the debate centered not so much on whether to build the factory, but how the village should adapt to this *fait accompli*.

In 1973 the first completely detailed *Schiţa de Sistematizare* was prepared by the Brașov County Planning Institute (Institut Proiect-Brașov 1973). According to the usual procedures, the plan was formulated in two separate variants. Each variant was in turn elaborated in both an initial (1974-1980) and a long term (1980-1990) stage. Drafted down to the most minute details, each variant included designs of a projected "civic center" for Feldioara for the year 1990. Variant I was estimated to cost 32.5 lei ($2.5 million) and Variant II 30.1 lei ($2.3 million).

The proposals were very much the same, except for two essential differences. First, apartments in Variant I would be built on the site of existing housing, thus necessitating the immediate demolition of about 20 houses, with additional demolitions at a later time. In contrast, housing construction for Variant II would be carried out on empty lands. Second,

Variant I would introduce more new services (e.g. clinic, bank, school) in the initial five years of the plan, while Variant II left most of these to the post-1980 or even post-1990 stage.

In April 1974, planners and officials from Braşov came to Feldioara to confer with the Executive Committee of the Comune People's Council and heads of local economic enterprises (altogether about ten people). Throughout 1974 the plan was further reviewed and refined. In November, as the Systematization Law was being enacted, planners and Party representatives from Braşov again returned to Feldioara. The delegation was led by the President of the County People's Council and First Secretary of the County Party Committee, Mr. Virgil Trofin (Mr. Trofin subsequently held several ministerial positions in Bucharest being discharged and expelled from the Party's Central Committee in 1981). The purpose of the meeting was to examine the ways in which the new law would affect the proposed plan.

Mr. Trofin proposed that Variant II be revised in accordance with the Law's strict zoning regulations to prevent sprawl. He proposed a new "Variant III" which would add 200 apartments in the first five years; this would entail the early demolition of 22 houses (46 families or 150 persons). An additional 1040 apartments would be constructed in the 1980-1990 stage, with only two additional houses being demolished. There would be a total of 69 apartment blocks, and space would be set aside for 14 two-family duplexes (*duplexuri*) which could be built privately. The apartments would vary in quality and in the number of rooms, so as to take account of diverse economic levels and family sizes. (The quality levels, called *confort* 1, 2, and 3, refer to fringe items such as the number of tiles in the bathroom, kitchen specifications, etc. The average size of the apartments is $30m^2$. Since official guidelines specify $10m^2$ living space per person, it appears that these would be technically legal only for those families with one child.) Variant III would entail building a new school, kindergarten, hotel and sports area; the present town hall would be moved into the old school building and replaced with a historical-ethnographic museum.

While Variant III was being worked out in more detail, the old Variant I was similarly upgraded. The second phase of the plan was prolonged from 1980-1990 to 1980-2000, thus making the plan more ambitious. Instead of the initial 180 apartments, the second phase now projected 820 to be built.

During the meeting in which he proposed Variant III, County Party Secretary Trofin made several other urgent recommendations. These included speeding up construction of the new factory, recruiting local workers rather than in-migrants (who required housing), improving the efficiency of infrastructural investments, assuring that apartments are put as close to the village center as possible, suggesting the building of a local slaughterhouse and proposing that light industry be established to utilize the surplus female labor force which would enter Feldioara with their husbands.

In December 1974, eight members of Feldioara's Systematization Commission met with planners in Brașov to bring up certain requests with regard to the plan. They sought assurances that the forthcoming apartments would be differentiated so as not to become monotonous six-story blocks; they also requested a new veterinary dispensary for local livestock and that a "sports complex" rather than simply a playing field be built in the village's recreational zone. The placement of certain buildings was also discussed and slightly revised. The meeting ended with the plan for Feldioara's "civic center" being approved; however, the record shows that two votes were cast against the plan proposal, a rarity in Romanian political life, where voting is almost always unanimous.

Throughout 1975, planners visited Feldioara for further inspections and consultations, most of which concerned the factory, the railroad siding and apartment construction. In August 1975 a newly revised, 90-page planning dossier was completed (Institut Proiect-Brașov 1975b). Two variants were still present—but they were Variant I and Mr. Trofin's proposed Variant III. The principal differences again lay in the 1980-1990 phase, specifically in the question of how many workers for the new minerals would be recruited locally and how many would be in-migrants. An in-migrant work force meant that more new housing would have to be built. According to the plan, the factory's labor force would eventually reach 1,000 workers; these would be composed of 100 from Feldioara, 200 commuters from Brașov City, 250 unmarried migrants and 350 migrants with families. The wives of migrants would be prime candidates for jobs in the aforementioned light industry. The prognosis was that after 1980 an additional 100 Feldioarans would relinquish their jobs in Brașov and take up employment at the factory. (In fact, this number was surpassed by early 1978).

According to the new planning dossier, the number of apartments to be built would now increase in the initial phase and social services would be extended. The existing headquarters of the State farm would be converted into a home for pensioners, and the commercial complex would be greatly enlarged. The two variants still differed with respect the placement of apartments, however; Variant I would build on the existing housing stock, thus necessitating more demolitions than Variant II.

In October 1975 County planners against visited Feldioara to meet local representatives. Pressure was building to finalize the plan, as Romania's forthcoming Five Year Plan was to take effect in January 1976. Despite the obvious importance of this meeting, local representatives received only one day's notice. Seven local leaders attended: mayor, vice-mayor, factory director, heads of agricultural and consumers cooperatives, the local trade union leader and the high school vice-principal. These individuals met with County planners for two hours, discussing various aspects of the urbanization scheme for Feldioara. The locals asked for a large bakery so as to end their dependence on bread delivered from Brașov. They also requested a modernized dairy complex for bottling and sale of milk and repeated their plea for a local slaughterhouse first suggested by County Party Secretary Trofin a year earlier. Brașov officials took note of these requests, only to reject them a month later as unworkable. Their rationale was that provisioning Feldioara would decrease the productive efficiency of Brașov's enterprises. Feldioara may have been preferred to other villages, but it would have to remain subordinate to Brașov in the competition for resources, factory capacity and the like.

The fate of Feldioara's high school was also discussed at the meeting but left undetermined. Rumors had been circulating that the high school would be converted into an agricultural or trade school or phased out altogether. This was causing considerable anxiety among teachers, parents and aspiring university students. The high school's 12th grade had already been eliminated, and from September 1976, both 11th and 12th graders would have to attend school in Brașov if they wanted to obtain their baccalaureate, which is required for university admission. It was understood that these grades would soon be restored to Feldioara and the high school re-organized to train students for the chemical industry, in conjunction with the new factory. This re-organization has not occurred, and it appears that Feldioara has irrevocably lost its high school. Parents of high-school students must now face the difficulties of finding housing for their children in Brașov—in a dormitory, with relatives, or in a rented room—or having their children commute each day to the city. In the sphere of education, the aspiring new town of Feldioara remains subordinate to the requirements of the county and the Education Ministry's rationalization of schools.

During 1975 alone, the systematization plan for Feldioara was altered three times. In December 1975 the latest, "final" version of the plan was debated and approved by a joint meeting of the Commune People's Council and Commune Party Committee (most of whose members overlap). This meeting was part of a nation-wide campaign in which all localities were required to debate and endorse their local 1976-1980 Five Year Plans. Although *Drum Nou* referred to several mass meetings being held around Brașov County, the session at Feldioara was confined to about 35 people: deputies of the People's Council, members of the Commune Party Committee, heads of key institutions and invited guests. Among these guests were First Secretary Trofin and seven planning officials who arrived with sketches, charts and prepared speeches about Feldioara's urbanization.

At this meeting the revised Variant I and Mr. Trofin's Variant III were presented as the two alternatives. In essence, the two variants were joined for the initial period and retained as options for the post-1980 phase. According to this revised scheme, the expansion of the factory's work force would require 280 new apartments by 1980 and another 540 in the 1980-1990 phase. By the year 2000 there would be 1,600 apartments and ten privately built duplexes. New services would include an enlarged school building, nursery, kindergarten, dormitory for unmarried workers, hotel, restaurant, retail complex and a sports area. The new apartments and stores would form a second civic center just behind the existing one.

This particular meeting lasted over three hours. During the "debate" phase, the factory head requested immediate housing and services for the increasing number of in-migrating workers, hundreds of whom were being housed in Brașov and driven to Feldioara daily. Community leaders—supported by First Secretary Trofin—countered by asking the factory for additional financial support and labor allocations to aid the local building effort. It was a clear case of conflict between the enterprise and the locality, each one claiming to be providing resources for which the other was benefiting uduly (cf. Taubman 1973 for similar instances in the USSR). At a deeper level, it is also a conflict between local needs and State priorities, since the factory is controlled not by Feldioara but by the Construction Ministry in Bucharest.

Mr. Trofin brought up the idea of a vinegar distillery to employ surplus female labor, while from the floor there came renewed requests for a slaughterhouse and for a lavender-processing unit to be built in conjunction with the collective farm. A County agricultural official complained bitterly about the lack of apartments for in-migrant tractorists at Feldioara's machine tractor station, scolding local leaders for not offering these young men local accommodations. There was heated debate about about low productivity on the collective farm and whether the cause was bad weather conditions or poor organization. Mr. Trofin had no hesitation in asserting that poor organization was to blame for Feldioara not having finished its culture house and having fallen behind in its plan to construct 120 apartments by 1976. The mayor's earlier complaints about the factory were rationalizations for poor mobilization on his part.

A dominant topic of discussion at the meeting was the placement of new construction and the extent of projected demolitions. Planners reiterated that "a few barns" would have to be torn down in the first years of the plan, but that further demolitions would be delayed until after 1980. It was also agreed that the central park running down Feldioara's main street would be left untouched and that the new recreation area would be located far enough from the Saxon church so as not to disturb its religious ambiance.

Having criticized Feldioara as a whole and mediated between the local administration and the factory leaders, Mr. Trofin adjourned the meeting, imploring local officials to "take all the necessary organizational measures so that Feldioara would *merit* the distinction of becoming a town." To be selected for urbanization was not just an administrative decision, but a *reward*. It was something the villagers must work for.

In the weeks after this final meeting, two more follow-up consultations were held between county officials and members of the local Systematization Commission. In ironing out further details, the collective farm's zootechnic engineer asked for additional apartments to be built for in-migrant workers in that section. Because their work required a 7-day work week, they needed to be relatively close to the stalls. The vinegar distillery formerly proposed by Mr. Trofin would be approved pending agreement on transport arrangements for trucking in raw materials and machinery. When the construction of the minerals factory had been completed, some of the construction workshops would become the site of the projected distillery. Records for the two meetings state no other suggestions.

On January 15, 1976, Feldioara's systematization plan for 1976-1980 was unanimously approved by the local People's Council and passed upward to the County level. Three days later the Braşov County People's Council unanimously approved the plans for all nine towns and 43 communes (150 villages), including the three future towns. With this declaration, the role of local and regional bodies in formulating Feldioara's plan officially ended. The plan was now passed upward to the State for possible alterations, approval and eventual measures of implementation.

In May 1976 a 10-page "planning summary" was prepared by one of the architects responsible for Feldioara (Institut Proiect-Braşov 1976b). Basically a statistical profile, the summary detailed the projected rise in Feldioara's population, decline in agricultural work force (owing to a reduction in the number of part-time female collective farmers) and a decrease in the number of incoming and outgoing commuters. The report noted the planned increase in agricultural production, the building of 240 apartments by 1980 and 200 more by 1990 (an unexplained drop from previous estimates) and the addition of new services. These included 16 new classrooms, a kindergarten, nursery, pensioners' home, hotel, sports area, retail center, TV repair outlet, auto repair shop, new cafe, restaurant, expanded culture house, cinema and administrative building. Though local representatives had requested that the school, vinegar distillery, sports complex and retail outlets be added in the early phase of the plan, the summary report reaffirmed the decision to delay these improvements until the post-1980 phase.

The plan appeared to have been finally worked out, but the earthquake of March 1977 soon led to further alterations. The earthquake damage necessitated large-scale efforts to rebuild apartments, factories and public buildings. Although only Romania's southeastern region had been affected, these rebuilding efforts spurred President Ceauşescu to call for revamping plans for all of Romania's cities and prospective new towns. During August 1977 President Ceauşescu visited Braşov. He severely criticized plans for the new towns (and for the city itself), upbraiding the planners for their lack of imagination. Rather than creating new, socialist towns, planners had carried out only piecemeal extensions of villages. The plans would have to be enlarged and qualitatively transformed so as to truly reflect the socialist transformation of the countryside.

Having worked and revised the same planning models for over five years, County planners were surprised by Mr. Ceauşescu's sudden rejection of their work. Some planners expressed sympathy with his remarks but his call for total revision meant that they would not be able to devote time to the existing problems of systematization in the countryside. One of these problems was that rural dwellers were constructing one-story houses instead of two stories, and building them outside the authorized building zones. The County Systematization Office had provided 42 different house-designs free of charge, but peasants were refusing or neglecting to utilize these models, either because of their increased costs or lack of sufficient building materials. Another problem that became known to County planners in 1977 was the reluctance of urban professionals assigned to rural localities to actually go and live in the villages in which they worked. Teachers, technicians, engineers and factory managers were retaining their urban apartments, hoping to be transferred out of rural assignments; many felt living in a village would mean a decline in living standard for themselves and their families. Improved transport links and availability of private cars made urban-rural commuting even more attractive.

The reluctance of rural specialists to leave Braşov City led to some embarrassing newspaper "raids" in Feldioara. In one instance, the collective farm's agricultural engineer was discovered arriving to work on the 9:00 A.M. train from Braşov, while peasants had already been in the fields for two hours. "Why didn't the engineer live in the village?" the article demanded (*Drum Nou*, August 10, 1977). In another example, the situation was revealed whereby a pharmacist's assistant from Feldioara commuted daily to her job in Braşov while her counterpart in Braşov commuted to the same type of job . . . in Feldioara! "Couldn't some type of arrangement be worked out," the article asked, "so that both parties would be spared the time-consuming trip between city and village?" (*Drum Nou*, August 14, 1977).

President Ceauşescu's demands to revise and upgrade the plans for Braşov County's new towns caused frantic activity in the County Planning

Institute. In a few weeks a new plan based on the more radical Variant I had been formulated. Under the new plan, the idea of preserving the traditional character of Feldioara's center was abandoned. The large Saxon dwellings lining the main street were now designated "irrational." They would be razed and replaced by rows of four-story apartment blocks. In the recast "civic center," the local town hall would be transformed into an "administrative complex" containing civil offices, Party headquarters, bank, credit union and offices of the collective farm and consumers cooperative. The building would be enlarged such that the main street would have to be rerouted aournd it. The new administration complex would became a symbol of socialist centralization, the physical expression of democratic (and bureaucratic) centralism in the rural community (cf. Sawers 1977 for a comparative analysis of Soviet and Chinese approaches to urban architecture).

Yet in a typical pattern of pervasive fluctuation, this plan, too, was altered before it could be implemented. As one planner explained, "the draftsman at the County Planning Institute had taken President Ceauşescu's remarks all too literally." Planners saw the need to upgrade the number of apartments and services, but they thought it unwise to demolish the large, sturdy houses lining Feldioara's main street. Here they were in agreement with local officials, who advocated converting some of the houses into apartments rather than demolishing them altogether.

By September 1977, some 60 apartments had been constructed, though 120 had been scheduled. The new culture house, planned for December 1976, was still unfinished, and the inadequate amount of voluntary labor was causing acute embarrassment for local officials. Social tensions rose to the surface when several villagers protested the placement of a proposed dormitory for young, unmarried construction workers. Residents felt that the workers would disturb this quiet atmosphere of the neighborhood with drinking and loud music; this was viewed as especially harmful to the young children.

On November 9, 1977 *Drum Nou* reported that a 3km water-main, 182 apartments and the dormitory for single workers were nearing completion in Feldioara. A few months later, however, local officials were publically reproached for the lack of services in the village. There was no textile workshop, no organized woodcutting services (for firewood) and no full-time auto mechanic (*Drum Nou*, February 3, 1978). The electrical repair shop was wholly inadequate to serve the large clientele, and the lone repairman commuted daily from Braşov. There were not enough shoemakers and other artisans, and most of these posts were occupied by commuters rather than local youth. The journalist demanded that Feldioara be able to provide its own work force and that it retain agricultural self-sufficiency as if it were an agrarian community instead of a worker village. This would be accomplished by encouraging all the citizens to deliver meat, milk and eggs to the local consumers' cooperative, by storing barns with hay instead of using them as garages, and by cultivating plots of land on the collective farm's *acord global* sharecropping system. In the Romanian conception, Feldioara's urbanization was not to transform the citizens from producers into consumers. By exhorting the citizens to be more self-sufficient, the State could hold food surplus from rural distribution channels and instead channel it to large cities or for export.

In their efforts to effectuate the new systematization scheme, planners and experts from Braşov visited Feldioara continually through 1978 and 1979. The five apartment blocks were completed, new tenants had moved in and construction of another five blocks has begun. Three houses, eight barns and eight gardens have now been expropriated. Feldioara's culture house was finally completed, three years behind the original schedule and two years beyond the "final" deadline set by the County Party Secretary. With the opening of the minerals extraction plant, Feldioara's population has grown to nearly 4000 persons. A tiny vegetable storefront has opened, and the local grocery store is now kept open round the clock, from 6 A.M. to 8 P.M.

Through 1979, County planners continued to react to national level inputs, causing further fluctuations in Feldioara's plan. During the summer of 1979, they received directives from Bucharest that Feldioara was to be "pushed" to be converted into a town by the end of the year. Rumors passed through the village that on August 23rd, the anniversary of Romania's 1944 armed uprising against the German army, Feldioara would be declared a town and be renamed "Petru Rareş City" after a famous Romanian prince who fought a bloody battle near Feldioara in 1529. August 23rd passed without a declaration or new naming ceremony. County officials now insisted that they did not know exactly when the declaration would take place. They maintained that it would in any case by by the end of 1980, at the conclusion of the existing five-year plan. However, this, too failed to occur.

By 1982, Feldiora had acquired more frequent bus service between the village and Brașov. Another 100 apartments had been built and a small grocery outlet existed in the ground floor of one of the apartment blocks. Those apartment dwellers who worked in the factory also benefited from regular meat rations given to all the workers. Other villagers chafed at this discrimination, since Feldioara's butcher was open only two days per week, and often had no meat at all. The village police station had moved into a house vacated by a Saxon leaving for West Germany. The old station was now the home of an electrical repair shop, though the repairman was still a commuter from Brașov City. The village had acquired a watchmaker, and a textile cooperative was now employing about a dozen wives of migrant workers. A third cafe was now in operation.

Nevertheless, Feldioara was not yet a town, but still "a village on the way to urbanization." In fact, not a single one of the 129 villages scheduled to be declared towns in 1980 had received "town" status. Romania's general economic retrenchment of the 1980s had led to limitations on new investments. Feldioara's "citification" seemed to be in a sort of holding pattern. Certain changes (planned and unplanned) had indeed occurred: the minerals plant was functioning, commuter links to Brașov had increased, and more workers had arrived in the village. Yet the stores had not grown appreciably with the population; they were more crowded and sold out of available goods more rapidly. Feldioara had also acquired a different social character. Many residents were strangers to each other, and people no longer exchanged greetings on the street as they had done just a few years before. The degree of lost rural "community" had not been compensated by urban services and social integration. For Feldioara, being a village *on the way* to urbanization had become a mixed blessing.

As for the final declaration of town status and eventual re-naming, a County official interviewed in 1982 now insisted that all 120 villages would be declared towns together at the end of the current five-year plan, in 1985. However, no one in Feldioara had any concrete information that this would be the case. If the evolution of planning activities in Feldioara is any indication, it appears that the villagers will be the last to find out exactly when the community is declared a town.

Feldioara's experience with the planners over the last ten years can be analyzed from two perspectives: one involves the interactions between planners and villagers during the period of the plan's formulation; the other perspective involves analyzing the structural and ideological foundations behind the plan itself. These will be discussed in turn.

Planners and Feldioara's Representatives

As a prospective new town, Feldioara has certainly not been ignored by the regional administration in Braşov. The record shows continuous meetings, hearings, debates, reformulations and revisions in the plan. These discussions took place both in Feldioara and in Braşov. In examining these meetings in more detail, however, it can be seen that planners came to Feldioara more to obtain technical information and inform villagers of decisions already reached than to actually debate planning goals or decide possible alternatives.

Despite planning guidelines which specify mass participation, there took place only one truly public meeting, and this was in the early stages of the plan. Otherwise, planner interaction with villagers was limited to meetings with the Commune People's Council or Party Committee (of whom 15 individuals represented Feldioara) or with even smaller groups of local officials.

It is significant that the one meeting (1971) where the planners confronted the villagers as a whole was barely remembered even by key participants and was not even deemed important enough to merit written record. The former mayor (interviewed in 1975) could not even recall the year in which it was held. It is evident that the numerous revisions effectuated since 1971 easily justified a second (or third) community-wide citizen's assembly. Such a meeting never occurred, nor was it even proposed by local leaders, to my knowledge.

Considering the ten announced meetings which occurred between planners and commune officials over the years, the participants usually numbered no more than the eight members of the Executive Committee of the Commune People's Council, the local Systematization Commission and a few invited guests. These persons thus constituted Feldioara's representatives to the planners; they were eventually called on to execute their directives as well. In dozens of additional consultations, the mayor was the village's sole representative to the planners.

With so much depending on so few persons, it is necessary to consider their administrative positions, continuity in office and social characteristics so as to evaluate their ability to reflect local interests. Those local officials who normally met with the planners consisted of the following individuals:

1) Mayor—changed in 1974, 1975, 1977, 1979, 1982
2) Vice-mayor—changed in 1975, 1979, 1980, 1982
3) Collective Farm president—changed in 1976, 1981
4) Consumers' Cooperative president—changed in 1976, 1977
5) Director of local road maintenance unit
6) Director of brick factory (Colonia Reconstrucţia)
7) Director of new minerals factory
8) School Vice-principal—changed in 1975, 1980
9) Local veterinarian
10) Regional Party activist (commutes from Braşov)
11) Local Party activist ("assistant secretary for propaganda problems," a new post created in 1977)
12) Chief of machine tractor station
13) Head of local post office (trade union representative)
14) Head of State farm unit

Recalling the "organized flow" chart from Chapter 6, we find that half of these leaders are either recent migrants to Feldioara (arrived within the last 3 years) or commute daily from Braşov. Three others—veterinarian, party activist, post-office chief—are also in-migrants but have lived in Feldioara for over 10 years; they lack complete integration into the community because the first is married to an in-migrant and the latter two are both unmarried. Thus, during 1975-1977, the period of most intense planning activity, only four of the 14 local representatives listed above had acutally been born in Feldioara. None of them were Saxons, none were industrial workers and only one was female. One must conclude that in certain respects, the local leadership was not wholly representatives of the community.

This does not necessarily mean that village leaders were opposed to the interests of Feldioara's locally born households; neither does it mean that they were without some local support. The problem stems not from these individuals' motivations but from their administrative roles. These roles generate corresponding obligations which tend to prevent elites from identifying local problems and from articulating village concerns. The heads of local institutions have obligations to higher authorities or to their own organizations which supercede any commitment they might have to the village. Feldioara's factory director, for example, is employed by the Ministry of Construction. He was reluctant to offer "his" workers to help build Feldioara's culture house for fear of not fulfilling the factory's plan. In similar fashion, Party activists and other enterprise chiefs have career ambitions for which their tenure in Feldioara is only the beginning. Because many local leaders (who represent the village to the planners) have not occupied their positions very long and because of the social complexity of the village, these leaders are often unable to identify the diverse interest groups within Feldioara. Moreover, to the extent that these leaders are tied to outside organizations, they may be unwilling to articulate these interests: they will assume that local and national interests coincide, so that any local deviation (or discontent) will be interpreted as village "provincialism" or "retrograde mentalities."

What exactly are these "local interests"? They can be seen as a reflection of the diverse social groups and political forces within Feldioara. First, there are the agrarian families who must retain their houses, barns, gardens or stalls in order to produce food products for home consumption and delivery to state coffers. Another interest group are the proletarian families, who seek more opportunities to satisfy their consumption needs. A third interest group would be composed of those households whose members work in both the collective farm and in industrial employment. A fourth group comprises specialists and professional cadres who live in Feldioara but may want to leave in the future for a more desirable location. Finally, a fifth interest group are the local residents who desire more community integration; they feel threatened by the social and economic transformation of the community, especially by the influx of migrants.

For all five groups, an improvement in public services and retail failities would be desirable. However, some aspects of the plan may represent a threat to certain groups. For the agrarian households, the physical transformation of the village may threaten the viability of their food producing household "enterprise." One planner summarized this contradiction in graphic terms: "You just can't have a town that smells like cow-shit." For the group of local villagers, the apartments and services planned especially for the in-migrants give no guarantee of being extended to include the rest of the village.

One must conclude that in terms of the type and sequencing of investment decisions, planners have placed the interests of the factory, migrants
and apartment dwellers above the interests of agrarian households, those
in one-family dwellings, and those desiring expansion of retail outlets
and services. These priorities are indicated not only in planner-villager
relations, but in the structure of the plan itself.

Analysis of Feldioara's Plan

It appears that the plan for Feldioara was formulated chiefly for the
future in-migrants. The new apartments will house the factory's workforce; 80% of the occupants will be in-migrants workers, 15% local functionaries (who are also mostly in-migrants) and 5% will be families whose
houses have been demolished. The extra retail space will benefit the apartment dwellers rather than local villagers. Physical transformation of
Feldioara will be confined to the village center, which coincides with the
old Saxon quarter. Saxon houses and gardens are being expropriated and
replaced by new apartments, with expropriation payments mandated
at 1 lei per square meter—well below the market value of these houses.
These new apartments will house future newcomers to Feldioara.

That the plan is constructred to serve in-migrants is best illustrated by
the policy for energy consumption. According to the plan, Feldioarans
will continue to heat their homes with wood-burning *terracotta* furnaces,
for which firewood is purchased at the local fuel deposit. While villagers
extol the virtues of wood heat when compared to coal or kerosene stoves,
its disadvantages are also well known: the wood must be brought, trans-
ported, cut and stacked in time for the cold weather. The fire must be
started each day and continuously attended to, and each room must have
its own stove. Baths must be prepared by a separate hot-water heater, also
wood-fueled. More serious than the time and effort to keep the stoves running has been the continually rising costs of firewood. Price increases are
justified by Romania's energy conservation measures, which require villagers to purchase 40% of their heating fuel in the form of soft coal. The
problem is that the coal tends to clog up the *terracotta* ovens. Hence,
instead of fostering a conversion from wood to coal, the State's directive
has compelled villagers to pay 40% more money in order to assure themselves adequate supplies of firewood. The excess coal often ends up in the
backyard, to be used for occasional outdoor burning. Sometimes it is bart-
ered or sold to those residents who own coal-burning stoves. The coal

"sales tax" has effectively increased the real cost of firewood in Feldioara. In addition, opportunities to procure firewood outside formal channels (i.e., in the forests) have been severely restricted by State policy of forest trails and penalties for unauthorized trucking. Consequently, home heating in Feldioara has become so expensive that in winter some households actually send one of their number to live with relatives in Braşov City. Remaining members live out the winter months in the kitchen.

Neither in its initial nor in its latter phases does Feldioara's plan provide for heating or hot running water to be supplied to the villagers' homes. Were central heating ducts to be provided on a village-wide basis, they would be both welcomed and affordable for most Feldioarans. Yet central heating will be supplied only to the more "rationally" constructed apartment blocks. In justifying their decision, planners and Party officials assert that single family homes are too dispersed, that costs of laying pipeline and energy losses would be prohibitive. Yet Feldioara is a highly nucleated village; houses adjoin each other row-style, and the population density is as high as any rural settlement in Romania. If investment in central heating infrastructural were economically rational for *any* village, it would be *most* rational for a village like Feldioara. One cannot help but conclude that the local residents are being discriminated against in favor of the needs of the factory and its apartment dwelling workers. Yet in a decade or two, most villagers will have ceased working in agriculture and will be without barns, workshops and storage areas. Most likely they will not relish the thought of having to chop wood while apartment dwellers have both central heating and hot water at their disposal. That one of the key symbols of modernization is being made available primarily for in-migrants makes it difficult for local residents to be enthusiastic about the plan.

As has already been noted, Felidoara's plan has been subjected to continual revisions in scope, scale and sequence. Since new conditions and new information should generate flexible planning responses, this fluctuation is not necessarily to be criticized. However, in Feldioara's case few of these changes were produced by local pressures on higher organs. They emanated from ministerial decisions to increase the factory's labor force (thus necessitating more in-migrants and more apartments), revisions affected by County planners, suggestions from County officials such as First Secretary Trofin, from officials in Bucharest, from President Ceauşescu himself, or from whoever decided that Feldioara's urbanization should

be "pushed," "revitalized" or held up without consulting or even informing the villagers. Most of the revisions were enacted without debate
between planners and citizens. The lack of debate should not be attributed wholly to the arrogance or elitism of planners or local elites, however.
Romania's administrative structure, due to its centralization and fluctuations, tend to produce unilateral decision making on the part of middle-
level officials. Administrative fluctuations in priorities and the sustained
pressure of higher-level units on lower level units tends to limit the degree
of local input which planners can assimilate. Consequently, lower-ranking
planners and officials are forced to take quick decisions in order to satisfy
their superiors. They can thus do little more than inform citizens about
higher level decisions rather than actually debating these with them. New
plans can proceed only schedule only if public debates are restricted and
grass-roots protests overlooked. Administrative pressure from above and
the improvizational activities at middle levels generate two consequences
at the community level: first, planners obtain inadequate information as
to local concerns; and second, the plans are not totally in accord with local
interests. That leads to problems in citizen participation and mobilization
(to be discussed in the following two chapters).

    Plan formulation in Feldioara was clearly affected by problems of
"administrative distance" (Cohen 1977) between planners, local elites
and citizens. At County offices, responsibility for Feldioara shifted from
one staff planner to another, while turnover in the planning office and
among Feldioara's elites meant that County and local officials were not
fully informed about specific local conditions.

    Even within the planning office there was uncertainty and confusion:
one draftsman went about making up a new revised plan only to see it
rejected as "too ambitious." Some planning documents were either out-
dated or statistically inaccurate. Feldioara's main planning map had such
embarrassing mistakes as the misnaming of one main street, an error that
could lead to a host of unwanted consequences.

    Public access to Feldioara's plan was restricted to a few local officials.
Villagers had little opportunity to see the detailed maps, graphs, charts
and tables showing population and work force projections, houses marked
for demolition and placement of future stores.

    After the plan had been finalized (December 1975), some outdated
posters hung in the mayor's office for a few months. However, the only

people who would even chance to see these documents were those having business with the mayor. As for Feldioara's planning dossier, it was kept in the mayor's safe, and he regarded it as highly classified, if not top-secret. In no way was this dossier considered to be in the public domain. A copy of the dossier was kept at the Systematization Department in Braşov, but this was for planners' use only. The reticence to open the plan to the public stems partly from bureaucratic inertia. Plans which are in the process of being formulated are usually classified "for internal use only" (*pentru uz intern*) or "working secret" (*secret de serviciu*). Restricting information to keep it from public scrutiny has been a standard feature of bureaucratic organization (Weber's famous essay on bureaucracy mentions "official secrets" as a logical outcome of this kind of organization). The secretive aspect is more pronounced in Romania, however, because of the State's military-strategic concerns. Virtually every roadway, bridge and factory in Romania is considered to be of military importance. Tourists are routinely warned not to photograph airports, bridges, railroad stations or public buildings; Romanian internal flights prohibit passengers from taking cameras as hand baggage. The problem is that plans for these strategic units affect human settlements and social communities. To date, the strategic considerations have been paramount so that access to the plan is limited until it has been officially approved. Hence, discussion of the plan is centered not only planning goals but on the best means of achieving them. To compensate for the lack of input from below, plans are altered by those at middle and higher levels, often without the citizens' full knowledge (or prior consent). From the citizens' perspective, plan formulation is secretive, capricious or uncertain.

The only truly public display of planning documents in Feldiora consisted of a billboard placed in the central square during the summer of 1977. The information on that billboard is replicated in Table 17 (following page—with explanatory remarks).

Apart from the billboard, Feldioarans' knowledge of the plan was limited to observations that apartments were being built. Further information could be obtained from occasional newspaper articles which usually had the mayor citing the kinds of statistics shown above, or from uninformed local gossip. Even those residents whose houses were to be demolished, or those living in full view of the new construction, had little idea of what was going to happen. When I asked numerous residents "What's going to happen in Feldioara in the future?", the most common reply was that

TABLE 17

"PLANS FOR THE URBANIZATION OF FELDIOARA COMMUNE"[1]

	1975	1977	1980	REMARKS
1. Population	4,500	5,626	8,000	Refers to Commune population not village
2. Number of Schoolchildren	450	740	1,000	
3. Commercial Space	960m²	2,820m²	5,000m²	
4. Number of Radios	850	1,200	2,000	
5. Number of Televisions	—	950	1,500	
6. Number of Telephones	4	185	300	
7. Number of Automobiles	—	60	100	Actual number was 100 in 1977
8. Number of Apartments	—	280	400	Actual number was 240 in 1977
9. Dormitory Rooms	—	—	60	

1   Translation from the Romanian title.

"the village would be made into a town" ("*Se face oraş*"). When asked for further details, however, the nearly universal response was "They'll build apartments" ("*Se face blocuri*"). A few residents mentioned the new factory or added that factory families would enter the village. Further details were completely lacking, however.

Uncertainty and ignorance of the plan encompassed not only the villagers but certain local officials as well. Pointing to the same plot of grass, one local leader stated that it would become a sports area, while another told me that it was the site of the future hotel. While one predicted delays and retrenchments, the other spoke of speed-ups and expansion. County officials sent to Feldioara were similarly confused on certain points.

The confusion and uncertainty of the planning process at the local level was typified by the 1979 rumors concerning the exact date of Feldioara's declaration as a town (August 23rd), and its rebirth under a new name (Petru Rareş City). As it turned out, neither rumor proved true. What is significant, however, is that right up until August 23rd, no one in Feldioara's administration nor even in the County planning office could unequivocally say that this could *not* happen. Since such decisions could be abruptly made by "higher organs" (*organele de sus*). County and local officials simply could not be sure. That Feldioara's urbanization is now in a "holding pattern" until 1985 is the latest example of the uncertainties in plan formulation. In fact, if any one feature marks the planning process in Feldioara, affecting planners, local elites and citizens alike, it is this *atmosphere of pervasive uncertainty* about the future.

Feldioara's plan also reflects two additional shortcomings. First, the needs of surrounding villages were not integrated into the plan. Three communities lying less than 5 kilometers from Feldioara (technically within the boundaries of another county) were not included in planning calculations; closer preparatory work would have revealed that residents of these villages often avail themselves of Feldioara's retail, service, transport and employment facilities. Aside from statistics on ten nearby villages, provisions for a maternity clinic and a few minor service outlets, no regional analysis of Feldioara and its hinterland was carried out. There was no prognosis for central place-hinterland relations other than the rhetorical statement about Feldioara becoming a "regional center." Needless to say, knowledge about the details of Feldioara's urbanization was virtually nonexistent in these surrounding villages.

Second, and most important, the plan failed to provide any kind of social prognosis for Feldioara's demographic and economic growth. Two nearby villages are to be depopulated and most of their residents moved into Feldioara after 1985. Yet there are no comments on how this procedure is to be effected. Other than the program to provide work for the wives of incoming factory workers, planning documents are silent about the social consequences of population increase, integration of new residents, cultural and psychological adjustment difficulties of young, unmarried workers and numerous other problems known to exist in rapidly urbanizing localities; many of these problems are documented by Romanian sociological researchers elsewhere. To the extent that the social consequences of urbanization are not taken into account, the plan for Feldioara was really only a physical plan.

Summary: Plan Formulation in Feldioara

Although there was continual contact between local leaders and County officials, this was in the context of execution, control and monitoring of national-level directives. Only a small minority of local citizens actually participated in formulating the plan. All were ethnic Romanians, and a disproportionate number were males, higher functionaries, in-migrants or commuters. Though some elites may have been well-intentioned, their administrative obligations and personal interests were not in concert with diverse interests of most of the residents. For example, since most elites have their own cars and must support the state's "general interest" for fuel conservation, they tacitly accepted the abrupt cancellation of Feldioara's bus service.

The needs of the new minerals factory took precedence over the community's needs. In fact, the plan seemed to be designed to make Feldioara a service outlet to the factory. The planners' placed the provisioning of the in-migrants above that of villagers. Service or utilities that might have benefited the village as a whole—retail facilities, bus transport, night school, upper grades in the high school and central heating—were either delayed or eliminated from the plan. Published directives to preserve the traditional Saxon architecture were overruled by the demand for urban style apartments and demolitions, only to be revoked later on. The priority of the factory and its labor force reflected national (ministerial) priorities for industrial growth over the interests of local communities.

In similar fashion, the needs of higher-order central places like Brașov City took precedence over smaller localities like Feldioara. Feldioara's urbanization functioned as a reward, but it was a reward with upper limits. Feldioara would remain subordinate to Brașov City.

County planners were subject to contradictory directives from their political superiors. In trying to reformulate and implement the plan at the community level, they had to act under the ambiguous ideology of "collective interest" or "national interest" as articulated by key ideologues like President Ceaușescu or County First Secretary Trofin.

The planning process was often rushed and haphazard. Meetings were called, postponed, hastily recalled and the results often nullified by subsequent events or new campaigns. Mass meetings that should have occurred did not. The population was ill-informed about the plan and its options, and the available procedures to convey information about key changes were badly used, partly because the responsible persons were similarly ill-informed.

The centralized and volatile mode of Romanian administration means that plans are never truly "finalized." Since any decision can be revoked, county planners, local elites and citizens are continually uncertain of what will happen. Changes can occur abruptly, while those events scheduled to happen never take place. What may appear to be a flexibility at higher levels appears as caprice or confusion at middle and lower levels. It can cause cynicism among planners and apathy on the part of local officials. Moreover, the long term result of confusion is resistance among villagers who are denied adequate information to discuss the plan from its formulation phase and in its larger perspectives.

Finally, the plan did not integrate Feldioara's hinterland into the urban scheme and failed to recognize the social consequences of such rapid change on a small community. The village became a site for the execution of a plan rather than a community involved in its own future. Feldioara became an object rather than a subject.

The preceding discussion has shown the distinctive combination of planner ideologies, socialist practice, Romanian conditions, regional constraints and specific local factors which enter into Feldioara's planning process. From the *general traits of planning* there arose problems of administrative distance, architectural determinism and urban orientation in planners' efforts to create a miniature town out of a worker village. From the *"socialist"* aspect came the priority of industrial requirements over services, the national scale, scope and hierarchical ordering of settlements. The centralization and bureaucratization of socialist planning was exaggerated by specific *Romanian conditions*. It was also made more flexible (and more capricious) by the personal priorities of President Ceaușescu. His preference for rapid and grand development schemes and the continual pressure to achieve quick results in all sectors kept planners off balance and local elites and citizens ill-informed. At the *regional* level, the pervasive uncertainty of the plan kept planners off-balance, citizens ill-informed and the plan continually in flux. Finally, from the *local* perspective, Feldioara's social composition—the in-migrants, the factory, the ethnic groups, the unstable cadre of local leaders—constrained the way in which individuals and households articulated their interests and hindered community acceptance of the plan. The result of these constraints appears in the character of household participation in plan execution and in the relationship between local elites and villagers. These are the subjects of the next two chapters.

It is at this point that we will look at people as active subjects rather than as passive objects of the plan and the planners. In examining household participation and elite mobilization of citizens, we will be able to make a fundamental distinction. It is the distinction between The Plan as it comes down to the village and the *planning process* as a mode whereby supralocal inputs are integrated into local social organization.

CHAPTER VIII

RESISTANCE, APATHY OR ENTHUSIASM?
THE DETERMINANTS OF HOUSEHOLD PARTICIPATION
IN FELDIOARA

Introduction

At the local level, successful execution of systematization depends primarily on the participation of individual households. The first half of this chapter sets out a model for explaining why households are enthusiastic, apathetic or resistant to planning inputs. The model will concentrate on two critical variables: (1) household economic resources and (2) the degree of household commitment to the village. The interaction between resource control and village commitment will determine the degree of participation of individual households in Feldioara, and influence the way these households must be mobilized to execute the plan.

The latter half of the chapter illustrates this interaction by discussing five types of Feldioara households and their expected and actual reactions to the plan. After establishing the determinants of household participation in Feldioara, it will then be possible to proceed back up the "vertical slice" and bring regional and local elites back into the analysis (Chapter IX).

A Model for Predicting Household Participation

With Romania's limited resources and ambitious development goals, household participation is an absolute necessity if plans are to succeed. It is "household" rather than "citizen" participation because in the village setting, it is households which constitute the significant social and economic units. Ultimately, they become the key units of participation, and where participation is not forthcoming, the units of mobilization. For example, it is household labor which produces animals for State agricultural contracts, which contributes to neighborhood associations (Dumitru 1977) and which cultivates the plot of land assigned them by the collective farm. Moreover, for many collective farm tasks and village work projects, the individual with a formal obligation can send another household member in his or her place.

Tentatively, one might predict the degree of household participation by evaluating the interpersonal relations (or animosities) which exist between specific families and the village leaders. Where relations were strong and multiplex, participation would tend to be more spontaneous. Where there existed relations of animosity, participation would be low and more mobilization activity would be required on the part of local elites. A theory based solely on the character of interpersonal relations has built-in limitations, however. In villages as large as Feldioara, the number of households is usually too large for personal relations to have developed between each family and the relevant local elites. Moreover, rural elites change positions so frequently that they may not have had time to create either confidence *or* emnity among most rural households. Hence, in addition to explanations based on interpersonal relations, it is necessary to identify structural and processual attributes which could distinguish "participatory" from "nonparticipatory" households.

Romanian social scientists, in accounting for differential household participation in planning activities, have highlighted diverse psychological and sociological explanations. These include such factors as attitudes toward the plan in question, the personal preference of household members, the household's socio-economic position, whether household members commute to other localities and even ethnic factors, where some groups have more ingraned "traditions of cooperation" than others (Dumitru 1977, Matei and Matei 1977). These "explanations" are in fact little more than associations. They tend to beg the questions of just why some households have "negative" attitudes toward the plan or why commuting to other localities should automatically entail less participation.

I propose to consolidate these diverse explanations into two critical variables (or predictors) determining the degree of household participation.

The first variable is the household's *resource control*, i.e., the household's control over its productive and exchange processes. Included within the village are a spectrum of household types: subsistence-agricultural, commodity-agricultural, mixed (peasant-worker) and fully proletarian households. Those households who perceive the plan as a threat to their control over domestic resources will be less apt to participate voluntarily and will have to be mobilized administratively.

Nonagricultural households control few or no productive resources. Their participation will be more affected by the second variable, *commitment to the village*. "Commitment" refers to the villagers' belief that the well-being of their own households depends on improvements in the welfare of the locality where they presently reside. The degree of village commitment will be affected by social position, local working conditions and by past and expected migration patterns. Households with a lower degree of commitment will be less concerned with the plan, and thus less apt to participate in planning execution.

The two variables of resource control and village commitment are clearly interrelated. Alterations in household resource control (e.g., expropriation of a barn and garden) can affect commitment to the village; an increase in commitment may lead a household to try and control more domestic resources. For analytical purposes, however, the two variables will first be discussed separately. Their interraction will be highlighted in the case studies which make up the latter half of this chapter.

Household Economies and Resource Control

Economic niches. The most important social unit in the Romanian village is the co-resident domestic household or *gospodarie*. The rural household endeavors to control as much of its production, distribution and consumption of key resources as possible. The household also functions as a unit of primary socialization. It establishes rights and obligations of kinship relations and it determines the kinds of social linkages its members may have with other households. For example, if two villagers have quarreled, it usually means that members of their respective households must also avoid each other.

In examining the economic aspects of peasant household organization in Romania, six different domains of resource control can be delineated:

1) control over *productive resources,* e.g., land, animals, tools, wagons; these resources can be (a) owned outright by the household, (b) accessible directly by virtue of membership in an organization such as the collective farm, or (c) accessible indirectly, i.e., through informal or illegal means.

2) control over *allocation of members' labor input* (the labor process); for example, exclusive control by the household can be opposed to control exercised by outside organizations such as the collective farm or factory.

3) control over the *scope of production* e.g., subsistence production, petty-commodity production or production of exchange values.

4) control over the *form of the product,* e.g. directly consumable, a product that must be processed by and sold to outside agencies, or the wage-form.

5) control over *disposition of the product;* e.g. to be consumed directly, given away to friends or kinsmen, exchanged locally, sold on the open market, or rendered over to the State as a quota, rent, tax or contract.

6) control over *exchange networks;* what resources the household can offer, what they themselves require and channels through which exchange occurs.

To the extent that a household is able to unilaterally determine the process of production and disposition of their product, the household can be said to possess a high degree of resource control. For example, the classic peasant household described by Wolf (1966b) or Chayonov (1968), has a high degree of resource control: it furnishes most of its own subsistence rather than purchasing it on the market; it controls its own labor process; it produces primarily for use and only secondarily for exchange/sale; and it disposes of its product by consuming it directly or via exchange with local networks of kin, friends and neighbors. In contempoary Romania, such autonomous households are confined to the uncollectivized mountain zones. In collectivized villages like Feldioara, *subsistence households* will be found principally among old couples who are retired from the collective farm. These couples spend their time raising food and livestock on their private plots, with any surplus being given to or exchanged with their children.

Throughout Romania, such households have become increasingly integrated with outside institutions, principally the State. Most agrarian households now combine subsistence production with production for sale to the State or on local markets. Such households can be designated *commodity agriculturalists.* In the Romanian context, commodity agriculturalist households combine work on the collective farm with production on the household "enterprise." The resultant surplus can be exchanged locally, sold on the free market, or sold to the State under contract. Commodity agriculturalists are thus intimately tied to informal markets and outside State institutions. Being more vulnerable to forces beyond immediate household control, they are also more vulnerable to State planning decisions. Their participation in planning will be problematic if these households feel that their resource control is threatened. (It should be emphasized that it is the *perception* of loss of control which determines whether household members participate in the plan. Party propaganda and exhortations—which frequently degenerate into orders and commands do little to combat these perceptions.)

Where subsistence and commodity households have variable amounts of resource control, this is not true of *worker households.* Worker households own no productive resources but their labor-power. Since household members work in factories or state institutions, control over members' labor inputs is taken out of the household and placed in the hands of the enterprise. The worker household controls its members labor and their product only during the so-called "second shift," i.e., labor carried on outside normal working hours (Cole 1981 discusses "second shift" labor in Romania in more detail). Members of worker households, instead of receiving the actual product of their labor in state enterprises, are now paid a wage. This tends to bind worker households to the state-administered retail system and its periodic shortages of key goods and services. The workers' wages are themselves determined administratively; this is so even under the various piece-work arrangements common throughout Eastern Europe (see Haraszti's 1978 critique of piece-work in Hungary for a detailed description of the way socialist managers manipulate piece-work wages). Finally, proletarian households are limited in their exchange transactions. They exchange no scarce products, but instead only their labor or cash.

Between the agrarian and proletarian "niches" lie the mixed *peasant-worker households.* The peasant-worker households combine cash income from wage labor with household agricultural production. As such, their resource control lies midway between agrarian and proletarian households on all of the six indices cited above. This is schematically illustrated in Table 18, where each of the indices is shown for various types of households.

Control is highest for subsistence-oriented, agrarian households. It then decreases along different dimensions as households evolve toward commodity production and wage labor. Fully agrarian households have the highest degree of resource control, but they also have the most to lose. Agrarian households who risk having their "irrational" estates expropriated will be most threatened by planning decisions to urbanize the village. On the other hand, until they are physically deprived of their resource base, these same agrarian households stand to prosper during the early stages of the urbanizationa process. During these early stages, the worker population grows rapidly, consumer demand for agrarian products increases unexpectedly, and (due to Romania's restrictions on private commerce), the State's retail supplies become quickly inadequate to meet consumer needs. Whereas spontaneous or incomplete urbanization may benefit agrarian households, then, planned and completed urbanization usually constitutes a threat to their resource control.

This is not true for mixed agro-proletarian households. Because they straddle two economic niches, they tend to be more adaptable during periods of rapid change. Finally, the proletarian households have such a low degree of resource control that they have little left to lose. In theory, as long as worker households have high local commitment to the community, they will have everything to gain by participating in planning activities.

Let us apply this model of differential household resource control to Feldioara's households. Table 19 classifies these households by their occupational profiles and by their potential for perceived threats to resource control under the conditions of planned urbanization.

Table 19 indicates that less than half of Feldioara's households are direct producers of agricultural goods. Nonagricultural households obtain their food supplies either via exchange networks of kin and neighbors or through State retail outlets and rationing. With the expanding, the new factory and migration of about 200 young worker families into Feldioara, the existing exchange networks will come under extreme pressure. Local agrarian families will be pressed to produce more surplus for local sale,

TABLE 18

FACTORS INFLUENCING HOUSEHOLD RESOURCE CONTROL IN RURAL ROMANIA

HIGH (autonomy) · · · · · · · · · · · · · · · DEGREE OF CONTROL · · · · · · · · · · LOW (dependence)

Dimension of Control	individual or mountain peasant	collective farm pensioner household	type of household collective farm household	mixed agro-proletarian household	fully proletariat household (incl. pensioner)
a) means of production	outright ownership or direct access	ownership of household resources; usufruct rights to collective's resources	ownership of household resources; usufruct rights to collective's resources	ownership of household resources; usufruct rights to collective's resources, no access to the resources of the enterprise	owns only labor power
b) control over labor process	fully controlled by domestic group	fully controlled by domestic group; possibility to work under the collective	partially controlled; household shares with collective farm organization	partially controlled; household shares with outside enterprise	none; household members labor in State enterprises; only control over "second shift" work

(continued on next page)

TABLE 18 (Continued)

| Dimension of Control | HIGH (autonomy) · · · · · · · · · · DEGREE OF CONTROL · · · · · · · · · · LOW (dependence) | | | | |
	individual or mountain peasant	collective farm pensioner household	collective farm household	mixed agro-proletarian household[1]	fully proletariat household (incl. pensioner)
c) type, amount of production	subsistence production; some surplus sold	subsistence production	subsistence PLUS commodity production. State contracts and collective farm obligations partially control type, amount of product	subsistence PLUS possible commodity production for household, collective, and State, but no control over product of members working outside the household	production of exchange values only. State/enterprise determines the type, amount of product
d) form of realization of the product; forms of payment	realized as "kind," possibly contracted or sold for "cash;" child allowances from the State	direct consumption plus payments paid out as both kind (grain, potatoes) and as cash; determined by collective farm	directly consumable household produce; other crops and cash payments determined by the collective farm; fodder and cash from informal exchange transactions; cash child allowances from the State. PLUS: cash wages or pensions; determined by State/enterprise	PLUS: cash wages or pensions; determined by State/enterprise	wage payments from State/enterprise; child allowances; pensions determined by State

(continued on next page)

TABLE 18 (Continued)

Dimension of Control	individual or mountain peasant	collective farm pensioner household	collective farm household	mixed agro-proletarian household[1]	fully proletariat household (incl. pensioner)
e) disposition of the product (in order of importance)	consumption, exchange, sale to State	consumption, gifts to kin	part to the collective farm; necessary household consumption; local exchange; accumulation; sale/contract to State	part to the collective farm; necessary household consumption; local exchange; accumulation; sale/contract to State PLUS: product goes to State/enterprise wages consumed or saved	product goes to State/enterprise. Wages are then exchanged for use value
f) types of exchange networks:					
1) offers:	produce, labor	produce, services	produce, labor, cash	produce, labor, services cash	cash, services, labor
2) seeks:	services, cash	labor, services	cash, services	produce, services	produce, services

TABLE 19

CLASSIFICATION OF FELDIOARA'S
HOUSEHOLDS BY OCCUPATION

	NO.	P.C.	DEGREE OF CONTROL	POSSIBILITY OF DECLINE
Agricultural only	120	15.2%	high/mid[2]	high/possible/low
Mixed[1]	236	29.9	mid/low[2]	possible
Worker households	433	54.9	low	none
	789	100.0		

1. Where "mixed" means that they must have livestock or at least one active member on the collective farm. As more household members enter nonagricultural employment, the resource control of the household decreases, but the threat of losing control nevertheless remains.
2. Depends on the degree of demands from outside markets or State contracting agencies.

Source: *Registru Agricole Feldioara*, 1976, plus interviews.

while migrant workers will be competing with local worker families for scarce agricultural produce. Thus, both the spontaneous and the planned aspects of Feldioara's urbanization create pressures which threaten the resource control and living standards of all three groups, albeit in different ways.

Demographic effects on resource control. Variations in resource control are not determined solely by economic niche, however. Numerous anthropological studies have described how individual households pass through "developmental cycles" in their internal demographic structure (cf. Goody 1958, Cole 1973). This cycle begins with the young couple forming a nuclear family. Eventually, the household expands to become a three-generation extended family. During this "expansion" phase, the household will be demographically flexible and economically highly productive. As children leave and set up their own families the household enters the "dispersion" phase; it may now consist of one married couple, an elderly parent or sibling, and the couple's dependent children. As elderly parents die, the household may end as an old couple, as a fragment (two widowed sisters, for example) or as a single person. Married children may move back onto the household "estate" or the old couple or widow may move in with the children. In either case, this constitutes the phase of "replacement," for a new head of the household now takes over.

Developmental cycles as described here should not be seen as timeless demographic laws but as historically conditioned social processes which vary according to the social and economic context in which the household finds itself. Each household undergoes its developmental cycle differently, depending on fortuitous demographic events (number of children surviving to adulthood), economic resources and external political conditions. In socialist Romania, for example, traditional household cycles have been altered by the collectivization of agricultural lands, proletarization of the rural work force, educational opportunities for the peasant offspring, rural industrialization and the possibilities for urban migration. Virtually all land is in the hands of the State, so parents have fewer resources to pass on to their offspring. Those resources which can be passed on—money, furniture, etc.—are easily movable. Since many children have now acquired specialized educations which necessitate their leaving their natal community, "inheriting" a house may in fact mean inheriting the right to sell it and pocket the money. These processes have all reduced initiative to remain with the parents on the natal "estate." Hence, the "expansion" phase has been gradually replaced by more dispersion into nuclear households at an earlier time. The developmental cycle of domestic groups has certainly not been eliminated in Romanian rural communities. However, it has certainly been altered by social and economic changes which have affected village life in general (see Cole 1976, Randall 1976, Kideckel 1977, Beck 1979, and Randall 1983 for examples of these changes in other Romanian communities, both collectivized and noncollectivized). The importance of the developmental cycle framework is that it avoids the error of analyzing nuclear families *as opposed to* extended families. It helps to reveal how nuclear families eventually pass into an extended family stage for a time, only to be dispersed into nuclear units again.

The development cycle of any given household can have direct implications for its degree of resource control. Given similar economic niches, households will be differentially vulnerable to outside forces (e.g., planning inputs) simply because they are at different stages in their development cycles. For example, let us compare two agrarian households, one an elderly couple, the other a "stem" family consisting of parents, one married son, his spouse and children. In several ways, the couple's resource control will be eminently more vulnerable than that of the stem family. Where the stem family contains four able-bodied workers, the couple contains only two. Where stem family members vary in age and types of skills, the nuclear family is more homogenous and probably lesser educated. Where the stem family has "generational depth," the couple has a depth of only one generation. Where the stem family is more self-sufficient, the old couple, at the end of their developmental cycle, is more dependent on their children to procure scarce resources as they age. In sum, the stem family is demographically resilient while the couple is demographically fragile. Hence, the couple will be less able to cope with threats to their resource control and consequently more vulnerable to planning decisions.

Household types in Feldioara. Feldioara's households reflect a range of economic niches among families at various stages in their demographic cycles. There are "young nuclear" households, "young extended" families containing parents plus one married child and grandchildren, "residual extended" families containing a couple plus an aging parent or unmarried sibling, elderly couples whose children have left the household (called "residual nuclear" families), family fragments and single person households. Table 20 classifies Feldioara's households according to economic niches and stage in the developmental cycle. "Young nuclear" and "young extended" families correspond to the "replacement" and "expansion" phases, respectively. "Residual extended" and "residual nuclear" families indicate early stages of household "disperson," while "fragments" and "single person" households represent ultimate degrees of dispersion.

Table 20 shows that most of the proletarian families are of the "young nuclear" type. This is a further indication that industrialization has reduced larger, co-resident domestic units; the phase of "expansion" is being replaced by more household "dispersion." However, the data also indicate that Feldioara's urbanization has failed to eliminate the extended family. Even in a village like Feldioara, at the forefront of urbanization and rural industrialization, extended families still comprise nearly one-fourth of the total households. The proportion of extended families would be higher if "single persons" could be re-classified according to the *qualitiative* relations with other households, rather than as separate units as in Table

TABLE 20

HOUSEHOLD STRUCTURE AND RESOURCE CONTROL IN FELDIOARA, 1977

	Degree of Resource Control (as indicated by economic niche)							
Type of household (stage in developmental cycle)	High (Agr. only)		Middle (Mixed)		Low (Proletariat only)		Total Cumulative	
	N	%	N	%	N	%	N	%
Young Nuclear (YN)	29	7.2	82	20.4	290a	72.3	401	50.8
Young Extended (YE)	4	4.5	51	58.0	33	37.5	88	11.1
Residual Extended (RE)	11	0.7	64	62.1	28	27.2	103	13.1
Residual Nuclear (RN)	43	9.4	21	24.1	21	26.5	87	11.0
Fragments (FR)	0	0	18	50.0	18	50.0	36b	4.6
Single Persons (SP)	33	4.6	n.a	n.a.	41	55.4	74c	9.4
TOTAL Cumulative	120	(5.2)	236	(29.9)	433	(54.9)	789d	(100.0%)

a Approximately 200 more Young nuclear proletariat families are expected to in-migrate by 1980-1981.
b Of which 19 were Saxons.
c Of which 15 were Saxons.
d Of which 140 households (17.7%) were Saxon.

(Continued on next page)

TABLE 20 (Continued)

YN = conjugal pair with children OR newly married pair without children; The "cut-off" between YN and RN is not so much age, as it is whether there are unmarried children living at home who are of marriageable age.

YE = must contain two conjugal dyads, with or without grandchildren (i.e. 2 or 3 generation)

RE = one conjugal dyad plus children, PLUS one or more co-resident adults; typically a nuclear family plus husband's widowed mother.

RN = an "old" couple with or without older, unmarried children over 35.

FR = sibling sets, parent-child pairs, households without a conjugal dyad.

SP = single person households, i.e. widows, widowers, pensioners. These people must live alone, at a different address from their kin, or otherwise function as a unit of social reproduction. Lacking qualitative data on the social exchange relations between Singles and nearby kinsmen, this number is probably overstated, while the number of Residual Extended families is correspondingly understated.

Dual residential households (to be discussed later) have not been calculated due to lack of intensive-qualitative data.

Source: *Registru Agricola Feldioara* 1976, plus interviews.

20. (For example, a widow living alone and her son's family down the street would be classified as separate households—"single person" and "young nuclear." As is frequently the case, the mother spends most of her day at her son's home helping with chores and caring for children, whereupon she returns home to sleep. While official census records would list the two families separately, the empirical observations could argue for re-classifying them into a single "dual-residential extended household." However, this kind of data can only be arrived at through intense observation, which is difficult in communities as large and diverse as Feldioara. Hence, most of the classifications in Table 20 have been based on official census data.)

The large number of extended households is significant for planning activities. Such households can respond more easily to planning decisions by shifting members into other economic tasks and by delegating one member to aid in the plan's execution. However, were an extended family to perceive the plan as a threat to their resource control, this same flexibility would be instrumental in helping them to impede the plan.

The data in Table 20 also suggest that by knowing the developmental stage of a household, one can predict the extent of resource control and by implication, receptivity to the plan.

The "young nuclear" households, for example, are overwhelmingly proletarian, the "young extended" and "residual extended" families mostly of the "mixed" type, while residual nuclear familes are in nearly half the cases agricultural. Moreover, Table 20 gives further evidence for the oft-cited flexibility of the peasant-worker household (Cole 1976). Where proletarian families tend to be "young nuclear" and agrarian families seem to dwell in the "dispersion" phase of the developmental cycle, the mixed households are found at all phases.

Recapitulating this section, the variable of "resource control" has been defined as the degree to which household resources can be channeled to fulfill household needs. Resource control is a function of both the household's economic niche and its developmental cycle. Control is highest among subsistence-oriented agrarian households, and further reduced with the proletarization of household members. Within the parameters of a household's economic niche, its resource control is also influenced by its internal demographic cycle. Hence, "young nuclear," "young extended" and "residual extended" households have a higher degree of demographic flexibility and will henceforth be less vulnerable. Residual nuclear families, fragments and single person households will be more vulnerable to outside influences. Because of the economic and demographic limits to resource control, household participation in the planning process will be most problematic for those households who perceive their remaining resource control to be threatened and are without the demographic flexibility to adjust.

Village Commitment

Several factors affect the degree to which household members will seek to identify their own well-being with the community in which they presently reside. These factors were discussed in the "organized flow" model presented at the conclusion of Chapter VI, where economic change and occupational mobility created both social complexity and social tensions within Feldioara. These factors will be recapitulated here so as to point out their implications for planning in Feldioara:

1) *In-migration of worker families into Feldioara* has resulted both from the village's fortuitous geographic placement near Braşov and its on-going industrialization. In-migration has produced a disproportionately high number of single males and young nuclear families. They find it difficult to establish the kinds of local exchange networks needed during the early urbanization period, where population increases faster than available consumer goods and services. To the extent that in-migrants find themselves unable to establish these networks, they will not obtain long-term commitment to the village.

2) *Emigration of local Saxons to West Germany* has resulted in a greater amount of demographically fragile households, elderly couples, lonely parents and widows. With their resource control already limited and with relatives in West Germany, Saxons are much less committed to Feldioara's future than local Romanians.

3) There has been a *demographic replacement* resulting from 1) and 2) above, where the newcomers, many of whom do not even know each other, come to occupy key positions in local structure, especially as political elites. Community mobilization is made more difficult by the social

heterogenity of the population, especially the gap between locals and new-comers.

4) Feldioara has experienced a *net increase in population* so that new services must be built with diverse clienteles in mind. There has been an increase in the number of household units, and more households (commodity producers and worker households) are critically dependent on outside institutions. Large numbers of nuclear households are individually less able to respond as viable units, making the village more vulnerable to planning decisions.

5) Feldioara has *emerged as a worker village* due to the in-migration of worker families and the *proletarization* of formerly agricultural families. For example, from 1970 to 1976, the total number of cattle owned by Feldioara's households declined by 22%, the number of milk cows by 46%, pigs by 48%. The worker households find themselves less tied to local resources and more apt to leave the village in order to pursue career goals or personal ambitions. They have a higher tendency to marry spouses from outside Feldioara, thus giving further stimulus to move to the spouse's home or to leave the village because of the spouse's lack of local ties. These features lead to reduced levels of commitment among worker households generally.

6) Feldioara has experienced acute *social tension* due to the contrasts between the newcomers' and locals' economic needs, household types, exchange networks, ethnic and regional backgrounds, lifestyles and ties to the village. Regarding "ties to the village," those who both live and work within Feldioara will have more local commitment than those who live there and work in another location, or those who intend to eventually more to Brașov.

The social stress and migration flows around Feldioara make it difficult to build up the kind of community spirit that fosters long-term village commitment. Neighbors see each other moving, emigrating and changing jobs. A lack of connection to the physical locality and social community of Feldioara has become the accepted norm. The village's population increase has made local Feldioarans feel somewhat overwhelmed by the newcomers, for the latter comprise many of the leading political cadres above them, as well as the mass of new apartment dwellers in the village center. In sum, several social forces have contributed toward a reduced degree of village commitment. This has had serious implications for the degree of household participation.

Households with the highest degrees of commitment are those who are agrarian, locally born, who have only one in-migraiting spouse, or who are in-migrant families resident in the village for over 10 years. In contrast, worker families, recent migrants, those who commute to Brașov, those assigned to work in Feldioara from elsewhere, and Saxons waiting for emigration permits will all have reduced levels of village commitment. That is, their well-being as households will not be tied to improvements in the quality of life within Feldioara, but to realizing household or personal strategies elsewhere. This latter group, being less concerned with the plan, will therefore be more difficult to mobilize.

Bringing the variable of household resource control back into the analysis yields the following hypothesis: households most disposed toward voluntary participation will be those who perceive no threat to their resource control and who possess long-term commitment to the village. For example, most of the worker households will not perceive a threat to their resource control because they have already lost most of it. However, since many of these worker families are low on the commitment index, participation will be problematic for them. Agrarian households represent the opposite situation: they have a high degree of resource control and high commitment to long-term residence in the village. Planning decisions will thus affect them differently than worker families.

Hence, the combination of household contol over key resources and commitment to living in Feldioara yields a range of responses to planning decisions. These responses will now be illustrated with five case studies of representative households in the village.

Resource Control and Village Commitment: Some Case Studies

Families with mixed agro-proletarian strategies. Anthropologists writing on Eastern Europe have attached special emphasis to the adaptive advantages of the mixed peasant-worker household strategy (cf. Cheetham and Whitaker 1974, Lockwood 1975, Bisselle 1975, Beck 1976, Cole 1976, 1981). Typically, the mixed household contains a wage-earner, a wife or mother on the collective farm, an older child and spouse working in a factory or office and a retired parent (or daughter-in-law) who carries out household chores, receives a pension (or maternity allowance), maintains a private plot, takes care of children and perhaps does some craft work. Romanian social scientists have recognized that "these 'peasant-worker' households are a necessity at our stage of development" (Constantinescu 1978: 78). In fact, such households are not just a means of weathering the transition period, as many Romanians believe. Rather they are being continually reproduced under the specific conditions of Romanian socialist development (Cole 1976, 1980, 1981). These conditions include the villagers' need for direct access to agricultural produce, inadequate state retail networks, the expansion of wage labor opportunities in the cities and countryside, and the administrative restrictions on urban migration. Because of these restrictions, some mixed households are kept together artificially. Younger members of these households might move to Braşov were they to receive permission to move there. However, since Feldioara lies within 30 kilometers of Braşov, villagers are required to commute (nationally, 30% of Romania's urban work force commutes from outlying villages; see Chelchea and Abraham 1978:76).

Family "A." represents a typical mixed household from Feldioara. Their three adult members and two children bring in a healthy combination of wages, agricultural produce, pensions and State child allowances. The monthly income for Family A. is shown in Table 21. As Father and Mother age, their cash income can be expected to drop. However, when Father turns 63, he will receive his pension from the collective farm, yearly grain allowances and a private plot; this will supplement his pension benefits to be earned from working in industry over the last 10 years.

Expenses for the A. household consist of heating fuel (kerosene, wood, coal), limited food purchases (baking their bread, extra meat for family festivals, vegetables, cooking oil), cornmeal and other fodder for their pigs and chickens, luxury beverages such as coffee, tea, beer and liquor (they make their own wine), house maintenance, taxes and, for the grandchildren, clothes, toys and private language tutoring. Most of the children's clothes are made at home or received as gifts from relatives or godparents.

The A. household is a subsistence-oriented, residual extended family. They raise pigs, chickens and vegetables for their own consumption; potatoes from the private plot provide food and fodder; additional food and fodder come from local exchange networks and through extra work on the collective farm. As a mixed household, Family A. has a healthy degree of

TABLE 21

MONTHLY INCOME OF FAMILY A. (1977)

Member	Age	Cash in lei[1]	Noncash income[2]	Source
Father[3]	59	1700/mo.		factory work
Mother	63	800/mo.	80kg/mo.	CAP[4] work in canteen
		250/mo.	20kg/mo. + private plot (0.15 hectares)	CAP pension
		170/mo.		widow's pension from first husband
Daughter (divorced)	36	1900/mo.	bonus kg.	office work at CAP
Elder grandson	8	500/mo.		allocation/child support
Younger grandson	6	400/mo.		allocation/child support
		5820/mo.		

1. 100 lei = $8.50 in 1977.
2. Payments of grain from collective farm.
3. Father left collective farm in 1970.
4. CAP = *Cooperativa Agricolă de Producție* (the collective farm).

resource control while their extended structure gives them maximum flexibility. Moreover, they have a long-term commitment to Feldioara. All were born there and the recently divorced daughter gave up her Brașov apartment to return to the village. (Paradoxically, the mother would one day like to purchase a house in Brașov; she finds the city's convenient central heating facilities and many consumer goods especially attractive.)

Feldioara's planned urbanization presents no special problems for Family A. Living at the fringe of the village, they are not threatened by expropriation. In fact, they have everything to gain from the plan. If services and salaries improved further, they could give up household agriculture completely. They have already stopped raising cows and have converted part of their stall into a storage area for firewood and for the children's toys. They even joke about building a garage for a future automobile. Maximum participation, however, will occur only if household members feel that the plan will bring them concrete benefits in the immediate future. For many of the families living on the fringe of Feldioara, these benefits will be a long time coming. Modernization of heating ducts, extension of telephone lines and asphalting of local streets will be provided only at the village center, chiefly in those areas housing new migrants. Hence, despite their long-term commitment, there is no guarantee that households such as Family A. will participate enthusiastically in planning execution. If innovations like those above are not provided, such families will have to be "mobilized." In fact, the patience of Family A. seems to have reached its limit, for in late 1982 the A. household had purchased part of an old house in Brașov City. Their motives were directly related to lack of provisions in Feldioara: first, they wanted the assurance of reliable and relatively inexpensive gas heating; second, they wanted to improve life changes for the two grandchildren by sending them to the presumably higher quality schools in Brașov. This sacrifice became more striking when considering the fact that their house in Feldioara now stays empty during the school year, and that the daughter must commute each morning from Brașov to her job in the office of Feldioara's collective farm. In the case of Family A., the gap between waiting for Feldioara's potentially higher living standard and the advantages offered by living in Brașov led to their decision to purchase a second residence. If Feldioara's urbanization is to involve citizen participation, it must also stimulate families like the A. household. As the years pass, and if promises are not fulfilled, their participation will become that much more problematic.

Nuclear families in agriculture. Despite bountiful wage-labor opportunities in Feldioara and Brașov, a large number of nuclear families (both "young" and "residual") have chosen to concentrate their energies in agricultural pursuits. Most of these families are pensioners who live as subsistence peasants, cultivating gardens and collective farm plots. However, there are some households which lack co-resident kin and wage-labor supplements, but who nevertheless have established highly productive commodity-agriculturalist "enterprises."

The most successful of these are households in which the husband and wife are in their late 40s to early 60s. The children have grown up or left home, thus leaving the mother free for "productive" labor. Most of these couples are members of the local collective farm, but in many cases their input is only minimal. For these commodity agriculturalists families, the collective farm functions not so much as a workplace but as a resource base. Its land, tools, horses, wagons, labor and expertise are "exploited" by members for the benefit of the *household*. They do not work *for* the collective but *on* the collective for the benefit of the household enterprise. The products of this labor (either cash or produce) are then donated to children or infirm parents, exchanged with kinsmen in the village, given as gifts to important persons, sold to worker families on the informal market, or sold to the State under contract.

Being composed of a single couple and working without machinery, these commodity agriculturalist households will prosper only if both husband and wife are in good health, willing to put in long hours and to forego frivolous or conspicious consumption. Commodity households are continuously laboring to procure enough fodder, intensify gardening, raise cattle, pigs, lambs and poultry and sell wool, skins, meat, milk and eggs.

Though tremendously productive, these households are also demographically fragile. The advanced age and low level of education of husband and wife usually inhibit them from seeking work in higher-paying nonagricultural jobs. Their children, even if they provide intermittent aid on weekends, cannot be expected to take over agricultural work if one parent becomes permanently ill or dies. In fact, the death of either of the couple usually leads to the disintegration of the entire commodity enterprise: the house will be rented or sold, and the widow will move in with a sibling or with her children as a dependent, housekeeper and babysitter. Such moves may also involve leaving Feldioara, or emigrating to West Germany in the case of Saxon households. Because of their demographic fragility, commodity agriculturalist households are especially vulnerable to any threat to their resource control.

In the specific conditions of Feldioara—an increasing worker population and insufficient supply of consumer goods—those families who elect to remain in agriculture can become quite successful. The incoming apartment dwellers lack animals, gardens and local exchange networks. They are literally at the mercy of local peasants when purchasing fresh produce or meat. Local prices can reach 3 lei per egg and 8-10 lei per liter of fresh milk (where factory wages average 10-13 lie per hour). The prosperity of agrarian households hardly goes unnoticed by other villagers. A common complaint, especially among local mothers with young children, is that these households would rather sell their produce at "market" prices to all comers, instead of giving it away "at cost" to kin and friends. Commodity agricultural couples may be criticized as being too hardworking, too ambitious, or too money-minded. They are condemned for hoarding their wealth instead of spending it (the usual figure cited is 100,000 lei in the bank). The perceived social distance may have some basis in reality, for many of these families work so hard that they are forced to cut back on certain social obligations. The men have little time to sit at the cafe (where they would have to buy a round for their colleagues). The wives can go for days without leaving the courtyard and thus do not participate in the rounds of visiting and talking with kin and neighbors which characterize village life.

The wealth generated by these agrarian "enterprises" does not reveal itself in conspicious consumption by the couples themselves. Showing too much of one's wealth, especially that earned in activities outside formal wage labor, is considered socially improper and politically unwise. Instead, profits are invested back into their offspring through gigantic wedding celebrations or elaborate baptismal feasts for children, grandchildren or godchildren; by offering cash gifts to help children procure a new car, apartment, clothing, or live-in maid in the city (usually an old woman); and by providing cash to pay for the upbringing of grandchildren, especially private tutoring. Additional food payments, sheepskins, homemade spirits or cash gifts may be used to curry favor with certain important persons or potential patrons. Their "gift list" invariably includes one or more doctors, a teacher, work supervisor, in-laws and godparents. Grown children often live in another locality, so that the couple's wealth is consumed in a way that does not aggravate status differentials between themselves and other households in Feldioara, and which does not arouse suspicion about unreported incomes. The children reciprocate by contributing labor in crucial periods and making their social networks available to their parents if and when they require them.

These agrarian couples are especially subject to changes in State agricultural policy as regards pricing, fodder and procurement of produce. Their vulnerability is all the more serious because of their advanced age; demographic fragility limits their ability to adjust labor inputs correspondingly. Being agrarian, elderly and usually uneducated, they have a long-term commitment to the village with little option for migration. Any urbanization plan could have serious repercussions for the resource control of these households. Finally, for those fully agricultural nuclear families living in the very center of Feldioara, urbanization can affect their enterprise in a more direct way.

An example of these effects can be seen in the case of Family "G." G. and his wife are both in their mid-50s. Their daughter has just finished medical school and has married a factory director in a nearby town. Their son is in his final year of high school in Braşov; after years of costly tutoring, he has managed to qualify for medical school in Bucharest. Both G. and his wife are members of the collective farm, entitling them to a private plot of 0.25 hectares. However, it is G.'s wife who fulfills the obligations to the collective, while G. concentrates on providing fodder to his 5 cows, 2 calves, 4 sows, 23 piglets, 20 sheep and 10 hens. G. even owns a small tractor which he uses for cutting hay on the collective's fields.

G.'s enterprise is a sophisticated combination of subsistence production, labor on the collective, and agricultural entrepreneurship. G. raises the calves on contract to the State, from which G. retains 50% of what he cuts. With the fodder, G. raises additional pigs, cows and lambs. A certain quantity of piglets, milk and eggs must be delivered to the State, whose buying prices are somewhat below those found on the free market. Because of this, most of G.'s production is sold outside State channels, either to friends in Feldioara or to contacts in Braşov. The remainder is consumed by his household and given as gifts to his children, in-laws or important persons. Though only a portion of his total production is delivered to the State, G. is still one of Feldioara's leading animal contractors, and he is a respected member of the local Communist Party organization. G. has in fact become quite wealthy as a result of his productive enterprise, rendering him both considerable local prestige and an equal amount of envy. At his daughter's wedding, no less than 400 persons attended, representing nearly every local Romanian family in Feldioara. G.'s agricultural talents also made him a likely candidate for a leadership position on the collective farm. Offerd the post of brigadier, G. turned it down "because the work would take too much time." But G. is clearly not afraid of work as such. What he really meant was that working on the collective would take too much time from building up his household enterprise. Though eminently successful by village standards, G. had the misfortune to have his barn and large garden on the site of future apartment buildings. G. had only vague notions about the plan and was uncertain about the future of his enterprise. His attempts to find out more details were rebuffed by local officials, who were themselves oftimes unaware of the changes emanating from the Braşov planning office. After all, it was not Feldioara that was building the apartments, but the Ministry of Construction in collaboration with the new factory.

In early Spring, just after G. had planted his garden, Feldioara's vice-mayor came to G.'s home and told him that his garden and barn were to be expropriated for the standard fee of 1 lei per square meter. G. understood the rationale for relinquishing his large, fertile garden, but he was dismayed at losing his barn. Without a barn he could neither store fodder nor keep sheep. G. cited his good standing in the Party and his status as a leading animal contractor in Feldioara. "What an embarassment it would be," he said, "to dismember an enterprise like mine."

During this period, several homes owned by Saxons had become empty due to the emigration of their owners. The houses had large courtyards, stalls, barns and gardens—all that was needed to sustain a household agricultural enterprise. G. pleaded with the vice-mayor for the opportunity to purchase one of the houses from the Feldioara People's Council, but to no avail. The houses were sold or rented to other individuals (among them Feldioara's mayor). Several of these buyers were uninterested in raising animals, and the stalls and barns would go unused. G. protested the expropriation decision, but the vice-mayor told him that "if he didn't like it he could go to the County offices and complain" (*du-te la judeţ!*). G. threatened to do so, and local officials actually became a bit anxious. However, to G.'s relief, there was a sudden delay in the implementation of the construction program. G. was now told that he could keep his barn "until the mid-1980s."

No doubt it was the inertia and caprice of the planning process rather than G.'s threats which forced the delay, G. himself has become quite wary of the urbanization plan in Feldioara, remarking on the haphazard way the plan was implemented, the callous attitude of officials toward him and his enterprise and the fact that the vice-mayor was able to retain *his* garden while others (including G.) had to relinquish theirs. (It is impossible to find any local conspiracy to juggle the expropriations in favor of certain individuals. However, Feldioara resembles most other rural communities, in that suspicion and gossip constitute sufficient proof.) G. criticized local leaders, mocking their earlier threats and later timidity about him taking the matter to Brașov. He is also skeptical about whether he can maintain production over the next few years. He now expects his barn and house to be expropriated at a moment's notice. Too old to migrate or to change jobs, G.'s household enterprise is especially vulnerable to the way planned urbanization is carried out in Feldioara. G. has long-term commitment to the village, but the plan's threat to his resource control make his participation in community actions especially problematic.

The case of G. illustrates the vulnerability of agrarian families in urbanizing villages. Such households can prosper in the early stages of urbanization, but they are directly threatened in its later stages. If loss of resource control is not compensated, voluntary participation will degenerate into a grudging acceptance, cynical apathy or overt resistance.

Migrant households and exchange networks. A household's degree of resource control and its village commitment cannot be determined solely by considering the household as an isolated unit. It is also necessary to evaluate the extent of the household's relations with other domestic groups, both within the community and beyond it. This can be demonstrated by comparing two ostensibly similar households, both of which are newlywed, nuclear and proletarian. The key difference between them is that one household is locally born, while the other consists of new inmigrants. This difference in natal origin produces significant differences in resource control, living standard, commitment and ultimately participation in the plan.

In one of Feldioara's new apartment blocks live "M." (for migrant) and his wife. They are both in their early 20s and have no children. The couple was lured to Feldioara from far-away Moldova after reading a newspaper advertisement promising them training, salary increases and modern housing in an urbanizing area. They signed a three-year work contract and arrived sight-unseen in Feldioara in early 1976. They now both work as chemical operator-trainees in the new minerals factory at the outskirts of the village. In the same building as M., occupying a similar two-and-a-half-room apartment, lived Family L. (for locals). L. is a clerk at the factory, his wife is a kindergarten teacher in Feldioara. L. was born and raised in the village. His wife comes from a nearby village. Married for over a year, they are expecting their first child.

Though the two households earn nearly identical salaries and occupy similar living quarters, L. and his wife lead a more comfortable existence while Household M. is under considerable social and financial strain. The key difference lies in the M.'s inability to establish exchange networks within Feldioara.

The L. household receives supplies of meat, dairy products, clothing, and domestic services (and eventually babysitting) from L.'s parents, who are collective farm peasants. L. returns these gifts by laboring on his parents' plot, helping with chores, or procuring special servies or supplies through his own network of village colleagues now employed in diverse enterprises throughout Braşov County. The exchange relations between L. and his parents are so interlinked that the two nuclear families function essentially as a dual-residential extended family. The depth of L.'s exchange network with his parents presents a sharp contrast to the shallow network of M. and his wife. Household M. receives some rations directly from the factory and occasional packages from home. Most of their food, however, must be procured in the village, either through the village stores or by seeking out local peasants to buy fresh produce or a cut of meat. In both cases the M. household is at a disadvantage; they must compete with local citizens who know the retail staff at the shops, or have special relations with the peasant sellers. Feldioara's agrarian households are obligated principally to other *local* families and only secondarily to the migrants (with the exception of migrant elites; see Chapter IX). In effect, M. receives what the shops have not sold under the counter and what the local peasants have left over, often at higher prices.

The food parcels from Moldova help, of course, but there are limits to the amount of corn meal one can send through Romanian mails. More importantly, parents cannot help with daily chores such as standing in line, buying food, preparing meals and washing clothes, all of which are especially time-consuming in apartments which frequently lack gas, heat, electricity and water. One can expect that these chores would increase were M. and his wife to have a child.

Now the M. household could improve their situation by establishing more social linkages with other Feldioarans. However, most of their colleagues at the minerals plant and all their immediate neighbors are also in-migrants. Many of them hardly know each other, much less the locals, and a sizable number will leave Feldioara sooner or later. M. himself has not a good word to say about Feldioara. He considers Feldioarans to be

unfriendly, jealous, greedy and snobbish. While Family L. is kept busy
by their extensive kin ties and village friendships, M. and his wife spend
their free hours at the local cafe or at home watching TV. Were they to
have a child, it would most likely to sent back to Moldova to be raised
by their grandparents. For the M. household, Feldioara has been a disap-
pointment. It combines rural underdevelopment, boredom and isolation.
It has all the disadvantages of urbanization without any of the advantages
of rural community. A small two-room apartment in a strange city is at
least in a city. The same apartment (poorly heated), in a far-off, poorly
provisioned, unfriendly village seems even more oppressive. M. and his
wife talk of leaving Feldioara for a larger city or returning home to Moldova as that region industrializes.

The case of M. should not be interpreted to mean that Feldioara's in-
migrants can never hope to establish significant social ties with the locals.
To speak of total segregation would be an exaggeration. Nevertheless,
when compared to L., the M. household is confronted with several obstacles. First, the M.'s are not just an isolated in-migrant family but one
of hundreds, all of whom are trying to establish ties with locally born
villagers. Second, the M.'s are not workers migrating to a peasant community, where complementary exchange of goods and services might be
expected, but workers migrating to a *worker village* where goods and
services are roughly equivalent (though scarce), and where the remaining
peasants already have exchange obligations to local workers. Third, most
of the migrants work in an isolated plant five kilometers from the village
or in Brașov. They have little opportunity for informal contact with other
villagers through their work or during pauses, as do those working on the
collective farm, or in Feldioara's schools, stores, town hall or clinic. Fourth,
M. and his wife have come to Feldioara as a simple couple. Since they both
work full-time and in the same isolated location, their social networks
are severely restricted. They have no old mother or relative who could
help them to keep track of network possibilities via waiting in line, gossip
networks, a local workplace, etc. Finally, M. and his wife chose Feldioara
for instrumental reasons rather than social commitments. While Moldovan
peasants may look forward to migrating to cities like Bucharest or Brașov,
they hardly hope to come to urbanizing villages like Feldioara, with its
depressing combination of rural hardship and an urban anomie.

Social separation between migrant and local youth has even reached
the point of actual fist fights when migrant men tried to dance with local

women at the village discotheque. Regardless of the mutual recriminations from one group that the other is "uncivilized," this is a further sign that migrants are poorly integrated into the community. It also indicates that the creation of long-term residential commitment will be problematic.

What of the comparative mobilization potential of local household L. and migrant household M.? It is evident that M. will benefit from the eventual increase in services that comes with urbanization. However, M.'s commitment to long-term residence in Feldioara is quite limited. He and his wife could seek work in Braşov or return to Moldova when their work contracts expire. M. is so negative about Feldioara that he would like to break the contract with the factory and leave immediately. His wife would like to remain for another year or two and see what happens. The M. household, then, in unaffected with respect to resource control but questionable on the factor of commitment.

Looking at the L. household, we find just the reverse. Both L. and his parents have long-term commitment to Feldioara. Yet the continued prosperity of L. depends partly on his parents' ability to provide him with agricultural goods and other services. Any threat to his parents' resource control would also be a threat to L.'s own living standard. Were his parents to be expropriated or fully proletarized, for example, L. and his wife might have to support them instead of receiving food from them as they do at present. L. and his parents will participate in the plan, but only so long as they see a plan which gives them concrete benefits. To date, most of these benefits have been aimed at attracting and keeping households like M. Local Feldioarans, overwhelmed by both the planned and unplanned urbanization of their community, have been left to fend for themselves.

L. and M. are two ostensibly similar households: young, nuclear, proletarian and apartment-dwelling. However, the quality of exchange relations with other households (or in M.'s case the lack of these relations) reveals quite different levels of resource control and village commitment. L.'s problem is to retain domestic control for himself and his parents. M.'s dilemma is to build a commitment to long-term residence in Feldioara in the face of social isolation. While the situation of the two households differ, the consequences for planning are the same: namely, problems in participation in planning execution.

Wage-laboring extended families. In Table 20 it was shown that at least 15% of Feldioara's *worker* households were either young extended or residual extended. The wage-laboring extended family sacrifices diversity of resources for sheer quantity of income. This income is then pooled for collective consumption.

Family P. can serve as an example. The father (age 55) and his married son (25) work in Braşov City as truck driver and typographer, respectively. The son's wife (22) is a secretary at the office of Feldioara's collective farm. A younger, unmarried son (20) works for the village consumer co-operative, but he will soon begin technical school in Braşov. Finally, P.'s wife (age 51) works occasionally at the local grocery outlet but is at home most of the time. The current total monthly income of this household exceeds 7,000 lei, of which 2,500 lei is used for food. Much of this is purchased in Braşov, where the selection is better than in Feldioara; the remainder is obtained via local exchange networks. During the week, father, mother and the unmarried son eat separately from the married son and his wife, but on weekends they eat together. Major purchases of fuel, household goods and services are carried out by the household as a unit. The married couple maintains a bank account of their own but they also contribute half their earnings to the mother. Much of the family savings have gone into modernizing the house, installing a convenient kerosene heating unit and an all-new bathroom. They also have bought a family car which father and son share. One indication of Household P.'s high disposable income is that father and son use the car to commute to Braşov, rather than relying on public transport as do most other villagers. Driving long distances to work six days per week is a costly luxury for most Romanians. The 44 kilometer round trip between Feldioara and Braşov costs about 3 hours' wages per day. These costs are partially offset by "supplementary" income earned by many truckers and car-owners who transport goods or people for cash sums or subsequent favors. (For example, hitchhikers in Romania normally pay the equivalent of bus or train fare to the driver.)

Household P. possesses no agricultural resources other than a tiny garden. Nevertheless, their combined salaries, supplementary incomes and wide-ranging exchange networks (in Feldioara, Braşov and through the father's contacts as driver/deliverer) more than offset the household's lack of resource control.

Wage-laboring extended families like P. constitute a viable alternative to the breakup into nuclear families which supposedly accompanies proletarization. What makes the extended worker household particularly suited for *rural* areas is the presence of pre-existing housing. Unlike crowded urban apartments, rural homes can easily be enlarged to retain household members during the "expansion" phase of the household's developmental cycle. Whereas urban worker families are usually nuclear and live in apartments, the rural worker family can be extended because they live in a house.

Especially in rural areas, *extended* worker households have advantages over nuclear ones. In a village like Feldioara, where consumer demand often outruns supply, extended families can procure food and special services more easily. They have more social networks at their disposal and can buttress their household with more wage-earners. An extended family has simply more ways of finding the right "contracts" and can afford to pay more for desired goods and services. Utilizing their village networks to exchange scarce resources and pooling their incomes collectively, each member of the wage-laboring extended family can contribute to and benefit from the security of the household unit. Hence, for rural families who are unwilling or unable to cultivate land, an extended family "strategy" has definite advantages. It is not just a relic from the past, but a modern adaptation to consumer scarcities in socialist Romania. One might also expect that in-migrant families will eventually bring some of their kinsmen with them, thus producing additional members of extended households among the workers of Feldioara.

There is nothing that prevents a high degree of voluntary participation in the plan from wage-laboring extended households like P. Their already limited degree of resource control is not threatened, and their collective consumption provides them with social and material security. The more they modernize their home, the more long-term commitment they achieve. Urbanization will no doubt improve their living standards. As more jobs and better services are made available in Feldioara, the city of Brașov will lose some of its attraction. This will further solidify their commitment to long-term residence in the village-*cum*-town. Though P. and his family do not expect profound changes in Feldioara in the near future, they are quite optimistic about their own household welfare. Indeed, they have every reason to be optimistic, for in many ways their living standard is higher than that of their urban counterparts and more comfortable than most Feldioarans. Conflicts will arise only if their heightened aspirations are not met by the pace of the plan as it is implemented in Feldioara.

The ethnic factor: Saxon households in Feldioara. The situation of Saxon households in Feldioara is hardly encouraging. Regardless of the currently benign ethnic policies in present-day Romania, Feldioara's Saxons have already endured post-war deportation to Soviet labor camps, mass expropriation of their lands and continuous migration to West Germany. None of these factors helps the remaining Saxons to maintain long-term commitment to the village.

A cursory examination of Feldioara's Saxon households shows a low number of demographically viable families (see Table 22). Their low birth rate and ongoing emigration have left an inordinately high number of fragmentary, single-person households among Saxons. This makes resource control more tenuous because those households in the later phases of their demographic cycles have fewer resources at their disposal. Without a balance of households—young and old, nuclear and extended—the exchange networks operate with greater difficulty. This is all the more true for Saxons, since they normally have tried to restrict exchange of key resources to their own ethnic group. Saxons can compensate for their vulnerability by increasing exchange linkages with local Romanians (with consequent implications for Saxons' internal unity) and by maintaining links with relatives in West Germany. Many of these relatives visit Feldioara during the summer months, often laden with gifts. The comparisons between life in West Germany and life in Feldioara—and between being a *Volksdeutsch* in Germany and a member of the tiny German minority in Romania—both work against the stimulation of Saxon commitment to Feldioara.

Saxons have traditionally occupied the very center of the village, with the wealthiest families living on the main street. Thus, Saxons are the first to experience Feldioara's physical transformation, e.g., installation of heating ducts, phones, asphalting of streets, new shops, etc. However, it is also Saxon houses and gardens that have to be demolished to build some of these amenities, including the new apartments and shopping complex. This is hardly encouraging for a group which has prided itself on its physical and social togetherness (*zusammenhalten*). The decline in the number

TABLE 22

CLASSIFICATION OF SAXON HOUSEHOLDS IN FELDIOARA

Type of household (= stage in developmental cycle)	Saxon households only		Total households		Saxons as percent of total households
	N	%	N	%	%
Young nuclear	48	33.7	50.8	401	12.0
Young extended	13	9.2	11.1	88	14.8
Residual extended	29	20.4	13.1	103	28.2
Residual nuclear	18	12.7	11.0	87	20.7
Fragments	19	13.4	4.6	36	52.8
Single Person	15	10.6	9.4	74	20.3
TOTALS	142	100.0	100.0	789	18.6

Source: *Registru Agricole Feldioara*, 1976.

of Saxon households and their markedly reduced demographically viability have led to a decline in village commitment. The Saxon "community spirit," so often lauded by Romania's ethnographers and by County officials, has always been more Saxon-than community-based. Under existing conditions, it is difficult to envision the revitalization of this spirit.

This does not mean that Saxons will overtly resist the plan to urbanize Feldioara. As the average Romanian would put it, "this is just not their style" (*"Nu e stilul lor"*). More likely, Saxons will exhibit a higher degree of apathy and cynicism toward the plan, as they do toward the Romanian regime in general. Those Saxons who would benefit most from the plan—the young families of skilled workers—are also those seeking to emigrate to West Germany. For the remaining Saxons of Feldioara, the plan will simply become irrelevant to them. With demographic fragility and declining commitment, the Saxons' participation will become problematic. And the more the Saxons have to be mobilized by administrative means, the more alienated they will become. To take one example of this alienation process, there is a Saxon family who recently had their garden, barn and house expropriated over the course of a year. This family had little sympathy for the rationality or "public interest" in Feldioara's plan. They saw the expropriation as just another in a long line of humiliations fostered on them by vengeful Romanians and their communist government, humiliations that began with the father's deportation to the Soviet Union in 1945.

The family did not raise a protest or resist. They simply moved in with relatives in Braşov and applied to emigrate to West Germany.

Over the centuries, Saxons have developed highly effective traditions of voluntary cooperation. How ironic that this participation is now lacking just when the State needs it most.

Summary: the Problem of Household Participation

This chapter has presented resource control and village commitment as the two key determinants of household participation under Feldioara's planned urbanization. These factors are subjective, in that they concern households' perceptions of threats to their resource control and their attitudes about the significance of Feldioara's future within the context of household economic strategies. Resource control is partly a function of the households' economic niche (fully agrarian, partly agrarian, subsistence or commodity producer). It is also a function of the household's demographic cycle, for at different points in the family's internal evolution, it will be differentially vulnerable to threats to its resource control. If households perceive their control to be threatened by the plan, they will be less likely to participate voluntarily and will thus have to be mobilized administratively. In many cases, household resource vulnerability feeds back onto their level of village commitment.

The degree of commitment derives from local-level processes of "organized flow" in Feldioara: emigration, in-migration, population growth, demographic replacement, proletarization and the increasing social complexity and social stress in the village. Households with a low degree of commitment will be less concerned with the plan and less likely to participate voluntarily.

The two variables and the case studies are represented schematically in Table 23, which distinguishes those households likely to participate from those who will be apathetic or resistant.

Table 23 shows that certain households will be more vulnerable to planning decisions than others. It is among these households that there will appear problems of participation. Ultimately, these will become problems of mobilization as well, for there is little reason to believe that households not disposed toward voluntary participation will be so readily mobilized by elites.

TABLE 23

| | Variables | | |
DOMESTIC RESOURCE CONTROL	VILLAGE COMMITMENT	EXTENT OF PARTICIPATION	TYPICAL EXAMPLE
severely threatened	long-term	resistance or apathy	agrarian nuclear family in village center, undergoing expropriation (Family G.)
severely threatened	short-term	apathy	Saxon agrarian household (expecting to emigrate)
partially threatened	long-term	apathy or acceptance	mixed, agro-proletarian households undergoing expropriation; "dual-residential" households where one unit is agrarian and one proletarian (L.'s parents)
unaffected	long-term or potentially long-term	acceptance	recently proletarized local households (Family L.); some in-migrant households (possibly Family M.); agrarian households at the fringe of the village (Family A.)
unaffected	short-term	apathy	Saxons expecting to emigrate; in-migrant households expecting to leave Feldioara (probably Family M.)
unaffected	none	apathy	worker households who commute to Brașov and are waiting to move there; temporary in-migrants assigned to Feldioara
maintained or strengthened	long-term	acceptance or enthusiasm	local proletarian households, both nuclear and extended; especially those who work in the village (Families L. and P.); permanently residing in-migrants, professional and elite cadres
maintained or strengthened	short-term	acceptance or apathy	in-migrant workers who want to leave; Saxons expecting to emigrate

Local participation (or lack of it) is thus contingent on structural and processual attributes of community households. If these structural and processual factors were better understood, Romanian planners and officials could foster more voluntary participation and have less need for administrative (or coercive) mobilization. As long as planners do not understand these factors, their complaints about villager's "poor attitudes," "retrograde mentalities" or "particularistic interests" will fall on deaf ears. The Plan will appear more irrelevant to household strategies and interests, and local elites will have an even harder task of mobilizing the population.

The next chapter examines how local elites try to accomplish these tasks, while mediating between the planners above them and the villagers below.

CHAPTER IX

VILLAGE ELITES AND MOBILIZATION

Introduction: "Leaders" or "Elites"?

Village elites in socialist Romania have two principal functions: they represent the community to the State, and they act as conduits of State power in the village. In this dual capacity, they channel local information back up to regional authorities and mobilize villagers to achieve national objectives. Yet within their administrative capacity, these individuals nevertheless remain *village* elites. As such, their behavior is circumscribed by the specific characteristics of rural social organization in Romania's villages. This chapter examines how the feed-back and mobilization functions of elites are carried out within the particular setting of an urbanizing village. The first part of the chapter deals specifically with Feldioara's elite cadres—their composition, recruitment and internal interaction. The latter half discusses the way elites interact with other villagers to achieve State plans and the kinds of "mobilization styles" they pursue when dealing with the citizenry.

The use of the term "elite" when applied to socialist soceites has been a source of controversy between Romanian and Western social scientists. Disagreements revolve around the different meanings attached to the term and the conflicting perceptions of the way in which these individuals function. The Romanian sociologist Cobianu-Băcanu (1977) believes that

233

"elite" cannot be usefully employed to describe Romanian's socio-political leadership. The term is unscientific, pejorative, even inflammatory. It conjures up images of "ruling clique," "upper class" or "special privilege," all of which are denied out-of-hand by official Romanian social science. Cobianu-Bacanu and Popescu (1977) have proposed that "elite" be replaced by the ostensibly more neutral "leader." This term implies a simple functional specialization between those who "lead" and those who "follow," such that neither is above the other. The "leaders" simply execute the "masses'" wishes. Where Western sociologists speak of "elites" the official East European conception speaks of "leading cadres." Where Western elites "rule" or "govern," socialist elites only "administer."

The substitution of "leader" for "elite" would be acceptable if the only persons under discussion were those holding formally constituted offices. However, in any Romanian village there exist persons who hold no formal leadership posts but who are nonetheless demarcated from the mass of villagers. Such persons may possess (1) high prestige in the local system of values; they might have (2) high social status or (3) special obligations accorded by the authorities outside the village; finally, such individuals might exhibit (4) a high degree of social cohesion with those villagers occupying the formal leadership posts. For people who fall under any of these four categories, the term "leader" is inadequate, if not wholly misleading, since *none* of these people hold formally constituted office. Precisely because of its generality, the term "elite" thus remains a more useful term than "leader" in discussing aspects of village political life in contemporary Romania.

Local-level elites' political and economic power is extremely limited. They cannot be termed a "new ruling class." Being constantly "on display" to the rest of the community, there are only limited grounds to even refer to elites as a "privileged strata." Yet there is still an unmistakeable inequality between these people and the rest of the villagers. This is not an inequality of wealth or privilege, but an inequality of duty. Village elites have *special duties*—toward the community, toward the State and the Party, and toward fellow elites. Since certain ordinary citizens (i.e., without formal office) also have such "special duties," a description of Feldioara's elite structure must encompass more than just the village "leaders." Hence in discussing local elites in Romanian rural communities, the following working definition can suffice: *village elites are those individuals whose formal office, high status or informal legitimacy gives them official or potential responsibilities for executing State policy.*

Feldioara's elites can be categorized according to their point of orientation (regional or local), the basis of their authority (formal or informal) and by their rank in the elite hierarchy (primary or secondary). These will be discussed in turn.

Elites in Feldioara

Regional elites. Regional elites are normally based outside the village, but they have special responsibility over local political, economic or cultural life. The regional elite is a specific type of county official. Like other county officials, he/she is normally based in the city of Braşov, but has jurisdiction over several communities beyond it. Since they oversee several communities, regional elites are unable to visit each village every day. Yet they are still "special people" whom villagers may respect, denigrate, gossip about or appeal to. Feldioara's most important regional elites are the Party *instructor* from Braşov (since 1979 the village has also has its own activist), the agent from the Union of Cooperative Farms, the official from the County Agricultural Bureau, a controller for the County Office of Consumer Cooperatives, and an inspector overseeing construction of new apartments. Regional elites are not required to live in Braşov.

In 1982, an engineer from Feldioara's minerals plant who had moved into the village was appointed Party *instructor* for Feldioara and four neighboring communes. He is expected to divide his time equally between his home village and the remaining 15 villages in his district.

Regardless of whether they live in an outlying village or in Braşov itself, all regional elites are expected to combine the functions of a local overseer, village mobilizer and cultural broker between the community and the State. They attempt to help villagers resolve immediate problems ("If you need anything, tell me about it.") Regional elites also articulate national policies, dispense information gathered from their wide networks of contacts outside the village and clear up the continuing spate of local rumors. This last duty is particularly important. Limitations on public discussion of policy conflicts, personnel changes, local disasters and crimes easily lead to underground channels of information distribution. These channels vary widely in reliability. Those least able to verify this information are the peasants, who become receptive to the most implausible of rumors. Regional elites have better access to accurate information and can thus clear up many local or regional-level rumors. (Inkeles and Bauer [1959: 159-188] report much the same type of problem in Soviet rural communities.)

Another important task of the regional elite is to mark off the limits of local demands on State resources or challenges to Party authority. It is the regional elite's job to insure that

> no deputy will ever ask for school reform, only for a new school in a certain community; no one asks for a change in transportation policy, only that a station on a branch line not be closed. (Konrad and Szelenyi 1979:164).

The position of regional elites is symbolically demonstrated during local meetings, for it is usually one of them who conducts the meeting and delivers the summary speech. Regional elites are not just visiting guests but an important part of the community elite structure. They are distinguished from other local elites because they form part of elite social organizations in several communities simultaneously and because they have social and political obligations beyond any particular village. Because of these obligations, regional elites can function not just as representatives of State power in local communities, but as State power itself.

Local elites. Feldioara's local elite structure can be divided into two broad categories: *formal* elites hold positions as heads of enterprises or institutions or as educated specialists; *informal* elites are those whose legitimacy derives wholly from within the local value system. The formal elites, to be discussed presently, can be further subdivided into those holding *primary* positions and those with *secondary* positions.

Primary elites. Primary elites are involved in most every major decision and campaign affecting village life. Such individuals are normally referred to as *"şefi de instituţii"* (chiefs of institutions) or *"cadre de conducere"* (leadership cadres). The primary elites in Feldioara include the following persons:

a) chiefs of political/administrative offices—Party chief/mayor, vice-mayor, local party activist, chief of militia;

b) heads of economic enterprises—presidents of collective farm and consumers' cooperative, directors of State farm, machine tractor station, brick factory, minerals factory and apartment construction sites;

c) heads of social institutions—head doctor at the clinic, head of veterinary unit, school principal, vice-principal, director of the culture house.

All these individuals are members of the local Party organization and sit on the Commune Party Committee. Most of them also serve as deputies on the Commune People's Council, which is the organ of State power in the village. The Party Committee and People's Council have alternating bimonthly meetings, such that the primary elites meet formally at least every four weeks. In fact, the exigencies of their tasks force them into more frequent contact.

Secondary elites. Secondary elites consist of those persons who hold lower rank within village institutions. In contrast to primary elites, these individuals are only activated to implement particular mobilization campaigns in the village. Feldioara's group of secondary elites includes the following persons:

a) Secretary of the Union, Head of Party Youth Organization; (In cities, where wage labor and youth activities are more organized, these two individuals would no doubt be classified as primary elites. In the village, however, they are of less significance.)

b) Second-ranking functionaries in political, economic or social institutions: the village notary, chief engineer at the collective farm, various assistants and bookkeepers.

c) Remaining members of the Commune Party Committee (of which there are 15 from Feldioara);

d) Remaining deputies serving on the Commune People's Council (of which there are ten in Feldioara);

e) Village professionals and specialists (Rom. *intelectualitatea*); that is, persons with higher educations who hold no formal leadership positions. Such people include doctors, dentists, veterinarians, engineers, technicians, teachers and priests. (The word *"intelectual"* is usually translated as "intelligentsia" by both Western and Romanian social scientists. In fact, as Mitchel Ratner's [1980] study of education and social mobility demonstrates, the Romanian *intelectuali* comprise a much broader group than East European "intelligentsia" or Western "intellectuals." In Romania, *intelectuali* are understood to include all those who have higher educations

and perform non-manual work. Ratner glosses the term as "professionals,"
and this seems more appropriate than "intelligentsia." Further discussion
of the social and political significance of East European intelligentsia/
intellectuals is provided by Gouldner 1979, Konrad and Szelenyi 1979,
Hirszowicz 1980:171-206 and Szelenyi 1982.)

Becasue of their special prestige within the village, the professional
cadres constitute the most important group of secondary elites for mobilization purposes. The professionals are frequently asked by primary elites
and regional Party instructors to perform extra duties which have little
relation to their formal training as doctors, engineers or teachers. Such
duties could include sitting on the local Party committee, chairing an ad
hoc commission, orgainizing a cultural event, supervising youth groups,
heading up voluntary brigades or presiding at public meetings.

The distinction between primary and secondary local elites is based on
observable power and influence in the local social organization. Because
this is a functional distinction, the exact division between primary/sec-
ondary positions will vary from village to village. For example, a doctor
or teacher may command such respect that he or she effectively functions
as a primary elite; alternatively, the head of a village school may be kept
in the dark about key decisions or excluded from the primary elites'
clique. Hence, primary elites are distinguished from secondary elites not
only by the posts they occupy but by their relatively greater authority
and internal group cohesion. While there do exist exceptional cases, the
primary elites' recruitment and interaction patterns usually assure an overlap between those who hold high posts and those who exercise real power
in the village.

Informal elites. Where primary and secondary elites derive legitimacy from
their office or professional status, informal elites derive theirs wholly from
within the local value system. This value system may be founded upon
criteria of financial success, prior positions of leadership, a family name
or individual moral character. Informal elites are wealthy, respected or
otherwise influential villages who hold no formal office or special occupation. Informal elites are those peasants, workers, clerks or pensioners who
can command a "following." They may be called upon to help mobilize
the population to execute the plan and they have the power to help impede the plans as well. Because of this, the Romanian State and Party have
used various tactics to either coopt, replace or neutralize informal elites.

Feldioara's elite configuration. Elites from each of the above categories will be found in every Romanian community. However, there will be wide variation in the absolute number, relative proportion and political significance of each of the elite categories. For example, in smaller villages, especially those which are not collectivized, the regional elites rarely appear; two local officials and the schoolteacher may be outnumbered (and outmaneuvered) by a large core of influential peasants who function as informal elites (Romanian Studies Collective 1977). In Feldioara, however, the informal elites play a more limited role. The Saxons have emigrated and pre-war elites have aged and died. The in-migrants are unfamiliar with the local prestige hierarchy and thus unable to confer legitimacy on potentially influential citizens. Similarly, local Feldioarans have found it difficult to grant informal elite legitimacy to any of the in-migrants. Because of Feldioara's rapid economic and social development, large numbers of professional cadres now work and reside in the community; this has further depleted the informal elites' influence. Finally, several new vacancies in village administration have caused many informal elites to be "drafted" into formal elite positions as these become available. In fact, Feldioara's informal elites serve as a reserve for future cadres of formal elites, both primary and secondary. Feldioara thus has relatively few informal elites. It seems probable that this kind of elite configuration may be typical for the 300 urbanizing communities with corresponding effects on mobilization potential. The use of informal elites as a reserve of cadres makes elite recruitment that much more important.

Elite Recruitment in Feldioara

During the immediate post-war period, when the Party regarded peasants with considerable suspicion, the number of qualified rural cadres was barely adequate. Hence, village elites were often installed by a regional apparatus which ignored local conditions or disregarded local conerns. Even today it remains undeniable that County officials and regional elites often take the initiative in selecting and confirming local leaders. By State law and Party procedures, the county apparatus still has the last word in village affairs. Nonetheless, it would be misleading to assume that the elite recruitment processes of the 1950s have continued unchanged through the 1970s. In Feldioara, elites are now recruited in a variety of ways. These include:

1) regional diktat, where the County places a villager or unknown outsider in charge of a local institution and subsequently legitimizes the decision via elections;

2) reactive decisions by the County, where local complaints cause the replacement of one elite by another;

3) nomination and election processes where villagers vote on a regionally proposed candidate, propose one of their own, or choose between two candidates running for the same post;

4) formalized consultations, where County officials solicit local opinions as to the best possible candidate for the post, and then decide for themselves;

5) informal, unscheduled and undocumented consultations among villagers, elites and County officials, ultimately leading to a reshuffling of elites.

The manner in which elites are recruited affects both their style of work and their eventual success in mobilizing population. The State has recognized that there are advantages in strengthening ties between local elites and citizens. Thus, various laws have been enacted and party cadre procedures reformulated so as to encourage more elite linkage with the masses. For example, two or more candidates now compete for the post of "deputy" in 90% of local elections to People's Councils. Nonparty members—invariably informal elites—now hold places on local administrative organs and in mass organizations. Graduates of universities and technical schools are preferentially assigned jobs in their natal communities, while commuting specialists are legally required to live in the villages in which they work, rather than in neighboring towns.

Nevertheless, these efforts to stimulate elite legitimacy have had to confront counter-tendencies toward administrative rationalization. In March 1975, for example, the number of People's Council deputies was reduced by 70% throughout Romania. This reduction has made it easier to assemble all the deputies for a meeting, as Feldioara's mayor happily stated, but it also means that remaining "deputy" positions will gradually come to be monopolized by primary elites. With fewer positions available, secondary and informal elites (not to mention ordinary citizens) have less opportunity to enter local political organs and influence decisions. Since many of Feldioara's primary elites are socially distant from certain segments of the community, the chances of their becoming truly isolated increase that much more.

Limitations on secondary positions thus render a special importance to mechanisms of recruiting local elites. These mechanisms will be illustrated with examples from Feldioara's posts of mayor/Party chief, collective farm president and consumers' cooperative president.

The mayor/Party chief: from diktat to consultation. Recruitment through regional diktat has been the most common means of selecting Feldioara's *political* elites. Given the Communist Party's tenuous hold on national power after the war, especially in the countryside, diktat could have been expected in this early phase. Support for the Party in Feldioara was generally weak, the Saxons and Magyars were unenthusiastic about the new regime, and potential village leaders (correctly) viewed political posts as involving considerable sacrifice and few rewards. Regional diktat meant not only that leaders were appointed by outside directive, but also that they often came from beyond the village. In several instances, they never even moved to Feldioara, preferring instead to commute from Braşov City.

The elites recruited by diktat have tended to be those with the shortest tenure in their posts. This is particularly true for the "mayors." (Since the early 1970s, Romania's measures to eliminate "parallelism" in State and Party administration have meant that the same individual holds leading State and Party posts at commune, city, county and national levels. The joining of the two offices in Feldioara took place in 1975, when the First Secretary of the Commune Party Committee automatically became the President of the Commune People's Council. The latter post is usually referred to as "mayor" (*primar*), and for simplicity's sake, "mayor" will be used here. (Further implications of Romania's merging of Party and State offices are discussed by King [1978; 1980: 106-109].) Since 1973 three of Feldioara's five mayors have resigned in disgrace, or, more accurately, been ousted from their jobs. In one instance, the cause was a combination of alcoholism, petty corruption, lackadaisical attitude and refusal to move into the village. The second case involved a series of administrative failures capped by a lurid paternity suit. The third mayor resigned after it was revealed that he had extorted extra payments while selling off State property and allocating scarce propane gas canisters. Moreover, this particular mayor had managed to alienate most of his fellow elites, staff and villagers with his extraordinary heavy-handedness: barging into the canteen and tasting the cook's soup, pushing a tractor driver off his tractor, physically assaulting a local technician who refused to get out of the way of his automobile, and accusing an American anthropologist of espionage.

In all three cases, the regional apparatus reacted to innumerable complaints from villagers and from local elites. Two of the cases appeared in newspapers, though only *after* the decisions to replace the mayors had been made. None of the three were brought to trial. They were asked to pay fines and received the Party's lowest level of censure, called *vot de blam* ("vote of blame"). *Vot de blam* can be followed by *vot de blam cu avertisement* ("vote of blame with a warning") and finally, outright exclusion from the Party. In most cases, criminal proceedings will be instituted only after the individual has been ejected from the Party ranks. Hence, all three mayors benefited from the "shield" of Party membership and received new posts in Braşov: one as head of a documents office in a forestry enterprise and another as Party activist in a factory. The mayor who resided in the village was rotated to the post of president of the local Consumers' Cooperative, a position for which he is unqualified by any rational educational standard.

The relatively light penalties inflicted on these ex-mayors have led some villagers to surmise cynically that Feldioara is a sort of dumping ground for cadres who could not succeed in the city. In Romania's strict system of spatial stratification, where villages rank below cities, some of those cadres sent to Feldioara evidently considered their tenure to be temporary. In order to fulfill the plan, please their superiors and be promoted, these individuals sacrificed their legitimacy among villagers. Feldioarans have complained bitterly about "foreign" mayors who tried to "squeeze out all they could get." A County official spoke of Feldioara's long period of "stagnation;" a schoolteacher bemoaned the elites' "*egoism;*" and a journalist commented, "It's as if Feldioara never had a mayor over the last ten years."

Certainly, these misfortunes are not the lot of every Romanian village. Feldioara has been particularly unlucky partly because of its intermediary (stepping-stone) position in the spatial network, its Saxon out-migration, and its population growth and fluctuations. Conversations with villagers and elites yield repeated images of Feldioara's history as one of missed opportunities and local incompetence. Saxons, for example, joke of the time in 1943 when Feldioara was offered the chance to link up with a natural gas line running through its territory. Village officials spurned this offer in the belief that the communal forests could forever supply their fuel needs. After the War, however, the forests were quickly nationalized; the price of wood has been increasing each year and villagers are now compelled to heat their homes with coal, which they regard as an inferior fuel. Meanwhile, the nearby village of Halchiu has comfortable gas heat.

With experiences of diktat behind them, County officials have sought other methods of recruiting qualified leaders. The recruitment of Feldioara's mayor in 1979 (resigned in 1982) is a case in point. Some years previously, County officials had visited Feldioara and had conferred informally with villagers about possible mayoral nominees. From the County's viewpoint, the qualified candidate would have to possess local legitimacy, political reliability and administrative expertise. Consultations with villagers and secondary elites revealed a likely individual who seemed to possess all three qualifications. "D." was a party activist from Braşov who was then attending "leadership training" courses at the Party Academy in Bucharest. Though born and raised in Braşov, D. was no stranger to Feldioara. He had attended high school with several village teachers and was on a first name basis with them. In addition D. had married into a well-respected Feldioaran family and thus visited the village frequently. Through his linkage to the secondary elites and via his wife's kin networks D. thus had a pre-established basis of legitimacy in Feldioara.

As a result of these informal consultations, officials and citizens came to an understanding. Upon finishing his education and obtaining more experience, D. could well be the solution to Feldioara's political "stagnation."

In Spring 1979, immediately after the most recent mayoral scandal, D. assumed leadership of the local Party organization. He told me that his selection was a complete surprise to him. By the summer of 1979 he had moved into Feldioara. Entering with an attitude of goodwill and social ties via his wife. D.'s work style was markedly subdued in contrast to the more "aggressive" (Rom. *"energic"*) style of previous leaders.

Recruiting a leader with strong local ties is not an automatic guarantee of success, however. Citizens view such persons with heightened expectations, which can easily be upset if the mayor favors his own kin or friends over other villagers. The mayor would quickly be subject to gossip or public accusations of favoritism or corruption. The problem is that while villagers may condemn such favoritism, the ethic of village kinship practically demands it [Sampson 1982, 1983b, 1984].

The new mayor's potential problems did not lie purely with the ambiguous nature of his local ties, however. There were also difficulties in working with a local cadre of elites who have their own social obligations and personal goals. Hence, it was not long before the mayor himself complained of lack of cooperation on the part of other local elites. Part of this problem consisted of quite normal interpersonal conflicts. These conflicts were exacerbated, however, by the continuous demands made on local elites to fulfill State programs.

Finally, though D. stated that he would take a job "wherever the Party sends me," he has personal ambitions which may override his interest in building local legitimacy. He had served as Party activist in Braşov, and in 1979 quite reasonably expected to be rotated to another post, preferably in a larger town. By 1982, D. had moved back to Braşov, having been transferred "at his own request for reasons of health." Needless to say, villagers proffered alternative explanations for his unexpected resignation. These included documented or suspected misue of his office, immoral personal behavior and alchoholism. D. was replaced by the vice-mayor, a native of Moldova who lives in the neighboring brick factory settlement which forms part of Feldioara Commune.

Despite D.'s having left Feldioara before his term expired it is clear that the County has placed new emphasis on local legitimacy and citizen consultation in recruiting new elites. These new procedures have avoided some of the problems caused by the diktat of earlier years. However, as the fluctuations in Feldioara's leadership cadres indicate, many problems remain.

The collective farm presidency: recruitment through consultation. Recruitment through consultation and an emphasis on local legitimacy have characterized the selection of Feldioara's economic elites, especially those chosen to head the local collective farm. Since its founding in 1950, the collective has had six presidents, all of whom were residents of the village. Four were born in Feldioara, and two were "colonists" from the mountain zone around Bran; they had settled in Feldioara in 1945 to take over Saxons' lands.

In late 1975 Feldioara's collective had degenerated into one of the worst run organizations in Braşov County (according to a County agricultural official). Members were retiring or resigning, production was down, payments were sporadic, three million lei had been paid to to migrant workers, 20 million lei was owed to the State, and the existing president had expressed a strong desire to resign.

County officials set out to find a new leader by means of formal consultations with the villagers. The upcoming General Assembly, where new officers for the collective were elected, was abruptly postponed. County officials came to Feldioara to examine records and discuss with the peasants. These "hearings" continued in Brașov for 3 weeks, as engineers, brigadiers, group leaders and members were called to County Party headquarters to give their views of the collective's problems and suggest viable candidates for the presidency. With villagers being abruptly called and recalled to Brașov, with possible candidates and their sympathizers jockeying for position, and with the usual secrecy and rumor which pervades Romanian political life, Feldioara was buzzing with gossip. Given the national policy of professionalizing agriculture, the County could have promoted the collective's chief agronomist or brought in a specialist from outside as president. Feldioara's case, however, demanded someone with local legitimacy; someone who could inspire the membership, or at least keep them for leaving.

After considering several candidates, the field narrowed to two: a young veterinary technician and a 55-year-old brigadier. Both had been born and raised in Feldioara. Both were well respected members of the community. Both were Party members. The technician had headed the local Party youth organization (UTC) and had the higher training deemed preferable for running a complex agricultural enterprise. The brigadier had extensive experience, an intimate knowledge of daily operations and a burning desire for the presidency.

The three weeks of hearings, deliberations, vacillations and rumors ended when County officials decided to support the brigadier. The man was then recalled to Brașov and "baptized" (!) in his post by the County Party Secretary. Only then did the collective's General Assembly take place.

The meeting was conducted jointly by the mayor and a visiting regional elite, the director of the County Union of Cooperative Farms (known as *UJCAP*). At the podium sat the outgoing president, the chief engineer, Party activists, and the brigadier. His selection as president had become common knowledge to most of the 300 collective farmers in attendance.

The General Assembly lasted seven hours, and all the collective's problems were discussed and debated. Members stood up and gave scathing accounts of waste, poor leadership and low payments. Elites responded by pointing out incidents of sloth or lack of discipline among members. Tempers flared as one women ended her remarks with the familiar Romanian axiom: "The fish always starts rotting at the head," implying that the fault lay with the leadership. She was harshly rebuked by the UJCAP director.

After several hours, the director proceeded to the elections of the collective's Administrative Council (*Consiliul de Conducere*). He began by saying: "The Commune Party Committee and the collective farm's [CAP] Party Organization have analyzed the problems of CAP Feldioara and proposed the following nominations."

The brigadier was then nominated and his election welcomed with a high-spirited, unanimous show of hands. Having gone from president-select to president-elect, the ex-brigadier thanked the CAP members for their support and appealed to them to "try and made CAP work as well as it did in the past, when it was among the "first in the County" ("*fruntaj in judeţ*").

Following this, Feldioara's mayor rose to say that he hoped that this would open a "new volume in the history of 'CAP Feldioara'." He lauded the outgoing president (who was also his close friend), reiterating that

> Comrade C_. had twice tendered his resignation, but the County had asked him to stay on even thugh he was ill and needed treatment. We should all thank him for his years of service and remember that the collective is like an orchestra: the orchestra may be good, but sometimes the conductor needs a rest.

Soon after taking office, the new president dispensed extra grain payments to the membership. This was an act of good faith and a plea to members to remain in the collective. While one can decry the backstage maneuvering which preceded his election, the new president could certainly not have been nominated without local support.

Expulsion of primary elites. Movement out of elite positions also furnishes evidence of the importance of local initiative and influence over regional authorities. In 1953, for example, County officials were startled when the collective farm's General Assembly refused *en masse* to re-elect their president.

As a faithful Party member, the president had become one of the County representatives to Romania's Grand National Assembly. Unfortunately, he was totally incompetent when it came to keeping track of the collective farm's expenses. Moreover, he was a Gypsy, having achieved his post partly because of his "healthy social origins." Since the General Assembly refused to risk another year with their president, County officials quickly yielded to their demands and nominated a brigadier from the collective. The new president was unanimously elected, and immediately received the backing of the County apparatus. He served for six years until falling ill and retiring.

Just as villagers' initiative can set limits on County efforts to impose unpopular elites, villagers can sometimes prevent the County from dismissing popular leaders. In 1976, the County sought to replace the president of Feldioara's Consumer Cooperative after the organization had had two years of poor performance and several financial irregularities. The president of the cooperative was an economist who lived in Braşov and commuted to Feldioara daily. Though without any particular local ties, his unusually soft-spoken manner and relaxed style had made him extremely popular with his employees. Some of them even considered the president "too weak" a leader, too quick to excuse those who were harming the cooperative via absenteeism, pilferage, and unauthorized use of its resources. The president's leniency may have been one reason behind the irregularities in the organization, which encompassed over 100 retail and service outlets dispersed over four communes (14 villages). (Feldioara's administrative difficulties must have been a more general phenomenon, for in 1977 all of Romania's regional Consumer Cooperatives were broken up into individual commune level organizations, a rare instance of administrative *de*-centralization in Romania.

When it came time for the General Assembly of the Consumers' Cooperative, County officials arrived prepared to oust the president. By the start of the meeting, most of those in attendance knew of the plan. They had even heard that the replacement would be an economist from neighboring Covasna County. When the floor was opened for "debate," the first speaker made an impassioned defense of the President, virtually pleading with County officials that he be retained. This was followed by other speakers who, while explicit about the problems of the Cooperative, nevertheless supported the President. County officials were somewhat taken aback by this unexpected outpouring of mass sentiment. One admitted to the Assembly that they had indeed planned to call for the President's dismissal, but changed their minds when confronted by "the will of the members." To the jubilation of the members, the President was renominated and re-elected for another year.

The President, who had been silent throughout the meeting, made a short, self-effacing speech, thanking the members for their vote of confidence. The County official then rose to give the cooperativists and their president his full support, but he also warned that they faced serious problems ahead. These problems could be overcome only through strong leadership from above and vigilant discipline from below. The meeting then adjourned to the local restaurant, where a full course dinner was served to the 150 members present (further depleting the cooperative's treasury).

Apparently, neither the leadership nor the discipline proved strong enough, for some months later the President's own chauffeur was caught in neighboring Buzau County with a trunk full of women's clothing—obviously on an improper, unauthorized and probably illegal mission. The President was not directly implicated, but he refused to dismiss the culprit and was soon forced to resign by higher authorities. He now works as an economist at the City Consumers' Cooperative in Brașov carrying out much the same work as he did in Feldioara, though without the aggravation of commuting.

The president was replaced by his assistant, a bookkeeper from the Bran area who had difficulties commuting the 40 kilometers to Felidoara each day. This individual soon resigned and was replaced by *his* bookkeeper, who was subsequently replaced by the locally resident ex-mayor after his dismissal. It was understood that the ex-mayor would be a temporary replacement until a qualified economist could be found to head the cooperative. In fact, the mayor has now been at his post for over five years.

The significance of "rotation" in primary elite recruitment

A recurrent feature of primary elites' career patterns is the tenacity with which they retain roughly equivalent positions even after being dismissed from their original jobs. As long as one remains a member of the Party (even a "censured" member), downward mobility rarely occurs. Rather than demotion it is *rotation* which selects functionaries for specific posts. The Hungarian sociologists Konrad and Szelenyi, in their analysis of the East European intelligentsia (1979), have explained rotation as a sign that political qualifications override technical competence. Party membership and ideological loyalty are seen as taking precedence over expertise. These political qualifications are reenforced by the system of Party training schools, which not only inculcate the correct ideological knowledge, but also help form a coherent group. Hence,

> diplomas acquired at the higher party schools entitle their holders to assume any kind of leadership position. From one day to the next a general can become a publishing executive, a political policeman an aesthetician, or vice versa, a newspaperman a colonel, and a bishop Foreign Minister or the chief political commentator of the State radio network (Konrad and Szelenyi 1979:152).

One cannot help but apply Konrad and Szelenyi's analysis to the elites of Feldioara, where the interchangeability of cadres is repeatedly illustrated. A shepherd from the Bran highlands has served as Party Chief, mayor, and in 1958 was selected to become president of a lowland collective farm. In 1975, a grocery store manager was drafted into the post of vice-mayor. In 1977, a deposed mayor (formerly a veterinary technician) somehow "qualified" to become director of a retail and service organization; while in 1981 a village electrician assumed the presidency of the collective farm. The notion that any member of the local party committee is qualified for *any* position is re-affirmed even by village gossip: frequently mentioned future mayors have included a local schoolteacher, a young clerk who recently completed Party school in Braşov and an engineer at the minerals plant. The gossip proved reasonably accurate, for the young clerk eventually became vice-mayor (though soon lost his post) and the

engineer was appointed regional Party *instructor* for Feldioara and surrounding communes.

A second conclusion to be drawn from the examination of primary
elite recruitment processes is the negligible role of elections. On most
occasions, the leading posts changed hands *between* elections, with actual
voting serving to simply legitimize the prior selection of the candidate. An
elite's "term of office" is rarely demarcated by winning and later losing an
election. The elite's rotation, promotion or dismissal seems to take place
in another rhythm entirely.

The contradiction between the necessity to rotate cadres and the need
to assure their stability in office has been taken up by none other than
President Ceauşescu himself:

> It is likewise imperative for us to see to securing a greater stability
> of cadress. . . . Examples have been provided as to the change, with-
> in barely a few years, of 3 to 4 managers, of 3 to 4 chairman of co-
> operatives, of 3 to 4 mayors. Such an attitude is not to be tolerated!
> At least over the period for which they are elected—besides excep-
> tional cases—the cadres are supposed to carry out their duties
> (Ceauşescu 1979:76).

The quotation is testimony to the enigmatic character of "rotation of
cadres." Rotation was originally conceived as a policy for improving *party*
cadres. Yet none of the above posts are Party posts; and cooperative chair-
men and mayors are supposed to be elective offices for which rotation
could hardly apply. Hence, there is a conflict between trying to foster local
legitimacy and assuring stable and reliable cadres.

In the case of Feldioara, it can be seen that regional officials have
tried to solicit local input in nominating the best candidates, even if their
election is a foregone conclusion. Instances of regional diktat still appear,
but formal and informal consultations have become a regular feature of
primary elite recruitment in Feldioara.

Recruiting secondary elites. The rotation which characterizes primary
elites gives way to *turnover* in the case of secondary elites. This can be
illustrated by the People's Council elections which took place in Feldioara.
In March 1975, five of Feldioara's 9 deputies were voted out of office

(six seats had been contested by two candidates). In 1979, only one of the ten deputies was a holdover from 1975. The cadre of deputies then elects Feldioara's mayor and vice-mayor. During the 1982 elections, the current vice-mayor, running in the neighborhood of apartments inhabited largely by in-migrant workers, was unexpectedly defeated in his bid for re-election to Feldioara's People's Council. His opponent was the well-known manager of the neighborhood bar. The young vice-mayor did not live in the migrant neighborhood but in a house at the edge of the village, among native Feldioarans. The vice-mayor had served two years in his post; he had been to Party training school in Braşov and was being groomed for further tasks in the local or County party apparatus. His unexpected defeat brought his career to an abrupt standstill. Having failed to be elected "deputy," he could not hold a post in local administration. Nothing prevents him from holding Party functions, however, and by 1983 he was working in the County Party youth organization (UTC).

The tendency toward rapid turnover among the secondary elites also stems from their relatively more passive relationship to the Party organization. Most secondary elites are Party members, but not all of them are Party activists. Not having assumed the activist's obligations, they cannot benefit from the Party's "shield" if they commit errors. Hence, secondary elites have a higher propensity to resign or be summarily dropped from elite ranks if they commit errors or make life difficult for primary elites.

Of all the secondary elite categories, the village professionals (or "*intelectuali*") have special tasks in achieving citizen mobilization. High-level speeches and newspaper articles continuously emphasize the professionals' responsibility to enrich social and cultural life in the village. Because of their special status, *intelectuali* are frequently "requested" to take on extra tasks which bear little relation to their formal training. Those professionals who refuse these additional tasks will be subject to local gossip or to the complaints of other elites who must assume these burdens. The professionals' obligations to take part in the political life of the community were clearly illustrated during a yearly meeting of Feldioara's collective farm General Assembly. A presiding County official expressed his dismay that not a single *intelectual* was in attendance:

> Where was the doctor? Why was there no one from the school? The cooperative farm belongs to the whole community, and the *intelectuali* should actively take part.

Actually, the doctor and some teachers had been at the meeting but had quietly left after some hours.

The official expectation is that village professionals be fully integrated into the village social fabric so as to raise "its level of civilization." Yet integration is hindered by the professionals' spatial mobility and general lack of roots in the community. Engineers at Feldioara's minerals plant have been *assigned* to the village. They can expect to be transferred again when they are needed elsewhere. Similarly, newly educated teachers and technicians will have been *assigned* to jobs in Feldioara upon graduation, or will have selected Feldioara simply because it was close to Braşov City. In fact, more than half of Feldioara's 35 schoolteachers live outside the commune. Many professionals thus consider their stay in Feldioara to be temporary. They hope to migrate to larger cities or to return to their home districts. Feldioara's problems are less severe than Romania's more underdeveloped zones, where the mobility of rural specialists is especially deleterious to village life. A study in Iaşi County, for example, reported two-thirds of the rural cadres to be in-migrants or commuters to the localities in which they work (Miftode 1978:163). In one of the communes, a peasant complained that:

> At night not a single *intelectual* remains in the village. By evening all of them have gone back to Iaşi (ibid.).

When Miftode refers to the professionals' lack of integration into village political, social and cultural life as a "dysfunction," he is understating the seriousness of the problem. In the case of Feldioara, County planners have had difficulty convincing *intelectuali* to move into the new apartments, for it would mean that they would give up their residential permits for Braşov City. The professionals' patterns of spatial mobility and their career goals thus keep their legitimacy solely on the formal level of "educated specialists." As a result, their mobilization ability is also hindered, putting pressure on primary elites to accomplish State plans via so-called "administrative measures."

Recruiting informal elites. Under Feldioara's urbanization process, the most promising and most reliable informal elites have been drafted into formal positions (especially secondary ones). The process usually begins with an invitation to join the Romanian Communist Party. Once in the Party, candidates find it difficult to refuse promotion into elite positions, for this is their duty as Party members. In 1975, for example, the manager of Feldioara's grocery store was drafted into the post of vice-mayor. Though he seemed not to really want the job, he was obliged to do his duty (*"fac datorie"*) to the Party and to the village. Under the circumstances, he performed adequately until being forced to resign in 1979 due to his silence over his boss' gross malfeasance. He is once again running the grocery store and clearly enjoys the relative calm of his life. Unlike other dismissed elites, he is seen more as a victim than a wrongdoer. And the villagers have remarked that the store is much better supplied since he has returned as manager.

The two advantages of drafting informal elites are their intimate knowledge of local conditions and the fact that elites' own social networks become available for mobilization. For instance, the new president of the collective farm had trouble filling the post of brigade leader. He asked several collective farmers to take the job, which involves closer supervision of other villagers, taking the "heat" from visiting officials, long hours of meetings and consultations, and a host of other headaches (cf. Kideckel 1979 for an extensive discussion of the brigadier and his "middleman" problems). Eventually, the president-elect appealed to his son's father-in-law, known in Romanian as *cuscru*. Because of their special relationship, it was virtually impossible for his *cuscru* to refuse the position. Other posts requiring long hours and a degree of personal responsibility were similarly filled from the ranks of the president-elect's close kin.

From the moment of their recruitment, new elites are courted by villagers who now envision a newly empowered patron, and by existing elites welcoming a new colleague. From villagers come offers of agricultural produce, labor service, profuse hospitality, and requests to be godparents of their children. The new elite will no longer have to wait in line at the bakery. ("After all, they are too busy. Only old ladies wait in line.") On entering the cafe, they will now be invited to use the private "back room," something which "special people" will find in even the smallest establishment. Moreover, newly recruited elites are expected to procure materials or services for their village clients. It is an image which some elites enjoy cultivating, even when their "miracles" are nothing more than the normal execution of their mandated duties (Cole 1980).

When drafted into formal offices, informal elites run the risk of losing their legitimacy in two particular ways. One way is to show overt preference to kinsmen in allocating scarce resources or to publically flaunt one's kin connections. Examples of such behavior occur frequently in Romania, since there are so many scarce resources, and since access to these is often obtained by virtue of a position in an organizational apparatus. The crudest forms of nepotism are roundly condemned, both in Romanian newspaper exposés and in village conversations. However, the Romanian ethic of kinship obligations virtually prescribes such behavior as an indication that one takes care of one's own. (Perhaps this is why the blatant nepotism of President Ceaușescu, himself of peasant stock, hardly surprises most Romanian villagers.) Feldioara's newly elected collective farm president was quite cognizant of the possibility of nepotism accusations. He went to his in-law only after several other villagers had refused the brigadier position, so as to avoid any hint of favoritism. For the same reason, the president waited several months before hiring his sister to run the collective's canteen and his niece to work in the office as bookkeeper. None of these posts is very well paid, but they all offer the potential for exploiting the resources of the collective in an informal or even illegal fashion. The three individuals have access to confidential records, the collective's inventory of fodder, deliveries of meat, visiting officials who happen to drop in, privileged conversations among the collective's leadership and drivers going to Brașov. All three individuals seem competent. Because of their obligations to their kinsman-president, they must actually work harder than they normally would. The sister tried for over a year to leave her post, but was talked into remaining by her brother. Given that most villagers are equally qualified for these special posts, the presence of three close kinsmen in the collective farm's staff can easily create the suspicion of nepotism. Were these individuals to overtly exploit the collective's resources, or were they to perform incompetently, these suspicions would be given further credence. It is at this point that the president's ability to mobilize the collective farmers would be severely threatened.

The second way informal elites can lose legitimacy is to neglect their original local networks and hobnob with other elites. Again, the collective farm president provides an example. After several years in his position, and burdened by numerous other duties connected with elite status, he gradually became one of "them" where formerly he had been one of "us."

Though he had done nothing overtly wrong, he visited his kinsmen less often and the visits themselves were often motivated by task obligations. He gradually began to lose some of his initial following among kinsmen and neighbors. Villagers began to criticize his favoritism in hiring and complained of his impatient mode of command when dealing with fellow colelctive farmers. Having lost a degree of his informal prestige, the president was forced to bear down that much harder to achieve effective mobilization. From a more egalitarian style, he came to adopt a more bureaucratic style of mobilization.

The pressures of kin obligations, the multiplicity of tasks to be performed, the tensions within the elite cadres and the elite's own personal ambitions are often in serious conflict. In fact, local elites often contract the classic illnesses of the harried manager—ulcers, stomach trouble, "nerves" and high blood pressure (the latter aptly called *"tensiune"*). These social pressures may be resolved if the elite resigns and rejoins the common people, as the grocery manager was forced to do, and as the presidents of the collective farm eventually did in 1976 and again in 1981. Alternatively, an elite may elect to consolidate his or her position among elite cadres so as to assure their being rotated instead of being dismissed. In such cases, the opportunities and arenas of elite interaction in Feldioara take on crucial importance.

Elite Interaction

The newly recruited elite assumes more than simply a new job. Elites in Feldioara assume new social responsibilities—towards their workplace, their Party organization, higher organs, fellow citizens and toward fellow elites. Because of Romania's inadequate resources and its ambitious development goals, elite cooperation is imperative if plans are to be fulfilled. This cooperation takes place in three specific social arenas: work tasks, informal organization and through membership in corporate associations such as the Party.

Task fulfillment. Labor mobilization on Feldioara's collective farm is a prime example of elite cooperation for specific task fulfillment. The fall potato harvest demands a labor force which greatly exceeds the number of collective farmers or paid migrant workers. The president of the collective is compelled to "borrow" laborers from other village institutions. These negotiations typically occur at a meeting of the Commune Party Committee or the People's Council, where the "agricultural campaign" is on the agenda. Joining the president will be the primary and secondary elites, regional Party officials and additional invited guests. The president will begin by emphasizing the urgency of completing the harvest before the rains come. He will appeal to each of the village institutions to donate as many workers as possible in the spirit of local patriotism and responsibility to the collective. Estimated labor needs will be discussed, with the Party activist repeating that the collective farm should be the concern of the entire community, including those who are not peasants. Quotas will then be suggested for the school (teachers and pupils), consumers' cooperative, brick factory, minerals plant and construction site. For his part, the mayor will propose a door-to-door campaign to round up available housewives, idle youth and healthy pensioners (i.e., those not part of any village "institution"). The chief of militia will arrange for day and night watchmen in the fields to prevent iilferage. The regional Party *instructor* will arrange to import school children from Brașov to help with the harvest. Posters and written appeals stressing the urgency of the campaign will be diffused throughout the community.

In 1976, the resulting mobilization was impressive. The upper school closed as 150 students and 10 teachers went out harvesting. About 100 members of the consumers' cooperative joined them as shops shut down except for short periods in early morning and evenings. The brick factory, minerals plant and construction site each released about 30 workers. The town hall, post office and clinic were closed as mayor, vice-mayor, notary, secretaries, postal clerks, doctors and nurses all went into the fields. They were joined by housewives, some pensioners, vacationing youth. One hundred schoolchildren from Brașov were brought out by train each day for a week and fed lunch in Feldioara's canteen. While the work routines of all these organizations were interrupted, the elites' cooperation through their respective institutions was effective enough so that the harvest was completed only a few days behind schedule. Moreover, though the voluntary contributions of village laborers and the Brașov schoolchildren, Feldioara's collective farm was spared from having to hire even more migrant workers.

The harvest plan was not completed without a degree of conflict, however. The factory director protested that if he had to give 30 workers to the collective, he would be unable to fulfill his own plan. The mayor reminded him of his community obligation, supplementing this with a veiled threat to call Braşov. After the harvest was completed, the mayor reproached the collective farm president for giving priority to the *collective's* harvest while neglecting to help the *village* achieve its campaign for household agricultural deliveries. Whenever such disputes arose, the regional elites would try to arbitrate the conflict to the mutual agreement of the contesting parties.

With mobilization campaigns occurring in virtually all sectors of village life, there remains a continuing expectation of aid among the elites. When the collective farm president needs labor he can count on the school principal to donate it. When the Party activist needs spectators for a propaganda film she can call the factory director. When the factory director desires extra meat rations for his workers, he can contact the Party activist to intervene with county authorities. This is not a direct mobilization of the village population. Rather, it is a mobilization *via elites* through their respective *organizations*. With inadequate institutional resources, elites must rely on outside help to achieve their immediate goals. Elites thus have a continuous need for each others' institutions as "banks" of potential resources.

Elites' informal interaction. The necessity for elite cooperation in task fulfillment also generates patterns of informal organization among elite cadres. Echoing the interactions between elites and ordinary villagers, elites try to cement ties among themselves with mutual presentations of food, favors, materials or services. However, they do not just exchange what they themselves own. Being elites, they are in a position to utilize the social and material resources of their respective institutions. Thus, the collective farm president may offer the school principal a crate of fresh strawberries before they are shipped to market in Braşov. A small load of cabbages will be dropped off at the mayor's doorstep, delivered by one of the collective's agronomists. The doctor may arrange for a ride into town in the factory's private car. The State farm engineer will offer the vice-mayor a sack of fertilizer for his garden. A school teacher offers the doctor's child extra tutoring. The chief of militia brings his car to the collective farm's tractor garage for a tune-up. A veterinarian is able to "borrow" some cement from the construction site for his household repairs, and the foreman may even release two workers to help him. The doctor recommends a specialist in Braşov who can treat the engineer's child. And so on.

In purely material terms, these mutual presentations are not large. If (and when) they exceed "custom," villagers are quick to gossip and eventually report it to authorities, newspapers or control commissions. The transactions of Feldioara's elites differ little from those of ordinary peasants, both in Romania and elsewhere. The essential difference is that the elites have more resources at their disposal.

There is one particular resource which is particularly crucial. That resource is *information* and especially that form of information which Ratner (1979:25) has termed "system knowledge." Almost immediately upon recruitment, new eilites will solicit and receive warnings about whom to trust, whom to watch out for, what the proper procedures are, what one can get away with, which tasks must be supervised personally and which tasks can be delegated to others.

There are two grounds for designating information as a crucial resource for elites. First, since they have the possibility of achieving positions quite unrelated to their areas of technical competence, there is more likelihood of elites' social and spatial mobility. This leads to considerable jockeying for power among elite cadres. Second, the socialist political economy in Romania rules out the possibility of elites ever owning vast amounts of resources. *Ownership* is in the hands of the State. Instead, there will be competition over *access* to these resources. Information (and its counterpart, secrecy) replaces money as the most valuable circulating commodity; but like all commodities, it must be continuously renewed. Hence, informamation gathering takes up a considerable amount of the elites' working and leisure time. Indeed, they do not have time to wait in line at the bakery, *unless* there is some important gossip to be picked up while waiting. Elites' information gathering is aided by the fact that their work involves more variety and less supervisory control than that of ordinary workers. Local officials, doctors and teachers often visit villagers in their homes (without calling first). Since these elites also attend meetings and conferences with counterparts in Braşov, they also obtain access to goings-on in other parts of the County as well.

It could well be argued that information is a universal commodity, possessed by peasants, workers and clerks. Undeniably, everyone knows something of value. However, because the elites' networks are more extensive, their information tends to be more detailed, more important and eminently more reliable than that of ordinary citizens. The accuracy of the ordinary Feldioaran's information is usually limited to the immediate neighborhood or network of village contacts. The elites tend to have networks which cross-cut neighborhood and kin networks; in addition, they can utilize those of fellow elites. Furthermore, they are much more likely to have reliable regional-level information; for example, local elites will know exactly why a certain Party official in Brașov lost his job, while villagers will have to suffice with the most outlandish rumors.

Their higher quality "system knowledge" means that when two elites meet each other they can truly *exchange* information. When elites interact with citizens, the merely *dispense* it. Citizens provide elites with gossip, "scandal," tidbits of personal and neighborhood information, and unlimited rumors, most of them unfounded. Elites gossip too, but they have forums where they come together to evaluate the reliability of gossip. In the local setting, elites never have to resort to rumor. On the contrary, elites clear up rumors.

The need to obtain access to resources, the constant search for information, the rotation of posts and interlocking memberships in corporate organizations all combine to lend a village-like character to the largest Romanian city. (Perhaps this is why real power in socialist countries is never held by those with direct access to material resources—the Economics Minister or factory chiefs; real power lies with those who have the information dossiers—the Party Secretary responsible for organization, the faceless Chief of Cadres, the Head of the "secret" police.)

Exchange of resources and information among elites occurs both during formal meetings and in the context of informal social networks. Feldioara's elites divide into an ever-shifting number of cliques based on age, sex, neighborhood, workplace, kin and ritual kinship, similarity of occupations (intellectuals vs. politicians), natal origins (Feldioarans vs. in-migrants/commuters), ethnic origins (Romanians vs. Saxons), hobbies (drinkers, card players, chess enthusiasts), childhood friendships and romantic involvements. (Elites tend to have extra-marital affairs with fellow elites, whom they can trust to keep secrets.) During organized mobilization campaigns and cooperative task fulfillment, information exchange takes place within each of these cliques and across them.

Interaction in corporate groups. In cases where task obligations and informal social networks are insufficient to forge elites into a cohesive
social group, their overlapping membership in corporate associations
fills the missing gaps. The most important of these corporate groups is
the Romanian Communist Party. The 250 Party members in Feldioara
are organized into several "basis organizations (*organizaţii de basă*) linked to the major workplaces—the collective farm, consumers' cooperative,
brick factory, minerals plant, school and People's Council staff (which
includes post office and clinic). Delegates from each of the separate basis
organizations are chosen to serve on Feldioara Commune Party Committee, of which 15 members come from the village of Feldioara. The activity of Feldioara's Communist Party is carried out largely during the bimonthly meetings of the Party Committee. In the interim, the Party is
led by its Executive Bureau, whose six members are usually co-terminous
with the leading formal elites in the village. Finally, the First Secretary
of the Party Executive Bureau also functions as mayor, i.e., President of
the Commune People's Council.

Feldioara's Communist Party members are neither a select clique nor
special class. To be sure, most village elites are Party members, but there
are dozens of ordinary peasants, workers, clerks, and pensioners in its
ranks. The Party is certainly not the rural "revolutionary vanguard" which
its statutes say it should be. Party members in Feldioara do not formulate
any policies but they do discuss these policies, re-interpret them, contest
them and sometimes ignore them. The principal duty of the local Party
organization is to "translate them into life" in one form or another. This
is done via the hard work, strict discipline, and conscientious application
of higher level directives.

The village Party organization has one major functional utility: in a
situation where elites and their institutions are so interdependent, the
Party brings under a single institutional umbrella virtually every "special
person" in the village: formal and informal elites, those in primary and
in secondary positions, and most of the village professional cadres (except
the priests). If the Party is effective at recruiting and promoting local
specialists, informal elites, conscientious youth, model workers and "proper peasants" (Fel and Hofer 1969), it can assure itself a continuously
renewable cadre of potential leaders. In pronouncements from Bucharest,
the Party is called "the leading force" in Romanian society. Yet in the

village, the Party could be more aptly termed a "stable for leaders," it is the base from which the rest of the citizenry is mobilized to realize Party-designated national goals. With the Party Committee functioning as the core, mobilization is carried out through the village institutions (collective farmers, consumer cooperative members), through the mass organizations (of women, youth, trade union, pioneers) and during local political events such as elections to the People's Council.

Feldioara's local elites are also brought together in other forums besides the Party. The collective farm president, who heads the collective's basis organization and sits on the Commune Party Committee, is also a member of Feldioara's People's Council, the village cultural committee, the county agricultural association, and the County Party Committee as well. The school vice-principal, who is Party secretary for agitation and propaganda, also takes charge of youth activities, oversees the local cultural house, and organizes a chorus group composed of teachers and other Feldioarans. Continuous demands from Bucharest for the active mobilization of the rural population—most recently in campaigns for household agricultural self-sufficiency, energy conservation measures and in the "Hymn to Romania" mass folklore competitions—impel local elites to organize and supervise new voluntary associations within the village. In carrying out these duties, elites can then be judged on their "style of work" (*stil de muncă*) with the population and their organizational talent.

Elites execute these extra-curricular tasks through their individual interactions with the population and through informal consultations with other elites. However, much of their work is carried out within the context of *meetings*. If there is one activity which most clearly sets elite behavior off from the rest of the villagers, it is their continuous running to and from meetings. There are mobilization meetings, orientation meetings, follow-up meetings, Party meetings, People's Council meetings, meetings of local commissions (sanitation, youth, recreation, systematization), General Assemblies of village institutions, ad hoc meetings with the mayor, surprise meetings with visiting County officials, intermittent calls to come to Brașov for consultations, regional conferences in Brașov, national congresses in Bucharest and short refresher courses in problems of politics, education, culture or administration. The list is endless, to the extent that Romanians have coined a word, *ședințomanie* (meeting-mania), to describe this devastating overabundance of formal gatherings.

(This has led to a recent joke: The day after a Party meeting, the local Party activist sights "Bula," a stereotypical buffon-type character and frequent subject of Romanian jokes, "Comrade Bula," the activist asks, "where were you at the last Party meeting?" Bula is startled and replies, "But Comrade Activist, had I known it was the LAST Party meeting I would have been there!")

Due to the capricious and often sudden nature of the campaigns, local meetings are frequently delayed, cancelled, or abrupty rescheduled. Quite often, the mayor will be forced to send young children scurrying around the village to find missing participants. Like most public gatherings, village meetings in Romania do more than discuss public issues or resolve pressing questions. Meetings function both as a forum for public mobilization and as a secular ritual: "sacred" socialist values are reaffirmed, and symbolic messages are exchanged between local elites and citizens and between regional authorities and Feldioarans (Kideckel [1983] discusses the symbolic functions of meetings in another Romanian village). In fact, many of the real problems are resolved before the meeting actually starts. Informal conservation and information exchange between elites means that nominations and speeches are pre-arranged. Further practical activities take place informally, after the meeting ends.

The bimonthly sessions of the Party Committee and People's Council are especially important for regional-local communication. It is here that regional elites can confront the entire cadre of village elites, lauding their successes, criticizing their failures, hearing their pleas, overseeing their arguments and proposing "organizational measures" which can be "translated into life." These meetings are the principal forum for local citizens to articulate local (or sectoral) interests. A teacher can stand up and say that he feels Feldioara has been "cheated" by the County after promised funds for establishing an evening school never materialized. It is also at such meetings that the regional Party activist can castigate local elites for incompetence or indiscipline, to the point where he deems Feldioara undeserving of becoming a town.

Since many key decisions are decided upon before the meeting, and since many Feldioarans know this, secondary elites and citizens will attend only if invited or to present grievances. Visiting officials and regional elites are frequently upset to find only half the local deputies present. The absent individuals are cited as evidence of the primary elites' (or Party

Committee's) "poor organizational ability" and "citizens' lack of community spirit."

Elite conflicts. Elites' interaction in task fulfillment, informal organization, corporate groups and meeting activity all serve to demarcate them from the rest of the villagers. However, this does not make the elite group free from internal conflicts. For example, some elites are more apt to go "by the book" while others are more indulgent or at times so flexible as to be "corrupt." If this misbehavior tends to interfere with the tasks or harm the prestige of fellow elites, or if outside authorities are known to be considering an inquiry into a local leader's conduct, local elite unity quickly dissolves. In the case of one former mayor, for example, his malfeasance became so overt that the local Party activist was practically shamed into reporting him to County authorities, lest she, too, be implicated.

Another mode whereby elite unity can be undermined lies in the ability of villagers to play off elites against each other when soliciting elite patronage. Citizens are aware that elite responsibilities tend to overlap. Elites connected with the Party apparatus have a sort of mandate to intervene in any domain of village life, a trait which Maria Hirszowicz had designated "power without responsibility" (1980:137). In concrete terms, this means a collective farmer dissatisfied with grain payments need not be content with the collective farm president's judgement against him. The peasant can take his case to the mayor, who has ultimate responsibility for achieving Feldioara's agricultural plan. Moreover, he may also appeal to the local Party activist or regional Party *instructor,* both of whom oversee village affairs. These individuals have the power to negotiate or override local elites' decisions, should the peasant be justified. The overlapping of competence and vagueness of responsibility does not automatically mean that the peasant will get his way. If prior conditions of social interaction have forged local elites into a cohesive social unit, a common front will appear and the peasant will either have to drop the matter or appeal to County or national authorities (e.g., letters to the newspaper, seeking an audience with the County Secretary, letters to the Central Committee, or to President Ceaușescu himself).

The combination of elites' overlapping areas of competence and the Party's "power without responsibility" gives the citizens a unique ability to appeal to several elites with the same problem. This tends to set limits on elite authority, and may even undermine elite social unity. These limits are best illustrated in the concrete problems of citizen mobilization in Feldioara.

Elite's Mobilization Styles

In fulfilling State goals in the village, local elites interact with the citizens in a particular "style." For example, the elite might simply instruct the citizen what he or she must do, basing the appeal on legal directives or the threat of negative sanctions. This style can be designated *bureaucratic*. At the opposite extreme, the elite might ask fellow villagers for their aid in accomplishing some common task, a style which might be called *egalitarian*. Mobilization styles will vary with specific tasks and with the elite's personality. However, there also exist structural constraints which determine the use of a specific style. These constraints derive from the functions of local elites in Romanian communities, their mode of recruitment to their posts, the kinds of social links they have to their constituents, their commitment to the village, and the kinds of value orientations used to mobilize the citizenry.

The fundamental structural constraint is the elite's duty to execute State policy in the locality. Elites have to cope with frequent turnabouts in these policies; they are poorly informed about the reasons for these changes and closely supervised by County and State officials. Elites may thus be compelled to act in a manner which appears haughty or insensitive to their constituents. Herein lies one explanation for the striking contrast between the elites' authorative public demeanor and their friendly, down-to-earth behavior in the personal sphere. This contrast is indicative of the kinds of pressures to which local elites are subjected. It is these pressures which impel elites toward a more bureaucratic style of mobilization even when they might be inclined to be more egalitarian in their interaction with the citizens.

A second constraint affecting elites' mobilization styles revolves around their mode of recruitment. Elites recruited via diktat or appointed from outside begin their tenure without any social relation to their constituents. They are one of "them," and will be more prone to using a bureaucratic mobilization style. Those elites born in the village or selected by virtue of their personal prestige will be one of "us"; they will be more likely to operate with an egalitarian appeal.

A third constraint on elite mobilization behavior lies in their linkage to the community. Regional and commuting primary elites are tied to outside institutions; they will tend to use a bureaucratic style simply because it involves fewer personal obligations. Resident elites, being more enmeshed in local social networks, will tend to be more egalitarian in their mobilization. This applies especially to secondary and informal elites, who are more likely to be cast back in the rank of the citizens at a moment's notice.

A fourth constraint involves commitment to the village. Elites who view their tenure in Feldioara as temporary will use any possible means to achieve results. Interested in pleasing their superiors, often with ambitious career goals, such people will tend to rely on a bureaucratic style of mobilization. The bureaucratic style is particularly suited for simplex (single-stranded) relations of a short-term nature. It neither presupposes nor creates additional social obligations between elites and citizens. Hence, it will be preferred by those elites who do not wish to create these ties, i.e., elites who have low commitment to long-term residence in the village. Conversely, those elites who reside more permanently must reckon with the long-term consequences of their behavior on their relations with fellow villagers. Being more likely to form multiplex social bonds with the citizens, long-term elites will tend to employ an egalitarian style of mobilization.

It should be emphasized that the bureaucratic and egalitarian styles are not equally conterposed. Egalitarian elites can always revert to the bureaucratic style, whereas bureaucratic elites are limited in their ability to act "egalitarian." Bureaucratic elites, because they come from outside, are without the intense relations which enable egalitarian appeals to operate in the first place. Outside elites must confine themselves to bureaucratic mobilization (until they become "insiders," at least). The asymmetrical character of the two styles means that an elite able to use the egalitarian style maintains an advantage because of flexibility of tactics. The egalitarian elite's advantage has a built-in limitation, however. More intense social relations between elite and citizen presuppose more mutual obligations between them. The egalitarian elite thus gets more out of the citizen, but the citizen is able to demand something in return. Egalitarian elites produce results by virtue of their legitimacy, but may alienate their constituents if they press too hard. In contrast, the bureaucratic elites will generate results so as to please their superiors, but will do this without even wanting to enmesh themselves in local ties of reciprocity. Hence, both types of mobilization style create distinct problems.

There are several ways these problems can be resolved. One way is to resign (frequently for reasons of health); hence, the turnover among secondary and locally born elites, who probably experience the most tension in their relations with other villagers. Another strategy is for the bureaucratic elite to try and become more egalitarian, with the consequent risk of creating obligations which cannot be fulfilled. A third possibility is for egalitarian elites to become more bureaucratic, hoping to permanently remain in elite ranks. A fourth strategy is to rely on "formalism," i.e., to reduce demands on citizens to a realistic minimum, thereby maintaining legitimacy; in this case the elite must endure the possibility of failed plans or angry superiors.

One can find examples of all four strategies among Feldioara's elite cadres. That these are structural problems of socialist development rather than purely personal problems of leadership are amply illustrated in comparative studies of local elites elsewhere in Romania (Romanian Studies Collective 1977, Cole 1980, Kideckel 1979) as well as in Hungary (Bell 1979) and the Soviet Union (Inkeles 1950:67-135, Fainsod 1958:138-53).

Value Orientations in Mobilization

Operating under these diverse structural constraints, local elites use more than simply the power of their office or threat of coercion to mobilize the population. Through personal contact with the citizens during formal meetings and informal interactions, local elites utilize specific value orientations to stimulate desired citizen behavior. Five of the most commonly invoked values are those of "work," "self-reliance," "discipline," "duty" and "social ethic."

Work. "Work" (*munca*) is embedded in the doctrine of the Romanian Communist Party. It is a frequent theme in newspaper articles, in President Ceauşescu's speeches, and in local meetings. In the words of the President:

> Communism cannot be built without work! . . . Without discipline, without order, without work, we shall not be able to implement what we have envisaged (Ceauşescu 1977:49).

Work, useful social activity, is the determining factor in the mould-
ing of socialist consciousness, in the moral and political education of
the masses . . . . The slogan "neither work without bread, nor bread
without work" should be permanently kept alive in the minds of our
children, of the youth, in the minds of all citizens of our 'homeland'
(Ceauşescu 1978:66-67).

A genuine "work ethic" also appears in informal conversations with
Feldioarans. For instance, the highest tribute one peasant can pay to another is to salute his work ability: "He worked—all his life he worked," is
a common refrain at funerals. An agricultural technician will insist that,
"any collectivist who wants to work can made a good life for himself; the
peasants should stop complaining." And a teacher from a nearby village
where the soil is especially poor complains,

> If only *we* had the kind of land Feldioara had, we would be rich.
> Feldioarans don't know how to work. We do.

The counterparts to work are sloth and theft. Thus, local trouble-makers
and Gypsies are placed at the bottom of Feldioara's social pyramid partly
because "they refuse to work." Villagers gossip continuously about those
who obtain resources without working, i.e., thieves. Anyone suddenly
exhibiting extra wealth—even a new dress—is subject to rumors that they
have come by their money illicitly. Theft in Feldioara is not common, but
it is a common topic of conversation.

Newspapers, when not saluting the model worker, revel in exposing the
slothful ones, those "lounging in the cafe," "taking an extended break,"
or "not paying their debt to society." The work ethic underlies the periodic
campaigns against petty corruption and bribery (Rom. *bacşiş, ciubuc,
mită*), where persons are caught receiving gifts or money that they haven't
really worked for.

In formal meetings, Feldioarans are instructed that they must *work* to
achieve "town" status. Urbanization is not a gift from the State but a
reward. As such, it must be earned.

Thus, the Party activist intones:

Villagers must not go around thinking that the State will do the work for them. It is through our own self-reliance and hard work that we construct socialism.

Self-reliance. Closely tied to the work ethic are the constant invocations for "self-reliance" (or self-responsibility, translated *auto-răspunderea*). Self-reliance is reflected in Romania's "independent" foreign policy and its program for economic development. At the local level, self-reliance campaigns emphasize enterprise "self-management" (*autoconducerea*) and community "self-administration" (*autogestiunea*). In concrete terms, these involve calls for more judicious use of raw materials, recycling waste, conserving energy, reduction in State subsidies, and self-sufficiency (*autoaprovizionarea*) in food production. Self-reliance thus extends to each individual household. Each must produce vegetables, eggs, and animals for its own needs, so that Romania's food distribution network can provide for urban workers and fulfill export obligations. Self-reliance is also an underlying theme in the campaigns for village voluntary work projects (to be discussed in more detail below). Calls for self-reliance have little to do with self-determination or genuine autonomy. In the Romanian context, self-reliance refers to measures taken by counties, villages, enterprises or households which save costs for the State or transfer administrative burdens from the State to local bodies.

Discipline. Where "work" and "self-reliance" characterize both villagers' and elites' world views, the theme of "discipline" (*disciplină*) is employed chiefly by the elites. The Party Program, the Five Year Plan, and enterprise organizations all represent disciplined forms for achieving goals. Plans and policies which go awry are never in themselves wrong; they have simply not been implemented correctly. Surprise visits by journalists to factories, villages, youth clubs or collective farms are replete with condemnations of "poor leadership," "weak organization'" "indiscipline," "pure chaos," "people coming and going," or "total lack of control." The Party activist constantly asserts that Party goals must be "translated into life," not haphazardly, but "by the book" (*"după carte"*). "We have to take measures" (*Trebuie luate măsuri!*) he exhorts. Such measures involve creating coordinating councils or commissions or replacing personnel. Organizational campaigns invariably include a call for stricter discipline.

Duty. By achieving the plan via self-reliant hard work and strict discipline, Romanians fulfill their "duty" (*datorie*) to society. Local elites have specially defined duties, of course, but in fact all Romanian citizens must "carry out their duty" (*fac datorie*) to their workplace, family, community, Party or country. Factory workers have obligations to their plant and peasants to their collective farm. It is a mother's duty to bear children in order that Romania will have a sufficient labor force. Parents should raise children to be good citizens, and children should help their parents in their old age. Communists are duty bound to be model citizens and to help implement Party policy. Villagers should assist the collective farm during harvest periods, contract to deliver agricultural produce to the State, and volunteer for community improvement projects. Each household has a duty to achieve self-sufficiency in food production, thus helping Romania to achieve its development goals. Finally, all Romanian citizens have a duty to build socialism and defend the fatherland from internal and external enemies.

Those who shirk their duty by not working, not delivering produce, not having children or by seeking to leave Romania—are placing their "personal interest" above the "general interest." Such people are "*egoişti*," and are actively harming the whole of Romanian society. The ultimate *egoişti* are those seeking to emigrate to the West. Emigres are seen as nothing less than traitors (*trădători*), according to some speeches by Romania's president; thus, "leaving the country they were born in is a shameful action, a humiliating action." And, "We do not need those who betray their homeland . . . since he who betrayed once, will betray always, and will remain a traitor forever!" (Ceauşescu 1979:114, 117-118).

Needless to say, the ideology of "duty" is more commonly articulated by elites than by citizens, for most ordinary citizens, their duties are executed by adhering to "the social ethic."

The social ethic. The social ethic involves "obligations" (*"obligaţii"*) of kinship, friendship and neighborliness which are germane to community life. Whereas "duty" specifies relations between individuals and impersonal institutions, the social ethic is a kind of duty within the sphere of interpersonal relations. The principles of the social ethic are articulated through day-to-day social interaction and during periodic mobilization campaigns. The most important obligation is the bond among immediate family members. Newspaper articles and television programs give scathing accounts of irresponsible children who bring anguish to their parents, drunken fathers who neglect their families, mothers who leave their children, and couples who hold huge wedding celebrations in order to obtain cash gifts, whereupon they divide the "take" and divorce.

The social ethic encompasses more than just family obligations, however. It includes social relations manifested in mutual gift-giving and moneylending, helping friends to obtain scarce resources, reciprocal labor exchange, social visiting, eating, drinking, gossipping (information exchange) and attendance at family celebrations. Many of the informal, illegal or otherwise undocumented exchanges which comprise Romania's "second economy" are the material manifestations of these social obligations (for a social perspective on Eastern Europe's "second economy" see Kenedi 1981 and Sampson 1983a).

Those who neglect their social obligations are a common topic of village gossip. Often they are people "in between," people on their way up or down the social ladder. As such, they are in the process of establishing relations with another network or clique. These people have not really forgotten the social ethic; they are simply transferring it to another group. An obvious example is the newly drafted elite who stops visiting (or has no time to visit) village companions and is now seen in the company of other elites.

While the social ethic is especially important for Feldioara's citizens, the local elites are hardly exempt from its sanctions. Elites' "moral comportment" is just as important as their professional capability. A local mayor was removed from office largely as a result of an extra-marital escapade, another local elite was demoted because of an affair. A village professional with an important Party function had left his wife and child; when threatened with possible exclusion from the Party because of his "bad moral example," he quickly returned home.

Villagers' expectations concerning the social ethic are more strict for locally resident and informal elites than for commuting or short-term leaders. They will tolerate behavior among "outsiders" which they do not accept among their own. This is quite logical, since the egalitarian mobilization style of locally resident leaders is linked to the social ethic. Elites who utilize the social ethic not only solidify their ties with the citizens, but mobilize them in the process. The problem for these elites is that relations of kinship and friendship may end up conflicting with Party "discipline" and "duty." From this conflict arise the possibility of "deviations," "errors," "weak leadership" and even "corruption."

The value orientations of mobilization are in conflict because the State considers the social ethic to be subordinate to "discipline" and "duty," and to the State's "general interest." The priority of the "general interest" is immutable. As expressed by President Ceaușescu, "there are no friends, no relatives, when general interests are concerned" (1977:616).

Of all the value orientations used in mobilization, the social ethic is both the most effective and the most hazardous for the elite. This will be illustrated in the following case studies of mobilization styles in Feldioara.

Mobilization Styles in Feldioara: Some Case Studies

Mobilization activities in Feldioara take place in a variety of domains. The most important are expropriations, voluntary work brigades, household contracting of animals and farm plots, villagers' assistance in the collective farm's harvest and local participation in public ceremonies. These kinds of mobilization activities take place in all Romanian villages, including those undergoing planned urbanization. Feldiora is special because (1) planned and unintended changes have sharpened the gap between elites and citizens and (2) State demands on elites have continuously increased. The following cases illustrate the constraints on elite behavior and the range of strategies they use to "get things done" in Feldioara. The "bureaucratic" and "egalitarian" mobilization styles will serve as the conceptual focal points of the analysis. The first case examines the most sensitive of the elite's tasks—expropriating peasants' lands.

Expropriation activities. By 1977, 12 gardens, 7 barns and four houses had been expropriated to build Feldioara's new apartments. Chapter VIII discussed the case of G., who feared losing his barn but was saved at the last moment because of a delay in the implementation of the plan. At the same time, it appeared that the gardens of several local elites were to be spared expropriation, while other citizens were scheduled to lose theirs. When some of these elites sought to connect their houses into the apartments' central heating system, local gossip began spreading that they had manipulated the plan in their favor. As it turned out, two elite families lost a *part* of their gardens, while two other families did manage to hook up to the central heating lines. There is no concrete proof that elites have manipulated the plan, yet the image of manipulation certainly exists for many citizens in Feldioara. Like the paranoia about theft, this image is probably linked to the relative socio-economic equality between elites and citizens in Feldioara. Differences which may be relatively slight or advantages allocated on a chance basis become that much more exaggerated because of the relative equality among most of Feldioara's citizens. Similar phenomena have been pointed out in other European community studies, notably France (Wylie 1963:194-206) and in Hungary (Bell 1979: 171-175).

A second example of expropriation illustrates the problems of elites who draw the wrath of regional officials for not going "by the book." An old widow in Feldioara was informed that she had to donate part of her garden for the building of a new veterinary dispensary. The woman was a collective farm pensionist living alone. She maintained that the garden was all she had, and categorically refused to give up any portion of it. The mayor, an in-migrant to Feldioara, did not take her refusal very seriously. He sent one of the local militia to her house to instruct her of the law about expropriating lands "in the public interest" and to remind her of her "duty" to help Feldioara develop. In return for her lost garden, the woman was offered a plot of land at the edge of the village. Still she refused, insisting that people would steal from her garden if it lay so far from her house. The policeman told the mayor that the old woman "was ready to throw herself in front of the bulldozer."

The widow's refusal was soon brought up during an informal gathering of the mayor, vice-mayor, veterinarian, village notary and regional Party *instructor*. They all agreed that the woman was "crazy." She would have to be "educated" about the necessity of the "general interest" and her "duty" to the community. Since she already possessed the maximum legal allotment of garden land on her collective farm plot, the commune was perfectly within its rights to expropriate it without compensation. For the Party activist from Brașov, the matter was simple: "The individual interest of this crazy old woman cannot stand in the way of modernizing the dispensary."

The mayor agreed, but he felt that he could not act so hastily: "That's easy for you to say, but people will say it's the mayor's fault if that crazy woman throws herself in front of the bulldozer!"

The Party *instructor* reiterated that there should be no compromise: "The law is the law," he said. "And everybody has to respect it."

Having reminded the mayor of his duty to implement Feldioara's development in a responsible way, the activist returned to Brașov. The mayor delegated the case to his vice-mayor, a recently drafted informal elite and an acquaintance of the woman's family. The vice-mayor called the family members into the town hall, and in a heart-to-heart talk, implored them to get their mother to give up her garden. The vice-mayor would assure them that she would get a double-sized garden of equal fertility in return. With the help of family pressure, the woman soon "capitulated" and construction of the veterinary dispensary began.

As the activist says, "the law is the law." But for *village* elites, who must deal with constituents on a long-term, multiplex basis, the law can be implemented in different ways. What the activist describes as elite "indiscipline" or vacillation is in reality the elites' flexibility in solving day-to-day problems within the local setting. By relegating a sensitive task to an informal elite, and by the vice-mayor's utilization of the social ethic and his personal relations, the expropriation was accomplished with a minimal degree of conflict.

Agricultural contracting. National directives and Party propaganda exhort all communities to be self-sufficient in food production. Villagers have a duty to sell a given quantity of pigs, calves, milk, eggs, lambs or wool to the local consumers' cooperative. In addition to cash payments, those who deliver produce can purchase State-owned fodder at favorable prices. However, the State's acquisition prices are lower than what peasants receive on the informal market, and fodder provisions are often inadequate. Hence, for local elites, contracting campaigns involve a considerable amount of mobilization activity. In January of each year, all household heads are called to Feldioara's town hall to negotiate their produce deliveries and sign contracts.

Mobilization for agricultural delivery contracts is carried out in conjunction with the collective farm's campaign to cultivate plots of land on the *acord global* system (*acord global* is roughly translated "comprehensive piece-work"). Under *acord global*, each person or enterprise is assigned a plot of potatoes or sugar beets which they weed, harvest and deliver, in return for cash and fodder payments. For example, a housewife is assigned

0.30 hectare; a commuter 0.10 hectare. The village administrative staff cultivates 2 hectares, the brick factory 12 hectares.

Both the contracting and the *acord global* campaigns provide material and moral incentives to the villagers. From a material standpoint, families were assured that for each pig delivered, they could obtain such cheap fodder that they could raise a second pig free for home consumption. Cultivating *acord global* plots would assure extra cash, vegetables and fodder for the household. Villagers also had a moral *duty* to help the collective farm reduce its need for outside labor, to help Feldioara become agriculturally self-sufficient and to maximize all available productive resources. Hence, a school-teacher couple who had an unused pigsty (their food needs were supplied by their parents down the street) suddenly found themselves required to contract for two pigs. Families who ignored these "incentives" or shirked their moral responsibilities were called into the town hall to explain themselves.

Despite the material and moral incentives, the two campaigns went poorly in Feldioara in 1976. Perhaps the plan was too ambitious. In any event, worker households were upset at the extra burdens. Peasants were skeptical as to the promised fodder supplies or they preferred to sell their produce on the informal market at higher prices. As a result, the plan for allocating land on *acord global* fell short by 40% (only 128 hectares out of a planned 200 were allocated). Contract statistics for 1976 revealed that only 22 pigs had been delivered out of 352 contracted, only 126 of 196 calves (calf prices were notably better, and restrictions on their illegal slaughter much stiffer), only 9 of 80 lambs, only 280,000 of 440,000 liters of milk and only 1548 kg of 2700 kg. originally contracted for wool.

In trying to achieve the plan, local elites resorted to a variety of strategies. Citizens' requests to utilize elites' institutional resources were now linked with the mobilization campaign. Thus a peasant's request to borrow the collective farm's wagons for her daughter's wedding celebration was granted only after the president had her sign a contract to take out an additional 0.30 ha. on *acord global*. The vice-mayor and village notary went house to house, trying to convince people to sign contracts to deliver pigs, milk and eggs. All local elites were expected to set an example by raising animals and cultivating *acord global* plots.

In one instance, a recalcitrant peasant was called to the town hall to explain why he hadn't signed a contract. The peasant confronted the vice-mayor, who also happened to be his nephew. He unabashedly complained that procuring fodder was too difficult, that he had contracted one calf which he thought was enough, and that he would rather raise pigs for his own consumption and for private sale. The vice-mayor, having been selected partly because of his prior legitimacy, did not enjoy pestering a kinsmen over his contract obligations. After listening patiently to the old man's complaints, the vice-mayor asked him to sit down and then said:

> Look, Uncle Ion, *everybody* has to take on some more contracting. The County wants to have more. We have our own plan and we know you can come through with 2 or 3 calves and some piglets. We'll try to get you some more fodder. You know I'm just trying to do my job here. Now why don't you help me and sign the contract for two more calves. I promise you on my word of honor that we won't bother you after that. Now how about it, Uncle Ion? Come on, how about it?

The vice-mayor's mobilization style was undoubtedly of the "egalitarian" type. He was appealing to a fellow villager, a kinsman, asking him for a favor, a favor which happened to coincide with the interests of the State plan. The appeal, "I'm just carrying out orders, we're all in this together," seemed effective in convincing the man to sign a new contract. At that moment the mayor walked in. Listening to the conversation he admonished the peasant in typical "bureaucratic" style:

> Stop griping. You know that everyone in the village has to take contracts and that we have a plan to fulfill. Those are the rules and if you don't want to follow the rules you'll be fined and that's it. If you want more fodder go out and cut some hay yourself [on the collective farm's *acord global* arrangements].

The man eventually signed, swayed probably by both the egalitarian appeal of the vice-mayor and the bureaucratic authority of the mayor. In fact, the mayor really has no power to fine anyone for nonfulfillment of a "contract," for it is really a household *plan*, and villagers cannot be fined for nonfulfillment of a plan. The mayor had been bluffing, counting on the peasant's fear of authority. That the old man signed drew no words of gratitude from the mayor. The peasant was simply doing what was expected of him, i.e., fulfilling his duty to the State. For the vice-mayor, however, his uncle's signing meant that he had acquired new social obligations: to arrange for cheaper and more available fodder and to grant a future favor if the peasant asked him for one. Since these contracts are renewed each year, the peasant could hold the vice-mayor to these obligations when the next mobilization campign took place.

Here is both the strength and the weakness of the egalitarian mobilization style. It produces results while simultaneously creating new obligations. Because the subsequent obligations are tied to the social ethic, they may conflict with his "duties" to higher organs. The structural aspects of these problems are elaborated in Alex Inkeles' (1950) analysis of party agitators in the Soviet Union.

Inkeles writes:

> The very element that gives him this increased effectiveness also acts as a real limiting factor on that effectiveness. For at times when the agitator is being pressed most by the party for more intensive criticism of lagging workers, or when he has to introduce measures which meet the displeasure of the workers, his personal relations with those workers will then most induce him to temper his criticism or to soft-pedal the measures as much as it is within his power to do so. Furthermore, insofar as he behaves as a good party man at such times and carries out the instructions of his party to the letter, then he runs the risk of losing that close contact with his fellow workers which was the basis of his authority in the first place (Inkeles 1950:90).

For Inkeles, then, the "problem of the quality of Party cadres" is really a false problem. What determines the quality of Party cadres (or in my terms, the style of mobilization) are the structural contradictions inherent in their role as local elites subordinated to continuous higher level demands. In Feldioara it is a problem of "village elites" versus "elites who are villagers."

Voluntary work brigades. An additional duty of all villagers between 18 and 55 years of age is a community tax which can be paid off in money or labor (*"contribuţie în bani şi în munca din partea populaţiei"*). These contributions usually vary from 4-6 days per year per individual. In addition to these legal obligations, there are also more spontaneous voluntary work tasks (*muncă voluntară*) in which groups of villagers, including school-children and pensioners, can contribute to specific community projects. In practice, the legal *contribuții* and "voluntary work" are often blended together. Even President Ceaușescu has remarked that what was supposed to have been a wholly voluntary, citizen controlled effort used only for special projects has become bureaucratized:

> . . . The way of applying the law was misinterpreted. In practice, the voluntary contribution has become a sort of compulsory tax; the people's councils have sent out office workers who simply made lists with how much each citizen should contribute (Ceaușescu 1973: 577-78).

Contributions and voluntary labor tasks can include physical labor, cleri-cal work or sitting on Feldioara's "citizen court" (*Comisie de Judecată*). Outdoor work brigades usually occur on Sundays, when those who com-mute to Brașov are available. Schoolchildren are active in local clean-up campaigns, planting trees and beautifying the local parks. Oftimes, in-dividuals execute their work contribution through their enterprise. For example, the collective farm's construction brigade may work as a unit to help the village construct a nursery.

Those who fail to execute the full complement of work-days are fined 50 lei per day, the equivalent of about half a day's unskilled labor. The commune uses the fines to purchase materials or hire skilled labor not budgeted by the State, but local officials would much prefer to have the labor than collect fines. Nevertheless, younger, skilled workers and com-muters with scarce leisure time are content to pay the fine. Older villagers and agriculturalists usually participate via labor, or send their children in their places.

Feldioara's urbanization plan demands voluntary contributions of work/money for laying sidewalks, digging sewage run-offs, repairing communal facilities, building flood dikes, planting trees and shrubs along the main streets and otherwise "beautifying" the village center. In the late 1970s, the most important project was the construction of a new culture house, used for weddings, meetings, films, dances, youth activities and, eventually, a library. It has taken over five years to build the culture house. In the final year, villagers were assessed an extra tax of 150 lei and people's contribution increased from four to six days. As it lay half-finished on the main street, the two-story structure was seen more as an eyesore than an inspiration. One Feldioaran commented how a neighboring village had

> managed to build their culture house in just two years, but Feldioara could not organize itself to build theirs in five. Besides, if we became a town, the State will have to come in and construct it using their own funds.

In late 1976 only 60,000 lei had been collected of the projected 138,000 lei in voluntary work/fines. Many of the Sunday work brigades were badly organized and poorly attended. Sometimes the elites scheduled to lead them did not appear until those assembled had already gone home. On other occasions, a needed truck or cement mixer never showed up, so that work could not begin. The effective work "day" hardly ever exceeded four hours. Delays in finishing the culture house were expecially irritating to regional elites and visiting County officials. Addressing local meetings, they scolded the villagers using all the mobilization themes of "work," "self-reliance," "discipline," "duty," and even "the social ethic":

> What are you Feldioarans waiting for? Don't think the State is going to do it for you!

> You've got to take measures and get yourselves organized!

> Delegate the tasks and stimulate more discipline. Everybody—chiefs of institutions, deputies, Party members, youth, commuters—you all have to do your parts.

> Have the deputies go house-to-house and get the citizens out on Sundays. Get your own family members out, too. This culture house is for you!

> Raise the fines if you want, increase the work days, but get that culture house done by August 23rd at the latest!

This was hardly a fortuitous date: August 23rd commemorates Romania's anti-fascist uprising and is marked with mass rallies and meetings. As part of the celebration, the culture house would have been inaugurated that day. Feldioara's mayor thus had to solicit labor from other local institutions. He asked the school principal for 20 pupils to help lay a sidewalk. From the head of the factory, he requested a truck and two laborers, and from the construction site three skilled workmen. When the directors of these institutions protested, they were reminded of their "duty" to the community, and of the fact that he "had orders from the County" to get the task finished. Yet despite County orders and the elites' contributions, August 23rd passed without a new culture house. In fact, the building was not completed until mid 1978, eighteen months after the "final" deadline.

Why the difficulties mobilizing citizens for projects which appear to be for their own benefit? Is it just a matter of the citizens' insufficiently raised *conştiinţa* ("consciousness," "attitude")? In Chapter VIII it was suggested that local participation would be contingent on both the perceived threat to household resource control and the villagers' degree of commitment. Clearly, those citizens who expect to move have little motivation to help the village construct its culture house. In addition, the option of contributing in either labor *or* cash had worked to Feldioara's disadvantage. The skilled workers have enough disposable income so that they would rather pay their fines than contribute their valuable labor skills. This is regrettable, since it is these workers who will come to benefit most from the future urbanization. The village mobilization campaign has thus become an unintended victim of the success of Romanian industrialization. Bureaucratized mobilization and apathetic cash payments have come to replace spontaneous participation and social commitment.

It would be misleading to attribute poor mobilization solely to the citizens' apathy. In a sense, County officials are correct when they cite "weak organization" among local elite cadres. These organizational difficulties are caused by structural problems rather than purely personal shortcomings, however. Enterprise heads see their first duty toward their factory, institution or ministry rather than to the community. After all, the minerals plant is directly subordinated to the national ministry, while Feldioara has little real power to impose its will on the factory. (Similar conflicts are reported by Taubman [1973] and Hough [1969] for the Soviet Union.) Moreover, fluctuation in elite positions has meant that some of

Feldioara's leading cadres do not fully comprehend the plan and their roles in carrying out voluntary projects. In 1979, I asked an official of the minerals factory, the newly elected mayor and the new vice-mayor why the total voluntary work contribution would remain stable at 138,000 lei during the forthcoming five years, even though Feldioara's population would grow by several hundred. Would this growth not mean a gradual increase in the sum total of labor/money contributed by the residents? "No," they all insisted. The 138,000 lei figure would remain stable, while Feldioara's urbanization would lead to the work burden being distributed among more people. As the population grew, the *per capita* contribution would be reduced. Presumably, it would one day become negligible. For these elites, then, voluntary work was but a temporary inconvenience, an unfortunate concomitant to Feldioara's underdevelopment. They were confident that as Feldioara urbanized, State budgetary allocations would eventually relieve elites of the need to mobilize villagers for voluntary projects.

Feldioara's newly appointed Party activist expressed a diametrically opposing view, however. The activist, in charge of "ideological and propaganda activities," insisted that the total voluntary work contribution would increase in direct proportion to the increase in population. The original plan for a constant 138,000 lei was being upgraded accordingly. Invoking the principles of "work" and "duty," she asserted that, "villagers would *always* have to contribute. They could never escape their obligations." With such misunderstandings within the elite cadres, it is small wonder that voluntary work brigades had difficulties organizing.

Given the structural factors inhibiting elite-citizen linkages, and the elites' differing views on the importance of citizen mobilization, it becomes clear why elites must frantically borrow laborers from other elites' institutions, recruit school-children for special tasks, and hire paid labor from commune funds. The Party activist is aware of the problem, and she has been working conscientiously to enlighten fellow elites and to mobilize citizens. Yet her individual efforts are up against the social complexities of a changing community, County and State demands on hard-pressed local organs and the structural constraints of elite social organization. Given these problems, what is remarkable are not the problems encountered but the degree to which they are ultimately resolved.

Summary: Getting Things Done in Feldioara

Elite mobilization activities in Feldioara reflect the structural features of Romanian planning, the characteristics of elite social organization, and the tension between egalitarianism and hierarchy in villager-elite relations. This combination of factors leads to styles of mobilization ranging from the "bureaucratic" to the "egalitarian." Table 24 (next page) shows more precisely the characteristics of elite behavior according to each style, where "bureaucratic" and "egalitarian" are employed as ideal types.

Both mobilization styles generate problems for elites and for the citizens, but they are quite different types of problems. The bureaucratic style relies on negative sanctions, thus reifying the power differential between elite and citizen. A bureaucratic elite can mobilize citizens, but cannot foster their voluntary participation. Use of such a style hinders the formation of multiplex ties, or restricts them to the most instrumental type of patron-client relations. The personal efforts of bureaucratic elites may ameliorate some of these negative tendencies (e.g., the indulgent president of the consumers' cooperative), but these efforts will not automatically produce multiplex social ties. An indulgent leader *who remains an outsider* will simply be giving the villagers license to exploit the system either informally or illegally, for this type of leader can employ only negative, bureaucratic sanctions.

The egalitarian style is an effective means of citizen mobilization because it reduces social distance between elite and citizen. The problem is that maintaining this close relationship creates its own contradictions. The elite who forms and fulfills reciprocal obligations with constituents may fall victim to accusations of favoritism or corruption. From above, the egalitarian elite's flexibility may be viewed as a "lack of discipline," i.e., a deviation from administrative rationality. An egalitarian elite who recognizes this dilemma can then choose either to opt out of elite ranks by resignation, or to carry out his tasks with a degree of formalism or indulgence so as to avoid alienating fellow villagers.

The problem of egalitarian elites is especially acute in rural communities. Only in the village are local elites so clearly visible. They cannot hide behind barbed-wire compounds and do not qualify for elite material privileges or special shops. It is in the village that demands from above become so incessant, that relations between citizens and elites are so intense, and that problems of mobilization become most acute.

TABLE 24

FACTORS DETERMINING ELITE-CITIZEN MOBILIZATION

	MOBILIZATION STYLE	
Factor	Bureaucratic	Egalitarian
Elite role	executor monitor	local partisan monitor

Elite category	all regional elites
	local formal primary
	  elites
		local formal secondary
		
		informal elites
		informal elites recently
		  drafted into formal
		  positions

Elite Residence	commuter temporary in-migrant	long-term resident
Elite Recruitment	via diktat	via consultation via election

Legitimacy	derives from administrative
	  role
		derives from local
		  value system

Elite Interaction	task fulfillment corporate groups (Party) meetings	task fulfillment corporate groups (Party) informal groups
Mobilization forums	formal meetings	formal meetings/informal interaction
Value orientations	"discipline" "duty","work" "self-reliance"	"the social ethic" "work"
Elite-citizen relations	simplex formalized	multiplex personalized

There thus seems to be a trade-off between the two styles of mobilization: the bureaucratic style is effective for short-term, onerous tasks but reenforces social distance between elites and citizens. The egalitarian style yields more effective citizen mobilization, but leads local elites into long-term multiplex social obligations which may conflict with administrative duties and Party discipline.

Romania's State and Party officials are aware of the problems brought on by citizen-mobilization in the villages. Measures taken to "improve the quality of elite cadres" include: drafting informal elites, local consultations to identify potential leaders, competitive elections at local levels, sending native-born graduates back into their home villages so that they can utilize informal ties, and teaching courses in "leadership science" at Party training schools (these strategies are described in Sampson 1984).

Nevertheless, the role of village elites as executors of State power has not been altered. If anything, this role must increase as Romania's development plans sustain their ambitious level and villagers are asked to sacrifice for a future which seems more and more remote (in numerous speeches, sacrificing "for our children" has now been replaced by sacrificing "for our descendants" [*pentru urmașii noștri*]). Elites will continue to suffer from haphazard information from above, capricious rotation into posts for which they are not trained, and confusing improvizations in the plans. All these will complicate their relation to their constituents.

The State's efforts to consult with citizens and draft informal elites are laudable steps in building elite legitimacy and improving cadre quality. But the purpose of these measures seems to be to make State authority over local communities more effective. The structural constraints on elites have not been altered. Could local elites ever achieve a role in local policy formation, transcending their primary function as executors of State plans? Could the increasing number of locally born, egalitarian elites ever become partisans for their communities without being denounced from above as chauvinists? Could they (to use Konrad's and Szelenyi's example) begin to question transport policy instead of simply pleading for a new bus route? If so, their local legitimacy would have a more solid foundation, and some of the constraints generated by supralocal structures would be less threatening. Letting elites speak for local interests would be confirmation of the fact that village-State relations are both administrative and political. The State would have to recognize that plans will succeed only if local-level informal structures are accepted or reenforced, with its inherent dangers to State power.

Recognizing the validity of local structures would not solve all the elites' problems, of course, for they still remain *village* elites, compelled to exert authority over people with whom they interact on a long-term multiplex basis. Yet there seems every reason to believe that altering the structural position of the elites would produce changes in mobilization style—from bureaucratic to egalitarian. And that the problems generated by egalitarian style would be reduced from the realm of "politics" to that of "social relations."

The contradiction between the two styles is best illustrated with quotations from two of Feldioara's former mayors (both of whom were forced out of office):

> We are a family. We should treat each other like a family. (Spoken at a meeting of the People's Council, 1975).

> I'm the shepherd around here, and these people are my sheep. (Spoken to a visiting anthropologist, 1977).

Both these metaphors distort the reality of villager-elite relations; they do not even constitute a viable ideal. It is significant that despite their diverse leadership "philosophies," both mayors were forced to resign. Their attempts to carry out their fundamental duty of citizen mobilization led to citizen alienation and hostility. Both men were condemned as "poor leaders," with an "improper style of work." But the problem of "poor leadership" cannot be solved simply by replacing personnel. As shown in this chapter, there remain more fundamental factors which determine the way villagers are mobilized.

Getting things done in Feldioara is hardly a family affair. And it is a far cry from sheepherding.

CHAPTER X

SUMMARY AND CONCLUSIONS:
PLANNING, SOCIALISM AND THE STUDY OF COMPLEX SOCIETY

Planning as a Process

This book began by expressing dissatisfaction with the way many anthropologists have studied complex society. Specifically, the need to understand processes of national integration had become overshadowed by the intensive analysis of bounded social units such as the community or region. Rejecting this "concentric circle" approach, this study employed a "vertical slice" procedure. Emphasis on the bounded unit was replaced by a focus on a specific societal institution and the processes by which different societal levels were integrated into a single social whole. Where the concentric circle model presupposed a dichotomous opposition between village and nation, the vertical slice approach assumed systematic linkage between them. This linkage also generated systemic contradictions, but these contradictions were intrinsic to the functioning of an institution rather than extraneous to it.

The vertical slice approach was applied to Romania's planning institution. Because there existed a codified set of frequently articulated public goals (e.g. "development," "communist society") and a formal bureaucratic apparatus assigned the task of realizing these goals, analyzing the planning "slice" seemed the most effective way of elucidating Romania's national integration processes. The vertical slice procedure focused on the plan to restructure Romania's national settlement network, a plan known as *sistematizare* ("systemization," "territorial planning"). The goal of Romanian systematization was to reorder the ties between smaller and larger settlements so as to create a fully integrated national settlement hierarchy. This would be accomplished by transforming 300 villages into small towns and by gradually regrouping or phasing out the dispersed or otherwise "irrational" settlements.

The initial focus on systematization had assumed a more or less "pristine" plan divorced from its social or political context. As it proceeded from national-level offices to regional planners to local communities, the plan would then confront various extraneous factors which could distort or corrupt it. The degree of this distortion constituted the gap between the official policy and the realities of plan execution.

The analysis of Romanian systematization showed that the "pristine" model of planning was unworkable. The model was unworkable because it insulated the corporate, bureaucratic features of planning from its more elusive but equally significant noncorporate features. The model had assumed that "the plan" as a technical, rational institution could be analyzed separately from the social milieu in which it functioned. In fact, there never was—nor could there ever be—such a "pristine" plan. The factors elucidated in the vertical slice framework—i.e., planning-in-general, socialist ideology, Romanian priorities, regional conditions, local social structure and elite behavior—these factors were not extraneous to the plan but as integral to it as the technical calculations and administrative decisions. These factors were not outside the plan; they *were* the plan. It became clear that what integrates Romanian society is not the overt plan as such, but a more subtle and more complex *planning process*.

On the surface, the plan may appear simply as a formal administrative structure. As part of the planning process, however, the plan was tied to a social dynamic and cultural logic which lie just below the institutional surface. Administrative behavior seemingly based on rational decisions and technical expertise was pervaded by informal social structures, underlying political tensions and inherently conflicting value orientations. The interaction between the surface and "hidden" features of planning occurred in both the formulation and execution phases, at each level in the national-regional-local hierarchy. The participants in this wider planning process included more than the planners and administrators attached to the institutional apparatus. Regional officials, community elites and individuals households also influenced the plan, while they themselves reacted to and executed planning decisions. Hence, Romania's planning process had ramifications far beyond the formal boundaries of the planning apparatus. In fact, the planning process (and not "The Plan") constituted the key integrating mechanism in Romanian society, much like tribal societies are said to be integrated by relations of kinship.

Using the vertical slice framework, the factors which directly shaped Romania's process could be readily elaborated. At the national level, Romanian systematization reflected a blend of development planning in general, socialist ideology in particular, and the specific national priorities of Romania's political leadership. Romania's development planners had a generalized conception of "the public interest" which they equated with their own version of rationality. Systematization was urban oriented, insofar as villages were to be created in the image of cities, and rural areas maintained to serve urban needs. Planners' ideas of citizen participation consisted of "informing" and "consulting" with the citizens so as to find more effective ways to implement the *planners'* decisions.

From this perspective, "the planning factor" in Romania operated much like it does in other countries. Phenomena that may have appeared typical of socialist planning or idiosyncratic to Romanian society actually derived from the nature of development planning itself.

Nevertheless, the similarities between Romanian planning and that of developing countries were overshadowed by its distinctly "socialist" character. The socialist countries have a common ideological foundation in Marxist principles. Yet before long term goals could be pursued, socialist planners were faced with the task of achieving the high level of development which was supposed to have occurred under capitalism. Socialist planning thus became a special form of development planning. "Socialist development" entailed realizing several priorities set by Marxist ideology: an end to urban/rural differences, alleviation of regional inequalities, dispersion of productive forces and social surplus to all classes, ethnic groups and regions, and the creation of a rational network of settlements. These immediate development goals were a means to a higher end—a classless, communist society. To achieve both the intermediate goal of "development" and the ultimate goal of "communism," socialist states have the authority to mobilize financial resources, qualified expertise, popular support and community labor. Priority projects such as Romania's three hundred new towns are indicative of the long range, wide scope, nation-wide scale and economic primacy that characterize socialist planning. In order to realize grand national objectives, local requirements and interests must be subordinated to national priorities. To this end, the socialist plan requires citizen participation as both a civic duty and an economic necessity. All the above characteristics make for similarities in the planning process of socialist countries, including those with quite unequal levels of development.

These countries are marked not only by similarities in their plans but by the social, political and symbolic functions of planning. No socialist country can be termed a "planned society." Yet each is a *society with a plan.* The symbolic signficance of "The Plan," both reaffirms and elevates its political and practical functions. By its "sacred" character, the planning mechanism assumes a dominant role in socialist society.

Within the socialist camp, there certainly exist national differences in planning policies and in the kinds of factors which influence the planning process. These national differences stem from (1) the historic conditions under which socialism emerged in each country, (2) the specific national priorities and their degree of relative importance, (3) the means by which these national goals are to be accomplished, and (4) the effects of these conditions, priorities and means on the planning bureaucracy, relevant social actors and local communities.

Socialism came to a Romania which was largely agrarian and rich in natural resources, yet without the infrastructure to exploit them. Along with a generally low level of development, the country possessed wide variations in settlement types and in regional economic levels; urbanized industrial regions existed alongside backward agrarian zones. Moreover, Romania's long history of political and economic subjugation under foreign powers was deeply embedded into the national consciousness. These initial conditions were typical of the Balkans and Third World countries generally. Overcoming these conditions became imperative after socialist Romania embarked on its more autonomous political course, around 1964. To sustain its emerging political independence vis-a-vis the Soviet Union, Romania sought to achieve "multilateral development" via an ambitious program of rapid industrialization. All other goals, including the "socialist" goals of regional equality and town/country homogenization, were subordinated to this end. To achieve industrialization it was necessary to maintain a high rate of primary accumulation, to concentrate on priority projects, to subordinate localities to the needs of the national economy, and to supplement State resources with citizen contributions.

The interaction of these conditions, priorities and means produced the distinctive characteristics of the Romanian planning process. This process was characterized, firstly, by an overwhelming preference for investment in "productive" over "unproductive" resources (e.g. housing, services, infrastructure). Second, because economically advanced regions and localities provided more rapid and more certain returns on investments, they were preferred over backward regions and localities. Third, the national priority for industrial growth through rapid accumulation led to a high degree of State centralization and a lack of coordination among sectors of the economy. Overcentralization tended to restrict local influence on planning decisions and prevent adequate feedback between local officials and central planning organs. Fourth, the requirements of localities and individual households had to submit to the ubiquitous "general interest" as embodied in Party programs and planners' decisions. Hence, there were no "local plans" per se, only national plans executed in diverse localities. This meant that any expression of local interests could legitimately be considered "chauvinistic." Fifth, the low level of economic development and the ambitiousness of the plans made citizens' participation in plan execution an absolute necessity. Constant pressure was exerted on regional and local leaders to mobilize the citizens, and citizens themselves were required to sacrifice their time, energy and immediate aspirations to achieve long-term national goals.

Romania's planning process is especially distinguished from that of other socialist countries by the *intensity* with which these national priorities are pursued. This applies not only to the high rate of accumulation but to the virtual military organization of citizen "mobilization" and the incessant campaigns for everyone to participate in plan execution. Hence, whereas Hungarian Party Secretary Janos Kadar has stated that "he who is not against us is with us," the situation in Romania could be summarized as "he who is not with us is against us." Romania's planning practice allows no room for spectators; citizens are expected to actively participate in plan execution, even when their immediate household goals or local interests are ignored in the process.

Romanian planning thus amalgamates the "planning," "socialist" and "national" factors brought out above. Selecting specific growth points as the means by which rural development is to be achieved corresponds with the "growth-center" ideology of general planning theory. In seeking to distribute these new towns evenly around the country, Romanian systematization also seeks to fulfill the "socialist" requirements for regional balance. Finally, rendering privileged status to these 300 settlements and elevating the urbanization of certain localities to a national campaign symbolizes Romania's national priority of rapid, concentrated accumulation.

The national-level factors generated their own contradictions, however. The socialist goal of regional equalization quickly succumbed to the need to place certain localities or regions ahead of others. Even within the group of 300 preferred villages, higher priority was accorded those villages with built-up infrastructure, pre-existing industry or an ostensibly more "rational" settlement pattern. Among socialist countries, Romania's rural settlement strategy is one of the most ambitious in the manner in which it seeks to revamp the the existing settlement network. It is not surprising that the "rationality" criteria became the source of conflicts within and between competing localities.

The premises used to determine whether a locality would be upgraded, maintained or phased out were especially noticeable at the county level of planning activity. Echoing the national priority given industrialized, labor-importing regions, planning priorities in Braşov County meant that the less developed zones were to receive their new towns only in the post-1985 phase, if at all. County planners faced the problem of respecting the national planning ideology while trying to mediate conflicts between individual localities, each of which demanded a share of scarce state resources. In planning for local communities, county officials were handicapped by a lack of information about local needs, an inability to satisfy these needs due to inadequate resources, social and administrative distance from the villagers, and by unrealistic notions of urban orientation and spatial concentration which were difficult to apply in the rural setting. Abrupt reversals of policy at the national level played havoc with county planners' efforts to forge effective relations with local communities. The sources of greatest potential conflict between planners and communities lay in the decisions to transform certain villages into towns and to phase out other villages. Within each locality, a major problem was to reconcile State priorities for productive investments with village desires for better housing, services and utilities. Villagers saw county planners as policy-makers, while the State considered them local executors of national directives. Because of their intermediate position, Brașov County's planners bore the brunt of this conflict, which was acted out in the problems of planning in local communities.

In the village of Feldioara, the planning process was affected by specifically local demographic, economic, social and historical factors. Feldioara's continuing population fluctuations and emigration of local Saxons had deprived the community of a stable social core which could articulate local interests, participate in planning execution or be mobilized by community elites. Feldioara's plan focused chiefly on the needs of the new factory, the in-migrant workers and apartment construction, while delaying the provision of services and utilities to local residents. The continuous alterations in Feldioara's plan were usually not the result of citizen input but of administrative decisions or sheer improvization. Plan fluctuations kept the citizens off balance and led to uncertainty, rumors, apathy and cynicism among many residents. Citizens' ignorance of the plan was aggravated by the continuing social cleavage between the locals and the newcomers, many of whom considered their stay in Feldioara to be temporary. Local participation in plan formulation was impeded by the plan's adverse affect on agrarian households, the low village commitment on the part of temporary migrants, and lack of integration of local elites (many of whom were also in-migrants). What local spirit still remained was further depleted by Romania's general economic downturn and the consequent slowing-down and rethinking of systematization's overambitious goals.

Since Romanian "community" planning consists only of national plans enacted in different localities, "local" development is permitted only insofar as it serves long-term national interests. This creates problems for community participation. It is feasible that long-term national goals can be compatible with short-term household strategies and local interests. When this happens, (providing local commitment is sufficiently high), one can expect a high degree of local participation in plan execution. Yet the nature of Romanian planning often produces situations where local and national strategies are either incompatible or directly contradictory. This is the case when the urbanization of the central core of a village turns autonomous producer households into consumer households dependent on inadequate State retail networks. In such situations, stimulating participation will become more difficult and may have serious effects on the plan's outcome. What should be emphasized is that even though the *plan* may come to a temporary halt, the planning *process* continues.

These effects were especially visible at the level of individual households in Feldioara. Local participation was a function of the degree of the household's perceived control over its domestic resources and its commitment to long-term residence in the village. Participation would be voluntary when household strategies and long term goals were compatible. Diverse levels of resource control among Feldioara's households reflected different economic niches and varying demographic compositions. Household commitment was also affected by length of stay in the village and the probability of migration. Because of the divergent degrees of resource control and local commitment, participation activities also varied: from active enthusiasm to passive acceptance, apathy and resistance.

Implementing the planning process in Feldioara precipitated social strains on elite-citizen relations as well. Elites sought to balance their roles as mobilizers in the planning bureaucracy with their social obligations as kin, neighbors or specialists. Elites' effectiveness in mobilizing the citizens was limited by (1) their origin outside the community, (2) their periodic rotation from post to post or from one locality to another, (3) their need to build effective relations with other elites, even at the expense of relations with fellow citizens, and (4) their administrative and Party obligation to place national concerns ahead of community interests or household requirements. Without sufficient local ties and pressured by national and regional demands, the elites often had to renounce the personal, egalitarian mobilization style for a style which was more bureaucratic; ultimately, this reduced their ability to mobilize long-term community support.

Administrative sanctions rather than social obligations came to form the basis for local mobilization efforts. As this happened, citizens became more difficult to mobilize and the plan's fulfillment further jeopardized. Elites were then under pressure from above to "take measures" which could further alienate them from their constituents. Hence, structural factors rather than personal inadequacies were the cause of the elites' problems in implementing the plan.

These structural factors were more clearly seen as a result of their being placed in a "vertical slice" framework. Instead of a formal plan being placed against the realities of informal "distortions," the two were integrated into a "planning process" which structurally incorporated these "distortions."

Implications for Development Planners

The analysis of Romanian systematization purposely highlighted its problems and dysfunctions. The causes for these seeming "aberrations" lay not in individual shortcomings or "retrograde mentalities" but within the structural contradictions of Romania's planning process: its goals, its means of execution, and in the patterns of interaction between planning bureaucracy and community members.

At the level of planning theory, the experience of Feldioara (and of Romania) demonstrates that any planning process involves more than a formal bureaucratic apparatus or the technical activities of experts. Planning is also a social arena for the acting out of power relations between diverse interests both within and outside the planning bureaucracy. The political nature of planning, thought it may be obfuscated by its technical veneer, is abundantly clear to those at the top of the political pyramid.

Conceiving of planning as a social and political process lends a new perspective to explanations of planning's "distortions" and "aberrations." The Romanian data suggest that distortions of planning are not incidental to the planning process but intrinsic to it. These alterations become more visible in Romania because of socialist planning's wide scope, national scale and ambitious development goals. More importantly, planning alterations assume a political character especially because they occur within a socialist society, i.e., a "society with a plan." Hence, to ask, "Why does the plan get distorted?" only perpetuates the artificial distinction between a formal institution and its social milieu. Instead of asking why plans fail, we should ask, "What are the underlying ideological and social forces which shape the formation of the plan and how do these forces play themselves out during the planning process?" By asking questions about planning as a process, we obtain a more accurate picture of how the planning mechanism works. For Romania, the processual emphasis can help show how planning fosters national integration within socialist societies, or within any "society with a plan."

This study has shown many consequences of planning which were unintended by the planners or unexpected by the citizens. However, such
consequences were hardly unpredictable. In fact, the Romanian data can
help generate specific predictions as to the kind and degree of alteration
to be expected with certain types of planning. One could hypothesize that
where planning policy is highly centralized and where plans are more ambitious in scope and scale, alterations in the plan will tend to be more probable and more extensive. The explanation for this lies in the nature of the
planning process: plans of larger scope automatically bring more social
forces into the planning "area." Planning alterations will thus be more common for societies where planning is the primary mechanism for achieving national integration, i.e., the socieites of Eastern Europe. Conversely, in
societies where plans are more limited in scale, or where "The Plan" has
not been elevated to a sacred societal integration mechanism, fewer social
factors will enter the planning process; hence, major aberrations or serious
unintended consequences will be less likely to appear.

These hypotheses, being based on the scale of planning, would appear
to represent an argument for decentralization. Clearly, a smaller plan will
be more manageable and thus yield fewer distortions. Yet smaller plans
may also be inadequate for the necessary societal tasks. The point of these
hypotheses is NOT to argue for decentralization. Large scale programs
will not necessarily fail; rather they will have more unintended consequences. In this sense, an overfulfillment of the plan by 50% is equally
as aberrant as a 50% underfulfillment. The unexpected results in both
cases are evidence of forces other than the formal institutional features of
planning. A more integrative model of the planning process which incorporates the informal, non-institutional factors can transform unintended
consequences into predictable ones.

By conceptualizing the plan as a social process, it becomes clear that
any development policy, no matter how well-intentioned, will generate
problems as it is mapped out onto local space. This is because the vast
majority of development plans—including most "community development" schemes—are invariably *formulated* on the basis of national requirements, whereas they are *executed* within local communities. The
interest of these communities, while they may complement or overlap
with national interests, can never be wholly identical with them. Herein lies
the potential for tensions or conflicts between localities and the State, as

well as the possibility for competition among communities for scarce State resources. Because of these inherent contradictions, some dysfunctions are the inevitable result of any development planning scheme. It is the task of the planners to expect these dysfunctions, to "plan" for them, so that they can be resolved in a nonantagonistic fashion. It is not utopian to expect that if dysfunctions could be discovered and explained, many of them could also be alleviated. The difficulties lie in the discovery process itself, in keeping track of the relevant factors and in providing both effective and humane means of resolving the problems. Planners will come to realize that there are other interests at stake besides their own. This can be accomplished only if all the relevant social groups (including those beyond the immediate planning bureaucracy) are included in the efforts to discover and resolve the conflicts. Explanations such as "inadequate information," "unintended consequences" or "conflicts of interests" are not sufficient. The real task to is to find out *why* there was inadequate information, *why* unintended consequences were not foreseen, *why* plans were formulated which contained conflicts of interest. Most planners, especially those in "societies with a plan," have tended to uphold the sanctity of the planning mechanism instead of asking these "why" questions. They have tended to believe that their "society with a plan" is really a "planned society." This is the danger which faces the development expert: structural or political problems cannot be reduced to problems of "expertise" or "getting the right information." As systemic problems, they require systemic solutions. The rationale behind the vertical slice framework used in this book was to make explicit these systemic aspects.

Implications for the Study of Bureaucracy

In revealing the workings of the planning process in Romania, this study focused on one segment of a socialist bureaucracy. The planning administration could function only by virtue of the "supplementary sets" which interacted with it (Wolf 1966:15). These noncorporate structures were a crucial part of the planning process. For those who study bureaucracies, especially socialist bureaucracies, this study of Romanian systematization suggests a need to rethink the traditional opposition between bureaucratic institutions and informal, noncorporate social relations (a more detailed "re-thinking" can be found in Sampson [1983b]).

All students of bureaucracy agree that informal organization plays an important role in helping the formal organization to work efficiently (e.g. Blau 1956). However, informal organization continues to be made subordinate to the supposedly increasing and inevitable institutionalization of social life (Eisenstadt 1971).

Informal ties of kinship, friendship and patron-client relations are seen as gradually decreasing in importance, becoming less significant to the effective functioning of society. This assumption has been called into question by anthropological studies of European societies (Cole 1977), urban areas (e.g. Basham 1978), and complex organizations (Britan and Cohen 1980). Wolf's "supplementary sets" are not only alive and well, but can actually thrive under bureaucratic organization. Informal ties may change in form and function, but they are not being replaced by corporate social organization. The strength of these noncorporate ties is daily demonstrated by the pervasiveness of "second economies" in Eastern Europe (Grossman 1977, Kenedi 1981, Sampson 1983a) and by the systemic linkages between bureaucracy and "corruption" (Wertheim 1964, Bayley 1966, Scott 1973, Blok 1974, Schneider and Schneider 1976). These linkages occur in all three "worlds"—East, West and "South." One could even argue that conditions for the emergence of these noncorporate forms of social organization directly increase with the institutionalization of social life. Resources once available only through private ownership, kinship, or ties of patronage are now "up for grabs" by being placed in the public, organizational domain.

The developmentalist view, with its emphasis on "creeping institutionalization'" permeates the work of many scholars on Eastern Europe. This includes those who see the bureaucracy as the new ruling class (e.g. Hirszowicz 1980) and those who see it in terms of a "corporatist" (Meyer 1964) or "institutional pluralist" model (Hough 1977). The developmentalist view also appear in two works on Romania, by Kenneth Jowitt (1978) and Daniel Chirot (1980), both of which use the corporatist framework.

Jowitt and Chirot argue that the Leninist Party apparatus has usurped the functions formerly carried out by traditional kinship and friendship relations. Jowitt notes the rise of "familism" even within the Party organization itself, but sees this as a pre-communist "survival" which will gradually wither away as Leninist institutionalization becomes more pervasive.

In a similar fashion (though much more inflammatory), Chirot argues that socialist Romania has actually realized the ideal of fascist corporatism.

Both these scholars are justified in pointing out the specific features of corporatist, bureaucratic institutions under actual socialism. However, in calling our attention to the existence of these formal structures, Jowitt and Chirot would like us to infer that society actually functions like a corporate organization, *that it is corporate forms that make society work.* The data from this study compel us to reject this inference. In reifying the corporate structures of Leninist Party organization in Romania—and by implication other socialist countries—Jowitt and Chirot confound the *institutional form* of society with its *actual social processes.* With their developmentalist assumptions, they have unwittingly swallowed the "Party line" of the very Leninist organizations they were supposed to be analyzing! Put simply, the line is that Party institutionalization and bureaucratic rationality are irrevocably replacing noncorporate social organization. Jowitt and Chirot have assumed that the omnipresence of the bureaucracy entails its dominance in society.

This study focused on what it supposed to be one of the more rational and bureaucratic of institutions, one whose *raison d'etre* is "calculation based on objective needs." Yet even here it was shown that beneath the institutional surface of the planning bureaucracy, there existed informal social relations, hidden political conflicts and unarticulated ideologies which form the very substance of social life. In opposition to the developmentalism of Jowitt and Chirot, *and* to the Leninist Party line, this study indicates that the informal features of society, though they will indeed alter their form and function, will hardly be supplanted by noncorporatist organization. Bureaucratic-corporate societies, including those dominated by Communist parties, are in fact crucially dependent on personalized, noncorporate social relations. Rather than disappearing one could hypothesize quite the opposite evolution; as the Leninist corporate organization matures, it could become an arena for competing interest groups and a "resource bank" for those wishing to realize individual strategies and patron-client-friendship obligations. As the bureaucracy becomes an arena for this resource competition, the re-emergence of "familism" within bureaucratic societies (or its perpetuation under circumstances quite unlike those connected with "Balkan mentality") is not as anomalous as seems on first sight (Jowitt 1978, 1983).

Instead of assuming that the bureaucratic monolith simply overtakes informal organization, our models should be based on their dynamic inter-action and dialectical relation. That this is evident to most ordinary Ro-manians is best illustrated by a joke about the initials "PCR". Officially *PCR* is the abbreviation for Romanian Communist Party (*Partidul Comun-ist Roman*). But with this "corporate designation" comes a noncorporate alternative. I am told by several Romanians (with a wink of an eye) that PCR is really a formula for getting things done: "connections, acquaint-ances and relations" (*pile, cunoştiinţe şi relaţii*)! What could be more il-lustrative of the functional interdependence between corporate and non-corporate organization than this dualistic definition of the Leninist party organization!

This is only to reiterate that the proliferation of bureaucratic *institu-tions* in socialist (or nonsocialist) countries should not be equated with the bureaucratization of *social relations*. Elements of informal organiza-tion—kinship, friendship, patronage, coalitions, i.e., forms of social rela-tions which we mistakenly refer to as "corruption"—these elements are not about to disappear. Informal ties are both the lubricant of corporate, bureaucratic organization and the safety-value for its inefficiency (these points are further elaborated in Sampson 1982, 1983a, 1983b).

Socialist Planning "As It Actually Exists"

The foregoing analysis of Romania's systematization has direct relev-ance to the ongoing debate over "actually existing socialism" undertaken by East European Marxists and their Western associates (cf. Bahro 1978, Konrad and Szelenyi 1979, Hirszowicz 1980, Wolter 1980, Rakovski 1980, Hegedus 1981, Schaff 1982; the journals *Critique* (Glascow), *Telos*, *Theory and Society* "Special Issue on Actual Socialisms," January 1980). From this perspective, the East European societies are not simply "transitional" formations somewhere between capitalism and socialism. Neither have the "degenerated" from prior conditions of genuine socialism (the Trot-skyist view); nor are they "state-capitalist" as the Maoists would have it. Rather, the East European societies represent new and historically unique social formations which cannot be analyzed with the concepts used to interpret capitalism and certainly not in terms of the way Marx envision-ed communism (as summarized in Ollman 1974). Coopting the terminology once used by his own Party theoreticians, the now-exiled East German Marxist Rudolf Bahro has given the name "actually existing socialism" to the East European social formations. "Actual socialism" replaces the normative socialism with the empirically observable reality of East European societies.

Bahro's *The Alternative in Eastern Europe* (1978) represents the fullest demonstration that the countries of actually existing socialism merit their own theoretical concepts (Wolter 1980 presents a discussion and critique of Bahro). Using Bahro's terminology, this study of Romanian systematization could be conceived as an analysis of "actually existing socialist planning." This type of planning has little in common with the notions of rational management envisioned by Marx or Lenin. The function of planning under actual socialism is to integrate lower-level units into the central Party-State bureaucracy. It is important to emphasize that societal coordination and national integration is carried out solely by the planning mechanism. In contrast to the multiplicity of institutions and the market forces of modern capitalism, socialist societies are "mono-organizational societies" (Rigby 1977). The entire social, political, economic and cultural life of society is coordinated organizationally. Achieving such coordination is a complicated task. Hence, actually existing socialist planning must absorb more social strains than does capitalism, where "economy" and "politics" are institutionally separated. These social strains are expressed in the distortions of the plan, and in the gap between actually existing socialism and the emancipatory socialism envisioned by Marx and Bahro.

In order to bridge this gap, fundamental changes must take place in the countries of actual socialism, changes which would affect their planning mechanisms as well. Such changes do not appear on the horizon, but there remain both the opportunity and the responsibility to help the system function more democratically and more efficiently within the existing institutional framework. Using Bahro's "actual socialism" as the conceptual framework and the Romanian data as empirical basis, I offer six proposals which could help transform actually existing socialist planning (as practiced in Romania) into a more genuine, emancipatory socialist planning. These recommendations include the following:

1) Access to information must be more widely diffused from planners and experts to the citizenry. Control over information is what upholds power relations between the planning bureaucracy and local communities.

If planners could make as much information as possible available to the local citizenry, and if this information could be furnished so that citizens help not only in plan execution but in formulation. Then the planning process could become both more effective and more democratic. Opening information channels and eliminating the pervasive "secret knowledge" would assure social equality between technical experts and ordinary citizens. It would help reduce social and administrative distance between them and would ultimately help local elites to mobilize their constituents more easily.

2) The dogmatic priority of "productive" over "unproductive" investments should give way to an equality between the two. Raising the living standards for the local population, i.e., adding more services, housing and infrastructure, must receive equal priority with factory construction. Socialist planners have tended erroneously to equate *unproductive* investments with *unnecessary* expenditures. Yet these social investments are required in order to reproduce the labor force. Since it is ultimately human labor-power, not factories, that produces the surplus which enables accumulation to take place, investing in services, housing and infrastructure is certainly as "productive" as building factories. More emphasis on the present needs of the rural labor force would constitute concrete evidence that the leadership takes seriously the rhetoric of equalizing town/country differences, uplifting backward areas and raising living standards for the rural population. These investments would yield genuine benefits for residents of these villages and make them more attractive to professional cadres as places of permanent settlement. In the case of Feldioara, more specialists might choose to remain in the community instead of leaving it when their contracts expired. Making the village a more desirable place to *live* in—and not just a place where one temporarily works or sleeps—would serve to increase village commitment and stimulate voluntary participation.

3) The ideologies of spatial centralization and settlement rationality need to be applied more flexibly, if not abandoned altogether. Vertical construction and spatial concentration are often counterproductive for household viability. The notion of settlement rationality sets localities and regions against each other in competition for state resources. Spatial organization is a reflection of social organization; to declare a spatial unit as unsuitable for the "needs of society" is to pass judgment on a social

group as well. Under actually existing socialist planning, Romanian planners have the power to make such judgments unilaterally. A more emancipatory socialist planning would accept the social realities of specific
settlements. Where a locality was judged "nonviable," the proper procedure would not be to eliminate it, but to make it viable again! Subsequent judgments as to the village's rationality would then be left to the
residents themselves: they could simply "vote with their feet." A "rationality" dictated by planners' decree or forced residence is not a socialist
rationality.

4) The political expedients of "general interest" and "national interest" should be discarded in favor of an institutionalized competition for
State resources among localities, regions and interest groups. The "general
interest" is so abstract, and so susceptible to political manipulation, that it
only masks the real struggle over planning objectives and means of achieving them. Instead of being suppressed as instances of narrowminded "chauvinism," regional and local power struggles should be incorporated into the
debate over development priorities and resource allocation. Recognizing
the inherent validity of "local" or "individual interests" would not only
aid in plan execution, but serve to recast the power relations between planners and communities; planners would be planning *with* the community
instead of *for* it. Ultimately, we would see the emergence of truly local
plans, a significant step toward the realization of Bahro's emancipatory
socialism. An additional result of relinquishing the hegemony of "the general interest" would be that local elites could legitimately speak for community interests vis-a-vis State interests without risking accusations of
"chauvinism" from their superiors. This would enhance elite-citizen contact and produce more reliable information. Local elites' flexibility in dealing with community problems would be evidence of community support
instead of "poor leadership."

5) Under actually existing socialist planning, the planners are either unaware or unwilling to acknowledge the social ramifications of their activities. The situation is especially delicate when plans call for the phasing out
of a settlement or a radical restructuring of large, socially diverse villages.
In view of the importance of the 300 new towns in the future rural settlement network, Romanian social scientists should focus more of their
energies on predicting the social ramifications of the plans and less in the

gathering of local statistics to serve the planners. Such "social impact statements," carried out with the active and equal cooperation of community members, could help villagers deal more realistically with local level transformations while showing planners possible unintended consequences of their plans. Since information is the key to the power differential between planning experts and the public, it would be imperative that the results of these impact studies be made available to those affected. At present, these studies are classified as "working secrets." To be sure, a well-done impact study would reveal several problems and contradictions, posing ethical issues for sociologists and political issues for planners and citizens. Yet if these issues are not brought out and resolved in the open, they will hardly disappear. Rather, they will result in citizen apathy, lack of participation or distortions of the plan.

6) Finally, the whole question of how planning goals are formulated should be taken up for deabate. Under actually existing socialist planning, local input serves purely as a feedback and control mechanism for implementing planners' goals. Goal determination remains the monopoly of the Party, which articulates its conception of the "general interest" through its planning policies. A more genuine socialist planning, however, requires a more open discussion of the planning goals. The plan's "sacred" character must be "secularized." Localities and citizens must be permitted to debate the most fundamental problems of Romanian development, including the meaning of "development" itself. This debate must begin by recognizing the inherent contradictions among household, community and higher level interests. Moreover, there must be established institutional channels for resolving these differences. If not, they will only appear in more indirect form, as "hidden" conflicts between advanced and backward regions, "viable" and "nonviable" localities, between the civic center and peasant periphery of a village, between agrarian and proletarian households in new towns, or between community members and local elites.

The six proposals outlined above can in part be implemented within the present framework of actually existing socialist planning. Yet they will be fully realized only in conjunction with a general transformation in the structure of actual socialism. When (if) such changes occur, we will see the emergence of a more genuine socialist-communist planning, clearly distinct from today's actually existing socialist planning.

This emancipatory planning will not be without its contradictions. The point is to expect them rather than to see them as aberrations. This view has been forcefully argued by none other than Romania's President Ceau-şescu, who (following Mao 1953), distinguishes between contradictions which are "antagonistic" and "nonantagonistic." Ceauşescu states:

> The existence of contradictions and the struggle between them con-stitutes a law of social development even under socialism. What is required is that we begin by recognizing the existence of contra-dictions and then study them in their essence and act conscienti-ously to keep these contradictions from being exacerbated, so that they do not become antagonistic and lead to violence. The role of . . . the party leadership, of the activity of the socialist state, consists not in closing our eyes and denying the existence of contradictions, but in recognizing their existence so as to understand them, to study them, and to find ways to attenuate or liquidate them . . . . (Ceau-şescu 1972:548-49; my translation).

The issue, then, is to keep nonantagonistic contradictions from evolving into politically dangerous antagonistic conflicts. This will be done only if the planning apparatus recognizes the contradictory nature of "local" and "general" interests. If this does not happen, it is not the fault of socialism as such, but of factors which blind us from recognizing these contradic-tions. To paraphrase Bahro's final prediction about communism, there is every reason to believe that genuine socialist planning "is not only neces-wary, but it is also possible" (Bahro 1978:453).

Conclusion: Anthropology and the Study of Complex Society

This analysis of socialist planning in Romania has applied anthropo-logical concepts and methods to be understanding of national integration processes. Local communities are integrated into larger societies through formal institutions and informal structures. Understanding these institu-tions and structures requires that we elaborate (1) the horizontal linkages between bureaucratic administration and informal social interaction and (2) the vertical linkage between nation, region and community. This is both the rationale for and the goal of the "vertical slice" framework as employed in this book.

For anthropologists, the analysis of supralocal institutions demands new kinds of data gathering techniques which may be incompatible with the ethnographic tradition of one person-one village-one year of fieldwork. Anthropologists thus need to acquire social science methodologies which are more applicable to the study of formal institutions. This does not mean that the anthropologist should seek to imitate the sociologist or political scientist, but only to complement and supplement their analyses. Hence, a focus on formal institutions by no means obviates the need for community studies and participant observation. It is only through communities, or similar social groups bounded by kin, friendship, workplace, class or ethnicity that formal institutions actually come to life. Hence, the "community study" remains the most effective *method* for understanding how formal institutions work.

The vertical slice perspective suggests that the success of a given plan or development strategy cannot be explained solely by its technical rationality, but also in terms of the relation between informal processes and formal structures. It is conceivable that by applying the vertical slice framework to other institutions besides planning, we could make general statements about the character of formal institutions in complex societies. For example, the relation of "The Plan" to its "distortions" is much the same as between the "official economy" and the "second economy" and between bureaucracy and "corruption" (Sampson 1983a, 1983b, 1984).

To be sure, the analysis of formal institutions generates problems for those anthropologists trained in qualitative approaches to bounded social groups. Using a vertical slice perspective requires a strict definition of the particular institution one is studying. There is a tendency to spread oneself thin as one moves between national archives and community social encounters. There are methodological pitfalls in drawing away from "the community," toward a more amorphous institutional network. One feels less and less like an "anthropologist" because one is not tramping in the mud with the natives. Yet the study of complex societies and bureaucratic organization must be brought within the bounds of the "anthropological project." For the anthropologist who seeks to understand how social systems work, who desires a full knowledge of human behavior in its cultural context, the question is not whether to leave the muddy village for the planners' office, but when, how, and with what obejctives.

This study of Romanian systematization has shown that socialist planning is a distinct form of national integration which restructures the relations between local communities and supralocal institutions. To accomplish this task, it was necessary to create false barriers between local and supralocal systems, and between formal and informal social organizations, and then to break down these barriers. Yet our task should not be to simply breach the artificial gap between national institutions and community social organization. Our task should be to do away with this gap altogether! If this book has contributed toward this goal, then it has fulfilled its own plan.

BIBLIOGRAPHY

I. Romanian Archives and Documents

Ausweiss über die Volkszahlung in ganzen Kronstädter District. *And* Orts Ubersicht von Bezirk Marienburg, 1832-1919. *In* Collection "Satele din Ţara Bîrsei," Arhivele de Stat, Braşov.

Church Records from Feldioara's Romanian Orthodox Church (baptisms, marriages, deaths), 1793-1975.

Church Records from Feldioara's Saxon Evangelical Church (baptisms, confirmations, marriages, deaths), 1864-1912.

Consiliul Popular ale Comunei Feldioara:

Contribuţii la Muncă Voluntară, 1975. (Contributions to voluntary work campaigns by household, revised yearly.)

Evidenţa Contractare ale Populaţiei (agricultural contracting plans and statistics).

Evidenţa Populaţiei (yearly population census and breakdowns by age, sex, occupation, etc.).

Protocole ale Şedinţe ale Consiliul Popular Comunal (minutes of People's Council Meetings).

Registru Agricole Feldioara, 1955-1976 (list of households with land and livestock holdings; updated every 5 years).

Recenţămîntul Animalelor (yearly livestock statistics).

Dare de Seama ale Cooperativă Agricole de Producţie Feldioara 1950-1976. (Collective farm yearly statistical summaries.) C.A.P. Feldioara.

Institut "Proiect-Braşov," Consiliul Popular al Judeţului Braşov
1970   Schiţa de Sistematizare a Comunei Feldioara: Studiu Agricol. Proiect no. 6064/70.
1972   Studiu de Sistematizare a Judeţului Braşov.
            Vol. I: Situaţie existenta
            Vol. II: Propuneri de sistematizare.
            Proiect no. 7065/71. M. Şuman, A. Tomescu, Jan. 22, 1972.
1973   Detailiu de Sistematizare Feldioara. T. Bredau. Nov. 6, 1973.
1974   Centru Civic Feldioara—Detailiu de sistematizare. Proiect No. 9142/74, T. Bredau. Dec. 24, 1974.
1975a   Schiţa de sistematizare a comunei Prejmer. Sinteza Proiect no. 11415/75. M. Şuman, P. Manu.
1975b   Schiţa Sistematizare Feldioara, Piese Scrise. Proiect No. 11.078/75. T. Bredau. August 25, 1975.
1976a   Schiţa de Sistematizare comună Hoghiz, etapa 1980, Piese Scrise. Proiect no. 11.415/A. M. Şuman, Director, April 26, 1976.
1976b   Schiţa de Sistematizare Comuna Feldioara, Piese Scrise. Proiect no. 11415/AA/75. M. Şuman, P. Manu, May 26, 1976.

Ocolul Agricol Feldioara (1945-1948). Documents dealing with land expropriations. Consilul Popular ale Com. Feldioara, Archives.

Feldioara Archives.
     Saşi Exceptaţi de Expropriare, July 1948. (Saxons exempted from expropriation).
     Tabel Cuprizănd Terenurile Agricole Expropriate din Comună Feldioara, 1945 (list of Saxons whose lands were expropriated).
     Tabel Nominal de Colonişti Improprietaţiţi in Comună Feldioara in anul 1946 care au Rămas Stabiliţi Definitiv in Comună, 1948 (list of colonists in Feldioara who have remained permanently in the community).
     Tabel Suplimentar de Locuitorii din Comună Feldioara Indreptaţiţi la Improprietariea, 1946 (supplementary list of residents entitled to receive land).

Osaci, Pavel, Croitoru, Nicolae and Mailat, Viorel
1968   Monografie Comunei Feldioara. On file, Consiliul Popular ale Com. Feldioara.

II. Other Sources

Aaby, Peter
    1977   The State and Guinea-Bissau: African Socialism or Socialism
                in Africa. Uppsala: Nordic Africa Institute.
Abrams, I. and Fracavighia, R.
    1975   Urban planning in Poland today. J. of the American Institute
                of Planners 41:258-69.
Adams, Richard
    1967   The Second Sowing: Power and Secondary Development in
                Latin America. San Francisco: Chandler Pub. Co.
    1970   Crucifixation by Power: Essays on Guatemalan National
                Social Structure 1944-1966. Austin: University of Texas Press.
Alavi, Hamza
    1973   Peasant classes and primordial loyalties. J. of Peasant Studies
                1:23-62.
Altshuler, Alan
    1970   Community Control: The Black Demand for Participation in
                Large American Cities. Indianapolis: Pegasus.
Amin, Samir
    1974a   (ed.) Modern Migrations in Western Africa. Oxford: Oxford
                University Press.
    1974b   Accumulation on a World Scale. New York: Monthly Review
                Press.
Anuarul Demografic al R. S. Romania
    1974   Bucharest: Direcția Centrala de Statistica.
Anuarul Statistic al R. S. Romania
    1975   Bucharest: Direcția Centrala de Statistica.
    1977   Bucharest: Direcția Centrala de Statistica.
    1979   Bucharest: Direcția Centrala de Statistica.
Apfelbaum, R.
    1977   The future is made not predicted: technocratic planners vs.
                public interests. Society 14:49-53.
Arensberg, Conrad and Niehoff, Arthur H.
    1964   Introducing Social Change. Chicago: Aldine.
Arnstein, Sherry
    1969   A ladder of citizen participation. J. of the American Institute
                of Planners 37:176-82.

Asad, Talal
  1972   Market model and class structure: a reconsideration of Swat
            political organization. Man (N.S.) 7:74-94.
Ash, M.
  1977   The new town and the nation. Town and Country Planning
            45:58-60.
Aspaturian, V.
  1974   Marxism and the meanings of modernization. *In* The Politics
            of Modernization in Eastern Europe: Testing the Soviet
            Model ed. by C. Gati. New York: Praeger, pp. 3-21.
Aya, Rod
  1975   The Missed Revolution. The Fate of Rural Rebels in Sicily
            and Southern Spain. Papers on European and Mediterranean
            Societies No. 3. Amsterdam: Antropologisch-Sociologisch Cen-
            trum, University of Amsterdam.
Bahro, Rudolf
  1978   The Alternative in Eastern Europe. London: New Left Books.
Bailey, Frederick G.
  1960   Tribe, Caste and Nation. New York: Humanities Press.
  1969   Strategems and Spoils: A Social Anthropology of Politics.
            New York: Schocken Books.
  1971   (ed.) Gifts and Poison: The Politics of Reputation. New York:
            Schocken Books.
Bailey, Joe
  1975   Social Theory for Planning. London: Routledge and Kegan
            Paul.
Banciu, Angela and Banciu, Dan
  1977   Cercetarea sociologică a manifestarilor deviate în rîndul min-
            orilor şi tinerilor. (Sociological research into manifestations of
            deviance among minors and youth) Viitorul Social 6:677-82.
Banfield, Edward
  1973   Ends and means in planning. *In* A Reader in Planning Theory
            ed. by A. Faludi. Oxford: Pergamon Press, pp. 139-49 (origin-
            ally published in International Social Science Journal vol. 11,
            1959).
Banfield, Edward and Banfield, L. F.
  1958   The Moral Basis of a Backward Society. New York: The Free
            Press.

Barnett, Homer
   1953   Innovations: The Basis of Cultural Change. New York: Mc-
               Graw-Hill Book Co.
Barth, Frederik
   1969   Models of Social Organization. Royal Anthropological Insti-
               tute. Occasional Paper No. 23.
Bax, Mart
   1975   On the increasing importance of the small community in the
               Irish Political Process. *In* Beyond the Community: Social
               Process in Europe, ed. by J. Boissevain and J. Friedl. The
               Hague: Netherlands, Department of Education and Science,
               pp. 134-143.
Bayley, David H.
   1966   The effects of corruption in a developing nation. Western
               Political Quarterly 19:719-732. Reprinted in A Sociological
               Reader on Complex Organizations, ed. by A. Etzioni. New
               York: Holt, Rinehardt and Winston, Inc., 1969, pp. 463-479.
Beck, Sam
   1979   Transylvania: Political Economy of a Frontier. Ph.D. Thesis.
               Anthropology Department, University of Massachusetts-
               Amherst. Ann Arbor: University Microfilms.
   1980   Uncooperativized but articulated: the myth of 'private' pea-
               sants in Romania. Paper presented at American Anthropo-
               logical Association Meetings, Washington, D.C., December 4-
               7. (On file, Dept. of Anthropology/Romanian Research
               Group, University of Massachusetts-Amherst.)
Beck, Sam and McArthur, Marilyn
   1981   Romania: ethnicity, nationalism and development. *In* Ethni-
               city and Nationalism in Southeastern Europe, ed. by S. Beck
               and John W. Cole. Papers on European and Mediterranean
               Societies (No. 14). Amsterdam: University of Amsterdam,
               pp. 29-69.
Bell, Peter
   1979   Social Change and Social Perception in a Rural Hungarian
               Village. Ph.D. Thesis, Dept. of Anthropology, Univesity of
               California at San Diego. Ann Arbor: University Microfilms.
               (to appear 1984 in University of California Press.)

Benet, Sula
1974 Introduction (Western and Eastern Europe). Annals, New York Academy of Sciences 220, Article 6, "City and Peasant: A Study in Sociocultural Dynamics" ed. by A. L. La Ruffa et al., pp. 522-23.

Berliner, Joseph S.
1959 Managerial incentives and decision making: a comparison of the United States and the Soviet Union. U.S. Congress, Joint Economic Committee, Comparisons of the United States and Soviet Economies. Washington, D.C.: U.S. Government Printing Office, pp. 349-76 (reprinted in Feiwel 1968:167-98).

Bettelheim, Charles
1959 Studies in the Theory of Planning. New York and Bombay: Asia Publishing House.

Bicanic, R.
1967 Problems of Planning, East and West. The Hague: Mouton.

Binns, Christopher
1979 The changing face of power: revolution and accommodation in the development of the Soviet ceremonial system, Part I. Man (N.S.) 14:585-606.

1980 The changing face of power: revolution and accommodation in the development of the Soviet ceremonial system, Part II. Man (N.S.) 15:170-87.

Bisselle, Walter
1983 The peasant-worker in Poland. Studies in European Society 1(1):26-39. The Hague: Mouton.

Blaga, Ion
1974 Repartisarea Toritorială a Forțelor de Produoția in România (The Territorial Distribution of the Productive Forces in Romania). Bucharest: Editură Științifică.

Blok, Anton
1974 The Mafia of a Sicilian Village 1860-1960. New York: Harper and Row.

Boesen, Jannik and Raikes, Phillip
1976 Political economy and planning in Tanzania. Copenhagen: Institute for Development Research, Ms.

Bogdan, Tiberiu et al.
1970   Processul de urbanizare în România: Zona Brașov (The Ur-
        banization Process in Romania: the Brașov Zone). Bucharest:
        Editură Politică.

Boissevain, Jeremy
1968   The place of non-groups in the social sciences. Man (N.S.)
        3:652-66.
1973   Friends of Friends: Networks, Manipulators and Coalitions.
        Oxford: Blackwell.

Boissevain, Jeremy and Friedl, John (eds.)
1975   Beyond the Community: Social Process in Europe. The
        Hague: Netherlands Dept. of Education and Science.

Bold, Ion
1965a   Contribuții la stabilirea conținutului studiilor de sistemati-
        zare a teritoriului agricol (Contributions toward establishing
        the content of planning studies for agricultural lands). Prob-
        leme de Economie Agrară 1:9-20.
1965b   Probleme ale sistematizării teritoriului agricol. (Problems of
        planning agricultural zones). Revista Probleme Economice no.
        11, pp. 84-95.

Bold, Ion, Matei, Mioara and Săbădeanu, Ion
1974   Sistematizarea Rurală. Bucharest: Editura Tehnică.

Bornstein, Morris
1975   Economic Planning East and West. Cambridge, Mass.: Ball-
        inger Publishing Co., pp. 1-21.

Britain, G. and Cohen, R. (eds.)
1980   Hierarchy and Society: Anthropological Perspectives on
        Bureaucracy. Philadelphia: Institute for the Study of Hu-
        man Issues.

Brutzkus, Eliezer
1975   Centralized versus decentralized urbanization in developing
        countries: an attempt to elucidate a guideline principle. Eco-
        nomic Development and Cultural Change 23:633-52.

Budișteanu, A. and Pop, Adriana
1977   Sistematizareea teritoriului: conceptul, obiectivele și mijloa-
        cele sistematizării teritoriului (Territorial planning: the con-
        cept, objectives and methods of territorial planning). *In*

Sistematizarea Teritoriului şi a Localităţilor: Culegere Tematica, ed. by A. Miu, Bucharest: Academia "Ştefan Gheorghiu," pp. 83-108.

Burke, Edmund M.
1979   A Participatory Approach to Urban Planning. New York: Human Sciences Press.

Cardaş, Mircea
1970   Sistematizarea teritoriului rural (Planning for rural areas). Arhitectura (Bucharest) 1:27-29.

Carter, F. W.
1975   Bulgaria's new towns. Geography 60:133-36.

Ceauşescu, Nicolae
1972   Report to the National Conference of the Romanian Communist Party, July 10, 1972. Bucharest: Agerpress.

1973   Romania On the Way of Building up the Multilaterally Developed Socialist Society. Reports, Speeches, Articles. March 1972-December 1972. Volume 7. Bucharest: Meridiane Publishing House.

1974   Report to the Eleventh Congress of the Romanian Communist Party, November 5, 1974. Bucharest: Agerpress.

1977   Romania on the Way of Building up the Multilaterally Developed Socialist Society. Reports, Speeches, Articles. October 1975-May 1976. Volume 12. Bucharest: Meidiane Publishing House.

1978   Romania On the Way of Building Up the Multilaterally Developed Socialist Society. Reports, Speeches, Interviews, Articles. May 1976-December 1976. Volume 13. Bucharest: Meridiane Publishing House.

1979   Bunăsterea Poporului—Obiectivul Suprem al Politicii Partidului Comunist Român (The People's Welfare: Supreme Goal of the Policies of the Romanian Communist Party). Bucharest: Editură Politică, pp. 117-12.

Chayonov, A. V.
1968   The Theory of Peasant Economy. Ed. by B. Kerblay, D. Thorner and R. E. F. Smith. Homewood, Ill.: American Economic Association.

Cheetham, Tom and Whitaker, Roger
1974   The Peasant-Worker of Eastern Europe. Report of a Seminar
        Held at Boston University Conference Center, January 6-9,
        1974. Seminar 4 of a Symposium on East European Peasant-
        ries. 37pp. (Sociology Department, Boston University.)

Chelcea, Septimiu and Abraham, Dorel
1978   Traditional values and new behavior models acquired in the
        process of industrial-urban adaptation. Viitorul Social (The
        Social Future, Bucharest), Special Issue for the Ninth World
        Congress of Sociology, Uppsala, Sweden, August 14-19,
        1978, pp. 73-80.

Chirot, Daniel
1976   Social Change in a Peripheral Society: The Creation of a
        Balkan Colony: Wallachia—1200-1800. New York: Academic
        Press.
1977   Social Change in the Twentieth Century. New York: Harcourt
        Brace Jovanovich.
1980   The corporatist model and socialism: notes on Romanian de-
        velopment. Theory and Society 9:363-81.

Chiţulescu, Traian
1977   Sistematizarea localităţilor urbane: conceptul, obiectivele şi
        mijloacele sistematizării localităţilor urbane (Planning for
        urban localities: the concept, objectives and methods of plan-
        ning for urban localities). In Sistematizarea Teritoriului şi a
        Localitaţilor: Culegere Tematică, ed. by A. Miu. Bucharest:
        Academia "Ştefan Gheorghiu," pp. 109-19.

Cliff, Tony
1965   Marxism and the collectivization of agriculture. International
        Socialism, No. 19, pp. 14-26 (1964/1965).

Cobianu-Băcanu, Maria
1977   A Romanian-American dialogue. Dialectical Anthropology 2:
        301-8.

Cohen, Richard A.
1977   Small town planning: case studies and a critique. J. of the
        American Institute of Planners 43:3-12.

Cohen, Steven S.
1968   Modern Capitalist Planning: the French Model. Berkeley: Uni-
        versity of California Press.

Cohn, Bernard S.
1971   India: The Social Anthropology of a Civilization. Englewood
          Cliffs, N.J.: Prentice-Hall.
Cole, John W.
1973   Social process in the Italian Alps. American Anthropologist
          75:765-86.
1976   Familial dynamics in a Romanian village. Dialectical Anthro-
          pology 1:251-66.
1977   Anthropology comes part-way home: community studies in
          Europe. Annual Review of Anthropology 6:349-78.
1980   In a pig's eye: political economy and daily life in southeastern
          Europe. IREX Occasional Papers vol. 1(3):3-24.
1981   Family, farm and factory: rural workers in contemporary
          Romania. *In* Romania in the 1980's ed. by D. Nelson. Boulder:
          Westview Press, pp. 71-116.
1981a   Ethnicity and the rise of nationalism. *In* Ethnicity and Na-
          tionalism in Southeast Europe ed. by Sam Beck and John W.
          Cole. Papers on European and Mediterranean Societies No.
          14. Amsterdam: Antropologisch-Sociologisch Centrum, Uni-
          versity of Amsterdam, pp. 105-134.
1982a   East European Anthropology as "Anthropology." Newsletter
          of the East European Anthropology Group 1(2):1-2.
1982b   East European Anthropology as "Area Studies." Newsletter
          of the East European Anthropology Group 2(1):2-4.
1983a   East European Anthropology as politics. Newsletter of the
          East European Anthropology Group 2(2):2-5.
1983b   (ed.) Social Science Research in Romania. Anthropology Re-
          search Report No. 22. Amherst: University of Massachusetts.
Cole, John W. and Wolf, Eric R.
1974   The Hidden Frontier: Ecology and Ethnicity in an Alpine
          Valley. New York: Academic Press.
Conklin, R.
1977   Participation versus expertise. *In* Inequality in the Peruvian
          Andes: Class and Ethnicity in Cuzco, ed. by P. van den Berghe
          and G. Primov. St. Louis: University of Missouri Press, pp.
          40-54.
Constantinescu, Virgil
1978   The cultural behavior of persons with double-occupational

status. Viitorul Social (The Social Future, Bucharest), Special issue for Ninth World Congress of Sociology in Uppsala Sweden, August 14-19, 1978, pp. 81-90.

Corwin, Lauren Anita
1977   The rural town: minimal urban center. Urban Anthropology 6:23-43.

Dahlberg, F. M.
1974   The provincial town. Urban Anthropology 3:171-83.

Dalton, George (ed.)
1971   Economic Development and Social Change: The Modernization of Village Communities. Garden City, N.Y.: Natural History Press.

Darwent, D. F.
1969   Growth poles and growth centers in regional planning: a review. Environment and Planning 1:5-31.

Davidoff, Paul
1973   Advocacy and pluralism in planning. In A Reader in Planning Theory, ed. by A. Faludi. Oxford: Pergamon Press, pp. 277-96 (originally published in J. of the American Institute of Planners 31:331-38, 1965).

Davidoff, Paul and Reiner, Thomas
1962   A choice theory of planning. J. of the Amer. Institute of Planners 28. Reprinted in Faludi 1973, pp. 11-39.

Denitch, Bette
1970   Social Mobility and Industrialization in a Yugoslav Town. Unpublished Ph.D. Dissertation, University of California, Berkeley.
1974   Why do peasants urbanize? a Yugoslav case study. Annals of the New York Academy of Sciences 220 (article 6):546-59. ("City and Peasant: a Study in Sociocultural Dynamics" ed. by A. L. LaRuffa et al.).

Diamond, M. (ed.)
1977   Special Issue on New Towns. Town and Country Planning (January).

Dienes, Leslie
1973   Urban growth and spatial planning in Hungary. Tijdschrift voor Econ. en Soc. Geografie 64:24-38.

Doherty, Joseph
1975   Urban places and Third World Development. African Urban
         Notes (Michigan State University), Series B, No. 2, pp. 1-17
         (also in Antipode 9:33-42, 1977).

Dragan, Ion, et al.
1970   Processul de Urbanizare in Romania: Zona Slatina-Olt (The
         Urban Growth Process in Romania: the Slatina-Olt Zone).
         Bucharest: Editură Academiei Republicii Socialiste Romania.

Dragomirescu, Romeo
1977   Conception and present problems concernign regional plan-
         ning and urban and rural settlement planning the Socialist
         Republic of Romania. Paper presented at the Seventh Inter-
         national Fellows Conference of Johns Hopkins University
         Center for Metropolitan Studies, Bucharest, July 1977, Offset.

Dror, Y.
1963   The planning process: a facet design. International Review of
         Administrative Sciences 29:46-58 (reprinted in Faludi 1973).

Drum Nou ("New Road")
1975-78   Newspaper of the Brașov County People's Council and County
         Party Committee.

Duggett, M.
1975   Marx on Peasants. J. of Peasant Studies 2:159-82.

Dumitru, Sandu
1977   Participarea locală (Local participation). *In* Sociologie și
         Sistematizare în Procesele de Dezvoltare by M. Matei and I.
         Matei. Bucharest: Editura Tehnică, pp. 138-50.

Dunare, Nicolae
1972   Țara Bîrsei. Vol. I. Bucharest: Editura Academiei Republicii
         Socialiste România.
1974   Țara Birsei. Vol. II. Bucharest: Editura Academiei Republicii
         Socialiste România.

Editură Politică
1967   Plenara Comitetului Central cu Privire la Imbunătățirea Or-
         ganizării Administrative-Teritorial a România și Sistemati-
         zarea Localităților Rurale (Plenum of the Central Committee
         Concerning the Improvement of Romania's Territorial Ad-
         ministrative Organization and the Planning of Rural Locali-
         ties), October 6, 1967 (republished in Scînteia Dec. 7, 1967).

1972   Conferința Națională a Partidul Comunist Român. July 6-10, 1972. Bucharest.

1974   Eleventh Congress of the Romanian Communist Party, Nov. 5-9, 1974. Bucharest.

1974   Legea nr. 58, din 29 Octombrie 1974, privind Sistematizarea Teritoriului și a Localităților urbane și rurale (Law No. 58 from Oct. 29, 1974, concerning the Planning of the Territory and of Urban and Rural Localities). Pamphlet. Bucharest. (Also published in Bulletin Official nr. 135, Nov. 1, 1974, pp. 369-95.)

Eisenstadt, S. N. and Roniger, L.
1980   Patron-client relations as a model for structuring social exchange. Comparative Studies in Society and History 22: 42-77.

Emmanuel, Arghiri
1972   Unequal Exchange: A Study of the Imperialism of Trade. New York: Monthly Review Press.

Enache, Mircea
1973   Towards a methodology for comprehensive planning in Romania: A Survey of the Urban Models and Associated Techniques and Their Applicability in the Romanian Context. Baltimore: The Johns Hopkins Center for Metropolitan Planning and Research, The Johns Hopkins University. Offset.

Engels, Friedrich
1962   Anti-Duhring. 3rd ed. Moscow: Foreign Languages Publishing House.

Epstein, T. Scarlett
1962   Economic Development and Social Change in South India. Manchester: Manchester University Press.

Erlich, Alexander
1967   The Soviet Industrialization Debate 1924-1928. Cambridge, Mass.: Harvard University Press.

1968   Economic reforms in communist countries. In New Currents in Soviety-Type Economies: A Reader, ed. by G. Feiwel. Scranton, Pa.: International Textbook Co., pp. 598-607.

Fainsod, Merle
1958   Smolensk under Soviet Rule. New York: Random House.

Fallers, Lloyd
  1956   Bantu Bureaucracy. Chicago: University of Chicago Press.
  1974   The Social Anthropology of the Nation-State. Chicago: Aldine.
Faludi, Andreas (ed.)
  1973   A Reader in Planning Theory. Oxford: Pergamon Press.
Farbman, David
  1960   A Description, Analysis and Critique of the Master Plan. University of Pennsylvania Institute for Urban Studies. Unpublished mimeo.
Fel, Edit and Hofer, Thomas
  1969   Proper Peasants: Traditional Life in a Hungarian Village. New York: Viking Fund Publications in Anthropology.
Feiwel, George (ed.)
  1968   New Currents in Soviet-Type Economies: A Reader. Scranton: Pa.: International Textbook Co.
Fisher, Jack C.
  1962   Planning the city of socialist man. J. of the American Institute of Planners 28:251-65.
  1965   Comment. J. of the American Institute of Planners 31:38-42.
  1966   (ed.) City and Regional Planning in Poland. Ithaca: Cornell University Press.
  1967   Urban planning in the Soviet Union and Eastern Europe. *In* Taming Megalopolis Vol. II: How to Manage an Urbanized World, ed. by H. W. Eldredge. Garden City, N.Y.: Doubleday and Co., Inc., pp. 1069-99.
Foley, Donald
  1973   British town planning: one ideology or three? *In* A Reader in Planning Theory, ed. by A. Faludi. Oxford: Pergamon Press, pp. 69-74 (originally published in British Journal of Sociology 2:211-31, 1960).
Fortes, Meyer
  1958   Introduction. *In* The Developmental Cycle in Domestic Groups, ed. by J. Goody. Cambridge: Cambridge University Press, pp. 1-19.
Foster, George
  1965   Peasant and society and the image of limited good. American Anthropologist 67:293-315.

Foster-Carter, Aidan
  1978   The modes of production controversey. New Left Review No.
            107, pp. 47-77 (republished as "Can we articulate 'articula-
            tion?'" *In* The New Economic Anthropology, ed. by J. Clam-
            mer. London: MacMillan Press, Ltd., 1978).
Frank, Andre Gunder
  1967   Capitalism and Underdevelopment in Latin America. New
            York: Monthly Review Press.
  1969   Latin America: Underdevelopment or Revolution. New York:
            Monthly Review Press.
Fraser, Thomas
  1968   Culture Change in India: The Barpali Experiment. Amherst,
            Mass.: University of Massachusetts Press.
Freedman, Maurice
  1968   A Chinese phase in social anthropology. *In* Theory in Anthro-
            pology: A Sourcebook, ed. by R. Manners and D. Kaplan.
            Chicago: Aldine, pp. 145-55.
French, R. A. and Hamiltion, F. E. I. (eds.)
  1979   The Socialist City: Spatial Structures and Urban Policies.
            London: John Wiley and Sons, Ltd.
Friedmann, John
  1968   The strategy of deliberate urbanization. J. of the American
            Institute of Planners 34:364-73.
Frolic, B. Michael
  1963   The Soviet city. Town Planning Review 34:285-306.
  1976   Noncomparative communism: Chinese and Soviet urbaniza-
            tion. *In* Social Consequences of Modernization in Commun-
            ist Societies, ed. by Mark Field. Baltimore: The Johns Hop-
            kins University Press, pp. 149-61.
Fuchs, Roland and Demko, George
  1979   Geographic inequality under socialism. Annals of the Associa-
            tion of American Geographers 69:304-18.
Gheorghe, Georgeta and Gheorghe, Nicolae
  1978   Gruparea satelor mici și a gospodărilor dispersate: analiza
            de caz (Regrouping of small villages and dispersed home-
            steads: a case study). Viitorul Social 7:276-82.

Gheorghe, Ion
    1977   Disciplină in activitatea de construcții-sistematizare; partici-
              parea maselor la acțiunea de sistematizare (Discipline in the
              activities of construction-planning; mass participation in plan-
              ning activities). *In* Sistematizare Teritoriului și a Localitați-
              lor: Culegere Tematică, ed. by A. Miu. Bucharest: Academy
              "Ștefan Gheorghiu," pp. 173-82.
Gilberg, Trond
    1977   Modernization in Romania Since World War Two. New York:
              Praeger.
Glass, Ruth
    1973   The evalution of planning: some sociological considerations.
              In A Reader in Planning Theory, ed. by A. Faludi. Oxford:
              Pergamon Press, pp. 45-67 (expanded version published in
              International Soc. Sci. Journal 11, 1959).
Gluckman, Max
    1955   The Judicial Process among the Barotse. Manchester: Man-
              chester University Press.
    1963   Order and Rebellion in Tribal Africa. London: Cohen and
              West.
    1968   Inter-hierarchical roles: professional and party ethics in tri-
              bal areas in South and Central Africa. *In* Local-Level Politics
              ed. by M. Swartz. Chicago: Aldine Pub. Co.
Goldfrank, Walter (ed.)
    1979   The World-System of Capitalism: Past and Present. Political
              Economy of the World-System Annuals, No. 2. Beverly Hills,
              Calif.: Sage Publications.
Goodenough, Ward
    1963   Cooperation and Change. New York: Russell Sage Foundation.
Goody, Jack (ed.)
    1958   The Developmental Cycle in Domestic Groups. Cambridge:
              Cambridge University Press.
Gouldner, Alvin
    1979   The Future of Intellectuals and the Rise of the New Class.
              New York: Seabury Press.
Graves, Nancy B. and Graves, Theodore D.
    1974   Adaptive strategies in urban migration. Annual Review of
              Anthropology 3:117-51.

Grossman, Gregory
  1968   Thirty years of Soviet industrialization. *In* New Currents in Soviet-Type Economies: A Reader, ed. by G. Feiwel. Scranton, Pa.: International Textbook Co., pp. 41-49 (originally published in Soviet Survey 26:15-21, 1958).
  1977   The second economy of the USSR. Problems of Communism 26(5):25-40.

Gundisch G.
  1937   Urkundenbuch zur Geschichte der Deutschen in Siebenburgen Vol. 4. Hermannstadt-Sibiu (no publisher).

Hall, Edward T.
  1969   The Hidden Dimension. New York: Doubleday and Co.

Halpern, Joel
  1967   The Changing Village Community. Englewood Cliffs, N.J.: Prentice-Hall.

Hamilton, F. E. Ian
  1970   Aspects of spatial behavior in planned economies. Papers of the Regional Science Association 25:83-109.

Hansen, Edward, Schneider, Jane and Schneider, Peter
  1975   From autonomous development to dependent modernization? The Catalan case reconsidered: A reply to Pi-Sunyer. Comparative Studies in Society and History 17:238-41.

Hansen, Niles
  1967   Development pole theory in a regional context. Kyklos 20: 709-25 (reprinted in Regional Economics: Theory and Practice, ed. by D. McKee, R. Dean and W. Leahy, New York: The Free Press, 1970, pp. 121-35).
  1968   French Regional Planning. Bloomington: Indiana University Press.
  1969   (ed.) Growth Centers in Regional Economic Development. New York: The Free Press.
  1971   Intermediate-sized Cities as Growth Centers: Applications for Kentucky, the Piedmont Crescent, the Ozarks and Texas. New York: Praeger, pp. 11-89.
  1972   Criteria for a growth center policy. *In* Growth Poles and Growth Centers in Regional Planning, ed. by A. Kuklinski. The Hague: Mouton, pp. 103-24.

Haraszti, Miklos
  1978   A Worker in a Workers' State. New York: Universe Books, Inc.
Hay, Richard
  1977   Patterns of urbanization and socioeconomic development in
            the Third World: an overview. *In* Third World Urbanization,
            ed. by J. Abu-Lughod and Richard Hay. Chicago: Maaroufa
            Press, pp. 77-101.
Hechter, Michael
  1975   Internal Colonialism: The Celtic Fringe in British National
            Development. Berkeley: University of California Press.
Hegedus, Andras
  1976   Socialism and Bureaucracy. London: Allison and Busby.
Helin, Ronald A.
  1967   The volatile administrative map of Romania. Annals, Associa-
            tion of American Geographers 57:481-502.
Hermansen, Tormod
  1972   Development poles and development centres in national and
            regional development: elements of a theoretical framework.
            In Growth Poles and Growth Centres in Regional Planning,
            ed. by Anton Kuklinski. The Hague: Mouton Press, pp. 1 68.
Herseni, Traian (ed.)
  1970   Industrializare şi urbanizare: Cercetări de Psiho-sociologie
            Concretă la Boldeşti (Industrialization and Urbanization:
            Empirical Socio-psychological research in Boldeşti Village).
            Bucharest: Editura Academiei Republicii Socialiste România.
Hirschman, A. O.
  1958   The Strategy of Economic Development. New Haven: Yale
            University Press.
Hirszowicz, Maria
  1980   The Bureaucratic Leviathan: A Study in the Sociology of
            Communism. New York: New York University Press.
Hobsbawm, Eric
  1969   Bandits. London: Weidenfeld and Nicholas.
  1971   Primitive Rebels: Studies in Archaic Forms of Social Move-
            ments. Manchester: Manchester University Press (orig. 1965).
Hoffman, George W.
  1964   Transformation of rural settlement in Bulgaria. Geographical
            Review 54:45-65.

1967   The problem of the underdeveloped regions of southeast Europe: a comparative analysis of Romania, Yugoslavia and Greece. Annals, Association of American Geographers 57: 637-66.

Holmberg, Alan
1965   The changing values and institutions of Vicos in the context of national development. Amer. Behavioral Scientist 8:3-8.
1971   Vicos: a peasant hacienda community in Peru. *In* Economic Development and Social Change, ed. by G. Dalton. Garden City, N.Y.: Natural History Press, pp. 518-55.

Hopkins, T. and Wallerstein, I. (eds.)
1980   Processes of the World-System. Political Economy of World-System, Annual, No. 3. Beverly Hills, Calif.: Sage Publications.

Hoselitz, Burt
1955   Generative and parasitic cities. Economic Development and Cultural Change 3:278-94.
1960   Sociological Aspects of Economic Growth. New York: The Free Press.

Hough, Jerry F.
1969   The Soviet Prefects: The Local Party Organs in Industrial Decision-Making. Cambridge, Mass: Harvard University Press.
1977   The bureaucratic model and the nature of the Soviet system. *In* The Soviet Union and Social Science Theory. Cambridge: Harvard University Press, pp. 49-70. (Originally published in Journal of Comparative Administration 2:134-68 [August 1973]).

Howard, Ebenezeer
1960   Garden Cities of Tomorrow ed. by F. J. Osborn. London: Faber and Faber (originally published 1898).

Inkeles, Alex
1950   Public Opinion in Soviet Russia: A Study in Mass Persuasion. Cambridge, Mass.: Harvard University Press.

Inkeles, Alex and Bauer, Raymond
1959   The Soviet Citizen: Daily Life in a Totalitarian Society. Cambridge, Mass.: Harvard University Press.

Ioanid, Virgil
 1967   Sistematizarea satelor in perspectivă civilizației socialiste (Village planning in the perspective of socialist civilization). Lupta de Clasa 47:65-72.
 1968   Innoirea Urbanistică a Satelor (Urban Innovations in the Village). Bucharest: Editură Agro-Silvică.
 1969   Sistematizarea Localităților Rurale: Sinteza Documentară (Planning of Rural Localities: a Summary and Documentation). Bucharest: Centrul de Documentare pentru Construcții, Arhitectura și Sistematizare.
 1974   Metodologii Moderne de Proiectarea in Sistematizare: Sinteză Documentară (Modern Methods of Design for Planning: A Documentary Summary). Bucharest: Centrul de Documentare pentru Construcții, Arhitectura și Sistematizare.
Ioanovici, Virgil and Popescu, M.
 1977   General conception of industrialization and environmental protection in Romania. Paper presented at the Seventh International Fellows' Conference, Johns Hopkins University Center for Metropolitan Planning and Research, Bucharest, July 1977. Offset.
Jarvesoo, Aino
 1974   Agrotowns in Soviet Estonia. Paper presented at Fourth Conference on Baltic Studies, University of Illinois Chicago Circle, May 16-20, 1974 (On file, Dept. of Agricultural and Food Economics, University of Massachusetts-Amherst).
Jekelius, Erich
 1929   Das Burzenland. Vol. 5(1). Kronstadt (Brașov): Verlag Burzenlandische Sachsen Museum.
Johnson, E. A.
 1970   The Organization of Space in Developing Countries. Cambridge, Mass.: Harvard University Press.
Jowitt, Kenneth
 1978   The Leninist Response to National Dependency. Berkeley: Institute of International Studies, University of California Research Series No. 37).
 1983   Soviet Neotraditionalism: Political Corruption in a Leninist Regime. Soviet Studies 35:275-298.

Kahn, Joel
    1981   Minangkabav Social Formations. Cambridge: Cambridge University Press.
Kamerschen, David R.
    1969   Overpopulation and underdevelopment: some common myths Economic Development and Cultural Change 17:235-53.
Kaplan, Barbara Hockey (ed.)
    1978   Social Change in the Capitalist World-Economy. Political Economy of the World-System Annual, No. 1. Beverly Hills, Calif.: Sage Publications.
Katsenelinboigen, Aron
    1977   Coloured markets in the Soviet Union. Soviet Studies 29: 62-85.
Kenedi, Janos
    1981   Do It Yourself: Hungary's Hidden Economy. London: Pluto Press.
Khodzhayer, D. G. et al.
    1972   Unifying and controlling the growth of cities in the USSR. Ekistics 34:410-13.
Kideckel, David A.
    1976   The social organization of production on a Romanian cooperative farm. Dialectical Anthropology 1:267-76.
    1977   The dialectic of rural development: cooperative farm goals and family strategies in a Romanian commune. Journal of Rural Cooperation 5:43-62.
    1979   Agricultural Cooperativism and Social Process in a Romanian Commune. Ph.D. Thesis, Anthropology Department, University of Massachusetts-Amherst. Ann Arbor: University Microfilms.
    1982   The socialist transformation of agriculture in a Romanian commune 1945-1962. American Ethnologist 9:320-40.
    1983   Secular ritual and social change: a Romanian Case. Anthropological Quarterly 56:69-75.
Kideckel, David A. and Sampson, Steven L.
    1983   Fieldwork in Romania: political, practical and ethical aspects. In Social Science Research in Romania, ed. by John Cole.

Research Report No. 22, Department of **Anthropology**, University of Massachusetts-Amherst.

King, Robert

1978 The blending of party and state in Romania. East European Quarterly. 12:489-500.

1980 A History of the Romanian Communist Party. Stanford: Hoover Institution Press.

Konrad, Gyorgy and Szelenyi, Ivan

1976 Social conflicts and underurbanization: the Hungarian case. *In* Social Consequences of Modernization in Communist Societies, ed. by M. Field. Baltimore: The Johns Hopkins University Press, pp. 162-80.

1979 The Intellectuals on the Road to Class Power. New York: Harcourt Brace Jovanovich.

Koropeckyji, I. S.

1972 Equalization of regional development in socialist countries: an empirical study. Economic Development and Cultural Change 21:68-86.

Krambach, I. and Müller, Jorg

1978 Interrelationships between settlement patterns, agricultural development and the social development of farmers in the German Democratic Republic. Paper presented at Ninth World Congress of Sociology, Uppsala, Sweden, August 1978.

Kudinov, O. V.

1975 Strategy of the spatial distribution of the productive forces and population in the USSR. *In* National Settlement Strategies: East and West, ed. by Harry Swain. Schloss Laxenburg, Austria: International Institute of Applied Systems Analysis, pp. 12-31.

Kuklinski, Antoni (ed.)

1972 Growth Poles and Growth Centres in Regional Planning. United Nations Research Institute for Social Development, Vol. 5. The Hague: Mouton Press.

Laclau, Ernesto

1979 Feudalism and capitalism in Latin America. *In* Politics and Ideology in Marxist Theory: Capitalism, Fascism, Populism. London: New Left Books, pp. 15-51. (Originally appeared in New Left Review 71:19-38, 1967.)

Lange, Oskar
    1968   The role of planning in a socialist economy. *In* New Currents
            in Soviety-Type Economies: A Reader, ed. by G. Feiwel.
            Scranton, Pa.: International Textbook Co., pp. 14-21.
Lăzărescu, Cezar
    1976   Probleme actuale ale sistematizării teritoriului național și
            așezărilor umane in România. Viitorul Social 5:31-38. Re-
            printed in English as "Current problems of organizing the na-
            tional territory and human settlements in Romania," Revue
            Roumaine des Sciences Sociales; Sociologie, No. 20 (1976),
            pp. 37-44.
    1977   (ed.) Urbanismul în România. Bucharest: Editură Tehnică.
Le Corbusier (pseudonym of Charles Edouard Jeanneret-Gris)
    1971   The City of Tomorrow and Its Planning. Translated by F. Et-
            chells from the 8th French edition of Urbanisme.
Lee, Tunney
    1977   Personal communication.
Leeds, Anthony
    1973   Locality power in relation to supralocal power institutions.
            In Urban Anthropology: Cross-Cultural Studies of Urbaniza-
            tion, ed. by A. Southall. New York: Oxford University Press,
            pp. 15-42.
Little, Kenneth
    1962   West African Urbanization: A Study of Voluntary Associa-
            tions in Social Change. Cambridge: Cambridge University
            Press.
    1973   Urbanism and regional associations: their paradoxical func-
            tions. *In* Urban Anthropology: Cross-Cultural Studies of Ur-
            banization, ed. by A. Southall. New York: Oxford University
            Press, pp. 407-443.
Littlewood, Paul
    1974   Strings and kingdoms: the activities of a political mediator in
            Southern Italy. Archives Europeenes des Sociologie 15:33-54.
Lockwood, William
    1973   The peasant-worker in Yugoslavia. Studies in European Soc-
            iety 1(1):91-110. The Hague: Mouton Press.
Logan, M. I.
    1972   The spatial system and planning strategies in developing coun-
            tries. Geographical Review 62:229-44.

Lonsdale, Richard E.
   1977   Regional inequity and Soviet concern for rural and small
          town industrialization. Soviet Geography—Review and Trans-
          lation 18:590-602.
Lundqvist, Jan
   1975   Local and Central Impulses for Change and Development: A
          Case Study of Mongoro District, Tanzania. Oslo: Norwegian
          Research Council for Science and Humanities.
Ma, Lawrence J. C.
   1976.   Anti-urbanism in China. Proceedings, Association of American
          Geographers 8:114-17.
Macesich, George
   1964   Yugoslavia: Theory and Practice of Development Planning.
          Charlottesville, Va.: University of Virginia Press.
MacMurray, T. C.
   1971   Urban planning in Poland. Town and Country Planning 39:
          117-22.
Malinowski, Bronislaw
   1938   Preface to Peasant Life in China by M. Fei. Oxford: Oxford
          University Press.
Mamdani, Mahmood
   1972   The Myth of Population Control. New York: Monthly Re-
          view Press.
Mangione, Enzo
   1977   Territorial social problems in socialist China. *In* Third World
          Urbanization, ed. by J. Abu-Lughod and R. Hay, Jr. Chicago:
          Maaroufa Press, pp. 370-83.
Mao-tze-dung
   1967   On Contradiction (orig. 1937).
          On the Correct Handling of Contradictions among the People
          (orig. 1953). Peking: China Books.
Marx, Karl and Engels, Friedrich
   1955   The Communist Manifesto (S. H. Beer, ed.). New York: Ap-
          pleton-Century Crofts.
Masser, F. I. and Stroud, D. C.
   1973   The metropolitan village. *In* English Rural Communities: The
          Impact of a Specialized Economy, ed. by D. Mills. London:
          MacMillan, pp. 235-48.

Massey, Doreen
 1979 The regional question. Capital and Class, January, pp. 1-21.
Matei, Mioara
 1960 Sistematizarea așezărilor sătești (Planning of village settlements). Bucharest: Editura Tehnică.
Matei, Mioara and Matei, Ion
 1973 Urbanizare: Elemente de Sistematizare (Urbanization: The Elements of Planning). Bucharest: Centrul de Informare și Documentare in Științele Sociale și Politice, Series "Progrese, Direcții, Tendințe" (no. 4).
 1977 Sociologie și Sistematizare in Processele de Dezvoltare (Sociology and Planning in the Processes of Development). Bucharest: Editura Tehnică.
Mayer, Robert, Moroney, Robert and Morris, Robert
 1974 Centrally Planned Change: A Re-examination of Theory and Experience. Urbana, Ill.: University of Illinois Press.
McArthur, Marilyn
 1976 The Saxon Germans: political fate of an ethnic identity. Dialectical Anthropology 1:349-64.
 1981 The Politics of Identity: Transylvanian Saxons in Socialist Romania. Ph. D. Dissertation. Dept. of Anthropology, University of Massachusetts-Amherst. Ann Arbor: University Microfilms.
Medvedev, Roy
 1972 On Socialist Democracy. New York: W. W. Norton.
Merrington, John
 1976 Town and country in the transition to capitalism. In The Transition from Feudalism to Capitalism, ed. by R. Hilton. London: New Left Books, pp. 170-94.
Meyer, Alfred G.
 1964 USSR Incorporated. In The Development of the USSR, ed. by D. W. Treadgold. Seattle: University of Washington Press, pp. 21-28.
Miftode, Vasile
 1978 Migrațiile și Dezvoltarea Urbană (Migration and Urban Development). Iași: Editură Junimea.
Mihailovic, Kosta
 1972 Regional Development: Experiences and Prospects in Eastern Europe. The Hague: Mouton Press.

Mitrany, David
  1951   Marx Against the Peasant. A Study in Social Dogmatism. New
            York: Collier.
Montias, John
  1967   Economic Development in Communist Romania. Cambridge,
            Mass.: M.I.T. Press.
Moseley, M. J.
  1974   Growth Centres in Spatial Planning. Oxford: Pergamon Press.
Murphey, Rhoads
  1975   Aspects of urbanization in contemporary China: a revolution-
            ary model. Proceedings, Association of American Geographers
            7:165-68.
Murray, L. W., Jr.
  1974   Socioeconomic development and industrial location in Po-
            land: the merging of growth poles and growth center theories
            in a socialist economy. Antipode 6:125-41.
Nader, Laura
  1980   The vertical slice: hierarchies and children. *In* Hierarchy and
            Society: Anthropological Perspectives on Bureaucracy, ed.
            by G. Britan and R. Cohen. Philadelphia: Institute for the
            Study of Human Issues, pp. 31-44.
Negoescu, V.
  1974   Prognoză privind construcția de locuințe in jedețul Brașov
            (Prognosis concerning the construction of housing in Brașov
            County). *In* Sinteze Socio-Economice, Culegere de Studii
            Aparută sub Indrumarea Comitetului Județean Brașov al
            P.C.R. Brașov, Romania: Laboratorul de Cercetări Eco-
            nomice și Social Politice, Brașov.
Nichols, Vida
  1969   Growth poles: an evaluation of their propulsive effects. En-
            vironment and Planning 1:193-208.
Ollman, Bertell
  1977   Marx's vision of communism: a reconstruction. Critique No.
            8, pp. 4-42.
Osborn, Robert J.
  1965   How Russians plan their cities. Transaction 3:25-30.

Osborn, Robert J. and Reiner, Thomas
    1962   Soviet city planning: current issues and future prospects.
                Journal of the American Institute of Planners 28:239-50.
Paine, Robert
    1974   Second Thoughts on Barth's Models. Royal Anthropological
                Association, Occasional Paper No. 32.
Pallot, Judith
    1979   Rural settlement planning in the USSR. Soviet Studies 31:
                214-30.
Pallot, Judith and Shaw, Dennis
    1981   Planning in the Soviet Union. London: Croom Helm.
Perroux, F.
    1955   Note sur la notion de pole de croissance. Economie Appli-
                quee 7:307-20. Translated in Regional Economics: Theory
                and Practice, ed. by D. L. McKee, R. D. Dean and W. H.
                Leahy. New York: The Free Press, 1970, pp. 93-105.
Petersen, W.
    1968   The ideological origins of Britain's new towns. Journal of the
                American Institute of Planners 34:160-70.
Pioro, Zygmunt
    1965   Comment on Fisher (1962). Journal of the American Insti-
                tute of Planners 31:31-35.
Pirenne, Henri
    1925   Medieval Cities: Their Origins and the Revival of Trade.
                Trans. by Frank D. Halsey (1969), Princeton, N.J.: Princeton
                University Press.
    1956   Economic and Social History of Medieval Europe. New York:
                Harcourt Brace Jovanovich.
Pi-Sunyer, Oriol
    1971   (ed.) The Limits of Integration: Ethnicity and Nationalism in
                Europe. Research Report No. 9, Department of Anthropology,
                University of Massachusetts-Amherst.
    1974   Modernization and development: a reconsideration of the
                Catalan case. Comparative Studies in Society and History 16:
                117-131.
    1975   Reply to Hansen, Schneider and Schneider. Comparative Stu-
                dies in Society and History 17:241-44.

Podea, Ion
 1938   Monografia Județului. Brașov. Brașov: Astra.
Popescu, Marin
 1977   Personal communication.
van Putten, J. G. (ed.)
 1971   Citizen Participation and Local Government in Europe: A
         Comparative Analysis of Fourteen Country Reports Pre-
         pared by the Research Staff of the International Union of
         Local Authorities. Studies in Comparative Local Government
         5(2):9-73.
Quadeer, M.
 1974   Do cities modernize the developing countries? An examina-
         tion of the South Asian experience. Comparative Studies in
         Society and History 16:266-83.
Radio Free Europe Research
 1976   Czechoslovakia Situation Report No. 8, March, 3, 1976, pp.
         5-8.
 1977   Romania Situation Report No. 17, May 25, 1977, p. 9.
Raikes, Phillip
 1975   Ujaama and rural socialism. Review of African Political Eco-
         nomy, no. 3, pp. 33-57.
Rakovski, Marc
 1979   Towards an East European Marxism. London: Allison and
         Busby.
Randall, Stephen G.
 1976   The family estate in an upland Carpathian village. Dialectical
         Anthropology 1:277-86.
 1982   The Household Estate under Socialism. Ph.D. Dissertation.
         Anthropology Department, University of Massachusetts-Am-
         herst. Ann Arbor: University Microfilms.
Ratner, Mitchell
 1979   Choose and be chosen: the transition from primary to sec-
         ondary education in contemporary Romania. Paper present-
         ed at Conference on Social Science Research in Romania,
         Amherst, Mass., January 1979 (to be published in Cole 1983b).
 1980   Educational and Occupational Selection in Contemporary
         Romania: An Anthropological Account. Ph.D. Dissertation,

Department of Anthropology, The American University. Ann
Arbor: University Microfilms.

Redfield, Robert
1941   The Folk Culture of Yucatan. Chicago: University of Chicago
Press.
1947   The folk society. American J. of Sociology 52:293-308.
1956   Peasant Society and Culture. Chicago: University of Chicago
Press.

Regulski, Jerszy
1972   Development poles theory and its application in Poland. *In*
Growth Poles and Growth Centres in Regional Planning, ed.
by A. Kuklinski. The Hague: Mouton, pp. 207-21.

Reiner, Thomas
1963   The Place of the Ideal Community in Urban Planning. Phila-
delphia: University of Pennsylvania Press.

Richards, A. I. (ed.)
1960   East African Chiefs. London: Faber.

Rey, Pierre-Paul
1975   Les Alliances des Classes. Paris: Maspero.

Rigby, T. Harry
1977   Stalinism and the mono-organizational society. *In* Stalinism:
Essays in Historical Interpretation, ed. by Robert C. Tucker.
New York: W. W. Norton, pp. 53-76.

Robinson, E. A. (ed.)
1969   Backward Areas in Advanced Countries. New York: St.
Martin's Press.

Rodell, Michael J.
1975   Review article: growth centers—two recent contributions.
Economic Development and Cultural Change 25:523-31.

Rodwin, Lloyd
1970   Nations and Cities: A Comparison of Strategies for Urban
Growth. Boston: Houghton-Mifflin.

Rogers, Everett and Shoemaker, F. Floyd
1967   Communication of Innovations. New York: Free Press.

Rohlen, Thomas
1974   For Harmony and Strength: Japanese White Collar Organization in Anthropological Perspective. Berekely: University of
California Press.

Romanian Studies Collective/Romanian Research Group (J. Cole, S. Beck, D. Kideckel, M. McArthur, S. Randall and S. Sampson)

1977   Between state and village: local elites in five Romanian communes. Paper presented at Symposium-Conference on Southeast Europe, Columbus, Ohio, April 1977 (on file, Romania Research Group/Department of Anthropology, University of Massachusetts-Amherst).

1979   Transylvanian ethnicity: a reply to Sozan's "Ethnocide in Rumania." Current Anthropology 20:135-40.

Rugg, Dean S.

1971   Aspects of change in the landscape of East Central and Southeast Europe. *In* Eastern Europe: Essays in Geographical Problems, ed. by George Hoffman. New York: Praeger, pp. 83-126.

Salaf, Janet W.

1971   Urban residential communities in the wake of the cultural revolution. *In* The City in Communist China, ed. by J. Lewis. Palo Alto, Calif.: Stanford University Press, pp. 289-323.

Samoff, Joel

1979   The bureaucracy and the bourgeoisie: decentralization and class structure in Tanzania. Comparative Studies in Society and History 21:30-61.

Sampson, Steven L.

1976   Feldioara: the city comes to the peasant. Dialectical Anthropology 1:321-47.

1978   Systematization in Romania: rational and irrational settlements. Paper presented at Ninth World Congress of Sociology, Uppsala, Sweden, August 1978.

1979   Planned and unplanned urbanization: the case of Braşov City Romania. *In* The Socialist City: Spatial Structure and Urban Policy, ed. by R. French and F. E. I. Hamilton. London: John Wiley and Sons, Ltd., pp. 507-24.

1982   Local level "bureaucrats" in Romania. Paper presented at the First International Conference on the Comparative Historical and Critical Analysis of Bureaucracy. Zurich, October 4-8, 1982.

1983a   Rich families and poor collectives: an anthropological approach to Romania's second economy. Bidrag til Oststatsforskning (Uppsala) 10(2). Previously presented at Conference on Second Economy in Eastern Europe, Bergen, Norway, November 9-11, 1982.

1983b   Bureaucracy and corruption as anthropological problems: a case study from Romania. Folk (Copenhagen) vol. 24 (in press).

1983c   The culture of the planners: some guidelines for the anthropological study of the planning process. Papers, Tenth Conference of Nordic Ethnographers, Copenhagen, October 8-12, 1982. (vol. 3). Copenhagen: Institut for Etnologi og Antropologi.

1984   Getting things done in Romania: styles of mobilization in Romanian villages. Sociologia Ruralis, vol. 24 (in press).

Sarfalvi, Bela (ed.)

1970   Recent Population Movements in the East Eurpean Countries. Studies in Geography in Hungary. Budapest: Akademiai Kiado.

Sawers, Larry

1977   Urban planning in the Soviet Union and China. Monthly Review 28:34-48.

Scott, James

1969   The analysis of corruption in developing nations. Comparative Studies in Society and History 11:315-41.

1973   Comparative Political Corruption. Englewood Cliffs, N.J.: Prentice-Hall.

Schaff, Adam

1982   Die kommunistische Bewegung am Scheideweg. Frankfurt: Europaverlag.

Schapera, Isaac

1938   Essay on field methods in the study of modern culture. In Methods of Culture Contact in Africa, ed. by L. Mair. Memorandum 15, International Africa Institute (originally published in Africa 3:315-38, 1935).

Schneider, Jane

1977   Was there a pre-capitalist world-system? Peasant Studies Newsletter 6:20-28.

Schneider, Jane and Schneider, Peter
   1976   Culture and Political Economy in Western Sicily. New York:
             Academic Press.
Schneider, Jane, Schneider, Peter and Hansen, Edward
   1972   Modernization and development: the role of regional elites
             and noncorporate groups in the European Mediterranean.
             Comparative Studies in Society and History 14:320-50.
Scînteia ("Spark")
   1975-78   Newspaper of the Central Committee of the Romanian Com-
             munist Party. Bucharest.
Seddon, David (ed.)
   1978   Relations of Production: Marxist Approaches to Economic
             Anthropology. London: Frank Cass and Co., Ltd.
Seers, Dudley
   1972   What are we trying to measure? Journal of Development Stu-
             dies 8:21-36.
Sfinţescu, C.
   1933   Urbanistică Generală. Bucharest.
   1942   Superurbanismul: Ideologie Tehnica. Bucharest.
Shah, S. M.
   1974   Growth centers as a strategy for rural development: India's
             experience. Econ. Development and Cultural Change 22:215-
             228.
Shanin, Theodore
   1972   The Awkward Class: Political Sociology of the Peasantry in a
             Developing Country. Russia: 1910-1925. New York: Oxford
             University Press.
Simic, Andre
   1972   The Peasant Urbanites· A Study of Rural-Urban Mobility in
             Serbia. New York: Academic Press.
Smith, Carol A. (ed.)
   1976   Regional Analysis. Vols. I and II. New York: Academic Press.
Sommer, Robert
   1969   Personal Space: The Behavioral Basis of Design. Englewood
             Cliffs, N.J.: Prentice-Hall.
Sovani, N. V.
   1964   The analysis of overurbanization. Economic Development and
             Cultural Change 12:113-22.

Stalin, J. V.
  1940a   Dizzy with success. *In* Problems of Leninism. Moscow:
           Foreign Language Publishing House, pp. 333-38 (originally
           appeared in Pravda, March 2, 1930).
  1940b   Reply to Collective Farm Comrades. *In* Problems of Lenin-
           ism. Moscow: Foreign Language Publishing House, pp. 339-58
           (originally published in Pravda, Apr. 3, 1930).
Stavenhagen, Rudolfo
  1964   Changing functions of the community in underdeveloped
           countries. Sociologia Ruralis 4:315-331.
Steward, Julian
  1956   The People of Puerto Rico. Urbana, Illinois: University of
           Illinois Press.
Stvan, J.
  1973   Physical, Socioeconomic and Environmental Planning in
           Countries of Eastern Europe. Document D4/1973. Stock-
           holm: National Swedish Institute for Building Research.
Swain, Harry (ed.)
  1975   National Settlement Strategies—East and West. Schloss Laxen-
           burg, Austria: International Institute for Applied Systems
           Analysis.
Swartz, Mark (ed.)
  1968   Local-Level Politics: Social and Cultural Perspectives. Chi-
           cago: Aldine Publishing Co.
Sweezy, Paul and Bettelheim, Charles
  1972   On the Transition to Socialism. New York: Monthly Review
           Press.
Sylverman, Sydel
  1965   Patronage and community-nation mediators in Central Italy.
           Ethnology 4:172-89.
  1974   Bailey's politics: review article. J. of Peasant Studies 2:111-20.
Szelenyi, Ivan
  1977   Regional management and social class: the case of Eastern
           Europe. Information der Arbeitsgemeinschaft fur Interdis-
           ziplinare Angewandte Socialforschung (Vienna). No. 1/2
           February.

1982   Gouldner's theory of intellectuals as a flawed universal class. Theory and Society 11:779-98.

Taubman, William
1973   Governing Soviet Cities: Bureaucratic Politics and Urban Development in the USSR. New York: Praeger.

Teutsch, F.
1965   Kleine Geschichte der Siebenburger Sachsen. Darmstadt: Wissenschaftlige Buchgesellschaft (orig. published 1920).

Thomas, Clive
1974   Dependence and Transformation: The Economics of the Transition to Socialism. New York: Monthly Review Press.

Tipps, Dean
1973   Modernization and the comparative study of societies. Comparative Studies in Society and History 15.199-226.

Tomniuc, Bucur
1974   Transformari în structura populaţiei din judeţul Braşov sub influenţa dezvoltării industriale: perspectivele demografice ale anului 2000 (Transformations in the structure of Braşov County's population under the influence of industrial development: demographic perspectives for the year 2000). *In* Sinteze Socio-Economice: Culegere de Studii Apăruta sub Indrumarea Comitetului Judeţean Braşov al P.C.R., ed. by I. Lupu and N. Prosan. Braşov: Laboratorul de Cercetări Economice şi Social-politice, pp. 173-84.

Trotsky, Leon
1937   The Revolution Betrayed: What is the Soviet Union and Where Is It Going? Garden City, New York: Doubleday, Doran and Co.

Tufescu, Victor
1978   Les villages disperses de montagne en presence de la systematisation. Rev. Roumaine Geologie, Geophysique et Geographie (Geographie) tome 22, no. 1, pp. 17-24.

Tunaru, M. and Rujan, D.
1976   Unele aspecte ale influenţei urbanizării asupra fenomenelor deviante (Some aspects of the influence of urbanization on phenomena of deviance). *In* Sinteze Socio-Economice: Culegere de Studii Apăruta sub Indrumarea Comitetului Judeţean

Braşov al P.C.R., ed. by I. Lupu and D. Rujan. Braşov: Laboratorul de Cercetari Economice şi Social-Politice, pp. 205-14.

Turnock, David

1970   The pattern of industrialization in Romania. Annals, Association of American Geographers 60:540-59.

1974   An Economic Geography of Romania. London: G. Bell and Sons, Ltd.

1976   Restructuring of rural settlement in Rumania. Slavonic and East European Review 54:83-102.

1977   Regional development and industrial growth: recent experience in Romania. Ms. Department of Geography, Leicester University, Leicester, England.

1982   The Rural Development Programme in Romania with Particular Reference to the Designation of New Towns. Ms. Department of Geography, Leicester University.

Verdery, Katherine

1983   Transylvanian Villagers. Berkeley: Univesity of California Press.

Vernescu, Dimitrie

1972   Oraşele viitorului şi viitorul oraşelor; opinii (Cities of the future and the future of cities; opinions) Arhitectura (Bucharest) 20:61-63.

Vincent, Joan

1977   Agrarian society as organized flow: processes of development past and present. Peasant Studies 6:56-65.

1978   Political anthropology: manipulative strategies. Annual Review of Anthropology 7:175-94.

Voskresensky, Lev

1976   Soviet village resettlement. Town and County Planning 44: 535-37.

Wachner, Heinrich

1934   Kronstädter Heimat und Wanderbuch. Kronstadt-Braşov: Buchhandlung Wilh. Hiemsch.

Wallerstein, Immanuel

1974a   The Modern World-System: Capitalist Agriculture and the Origins of the European World-Economy 1450-1650. New York: Academic Press.

1974b   The rise and future demise of the world capitalist system:
         points for comparative analysis. Comparative Studies in Soc-
         iety and History 16:387-415.
1979   The Capitalist World-Economy. Cambridge: Cambridge Uni-
         versity Press.

Watson, James
1970   Society as organized flow: the Tairora case. Southwestern
         Journal of Anthropology 26:107-24.

Weber, Max
1958   Bureaucracy. *In* From Max Weber: Essays in Sociology, ed.
         by H. Gerth and C. W. Mills. New York: Galaxy Books, pp.
         196-244.

Weitz, Rannan
1971   From Peasant to Farmer: A Revolutionary Strategy for De-
         velopment. New York: Columbia University Press.
1973   (ed.) Urbanization and the Developing Countries: Report of
         the Sixth Rehovot Conference. New York: Praeger.

Wertheim, W. F.
1964   Sociological aspects of corruption in Southeast Asia. Socio-
         logica Neerlandica 1:129-52. Reprinted *in* Political Corrup-
         tion: A Book of Readings, ed. by A. J. Heidenheimer. (New
         York: Holt, Rinehart and Winston, 1970) and *in* State and
         Society: A Reader in Political Sociology, ed. by R. Bendix.
         (Berkeley: University of California Press, 1974).

Wiarda, Howard J.
1981   Corporatism and National Development in Latin America.
         Boulder: Westview Press.

Wirth, Louis
1938   Urbanism as a Way of Life. American Journal of Sociology
         44:1-24.

Wolf, Eric R.
1955   Types of Latin American peasantry. American Anthropologist
         57:462-71.
1956   Aspects of group relations in a complex society: Mexico.
         American Anthropologist 58:1065-78.
1957   Closed corporate communities in Mesoamerica and Java.
         Southwestern Journal of Anthropology 13:7-12.

1959   Sons of the Shaking Earth. Chicago: The University of Chicago Press.

1966a   Kinship, friendship and patron-client relations in complex societies. In Social Anthropology of Complex Societies, ed. by M. Banton. London: Tavistock, pp. 1-20.

1966b   Peasants. Englewood Cliffs, N.J.: Prentice-Hall.

1969   Peasant Wars of the Twentieth Century. New York: Harper and Row.

Wolf, Eric R. and Hansen, Edward

1972   The Human Condition in Latin America. New York: Oxford University Press.

Wolter, Ulf (ed.)

1980   Rudolf Bahro: Critical Responses. White Plains, N.Y.: M.E. Sharpe.

Wood, Geof

1973   A peasantry and the State. Development and Change 5:45-75.

Wylie, Lawrence

1964   Village in the Vaucluse. New York: Harper and Row.

Zaslavskaya, T. N.

1978   The necessity of the planning by objective approach toward developing the agrarian sector. Paper presented at the Ninth World Congress of Sociology, Uppsala, Sweden, August 1978.

Zeitlin, Morris

1972   Guide to the Literature of Cities: Abstract and Bibliography. Part XI: Socialist Cities. Council of Planning Librarians Exchange Bibliography no. 328, October 1972.

Zimmerman, Franz, Werner, C. and Muller, G.

1892-1902 Urkundenbuch zur Geschichte der Deutschen in Siebenbürgen. 3 vols. 1892, 1900, 1902.

INDEX

343